a matrix

of meanings

Engaging Culture

WILLIAM A. DYRNESS
AND ROBERT K. JOHNSTON,
SERIES EDITORS

The Engaging Culture series is designed to help Christians respond with theological discernment to our contemporary culture. Each volume explores particular cultural expressions, seeking to discover God's presence in the world and to involve readers in sympathetic dialogue and active discipleship. These books encourage neither an uninformed rejection nor an uncritical embrace of culture, but active engagement informed by theological reflection.

a matrix

of meanings

finding God in pop culture

craig detweiler
and barry taylor

Baker Academic

A Division of Baker Book House Co
Grand Rapids, Michigan 49516

Published by Baker Academic
a division of Baker Book House Company
P.O. Box 6287, Grand Rapids, MI 49516-6287
www.bakeracademic.com

Printed in the United States of America

Library of Congress Cataloging-in-Publication Data
Detweiler, Craig, 1964–
    A matrix of meanings : finding God in pop culture / Craig Detweiler and Barry Taylor.
        p.   cm.—(Engaging culture)
    Includes bibliographical references (p.) and index.
    ISBN 0-8010-2417-X (pbk.)
    1. Popular culture—Religious aspects—Christianity. 2. Popular culture—United States.
I. Taylor, Barry, 1956– II. Title. III. Series.
BR115.C8D42   2003
261—dc21   2003052311

contents

LIFE WITH FATHER

ON SUNDAYs FA-
THER would put on
his church clothes
and go hunting FOR
Souls (and SOMETIMES squirrels)

preface

The first demand any work of any art makes upon us is surrender. Look. Listen. Receive. Get yourself out of the way. (There is no good asking first whether the work before you deserves such a surrender, for until you have surrendered you cannot possibly find out.)

C. S. Lewis, *An Experiment in Criticism*

The Rolling Stones began "Sympathy for the Devil" by singing, "Please allow me to introduce myself." Many view pop culture as the devil, as something to shun, avoid, and oppose. Rapper Eminem may be seen as the latest example of evil emanating from pop culture. His songs contain ample evidence of profanity, misogyny, and homophobia. He courts controversy, relishes a fight, openly plays the devil to enrage parents and other guardians of taste. Yet Eminem's film debut, *8 Mile,* also includes some surprisingly inspiring and spiritual undertones. The rap battles in the film take place at "the shelter," in a church basement. They are hosted by Future, a person of prayer who encourages Eminem's character, Rabbit, to "flip the script" onstage. Rabbit wins the rap contest by acknowledging his weaknesses, owning his embarrassments, revealing whatever secrets his opponents may use against him. Eminem's approach is summarized in the Academy Award–winning song from the *8 Mile* soundtrack, "Lose Yourself." He loses himself in the music, but the principle of self-renunciation, "flipping the script," finds surprising parallels in the words of Jesus.

In the Gospel of Luke, Jesus challenged his followers to deny themselves, take up their cross daily, and follow him, "For whoever wants to save his life will lose it, but whoever loses his life for me will save it" (Luke 9:24). Jesus' paradoxical teaching flipped the script on people's understanding of power, life,

7

and religion. You find life by losing yourself in Christ. Eminem may be the devil to some, but his *via negativa* has roots in Jesus' surprising strategies. It is easy to identify what's wrong with Eminem, but finding what's right, identifying and understanding what millions of teens connect with, takes much more work.

We want to flip the script on our understanding of pop culture, to look closer at what lies behind the music. Consequently, this book will offer "sympathy for pop culture," suggesting that God shines through even the most debased pop cultural products. Consider this a *via positiva*. Now, please allow us to introduce ourselves.

We approach popular culture first and foremost as fans. Craig grew up in Charlotte, North Carolina, in a basement featuring posters of the Miami Dolphins, U2's *Unforgettable Fire,* and Humphrey Bogart. He has compiled a journal of his lifelong film-going, complete with capsule reviews. Barry's love for popular music started in England, where he scoured record shops in search of American soul music. Our houses are filled with books, compact discs, and DVDs.

We write primarily as practitioners, artists involved in the day-to-day process of creating pop culture. Barry toured the world, creating the concert sound for musicians such as Marvin Gaye, Tony Bennett, and AC/DC. His original songs have appeared in movies such as *Green Dragon, Avenging Angelo,* and *Half Past Dead.* Craig graduated from the University of Southern California's film school and writes screenplays, including the teen comedy *Extreme Days.* We engage with popular culture out of genuine enjoyment, love, and respect.

We also write as pastors and teachers, having devoted ourselves to articulating a biblical faith for the twenty-first century. We love Jesus, even if we have our problems with Christianity. We both graduated from Fuller Theological Seminary in Pasadena, California. Fuller stands out as one of the world's largest, most diverse training centers for ministers, missionaries, and psychologists. We have worked in organizations such as Young Life and with churches such as Sanctuary and New Ground. We have invested significant time living among people in Japan, the Soviet Union, Europe, and urban America. We both treasure conversation, thoroughly enjoying the classes we teach at the Art Center College of Design, the Los Angeles Film Studies Center, and Fuller Theological Seminary. This book arises out of ongoing conversations with our insightful students.

We write for that bright, passionate audience of young people whom advertisers covet and the church is in danger of losing. We hope to offer some clues, some handles, some reference points for processing the sensory avalanche that pop culture creates 24/7. We hope to inspire the person of faith struggling with too much information as well as artists and culture watchers who dig God but can't stomach religion. We've always preferred the conversations occurring on the margins, with people heading either toward or away from God with passion and conviction.

We acknowledge that the entertainment industry generates plenty of products worth criticizing. Pop culture can transmit many allusions and delusions, leading unsuspecting audiences toward paths of destruction. As parents, we share many of the concerns raised about music, television, and film's contribution to escalating social violence. We wonder if video games desensitize habitual users. We would never condone bankrupt films such as *The Cell* or avowedly destructive bands such as Slayer and Cannibal Corpse. We worry about the sexualizing of our culture, about consumerism, about what art exactly is!

While recognizing people's legitimate concerns, we believe that the "sins" of pop culture have received ample coverage in previous books. Our book will concentrate on what's right with pop culture. We write for those with a love for P.O.D., a passion for *The Matrix,* and a commitment to *Friends*. Rather than attack pop culture, we've chosen to adopt the directive captured on the provocative poster for *American Beauty*. We want to "look closer," to examine where God might be lurking in the songs, shows, and films kids continually return to for solace and meaning. We celebrate the rise of pop culture as among the most profound, provocative, exciting expressions of legitimate spiritual yearning in at least one hundred years. We turn to pop culture in our efforts to understand God and to recognize the twenty-first-century face of Jesus.

We embrace pop culture because we believe it offers a refreshing, alternative route to a Jesus who for many has been domesticated, declawed, and kept under wraps. As the Christian church has often adopted the role of moral policeman, pop culture has assumed the role of spiritual revolutionary, subverting and frustrating those religious authorities who desperately cling to black-and-white answers in an increasingly gray world. We write this book in hopes of freeing Jesus from the chains that have bound him. We believe a bold, ancient, radical Christ stands on the sidelines of the culture wars, waiting (in the words of Creed) "With Arms Wide Open," eager to engage our hearts, our minds, and our culture.

We recognize that defending pop culture from a position of faith puts us in a small (but ever growing) group. Many of the conversations in religious circles begin with questions of morality. Our students often start with concerns about what they can watch. How much is too much? Where would Jesus draw the line in his pop cultural diet? We congratulate those who have sought to frame cultural engagement as a test of personal purity. Plenty of books have tackled those concerns with varying degrees of insight.[1] For those hoping to find clear prescriptions for what Christians should or shouldn't watch and listen to, *this is not your book*.

Instead, we write for students who have decided to live out their faith with feet planted firmly *in the world*—with all the messy but exhilarating complications such discipleship brings. We believe popular culture stands as a vibrant and vital arena of spiritual expression. It is the place where our faith and feelings are energized, tested, and refined. We've chosen to enter into the ambiguity that characterizes Western pop culture. In an era in which slain rapper Tupac Shakur can sing "Dear Mama," "F— the World," and "Only God Can Judge Me" on the same CD, we can't imagine any other option.[2]

At the same time, we have no interest in deepening generational divides.[3] We write in an effort to bridge the mutually frustrating gap between those who "get it" and those who aren't even sure what "it" is. We do not want to reinforce the recurring blind spot within the emerging postmodern church, "Thou Shalt Be Cool."[4] As the Jews demanded miraculous signs and the Greeks looked for wisdom, the next generation wants relevance. This book offers an overabundance of relevant and timely examples. But we don't hold up the cool, the trendy, or the pop cultural as the ideal. We need much more than relevance to negotiate our tumultuous era. We hope to communicate Christ crucified—the power, the wisdom, and the relevance of God.

Borrowing at least a page from theologian Karl Barth, we approach our faith (and this book) with the Bible in one hand and pop culture in the other. Most Christian attempts to engage pop culture have begun with the Bible, placing it as the standard against which pop culture must be judged. For many, this has created a gulf between what they hear in a worship setting and what they experience the remainder of the week. Frustration, confusion, and guilt can cripple those desperately trying to harmonize the Bible with their everyday lives. They want to understand how the same God can speak to them through R-rated films such as *The Shawshank Redemption* or *Braveheart* while calling them to "flee from sexual immorality" (1 Cor. 6:18). We have bridged that gap by reading our Bible *through* the grid of pop culture, what scholars call reversing the hermeneutical flow.[5] We construct our theology through a pop cultural matrix, allowing pop culture to speak for itself *before* we apply biblical interpretation.

We have found this approach helpful in understanding why Christian efforts to engage pop culture often end up communicating judgment and condemnation rather than love. In the New Testament, only the Gospels were written with the general public in mind. Yet many in the church read pop culture in light of Peter, Paul, and John's letters. Books of the Bible intended as "in-house" documents, designed to purify God's people, have been used inappropriately to correct the broader culture. So the warnings against sexual immorality in 1 Corinthians 7 get directed toward audiences Paul never intended. As he writes in 1 Corinthians 5:12–13, "What business is it of mine to judge those outside the church? Are you not to judge those inside? God will judge those outside."

Putting pop culture first has heightened our understanding of overlooked and underappreciated biblical texts. This method also allows us to "read" pop culture in its proper biblical context, alongside the section of the Old Testament known as "the writings."[6] For the Christian community, this is the middle of the Old Testament between the history and the prophets. In the Hebrew Bible, the writings come after the prophets and include (in this order) Psalms,

Job, Proverbs, Ruth, the Song of Solomon, Ecclesiastes, Lamentations, Esther, Daniel, Ezra, Nehemiah, and 1–2 Chronicles.[7]

We believe popular music should be heard in the same manner as the Psalms, as celebrations of the gift of God-given life. But the Top 40 charts also contain songs of longing, regret, anger, and doubt. Pop music has helped us hear the Psalms as prayers, formed in frustration, offered to a sometimes hidden God. We appreciate Job's sufferings even more after watching Mel Gibson's struggle in *Signs*. Proverbs' recurring emphasis on the danger of shortcuts, the snares of temptation, and the rewards of honesty finds expression in sitcoms such as *The Simpsons*. The Song of Solomon's obsession with love, with the celebration of the physical, dominates the radio dial. The weariness expressed in Ecclesiastes flows through the precincts of *NYPD Blue* and the suburbs of *American Beauty*. Lamentations deals with grief, which Eric Clapton captured so eloquently in "Tears in Heaven."

Like the Old Testament writings, pop culture is the collected wisdom of our era. It includes explorations of injustice, songs of sorrow, tributes to women. Like the Book of Esther, it may not mention the name of God. Like Ecclesiastes, it may suggest that in this life good doesn't always triumph over evil. Like the Song of Solomon, it may celebrate sex. It may not have a salvific purpose, but it still offers us essential perspective, comfort, wisdom. Its artistry often stands alone as smaller, isolated truths that endure the test of time.

We employ a diverse and multidisciplinary methodology in our investigation of pop culture. We use anthropology, sociology, philosophy, theology, and gut instinct to draw conclusions and work things out. Our commitment to Jesus' kingdom mission fuels our search. We examine different aspects of popular culture "not as ends in themselves but as means of unlocking their meaning in the culture as a whole."[8] What's "hot" changes constantly, causing some to question the study of such "disposable" forms. Infamous celebrities such as Heidi Fleiss or Monica Lewinsky rise and fall with seasonal fashions. Kurt Warner can lead the St. Louis Rams to the Super Bowl one year and to a losing season the next. Prince and Bruce Springsteen ruled the '80s. Nirvana and Pearl Jam had their moment in the '90s. The Backstreet Boys replaced New Kids on the Block, who perfected formulas developed by the Jackson 5. Christina Aguilera turned Mariah Carey into an old-school nostalgia act. Christina has been usurped by Avril Lavigne and Michelle Branch. And so it goes . . .

The realm of popular culture is so vast that our approach in this book must be subjective. We tackle issues and aspects of popular culture that we find interesting. They include (in order of impact): advertising, celebrity, music, movies, television, fashion, sports, and art. They are not the only "denominations" worthy of study. We leave the enduring appeal of NASCAR and country music to others.[9] Important volumes on the ten-billion-dollar video game industry will need to be written. But these arenas surely are central, serious, and worthy of careful theological reflection. It is difficult to analyze pop culture because of its interlocking, all-consuming power. TV underwrites sports. Movies and music create celebrities. Celebrities wear the fashions. Advertising tells us where to buy the clothes, using superstar athletes to push products on TV. Yet to criticize advertising as subliminal seduction or to reject capitalism for creating false demands seems too easy, especially given the collapse of communism and the spread of democratic capitalism. We hope to offer a conscientious response to a given, lived reality.

Neal Gabler encapsulates the triumph of pop culture in his brilliant book *Life the Movie*.[10] He makes a compelling case that moving images have not merely reflected or influenced reality. Our very lives have become "movies," with all of us playacting, stars of our own "lifies." We put on a costume almost every day, whether we want to appear classy, sporty, casual, defiant, unique, sexy, or religious. We cast ourselves, dressing like celebrities, imitating whatever pose we consider cool. We do not sit outside the culture, planning how to approach it. Pop culture *is* our culture, the air that we breathe, for better or worse.

Gabler cuts through the moral grandstanding, refusing to fall into the familiar and tiresome trap of lamenting the reach of electronic media. Instead, he builds a case by assuming pop culture's triumph in almost evolutionary terms. He recasts the debate as a struggle between "realists" and "post-realists," between those who think we "[stand] on a precipice" and those who think we "[stand] in a bright new dawn."[11] He doesn't answer the question but considers it central to the emerging epoch. Hopefully, we'll clearly communicate that we see a renaissance, a new dawn, the stirrings of a profound, spiritual renewal.

For the sake of space, we limited ourselves to recent examples of the subjects we discuss. We do not expect or aspire to make our chapters definitive histories. The sheer avalanche of information available guarantees that our readers will bring more expertise to particular areas of pop culture fandom. The chapters are intended as sketches to make you think more critically about your own fields of interest, rather than comprehensive answers. We offer our stories and perspectives not as *the* reading but as *a* reading of pop culture.

In fact, this book offers two distinct readings of pop culture. We will take turns, analyzing aspects of pop culture that appeal to our particular areas of interest. Barry covers advertising, music, fashion, and art. Craig writes on celebrity, movies, television, and sports. You will notice our distinctive styles, our divergent backgrounds. We write the book as a form of dialogue, a give and take, so important in a culture of pluralism expressed in a matrix of meanings.

More than anything, we hope our discussions will inspire your own theological engagement with popular culture—stimulating your curiosity, broadening your mind, deepening your faith. We aspire to much more than a snapshot at the dawn of the twenty-first century. We hope to identify a matrix of meanings that sharpens your own meaning-making activity. Pop culture is so broad that the opportunities for spiritual reflection and inspiration are endless. In light of this fact, we offer more of a first rather than a final word, joining an exciting, expanding, much-needed conversation. We hope you enjoy the ride and discover the divine emerging from the matrix.

acknowledgments

This book is an ongoing community project. It started at Sanctuary, an experimental faith community where we first tossed around these ideas. We're indebted to our academic community, Fuller Theological Seminary. We have been challenged by the sharp minds and urgent hearts gathered there. We especially acknowledge the insight and support of Robert K. Johnston and William A. Dyrness, editors of the Engaging Culture series. We've been richly influenced by the scholarship and friendship of Richard Mouw, Chap Clark, Wilbert Shenk, John Smith, Richard Peace, Eddie Gibbs, and John and Olive Drane. We also acknowledge Fred and Dottie Davison and Clay Schmit for their commitment to encouraging more reflection on these issues through the Brehm Center for Worship, Theology, and the Arts.

Dialogue with fellow students and friends provided invaluable insight and help in honing our work. Bob Gabriel, Michael Evans, and Rick Bonn offered essential suggestions above and beyond the call of friendship. Joe Park, Mike Kemmerer, Amy Jacober, and Garrett Lambert served as key pop cultural scouts. We're also thrilled to introduce our readers to the artists who enhance and illustrate our text: Don McKinney, who makes us laugh while delivering devastating insights, and Barry's students at Art Center College of Design in Pasadena, California. Thanks also to the Baker Academic community for believing in this theological conversation enough to give us the opportunity to write this book.

Finally, we acknowledge those closest to us, our friends and family, who lived far too much of this book with us. We are especially indebted to our partners, Caroline and Donna, for their encouragement and input. We proudly dedicate this book to our kids, the new "children of the revolution" who are just starting to sing the silly love songs of Jesus: Zoe, Theo, and Rylee.

introduction

Postmodernity in the Marketplace

When the forms of an old culture are dying, the new culture is created by a few people who are not afraid to be insecure.

Rudolph Bahro, quoted in *The Post-Evangelical*

Future Christianity is generating itself from the lives of those who have fled to the margins.

Sister Wendy Beckett

This book arises from a mutual love of two things: theology and popular culture. We want to explore the intersections between these two *seemingly* polar opposites.[1] Religious ideas and imagery float throughout our world, from the cross around Madonna's neck in her "Like a Prayer" video to the phrase "In God We Trust" on American currency. Pop culture returns the favor, offering God prominent billing, from Lauryn Hill's sublime song "To Zion" to Jim Carrey in *Bruce Almighty*. When the St. Louis Rams' quarterback Kurt Warner points a finger upward after a Super Bowl touchdown pass, sports fans join him in praising his Lord, whether implicitly or explicitly. Jesus makes regular guest appearances in all arenas of popular culture, including irreverent television shows such as *South Park*. God haunts the work of controversial Nigerian artist Chris Ofili. Theology and pop culture seem to have a mutual attraction and an intimate interrelationship.

Do not let a "serious" word like *theology* scare you. Theology involves talking about God, something you, your friends, and your music are already engaged in. We're all theologians to some degree, whether we realize it or not. *The Door* magazine named Buffy the Vampire Slayer its 2002 "theologian of the year." In this book, we want to look at theology through the lens of popular culture, to learn about perceptions of God in general, and to discover the evolving role the divine may play in our everyday lives. We aim to create a theology *out of* popular culture rather than a theology *for* popular culture. We want to join the theologizing already occurring *within* popular culture, outside the reaches of the traditional academy or religion.

We challenge you to "look closer," to discover the surprising messages God may already be broadcasting through the mass media. This is not a new divine strategy. God did something similar in Old Testament times, using the Assyrians (in Isaiah) and the Chaldeans (in Habakkuk) to correct his people. God's perceived "enemies" often prove much friendlier to God's purposes than initially imagined. Madonna's "Like a Virgin" carried a certain shock value twenty-five years ago. But looking closer, we see that what appeared to be a celebration of sexual intercourse was actually a prayer of longing and regret. Madonna says:

> At first, I mean, I was surprised with how people reacted to "Like a Virgin," because when I did the song, to me, I was singing about how something made me feel a certain way—brand new and fresh—and everyone else interpreted it as "I don't want to be a virgin anymore." . . . People thought I was saying I just wanted to have sex, when it meant just the opposite. It celebrates the idea of feeling untouched and pure. I like having the secret knowledge that what it said was good.[2]

Catholic priest Andrew Greeley acknowledges that Madonna's "Like a Virgin" video celebrates "a powerful erotic fantasy" but finds parallels in "the way we are in the presence of God." Greeley writes, "It seems evident that we are hearing the timeless cry of the human heart for renewal. Is not the gentle care with which the singer's lover treats her the way God alleges that He treats us? Is He not the lover Hosea of the Jewish scriptures?"[3] Or even the beloved in the Song of Songs?

Learning to "look closer" will take time; it will take work; it will take patience. But those willing to engage pop culture with eyes wide open may find themselves pleasantly surprised and spiritually energized.

The theological term behind learning to look closer is "common grace." It begins with an appreciation of the creative side of God, the goodness initiated in Genesis that continues through the Spirit's ongoing work of conscience. It finds biblical roots wherever God used questionable sources, such as Cyrus, the king of Persia (Isaiah 45), to restore his people, the Hebrews. Exhibiting a sense of humor and playful surprise, the God of the Old Testament speaks through such unlikely means as a burning bush, a donkey, and a dream. Jesus continues the unpredictable, inverted pattern. He chooses tax collectors and fishermen to initiate his kingdom. He befriends prostitutes and defends a woman caught in adultery. Social outcasts and pariahs such as Samaritans, widows, and orphans are singled out as particularly compelling (and surprising) role models. When Jesus parades into Jerusalem to shouts of praise and the waving of palm fronds, the religious authorities of that era demanded that he get his followers "under control." Jesus fired back, "If they kept quiet, the stones would do it for them, shouting praise" (Luke 19:40 THE MESSAGE).

Common grace explains why the most spiritual movies are often made by people outside the formal borders of the church. Robert Duvall offered an inspiring and humane portrayal of a Pentecostal preacher in *The Apostle*. Tim Robbins directed *Dead Man Walking,* a transcendent story of a death row inmate's spiritual journey with a nun. Vanguard Church in Colorado Springs considers Paul Thomas Anderson's sprawling *Magnolia* "their film, the closest approximation of what we're about."[4] When television shows such as *The West Wing* and *The Simpsons* feature sincere prayers to God, common grace takes a bow. When Dave Matthews sings, "Bartender, please fill my glass with the wine you gave Jesus that set him free," common grace claims another platinum record. Common grace subverts preconceived notions of how, when, and through whom God chooses to communicate. It makes God bigger and the evangelist's burden lighter.

In this book, we will search for today's burning bushes, talking donkeys, pillaging Chaldeans, dishonest tax collectors, and seemingly voiceless stones. We will look in surprising and humorous places to discover God's unlikeliest saints. We hope you will also find them, as we have, spiritually nurturing.

For ministers, missionaries, and those inside the church, pop culture can be our new best friend. For skeptics, scoffers, and doubters, both inside and outside the church, beware—ever subversive pop culture might be pointing you toward the divine. For those who find themselves regularly moved to tears, rage, and laughter via movies, music, or TV, welcome home. We're here to confirm what we all inherently sense—that something big, brash, and shockingly spiritual is happening.

Defining Popular Culture

> Culture is what your butcher would have if he were a surgeon.
>
> Mary Pettibone Poole

What is popular culture? Most of us have a rough idea from the very phrase itself, but some clarification will help for the sake of our discussion. Scholars generally make distinctions between popular culture and high or "elite" culture. High culture traditionally merited the most academic and scholastic attention. The word *culture* was reserved for human works of only the highest sophistication and quality. A symphony orchestra qualified, while a rock group did not.

Analysts of popular culture use broader definitions of the word *culture,* making fewer value, taste, or quality judgments. Movies, cartoons, comic books, T-shirts, ball gowns, symphonies, and rock bands *all* constitute "culture."

Our particular understanding of popular culture finds root in scholarship represented by the work of Russel Nye, a key figure in the development of popular cultural analysis as an academic field. This circle of scholars argues that popular culture requires a mass audience created by urbanization and democratization along with technologies of mass distribution, in other words, mass media in all forms. Nye writes that popular culture "describes a cultural condition that could not have appeared in Western Civilization before the late eighteenth century."[5] Ray Browne considers popular culture an indistinct term whose edges are blurred.[6] Yet within those blurred boundaries, he finds a widespread, common, usually commercial, and sometimes entertaining product. Those who study pop culture consider the everyday world of people, without necessarily determining who those people are exactly, and acknowledge that we are dealing with spectrums of popularity. Some elements of popular culture, such as jazz, do not reach as broad an audience as pop stars such as Linkin Park. Yet the enduring influence of jazz cannot be ignored. A definition of popular culture must include an acknowledgment of that which is—by virtue of its influence—worthy of attention and reflection.

This book falls within the broad and growing field known as cultural studies. Richard Hoggarth's 1957 book, *The Uses of Literacy,* is generally acknowledged as cultural studies' starting point.[7] Hoggarth focused on working-class life, offering a personal, subjective response to the changes coursing through postwar England. He criticized the imported American culture that threatened to colonize the British working classes through the growing mass media. From the beginning, cultural studies has championed the underclass, criticized capitalism, and berated America's dominance. Hoggarth founded the Centre for Contemporary Cultural Studies in 1964. The University of Birmingham and scholars such as Stuart Hall became the locus for most of the subsequent intellectual debate on the subject. Assuming Hoggarth's focus on politics and economics, scholars "read" pop culture from Marxist, feminist, and post-colonial perspectives. London's Routledge Press published most of the seminal overviews central to the discipline. Cultural studies has analyzed cultural practices in relationship to power structures, hoping to understand and undercut the dominant structures that undergird the cultural assumptions in capitalist society. It has trained people to read the signs and decode pop cultural texts to promote new forms of representation. Semiotics emerged as the study of pop culture's signs and symbols.

While we acknowledge our debt to pioneers such as Walter Benjamin, bell hooks, and Teresa de Lauretis, we seek to move beyond the politicized categories established in our field. With the fall of communism and the rise of postmodern feminism and queer theory, cultural studies has fragmented into an exhausting variety of subcategories rooted in competing agendas. How ironic that a discipline born in dissent outside the traditional centers of power would dissolve into a debate of elites connected almost exclusively to the academy. We seek to integrate and move past the fragmenting fields of dissent. Our cultural studies deals with politics, acknowledges gender, emphasizes narrative, and appreciates the subjective response of individual readers. But we hope to offer more than a critique. We want to encourage an appreciation for the arts and artists that create our pop cultural artifacts. We have chosen to concentrate on particular genres, from advertising to sports, in an effort to develop an interdisciplinary response to our overwhelming, all-consuming pop culture. Consider this book *a cultural studies reader,* borrowing from the best of what's gone before but adding a spiritual interpretation to pop culture's increasingly diverse texts.

Why Study Popular Culture?

> The very commonness of everyday things harbors the eternal marvel and silent mystery of God.
>
> Karl Rahner, quoted in *Virtual Faith*

Why should we pay attention to such a seemingly frivolous thing as popular culture? There are at least four reasons. First, and most simply, popular culture both reflects who we are as people and also helps shape us as people. The implications of both factors are profound. We've participated in a number of conversations about whether popular culture shapes public ideas or merely acts as a mirror reflecting our ideas back to us. These conversations have often arisen in the wake of traumatic events, such as 1999's Columbine High School shootings, in which particular elements of popular culture, in this case violent video games and movies, seem to have had a shaping role. Proponents for each perspective eagerly mount their defense or attack based on their particular view, while reality occupies a much more complex space. Popular culture can rarely be reduced to an either/or scenario. If it could absolutely shape and dominate our lives, pop culture would have a far higher success rate. The volume of films and music releases that fail to recoup their costs demonstrates the fragility of such an argument. Adolescents' steady diet of *The Eminem Show* and *Mortal Kombat* has been accompanied by a drop in statistics linking teens to violent crime. Overestimating pop culture's ability to influence frustrates those teens who rightly claim to think for themselves. Perhaps cultural watchdogs have overstated their case in order to generate more headlines for their cause.

Nevertheless, underestimating pop culture's shaping power can also be dangerous. Our perceptions of reality can be altered by the emphasis (or lack thereof) popular culture places on certain issues, persons, or places. Only recently have

African-Americans witnessed television shows built exclusively around them. For many years, black people were relegated to television roles as butlers, maids, and criminals, underscoring the marginalized position they already held in society. In the sixties, Bill Cosby and Diahann Carroll challenged perceptions on the TV series *I Spy* and *Julia*. The landmark miniseries *Roots* (1977) brought the painful history of slavery into millions of homes. Starting in the 1980s, with the runaway success of *The Cosby Show,* black viewers finally had several shows to call their own. MTV reluctantly embraced hip-hop culture every afternoon on *Yo! MTV Raps*. By the nineties, Martin Lawrence, Brandy, and the Wayans Brothers all contributed (both positively and negatively) to the changing racial climate.

Consider the evolving opinions about homosexuality accelerated by television's treatment of gay characters. The raging controversy around Ellen DeGeneres's coming out on her eponymous sitcom gave way to the wildly successful *Will and Grace*. Five years after *Ellen,* Viacom announced that its MTV and Showtime divisions were exploring a joint effort to create a gay network. PrideVision debuted in Canada in September 2001. Author Malcolm Boyd recalls, "Thirty years ago it would have taken a civil rights action to get something like this started. Now, it's a business decision."[8] Pop culture shapes who we are and who we're becoming.

Second, popular culture must be investigated theologically because it is already studied by the broader culture. Society already employs movies, music, and television as an arena of discourse, the primary forum for disseminating values, ideas, and ethics. Robert Mapplethorpe, Andres Serrano, and Karen Finley generated tremendous controversy and debate concerning what constitutes art and whether government should fund "obscene" work. Oliver Stone's film *Natural Born Killers* and Ice-T's song "Cop Killer" landed in court, used by both the defense and the prosecution to discuss murder. The satirical movie *Wag the Dog* initiated dialogue about then-president Bill Clinton's apparent indiscriminate bombing of targets in the Middle East as a means of deflecting attention away from his personal, moral problems. Spike Lee's poignant 1997 documentary *4 Little Girls* put the 1963 bombing of a Baptist church in Birmingham, Alabama, back in the public eye. Eventually, Ku Klux Klansman Bobby Frank Cherry was found guilty of first-degree murder for killing four black teens thirty-nine years after his heinous act.[9]

Within the broader society, popular culture stands as the place where certain ideas are elevated and others are condemned. Debates about racial stereotypes spill into passionate arguments for and against sports mascots such as baseball's Cleveland Indians and Atlanta Braves or the NFL's Kansas City Chiefs and Washington Redskins. The genial ensemble film *Barbershop* launched a storm of protests by joking about Rosa Parks and Martin Luther King Jr. The comments of *Politically Incorrect* host Bill Maher about American military cowardice after the 9/11 terrorist attacks were too political and led to his cancellation. MTV gets credit for electing Bill Clinton and the blame when kids imitate *Jackass*.

Controversy surrounding Eminem's homophobic lyrics on *The Marshall Mathers LP* grew to a firestorm after Elton John agreed to join him in a performance of "Stan" at the 2001 Grammy Awards. Public libraries become a battlefield for arguments about online access, Internet pornography, and kids. One must follow pop culture in order to understand key issues that clearly affect and shape our society culturally, politically, and spiritually—the same society we are called to engage with Jesus' message and person.

Third, pop culture serves as the lingua franca of the postmodern world, a point often missed by scholars. Allan Bloom's book *The Closing of the American Mind* raked America's places of higher learning over the coals for students' apparent ignorance. Bloom used literacy standards from earlier times, when American society was decidedly more homogeneous, much less pluralistic, and definitely less mediatized. Bloom and his followers refuse to recognize that young people have developed a new "canon" of literacy. This new canon draws from a broader range of influences and from a wider range of source materials, including classic literature and classic movies, songs, and even comic books. The new literacy is democratic, much less elitist, and decidedly influenced by the effects of mediatization. Bono and the Edge of U2 have replaced James Joyce as Dublin's most important writers. Philosophy teachers would be wise to use Richard Linklater's animated film *Waking Life* (2001) as an introduction to Nietzsche, Schleiermacher, and Hegel. For today's students, slain rapper Tupac Shakur stands as the most influential African-American poet. An English class at Oakland High School compared T. S. Eliot's "Love Song of J. Alfred Prufrock" with "The Message" by Grandmaster Flash. The teachers believe that "hip-hop can be used as a bridge linking the seemingly vast span between the streets and the world of academics. . . . Rap is literature, a worthy subject of study in its own right."[10]

A technological literacy complements this new canon. Information can now be accessed in any number of ways—computers, the Internet, video, television—and literacies are developed that are often far beyond the grasp of those raised in a more print-based culture. The next wave of students is capable of reading these visual texts and is more comfortable with fast-moving, fragmented pieces of information than were previous generations. Consequently, learning through popular culture allows them to draw on their existing literacies and analyze and think critically. This leads to the fourth point regarding popular culture.

There has been a tendency in academic environs to engage with only what can be viewed as high culture. Academia seems to be intoxicated with "ideas from above"—with the view that the best ideas, and those most worthy of study, emanate from the intelligentsia and trickle down to the rest of society (a very old way of viewing things in our opinion). But much has changed in Western culture in the past one hundred years, not the least of which is the onset of postmodernism with its "from below" perspective about ideas and values. Jean-François Lyotard, one of the key thinkers in the field, suggests that a hallmark of the postmodern age is that previously unheard voices can be heard and can influence society.[11] In an age of expanding democracy, the people's voice of choice became pop culture.

Yet Christian leadership often followed the academy rather than the people. To counter the rise of scientific modernism, the evangelical church tried to get serious about intellectual credibility.[12] Fuller Theological Seminary, founded by the most popular radio evangelist of his era, Charles E. Fuller, was founded on two key principles. Fuller wrote, "It should stand out first, as being absolutely true to the fundamentals of the faith and second, as a school of high scholarship."[13] At a 1948 convocation, founding president, Dr. Harold John Ockenga, stressed that "ministers had to have the 'best education' in order to answer rationalism, secularism, and evolutionary emphases." In a recurring practical joke by Fuller students, the first "o" in "theological" is removed, making "Fuller The logical Seminary."

Christian apologetics concentrated on "proving" the existence of God. Josh McDowell's *Evidence That Demands a Verdict* became an influential text. In a scientific era, many assumed that American society was secular, humanist, and godless, shaped by the rampant twentieth-century philosophical claims related to nihilism and the "death of God." But an engagement with the popular culture of the same period may have led to the development of an entirely different apologetic starting point. Fascination with Eastern mysticism and religion was voiced by bands such as the Beatles in the 1960s. Bob Dylan surprised his most ardent fans with his conversion to Christianity in the 1970s. *The Exorcist* scared filmgoers while treating spiritual warfare quite seriously. In contrast to the dearth of spiritually informed conversation in most academic circles, popular culture of the same time was abounding with the search for transcendence.

The best-selling Left Behind books of Jerry Jenkins and Tim LaHaye serve as a particularly vexing example. Literally millions of readers have latched on to the millennial thrillers. Yet the Left Behind phenomenon managed to unite the publishing intelligentsia and evangelical thinkers in mutual revulsion. Whether lambasting shallow character development or questioning the books' "fear-based" dispensational theology, critics of the Left Behind series cannot comprehend how these books captured the hearts and minds of a public that keeps buying each new installment.[14] America's enduring fascination with the end times flies in the face of twentieth-century rationalism. Yet interest in eschatology and the Bible's apocalyptic literature continues to rise in these uncertain times. Left-wing academics *and* credibility-hungry Christian scholars are both being left behind by an era of superstition, irrationality, and spiritual hunger.

At the turn of a new millennium, God has never been more alive in Western culture. In fact, one could argue that the definitive characteristic of the postmodern era is religion. America experienced a veritable religious awakening in the last decades of the twentieth century, and popular culture holds the evidence. Religion, or "spirituality," informs the lives of musicians such as Moby, DMX, Creed, Nas, Destiny's Child, Lifehouse, India.Arie, and the Beastie Boys. The film world experienced *Ghost, The Sixth Sense, Kundun, The Others, The Devil's*

Advocate, and a host of other films that have at their center questions and views about religion and the supernatural. This divide between the academy and the populace leaves modern Christianity, which took its theological cues from the academy, with a lamentable theological grid, one that does not speak to the questions being asked today. Most people we meet have no need for the proof of God's existence. Their issues and objections center around the institutionalism and practice of religion, around evil and life's randomness—time-honored questions of theodicy raised even by those still in the church.

These questions surfaced in *The Third Miracle* (1999), starring Ed Harris as a priest struggling with doubt. Polish filmmaker Agnieszka Holland crafted a deeply moving, faith-affirming film that looks at the issues of church authority, sainthood, and humanity. The film's producers organized a test screening, inviting a segment of the public to watch the film, fill out surveys, and answer questions from the filmmakers. Typical test screenings ask audiences whether they liked the main characters, how the story played, and if they would recommend it to others. As music supervisor on the film, Barry was in attendance, taking notes. At the end of *The Third Miracle,* the producers wanted feedback related to the relationship between the main characters and how the story played out. Instead, they got a heated conversation about faith versus rationalism, the potential dangers of church, and why the bulk of those who attended the screening held no organized religious affiliation yet viewed themselves as deeply spiritual.

There is a conversation about God going on in popular culture that the church is not engaged in and is often unaware of. If the Christian world continues in its scholastic mode, viewing popular culture as degraded and superficial, then the gap between church and culture will continue to widen. Our theological propositions will become increasingly redundant to a culture being influenced by other forces. The Gospels were written for "the people." Educated Greeks in the first century communicated in Attic Greek, a high cultural form that excluded many. But the writers of the Gospels preferred Koine Greek, a "street-level" language that communicated to the masses. We must get back to that street-level discussion, where our faith was forged.[15] People of faith need to become conversant with the new canon, the new literacy, and join the new conversation. Only in this way can we hear Jesus afresh. Only in this way can the Spirit quicken our spirits. Only in this way can we allow God to be fully God.

Postmodernity

Down is the new up.

sign on a hotel elevator in London[16]

In 1963, Bob Dylan released an influential song that captured the unrest and foment of change in America. He sang "The Times They Are A-Changing," and a generation rallied around it as an anthem for their populist revolution. In 2000, thirty-seven tumultuous years later, Dylan won an Academy Award for "Things Have Changed." This marks the postmodern shift: Things are no longer merely in the process of change; things, my friends, have changed. And by things, we do mean *everything*. Postmodernity doesn't mean a mere adjustment of modernity. It is a quantum leap into a new world of ideas, values, and ethics. All of Western society has been impacted, and nothing is really the same. Rationalism, faith in the future, and many of the ideas that fueled modern Western life have been discarded or, at least, reinvented.

Television's original picture of parenting, Ozzie and Harriet Nelson, has been supplanted by Ozzy and Sharon in *The Osbournes*. Hollywood stars such as Arnold Schwarzenegger and Sylvester Stallone have been replaced by new, multi-racial stars such as Vin Diesel and the Rock, who reflect the diversity of our era. Fervor once found at Billy Graham crusades now resides in U2's Elevation tour. Old categories of ethics, race, and religion have been reconfigured by postmodernity's new way of perceiving the world.

While we have no desire to engage in a lengthy discussion of the term *postmodern*, a brief description of how we understand the word may prove helpful. We believe in a "practical postmodernism," which we will call "postmodernity." The "real world," not philosophical thought, first brought us into contact with this reality. In our faith community, we did not discuss postmodernity as an idea but first experienced it as a lived reality. Understanding a slippery term such as *postmodern* can actually be made simple. We have heard any number of times, "The old ways, the old ideas, the way I was told the world works no longer ring true, and I am looking for another way of understanding it." Most people have not read the philosophical ideas behind postmodern theory; they've simply experienced them. Few have heard of Jean Beaudrillard or Jacques Derrida, but they have a practical knowledge that things have changed, and changed dramatically.

We recognize that not everything old needs to be dismissed or dismantled. History reveals recurring blind spots. The pendulum swings from scientists to artists, war to peace, doubt to faith. Many of last century's theological debates look foolhardy and shortsighted today. But we do not want to brush aside the twentieth century to create an equally narrow future. Modernism isn't the enemy. Postmodernism isn't the solution. But the recent changes are so significant, the current questions so intense, and the future opportunities so exciting that we find ourselves shaking people of faith who would rather shut their eyes and turn back the clock. We'd rather look foolish today than at the turn of the *next* century—not because we worship the new and unknown but because the current, postmodern reality should thrill those eager to put wheels on their faith.

We actually draw a distinction between postmodernism and postmodernity. Postmodernism comprises the theory, the philosophical views about the subject, and is for all intents and purposes dead in the water. There is already talk in many academic circles of *post-postmodernism,* the implication being that postmodernism is passé. The average person on the street has little interest in wrestling with the postmodern theorists; life is moving way too quickly, and the theories are diverse and lack cohesion.[17] But postmodernity is alive and kicking. It is the culture, the way of life, that rolls along with barely an acknowledgment of the theory that supposedly birthed it.

Theology does not occur within a vacuum—the changing times Bob Dylan sang about have swept through theology as well, breaking down the traditional lines and categories, changing the way theology is done. In his important work *The Shattered Spectrum,* Lonnie Kliever tracks these recent shifts in theology.[18] While diversity and change are endemic to theology, Kliever notes that "in the modern era theological disagreements . . . usually occurred along fairly predictable lines. . . . But this venerable theological spectrum has been shattered by the turbulent theological movements of the last quarter century."[19] He says that the new pluralism in theology "is largely an outcome of a long process of adjustment to certain structural and ideological changes within the wider culture."[20] Perhaps theologians, like the rest of our mediatized culture, draw from a new canon of literacy that informs their theological conclusions. We cannot underestimate the importance of learning this new canon. Kliever goes on to explore some of these twentieth-century theologies, theologies of hope, secularity, process, play, and narrative.[21] To these we would like to add another—a theology out of popular culture, forged in the marketplace, rooted in a matrix of meanings.

Jesus in the Marketplace

> Modern mass culture, aimed at the "consumer," the civilization of prosthetics, is crippling people's souls, setting up barriers between man and the crucial questions of his existence, his consciousness of himself as a spiritual being.
>
> Andrei Tarkovsky, *Sculpting in Time*

The bloody twentieth century can be viewed as a battle of competing "isms." The economic problems in post–World War I Europe gave rise to Adolf Hitler and Nazism. A depressed Italy regained pride and purpose under Mussolini's Fascism. Allied forces united in victory during World War II soon splintered into competing camps of capitalism versus communism. The Cold War traveled to Korea, Vietnam, and Cuba. So imagine the shock that accompanied the collapse of communism in the late 1980s. Countries that had succumbed to the Soviets forty years earlier now tore down barriers and smashed the walls.

Poland, East Germany, Czechoslovakia, Yugoslavia, Hungary, and even the Soviet Union were suddenly free. Only the communists in Cuba and China managed to retain power. Democratic capitalism emerged as the clear victor in the Cold War. The glory of the free market, spread by American pop culture's movies, music, and TV, undermined a half century of communism. We now live in a post-ideological era.

American pop culture fueled these profound, ideological victories. Massive military might could not unseat communists in Eastern Europe. But Victor Havel, a playwright, fueled by the rebellious sounds of the Rolling Stones, managed to free Czechoslovakia from the Soviet Union. Sights and sounds of America undermined the Berlin Wall and the Iron Curtain. The almost revolution in China's Tienamen Square came equipped with images (and recreations) of the Statue of Liberty. The ideas of democracy were spread by the products of democracy—our music, movies, and television shows. The arrival of borderless delivery systems such as the Internet only make the dissemination of "Americanism" more inevitable. Thomas Friedman credits the democratization of information: "Thanks to satellite dishes, the Internet and television, we can now see through, hear through and look through almost every conceivable wall. . . . The days when governments could totally isolate their people from information about what life was like beyond their borders or even beyond their village are over."[22]

The new global superpower is entertainment. The top of the charts measures the new military might. While Marxist critics bemoan pop culture's exploitation of the masses, we suggest that the masses actually want what the marketplace offers. The increasing gap between commercial success and critical acclaim rankles some. Accomplished films that fail to crack the top ten in their opening weekend are pulled, condemned to becoming cult items at best. A book gets discussed only after enough people have bought it. A painter's value is tied directly to the current price of his or her art. The exorbitant price the J. Paul Getty Trust paid for van Gogh's *Irises* turned the modest painting into a must-see event—"So that's what fifty million dollars looks like." Sales figures become the inevitable, essential means of lifting certain pop culture artifacts above the information overload. The post-ideological world traffics in dollars and cents. And the marketplace stands as the ground of our postmodern being.

Consider our work a tract for the times rather than a system for the ages. We will not attempt to reshape systematic theology. Instead, we seek to develop a "marketplace theology."[23] In his Gospel, Luke includes this comment from Jesus: "To what, then, can I compare the people of this generation? What are they like? They are like children sitting in the marketplace and calling to each other: 'We played the flute for you, and you did not dance; we sang a dirge, and you did not cry'" (7:31–32). The parable depicts two groups of children playing in the market—one group playing wedding music but unable to get the others to dance, the second group playing a funeral march and unable to get the others to act as mourners. Jesus sees a parabolic message for the religious leaders of his day in these two children's games. They symbolically frame life and death. Some may consider the pop cultural products that call us to dance frothy, superficial, or forgettable. Others may see far too much darkness, negativity, and depression in today's music. But Jesus calls us to pay attention to kids' music, to listen carefully to the songs emerging in the marketplace, whether they urge us to celebrate or to cry. We want to avoid the mistakes of those who called John the Baptist demon possessed and Jesus a glutton, a drunkard, and a tax collector. We invite you to listen to the cries of those who've been labeled demons and drunkards. Perhaps you will find surprising echoes of the prophetic voice of John the Baptist or the subversive teaching of the Son of Man.

Jesus spent a lot of time in public places, engaging people, hearing their stories, and telling his. He developed his theological approach within the marketplace, telling stories that made God's kingdom relevant to the people he encountered. At the same time, he directed blistering challenges to the prevailing trends within his own religious tradition. His approach differs from many of the theological methods developed within traditional theology that have been shaped by internal concerns about the church and its teachings. We contend that the marketplace (the cultural hot seat) was Jesus' academic arena, his theological context.

In the midst of the marketplace, Jesus developed his message of God's love. He discussed God's compassion and inclusion of the marginalized among the crowds. In Jesus' theological framework, women and children have access to God through prayer. Tax collectors and that strange category of people called "sinners" are welcome at a table God sets for us all. He used stories of the lives of common people to teach his own truths, truths that were often in conflict with prevailing religious ideas. Jesus heard from the marginalized how the official religion had often failed them. We need to hear the same thing.

The marketplace includes more than business and the routine of everyday life. Ideas are exchanged in the marketplace. The dramas of life, lived between the wedding song and the funeral march, are played out in the marketplace. It is where humans face the challenges of living and dying, in ways not adequately addressed by stock, religious propositions. The belly of messy culture is also the place where questions of ultimate existence and realities are posed in naked, stripped-down fashion, devoid of the religious language of etiquette and propriety. In the marketplace, the band U2 poses this question: "Jesus, can you help me? I'm alone in this world, and a f— up world it is too."[24] Tom Waits sings of the murder and rape of a young girl and asks the question, "Why wasn't God watching? Why wasn't God watching sweet Georgia Lee?"[25] In the marketplace, doubts are aired, gloves come off, politeness takes a rest. Pop culture is our marketplace—the arena we visit daily to encounter issues of life and death, to discover what it means to be human, to hear the questions society asks, to meet God. The marketplace can (and must!) inform our theology.

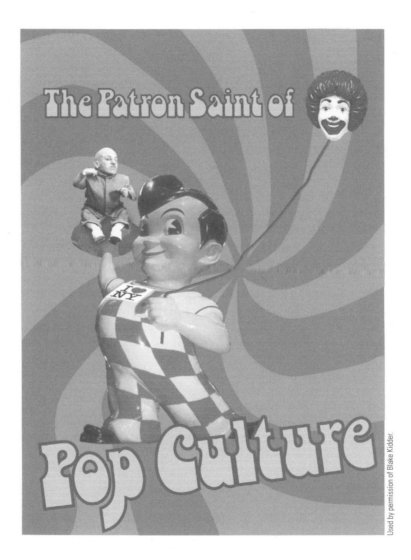

The Patron Saint of Pop Culture

methodology

1

A Matrix of Meanings

A theology mediates between a cultural matrix and the significance and role of religion in that matrix.

> Bernard Lonergan, *Method in Theology*

Trends, like horses, are easier to ride in the direction they are already going. . . . You may decide to buck the trend, but it is still helpful to know it is there.

> John Naisbitt and Patricia Aburdene, *Megatrends*

Blending, cut and paste, bricolage, cafeteria are all words that have been employed to describe the postmodern approach. The fragmented collages of Pablo Picasso hinted at the coming collision. Hip-hop music introduced the art of sampling. Now, DJs are considered musicians whether or not they play an instrument. The Wachowski Brothers' masterful trilogy *The Matrix* merged comic books, science fiction, Japanese anime, martial arts, mathematics, Eastern philosophy, and Western religion into something utterly new. That story ends with *The Matrix Revolutions*. But the postmodern shift is actually about "retrolutions." It doesn't shout, "Out with the old, in with the new." It rejects *recent* history but embraces our *cumulative* history. The old, or rather the ancient, serves as the new foundation. This "retrolution" presents "aspects of the future through terms set by the past, in order to make it palatable" today.[1]

We think of postmodernity as expressing a "consciousness of pluralisms." The veritable flood of ideas and information resulting from democratization and globalization has demanded "blending." Commentator Marshall McLuhan anticipated our global village, made smaller and more accessible by advancements in travel, technology, and science. At the same time, access to new ideas, values, and perspectives has exploded. The Internet allows instant access to virtually anything. Our understanding of time and space, geographical and political boundaries, has broadened and blurred. Previously elusive portions of the Vatican Library can be toured at anytime, from anywhere, by anyone with a computer and a phone line. Its vast contents can be discussed with any number of other interested parties around the globe without ever leaving the comfort of home. We find ourselves living in a world in which radically diverse worldviews emerge within the same society as alternative lifestyles, and belief systems exist side by side in ways not experienced before. The information overload has many calling postmodernity incoherent, but a close reading of the signs reveals highly discernible trends.

By approaching pop culture from the inside out, we find a matrix or pattern of meanings. Our theology will arise *out of* these recurring themes found in popular culture.[2] We search for patterns across disciplines, and a wealth of examples sharpens our understanding of God. Isolated cases within a particular pop cultural form need to be placed within the context of larger patterns of meaning in order for us to fully comprehend their contribution. This helps us avoid the trap of turning disposable examples into forgettable conclusions. These particular examples can then be viewed within the context of their own particular genre to determine whether their success reflects a change in the pattern or is simply an isolated creative uniqueness breaking through to capture the popular imagination for a moment.

Alienation and loneliness stand out as perpetual subjects in popular music. In one of Elvis Presley's first hits, "Heartbreak Hotel," we find him "down at the end of lonely street." Jackie Wilson's heart was crying "Lonely Teardrops" while Roy Orbison sang "Only the Lonely." This sense of alienation pervades virtually every genre of pop music right up through *NSYNC's "Bye Bye Bye" and Staind's "It's Been Awhile." What this says about life in the twenty-first century can possibly change our theological starting places when we engage culture in discussions about religion and faith.

The birth of the Cable News Network, the rise of world music, the influence of Chinese martial arts on Hollywood films, and the increase in foreign players entering the National Basketball Association suggest another burgeoning pattern. The world is getting smaller. German basketball player Dirk Nowitzki, Chinese movie idol Jackie Chan, and Columbian pop star Shakira may someday be remembered as asterisks within a much larger pattern—the blurring of borders brought on by globalization.

We have been amazed and encouraged by our discovery of Catholic theologian Bernard Lonergan. Only after we chose the title *A Matrix of Meanings* did a random web posting introduce us to his work.[3] Imagine our surprise when we learned:

It is Lonergan's position that . . . the shift from the classicist normative notion of culture to the [post] modern empirical notion requires that theology be conceived, not as a permanent achievement, but as an ongoing process of mediation between . . . a cultural matrix of meanings and values and a religion within that matrix. It is important to note, however, that Lonergan regarded the method proposed in *Method in Theology* to be a method for any discipline which draws upon the past to move into the future.[4]

As ubiquitous cell phone users say, "Can you hear me now?" A Canadian priest, trying to construct a theological method in 1972, looked at our changing culture and decided that fixed truths couldn't compete. He saw the future of theology as dynamic, ongoing, rooted in a cultural matrix of meanings. As with that of Lonergan, our theology starts by taking culture seriously. Only after careful inspection and reflection do we dare to locate values and religion within that matrix.

Consequently, this book can be read at least three ways. It is a study of the marketplace—driven by consumerism, fueled by advertising, whose highest aspirations are attained in celebrity. It is also a study of isolated artistic forms—music, movies, TV, fashion, sports, art—and what they may tell us about our world, ourselves, and our God. It is also a broad survey of culture that reveals several trends that cross art forms and invite serious, theological reflection. We're living in a post-national, post-rational, post-literal, post-scientific, post-technological, post-sexual, post-racial, post-human, post-traumatic, post-therapeutic, post-ethical, post-institutional, and post-Christian era (see fig.).

A Matrix of Meanings

	Music	Movies	TV	Fashion	Sports	Art
Post-national						
Post-rational						
Post-literal						
Post-scientific/technological						
Post-sexual						
Post-racial						
Post-human						
Post-traumatic/therapeutic						
Post-ethical/institutional						
Post-Christian						

Lived in the Marketplace   Driven by Consumerism   Fueled by Advertising   Attained by Celebrity

We are not suggesting that nations, science, or humanity is about to disappear. There will still be sex; there will still be Christians. But our assumptions and understandings of these concepts are being radically redefined. The discipline of cultural studies allows us to study the interrelationships of people and their practices. Postmodernism has already forced changes in philosophy and epistemology, our ways of thinking and knowing. Science and technology have pushed ethics into deep, uncharted waters. Anthropology must address the post-sexual, the post-racial, the post-human. Psychologists must wrestle with life beyond therapy, beyond Freud. Sociology tackles institutions, how we behave in group settings, for better or worse. Theology deals with institutions via ecclesiology, discussing what it means to be a faith community. All of these disciplines play a part in this book. These postmodern cultural shifts, studied in the context of the marketplace, manifested across pop cultural forms, create a lived theology that reveals the very nature of Christ and his kingdom. For best results, we recommend a thorough blending.

Post-national

> In a foreign country people don't expect you to be just like them, but in Los Angeles, which is infiltrating the world, they don't consider that you might be different because they don't recognize any values except their own. And soon there may not be any others.
>
> Pauline Kael, *I Lost It at the Movies,* 1965

> You're not a star until they can spell your name in Karachi.
>
> Humphrey Bogart

Globalization dominates international trade discussions. European nations have united around a new currency, the Euro. The United States, Canada, and Mexico signed the North American Free Trade Agreement. The World Trade Organization attracts economic leaders and fervent protestors. But pop culture is the new international currency, the language we all speak, the glue that binds a global youth culture together.

MTV is viewed in 342 million households, including households in Europe, Latin America, and Asia.[5] The National Basketball Association broadcasts to 600 million households in 190 countries.[6] China's Yao Ming was the first player drafted in 2002. Japan's greatest baseball star joined the New York Yankees. An Australian director borrowed from India's "Bollywood" musicals to create Hollywood's *Moulin Rouge.*

World music started out as a novelty, with left-field hits such as Harry Belafonte's calypso single "Banana Boat (Day-O)," Kyu Sakamoto's chart-topping "Sukiyaki," and Astrud Gilberto's Brazilian samba "The Girl from Ipanema."[7] In 1986, Peter Gabriel's "In Your Eyes" featured the lilting vocals of Senegalese superstar Youssou N'Dour. Paul Simon added the joyous sounds of South Africa's Ladysmith Black Mambazo to his Grammy-winning album *Graceland.* World music has become a legitimate subcategory of music, fueled by the unexpected success of France's Gipsy Kings, Cuba's Buena Vista Social Club, and Pakistan's Nusrat Fateh Ali Khan.

The travelogue *1 Giant Leap* demonstrates how global boundaries have blurred.[8] Two British musicians traveled the world armed with a laptop computer and a digital camera. They recorded as they went, creating soundtracks and music videos with musicians in twenty-five countries. They also interviewed thinkers about subjects ranging from sexuality to spirituality. *1 Giant Leap* combines singing and speaking, music and film, on a Grammy-nominated DVD and CD.

Strategically poised as the capital of the Pacific Rim, Los Angeles serves as the hub of Western culture's primary exports. Hollywood films now make more money overseas than at home. *X-Men, Lara Croft: Tomb Raider,* and *Spider-Man* play from Buenos Aires to Bangkok. Such roller-coaster films, marked by extensive action and minimal dialogue, translate easiest overseas. The French film industry was so steamrolled by American imports that it considered imposing a "cultural embargo." American movies allegedly undercut indigenous styles, creating a global youth culture united by Hollywood's version of America and its values.

Lurking in the ashes of the World Trade Center resides a fundamental rejection of our cultural exports, a resistance to "Americanization." The United States has foisted such a vigorous capitalism on the global economy that highly traditional religious cultures have resisted with equal aplomb. Yet the war rages on many fronts, from protests over Egyptian TV shows to Nigerians rioting over the Miss World Pageant. Sociologist Rodney Stark notes the irony: "For nearly three centuries, social scientists and assorted western intellectuals have been promising the end of religion. Each generation has been confident that within another few decades, or possibly a bit longer, humans will 'outgrow' belief in the supernatural."[9] British sociologist Colin Campbell predicted secularization's whiplash effect: "It could be that the very processes of secularization which have been responsible for the 'cutting back' of the established form of religion have actually allowed 'hardier varieties' to flourish."[10] As our cultural exports become more "godless," global instincts and longings become more god-focused.

What makes Islamic fundamentalists so hateful toward America?[11] Certainly, our cultural exports helped fuel their rage. Even before 9/11, international reporter Thomas Friedman noted, "What bothers so many people about America today is not that we send our troops everywhere, but that we send our culture, values, economics, technologies, and lifestyles everywhere—whether or not we want to or others want them."[12] Hollywood watchdog Michael Medved pointed out that most people—particularly those in developing nations—"get little chance to balance the negative impressions you draw from *The X-Files, Hannibal,* or *Natural Born Killers* with any firsthand experience with America or Americans. No wonder so many Islamic extremists (and so many others) now look upon the U.S.A. as a cruel, godless, brutal and vulgar society."[13] Writing in

1961, historian Daniel Boorstin warned, "Without reflecting on consequences, we have become preoccupied with creating 'favorable images' of America. Yet, by doing so, we may be defeating ourselves. Almost everywhere today American images overshadow American ideals."[14] While we felt attacked for our "ideals," we failed to own the responsibility for our very contradictory "images." Islamic fundamentalists attacked America and our way of life—the culture of looking good, feeling good, and buying more—that wires our televisions, radios, and brains. Yet the mullahs' efforts to turn back the clock, to shield their ancient culture from Western influence, have proven no match for the long arms of Sony, AOL Time Warner, and Viacom.

Post-rational

> What we've introduced at MTV is nonnarrative form. . . . We rely on mood and emotion. We make you feel a certain way as opposed to you walking away with any particular knowledge.
>
> Bob Pittman, founding chairman of MTV,
> quoted in *Dancing in the Dark*

Postmodernity cuts and pastes, scans and surfs. Yet multitasking proves we're more multi-attentive than attention deficit disordered. We're interactive and interrelated, practicing a different form of thinking. Some call it illogical. We call it free form. Some may dismiss postmodernity as a movement comparable to a Starbucks double latte, frothy and insubstantial. How much easier simply to acknowledge different areas of expertise? Some read books; some read comics. Some write dissertations; some make movies. It's not that postmoderns can't play by logical, modern rules; they simply choose not to. They'd rather scan images than words, splicing disparate sources together in a hip-hop-inspired visual sampler.

"Collage" sounds like a ridiculous style to apply to a building. So when Santa Monica architect Frank Gehry unveiled his mind-bending design for the Guggenheim Museo in Bilbao, we (Craig and his wife, Caroline) set our sights on Spain. We were willing to fly across the Atlantic to experience Gehry's cutting-edge creation. The ground of our being shook at our close encounter with the first building of the twenty-first century. We walked around it for hours, noticing the subtle changes in light reflected on its shiny, titanium cover. It works on every scale, from a faraway bridge to up close and profoundly personal. We spent one hour inside and eight hours outside. We stayed past sundown, surprised by the flames leaping from the reflecting pool. The building kept us looking, waiting, wondering, What's next? We had never been confronted by such a living, breathing edifice.

What makes Gehry's Guggenheim Museo so thrilling? The sleek surfaces, the organic forms, the chaotic flourishes all contribute to the overwhelming sense of a building still becoming. As the sun rises, the Guggenheim Bilbao is born anew every day. It "feels" like a rational impossibility. Inside, a three-story shaft of glass seems to fall from the sky. Following a century of rational right angles, the curves along the Guggenheim's every wall seem utterly impossible, an engineering nightmare. Gehry strives to break every rule, defy every convention, undermine every declaration of what's possible, what's practical, and what's appropriate. It is a kicking, screaming, gleaming tribute to what a post-postmodern world might look like. As we worry about security, about bombs bursting in air, Gehry's Guggenheim provides a defiant answer, a building that's already exploding.

Postmodern architecture flourished in the 1980s, featuring playful nods to the past. The cold, sleek high rises of the sixties and seventies were "softened" with humorous touches, such as Philip Johnson's Chippendale "flourish" topping his AT&T Tower in New York City. Robert Venturi became the architect of artifice, adding ancient columns to his late-twentieth-century designs. Po-Mo architecture brought much-needed humor to a profession rife with self-anointed "gods." Gehry's buildings, from the Guggenheim in Bilbao, the Experience Music Project in Seattle, and the Disney Concert Hall in Los Angeles, push waaaaay past

Guggenheim Museo, Bilbao, Spain. Used by permission of Craig Detweiler.

postmodernism in form, structure, and statement. He's not content to borrow from the past and wink at his audience with ironic, knowing gestures. Gehry's architecture waves to the past, forcing his contemporaries to play catch-up.

Why have tourists flocked to Bilbao? Photos cannot convey the magnitude, the audacity, the creativity of the Guggenheim. How did a grungy seaport like Bilbao transform itself into a must-see destination? Rather than engaging in slow, incremental rehab, Bilbao gave Gehry a huge blank canvas, prime waterfront property. Gehry gave them an experience, a building so bold, daring, and brave that what's inside is utterly immaterial. Many have criticized the postmodern mind as being superficial, irrational, incapable of embracing an overriding story. Gehry's Guggenheim whips past such criticism, illustrating how far it misses the main point. The Guggenheim Bilbao is not about what's inside. It is an overall experience, an overwhelming sense of what's possible rather than what's practical. The building stands as a monument to the miraculous. The *New York Times Magazine* called it "a shimmering, Looney Tunes, post-industrial, post-everything burst of American optimism wrapped in titanium."[15]

How did Gehry and the builders pull it off? Gehry used advanced computer technology and imaging to test the impossible. The height of rationalism, the end product of the twentieth century, the computer, made Gehry's cut-and-paste dream concrete. He does not work in an ahistorical vacuum. He draws on the history of architecture to create a new paradigm. *New Yorker* architecture critic Paul Goldberger said, "It's as if you had a serious composer writing a modern symphony that beat out everything on the Billboard charts."[16] The "superficial" titanium surface can be blinding. It can cause visitors to look at themselves, engage in navel gazing. But it also allows the building to change, to evolve, to reflect the changing "natural" environment. Cold titanium not only lasts longer, requires no toxic painting, and provides a rare uniformity but also reflects the brilliant warmth of the sun. Critics who carp about the superficiality of postmodern thinking are like art critics who complain about the sub-par paintings lining Bilbao's walls. They major on the minors, dwelling on one form of content while missing the overriding dynamism of what's happening. One bright, exploding idea transformed an entire economy, turned around a city at a dead end. Will others follow Gehry's irrational, emotional lead?

Does any of this make sense? Not if you're stuck in rational categories. In postmodernity, A plus B often equals Q, because people are thinking with their feelings first. Those longing for a consistent, systematic approach may find themselves flummoxed by a nonsystematic era. Pop stars Britney Spears and Jessica Simpson flaunted their bodies and affirmed their virginity *simultaneously*.[17] Films such as *Breaking the Waves* and *40 Days and 40 Nights* combine sex and religion with apparent ease. Missy Misdemeanor Elliott raps, "They Don't Want to F— Wit Me" while writing "Thank you, God, for being my inspiration" on the liner notes to her CD.[18] Christians For Cannabis make a biblical case for marijuana use (probably while listening to Missy Elliott sing "Pass the Blunt!").[19]

While the Osbournes cuss one another out, Mom Sharon suggests, "Through all the craziness, you see that there's a family that loves each other and are really close."[20] Such moral confusion will likely characterize the next hundred years. Those holding on to a more homogenized worldview express frustration with a generation that seems to hold coherent and paradoxical ideas at the same time, without inner turmoil. The deductive either/or thinking of the modern world has been replaced by a gut-level, both/and approach.

Post-literal

I can believe anything, provided it is incredible.

Oscar Wilde

There will be a road. It will not connect two points. It will connect all points. It will not go from here to there. There will be no there. We will all only be here.

television commercial for MCI

Our image-driven pop culture has caused many to wonder if we're becoming a post-literate society. Yet one million pre-orders on Amazon.com for the 896-page *Harry Potter and the Order of the Phoenix* suggest that reading is alive and well. The success of the series indicates that our society is not post-literate but post-literal.

Dictionary definitions of the word *literal* range from "according to the scriptures" to "adhering to fact." The past century of biblical scholarship took its cues from the scientific method, applying rigorous tests to Scripture in an effort to demythologize the faith. Rudolph Bultmann led the efforts to distill the facts from among the religious myths. Albert Schweitzer's Quest for the Historical Jesus eventually led to Robert Funk's Jesus Seminar. By the end of the twentieth century, scholars were voting on the veracity of each of Jesus' statements in the Gospels.[21] Postmodern philosophers engaged in an even greater deconstruction of myths, pointing out how unreliable, political, and loaded language can be. The large mythic stories (metanarratives) that underscored most faiths were declared "dead." What started with an emphasis on facts over fiction has now caused us to question knowledge itself. Aren't all facts just politicized fictions, the creation of others' agendas? A faith founded on the Word, committed to the Truth, may find a post-literal world frightening. A virtual faith may sound like no faith at all. Are there no more moral absolutes? Is everything relative?

Consider the many nuances inherent in the creation of docudramas. Screenwriters may alter the facts in order to fashion a more dramatic story. The Writer's Guild compares the source material, "the facts," to the finished screenplay before deciding on a credit. Networks fret over the distinctions between "based on" or "inspired by" true-life stories.[22] Major controversies erupted over recent Academy Award nominated cinematic biographies. Historical figures complained about the compression of multiple characters in *The Hurricane*. The negative press may have cost Denzel Washington a much deserved Oscar for his portrayal of Reuben "Hurricane" Carter (making his award for *Training Day* a belated correction). *A Beautiful Mind* faced complaints of fudging on John Nash's homosexuality, divorce, and out-of-wedlock child. Yet a nasty round of mudslinging did not prevent *A Beautiful Mind* from taking home the 2002 Oscar for best picture.

In *Christianity Today,* columnist Charles Colson bemoaned our "post-truth society," which produces liars such as Tawana Brawley, David Brock, and Stephen Ambrose. A few weeks later, reporters discovered that Anne Morse had written Colson's column about lying.[23] What all these games of gotcha fail to acknowledge is the major epistemological shift that accompanies this loss of absolute truth.

The literal truths, the cold, hard facts, are tired. The big mythological truths of *The Lord of the Rings, Harry Potter,* and *The Matrix* have taken their place. As postmodern philosophers announce that grand, overarching metanarratives are dead, Hollywood spends hundreds of millions of dollars on interlocking trilogies that garner global acclaim and interest. The end of stories? The death of the metanarrative? Moral chaos? A new generation rewarded J. K. Rowling a million times over for telling a ripping yarn about good and evil—everyday ethics couched in the mythological. *The Lord of the Rings* deals with the lure of power, the need to actively resist evil every step of our journey. We can obsess over the lost truths of traditional dogma or embrace the much, much larger picture. Are you blinded by *The Matrix* or capable of stepping outside the specifics long enough to truly see?

Sociologist Zygmunt Bauman called modernity "a war against mystery and magic."[24] For rationalism to win, "the world had to be de-spiritualised, de-animated, denied the capacity of the subject." Bauman concluded, "It is against such a disenchanted world that the postmodern re-enchantment is aimed."[25] Comic books have led the rise of re-enchantment. Big-screen, high-profile productions of *Superman* and *Batman* have been followed by *Spider-Man, X-Men, Daredevil,* and *The Hulk.* Television offered us *Smallville,* a sensitive and stirring study of Superman's awkward adolescence. These are much more than escapist fantasies. They are the post-literal cries of an audience suffering from a lack of metanarratives, searching for supra-human experiences to fill their transcendence gap.

A fan's reedit of *Star Wars: The Phantom Menace* illustrates why we should welcome this shift from literal facts to even greater truths. As a truly devoted *Star Wars* fan, "The Phantom Editor" cut out most of Jar Jar Binks's dreaded high jinks, creating his own, twenty-minute-shorter (and far superior) version of George Lucas's movie. Of course, Lucas tried to stop the spread of such an unauthorized version of his film. Religion professor Telford Work asked his students "whether the fluidity of these authorized and unauthorized editions confused them about where the real *Star Wars* story lies." A Westmont College student shrugged off the question. "Look at all the editions of the Bible."[26] The laughter that followed his comment spoke volumes about the postmodern mind. Students aren't fazed by different versions of the Bible. Matthew's additions to Mark or Luke's spin on the Q source don't cause them to question Jesus. "Biblical pluriformity has not weakened their appreciation of the story's ultimate integrity. In fact, it may have strengthened it. Only an eternal story could shine through so many centuries of spin."[27] At the end of all the demythologizing arises a profound commitment to remythologizing our culture and our faith.

Post-scientific/technological

> Descartes' dictum, "I think therefore I am" has been replaced by a new dictum, "I am connected, therefore I exist."
>
> Jeremy Rifkin[28]

> Science is always wrong: it never solves a problem without creating ten more.
>
> George Bernard Shaw

Science entered the twentieth century as an infallible god. We walked on the moon. We steered an expensive toy across Mars. We photographed the deepest recesses of black holes and hidden galaxies. Space is no longer the final frontier. Human DNA has been atomized into clonable portions. The Internet allows users to access ancient archives with the click of a button. We can talk to anyone in the world from anywhere in the world on a cheap, portable, and even disposable cell phone. Yet not enough attention has been focused on the implications of our insatiable need for speed.

Jeremy Rifkin, author of *The Age of Access,* notes, "The techno gurus promised us that instant access would lighten our loads and give us back more time. Is it possible, instead, that the nanosecond culture is enslaving us in a web of ever-accelerating connections from which there seems to be no escape?"[29] He attributes the rise in stress-related illnesses to information overload. "Road rage," "desk rage," and "air rage" followed our new 24/7 society. Around-the-clock "connectivity" has resulted in sleep deprivation, with our rest slipping from nine to ten hours nightly in 1910 to less than seven today. Rifkin worries most about the effects on the dot-com generation. While social conservatives blame our loss of civility on declining religious and moral values, Rifkin points to our hyper-speed culture. "Millions of kids, especially boys, are being diagnosed with attention deficit hyperactivity disorder in the U.S. Is it any wonder? If a child grows up in an environment surrounded by the fast pace of television, video games, computers and constant media stimulation, chances are that his neural development will condition to a short attention span."[30] And an even shorter fuse. More Ritalin is not the answer.

Even active parenting may not be the solution. *Newsweek* reported that "millions of parents around the country say their lives have become a daily frantic rush in the minivan from school to soccer to piano lessons and then hours of homework. But they're trapped, afraid to slow down because any blank space in the family calendar could mean their offspring won't have the resumes to earn thick letters from Harvard—and big bucks forever after."[31] Amen. Anne Quindlen laments overscheduled kids "deprived of the gift of boredom."[32]

Our electronic gadgetry leaves us more breathless than ever before. The search for silence, for inner peace, for mystery begins when we escape our technopolis. Unplugging will not be easy. Summer camp directors face an uphill battle. For today's campers, separating from computers, video game players, and cell phones can be as gut-wrenching as saying good-bye to Mom, Dad, and the family. Fifteen-year-old Sara Horowitz hated parting from her virtual family, *The Sims*. "I'm kind of addicted. I love my Sim family, but I think it's good that I have a break from it." At Cottontail Ranch's mandatory postcard dinner, Sara scribbled only three words: "I love you." She said, "It hurts my hand to write. I wish I could send an e-mail."[33]

Even new habits die hard. Will religious and educational leaders play hardball with kids hooked on instant access? Or will we pump up the volume in our teaching and preaching as our culture seeks a quiet, humane alternative? We fear that people of faith used to playing constant catch-up will embrace technology at the very moment the dot-com generation rejects it.

Post-sexual

> I think on-stage nudity is disgusting, shameful, and damaging to all things American. But if I were twenty-two with a great body, it would be artistic, tasteful, patriotic, and a progressive religious experience.
>
> Shelley Winters

> I've never even had sex, and already I can't stand it.
>
> from the teen comedy *American Pie*

The birth of the pill. The sexual revolution. Women's rights. Abortion rights. Gay rights. Passionate fights all rooted in sexuality. With almost everything out in the open, it's safe to say we live in a post-sexual era. After such a tumultuous sexual revolution, what is the new rebellion? A *Newsweek* cover story trumpeted "The New Virginity":

Rejecting the get-down-make-love ethos of their parents' generation, this wave of young adults represents a new counterculture, one clearly at odds with the mainstream media and their routine use of sex to boost ratings and peddle product.[34]

Statistics reported by the Center for Disease Control indicate that the number of high school students who say they've never had sex rose 10 percent in the past decade.

Is virginity more fashionable than ever before? Are more teens waiting longer to have sex? Then why does a cover of *USA Today* announce, "The Sexual Revolution Hits Junior High"?[35] Has the discussion of sex been reduced to such black-and-white choices that most adolescents wander in a hazy gray zone without any sense of direction? What's up with all the piercings and tattoos? Will women ever cover up their navels again? All these extreme examples of sexual restraint and physical "acting out" suggest that people of faith desperately need to develop an integrated theology of the body.

In 1972, less than 5 percent of fifteen-year-old girls and 20 percent of fifteen-year-old boys had engaged in sexual intercourse. Just twenty-five years later, 38 percent of fifteen-year-old girls and 45 percent of fifteen-year-old boys reported engagement in sexual intercourse.[36] In *What Our Mothers Didn't Tell Us,* Danielle Crittenden laments that "carelessly, thoughtlessly, casually, sex—in the short space of a single generation—went from being the culminating act of committed love to being a precondition, a tryout, for future involvement. If any."[37] The Reagan administration launched an assault on sexual promiscuity by allocating two million dollars a year to develop an abstinence-only curriculum.[38] Resulting public school programs such as Sex Respect and Teen-Aid offered an alternative to safe-sex messages. The Southern Baptist Convention joined the fight, launching an abstinence campaign entitled True Love Waits in 1993. Rallies held across America encouraged teens to take virginity pledges, promising to postpone sex until marriage. One million teens signed up. A wave of additional support groups followed, including STARS (Students Today Aren't Ready for Sex), Operation Keepsake, Friends First, and Free Teens. Joshua Harris "kissed dating good-bye" and created a best-seller. In January 2001, researchers from Columbia and Yale found that "adolescents who pledge are much less likely than adolescents who do not pledge to have intercourse. The delay effect is substantial and robust. Pledging delays intercourse for a long time. In this sense, the pledge works."[39] Even *Spin Magazine,* founded by Bob Guccione Jr., son of the creator of *Penthouse,* noted the virginity trend, acknowledging that 50 percent of high schoolers now graduate as virgins.[40] The abstinence movement took a well-deserved, collective bow.

Yet another study, conducted by the Urban Institute and also published in January 2001, found a shocking rise in "other kinds" of teen sexual behavior. Sixty-six percent of male teenagers had engaged in oral sex, heterosexual anal sex, and/or masturbation by a female.[41] Robert W. Blum, director of the Adolescent Health Program, found that "among many kids, there is a mythology that [non-coital sex] is safer or not a risk behavior. Teenagers see non-coital sex as protective because it protects against pregnancy."[42] Freya L. Sonenstein, author of the Urban Institute study, said, "Both parents and educators may be having difficulty imparting information about the riskiness of oral sex and anal sex. What we hope our study does is show that even though they are not talking about these behaviors with their kids, their kids are engaging in these behaviors."[43]

On college campuses, "hooking up" has replaced one-night stands, offering a no-strings-attached physical encounter without all the baggage of an emotional relationship. A *Journal of Sex* research study of sexual activity on college campuses found that 75 percent of undergraduates experience some form of hooking up, with one-third reporting intercourse with a stranger or acquaintance.[44] A student at San Jose State said that "dating" is nonexistent. "One of my friends hooked up with this guy, and I had taken a picture of him. She was so happy because she couldn't remember him or his name."[45] Such anonymous sex may stand as the final tribute to 1960s "free love." Sex without commitment may be free, but it's certainly anything but love.[46]

Are things getting better or worse than ever before? More teens are waiting for sex until marriage. And more teens are having sex and yet don't think they are. How does this compute? One of our Christian college students called it "rockin' the T.V." As he and his long-term girlfriend have struggled with waiting for their wedding day, they've passed the time by exploring T.V.—"technical virginity." Like many, they are trying to negotiate a post-sexual world. They see through the false promises of safe sex but are wrestling with areas beyond no sex. Where will teens turn for frank advice during these confusing times? After witnessing eighty priests being accused of child abuse in Boston, many teens may not be willing to trust the church. Most turn to pop culture, where the answers are fuzzy but the conversations are frank.

Television hasn't offered much help. The Kaiser Family Foundation found that two-thirds of prime-time programming contains sexual content, but only one in ten shows refers to the potential risks and responsibilities associated with sexual activity.[47] At the same time, the foundation reported in their biennial study "Sex on TV: Content and Context" that the percentage of shows with sexual content rose from 56 percent of all shows in 1997–98 to 68 percent in 1999–2000. In the 2001 season, the overall number climbed to 75 percent, with sitcoms mentioning sex in 84 percent of broadcasts. MTV's notorious *Undressed* demonstrates all manner of sexual combination with little discussion of the potential emotional repercussions. A few shows such as *Beverly Hills 90210* and *Dawson's Creek* have tried to handle the issues with the complexity they deserve.

Teen confusion can be found in the careers of four of the hottest female singers: Mandy Moore, Jessica Simpson, Britney Spears, and Beyonce Knowles. They made headlines for their chart-topping music, their belly-button-bearing fashion, and their commitment to abstinence. For some, these impulses seem contradictory. In the song "17," Mandy Moore flirts with sex, eager to "do something stupid." Yet Moore solidified her status as a virginal teen idol in her acting debut as Jamie Sullivan in *A Walk to Remember.* Moore plays the daughter of a minister and endures her peers' jeers but ultimately wins the respect (and heart) of the biggest hunk on campus. Moore reflects, "Playing Jamie has actually brought me closer to God and inspired me to go to church more. It's so nice to be part of a teen movie that's so positive."[48]

Focus on the Family criticized Jessica Simpson for her simultaneous desires to glorify God and turn heads. She grew up as the daughter of a Baptist youth minister in Dallas, yet her image evolved from "Sweet Kisses" on her first album to "Irresistible" on her second disc. Simpson defends her sexy style onstage: "I will wear sexy clothes. I'm not ashamed of my body, and I am not afraid of showing it. I just do it in a tasteful way. I just turned 20 and I want to show my body and that's okay because God gave me my body and I am proud of it and I worked for it, dang it!"[49] Yet Jessica also brought her True Love Waits virginity pledge into a high-profile relationship with 98 Degrees singer Nick Lachey.

Britney Spears maintained she was a virgin even after moving in with *NSYNC boyfriend Justin Timberlake. Yet in her film debut, *Crossroads,* Britney's on-screen character experiences sex for the first time. It may be read as a none-too-subtle acknowledgment that her public proclamations and private practices may diverge. The mixed messages of her songs, ranging from "I'm a Slave 4 You" to "I'm Not a Girl, Not Yet a Woman," magnify the discord.

The African-American community can find the same tension in Beyonce Knowles of Destiny's Child. She wears slinky outfits while celebrating her uncompromising Christian faith in the hit song "Survivor." Yet the black community doesn't seem bothered. In fact, spirituality and sensuality get downright cozy among black musicians. Little Richard, Sam Cooke, and Solomon Burke were practically nightclub preachers, sex symbols steeped in gospel music. Marvin Gaye, Aretha Franklin, Al Green, and Prince continued the sex and salvation legacy. Even today, R. Kelly, DMX, and Wyclef Jean celebrate their mothers, praise God, and offer booty calls all on the same album (and maybe even in the same song!). The dean of rock critics, Robert Christgau, wrote, "You get the feeling with many soul singers that the spiritual root of their music (call it God) and its emotional referent (call it sex) coexist at the center of their vision."[50]

Lauryn Hill serves as an "elderly" role model for tomorrow's sexy teen stars, one who wears both her sexuality and spirituality on her bare shoulders. At the 1999 Grammy Awards, Hill sang "To Zion," a deeply spiritual song thanking God for her illegitimate son. In accepting her numerous awards, she quoted liberally from Psalm 40 *and* acknowledged her lover, Rohan Marley. Attempts to reconcile her professed faith with her questionable actions end in frustration and confusion. Yet who can dispute the profound tears she shed previewing new, overtly Christian songs such as "I Gotta Find Peace of Mind" on MTV's *Unplugged*? For the next generation, the sacred and the profane are inseparable partners.

At least three frank films offer a peek into teens' competing notions of sexuality and responsibility, body and spirit. In *Pleasantville,* Reese Witherspoon begins the film as a floozy, trading her sexuality for campus standing. Her promiscuous, postmodern sexuality introduces "color" to the black-and-white world of the 1950s. Yet over the course of the film, Witherspoon abandons the sexual revolution she started. She learns to read, placing her education above her hormones.

American Pie stands out as the epitome of teen sex comedies, offering nubile nudity, oral sex advice, and embarrassing parent conferences. How surprising to discover in a *Rolling Stone* interview that *Pie* actors Chris Klein, Seann William Scott, and Thomas Ian Nicholas all profess a commitment to Christ. In an even more surprising bit of bait and switch, *American Pie* ultimately condemns rampant promiscuity, suggesting that sex for sex's sake is empty. The most passionate speech in the film occurs on prom night, when Jim yells at his closest friends:

> I'm tired of all this . . . pressure. . . . I hate sex! I don't want it, I've never wanted it, and I'm not gonna sit here busting my balls over something that just isn't that important. . . . Now, I'm gonna go hang out with that geek over there, 'cause at least she's got something else to talk about besides sex.[51]

Unfortunately, the film is mostly remembered for an apple pie, M.I.L.F., and bare-breasted exchange students.

40 Days and 40 Nights employs abstinence as a dramatic and comic device. Can hunk du jour Josh Hartnett resist the ovations of adoring women throughout Lent? He addresses Jesus directly, begging for understanding with a simple cry of "Dude?!" By incorporating the struggles of a priest-in-training brother, *40 Days* addresses the abstinence trend coursing through pop culture. Without affirming abstinence, *40 Days* addresses the religious roots of the tense struggle between body and spirit. Hollywood has continued to raise the messy questions, entering the gray zone that parents and churches have often oversimplified. A marketplace theology must enter the gray areas, willing to be attacked as too liberal by some conservative Christians and too uptight by a seemingly amoral culture.

Post-racial

> Once you begin to explain or excuse all events on racial grounds, you begin to indulge in the perilous mythology of race.
>
> James Earl Jones

> The racism, the sexism, I never let it be my problem. It's their problem. If I see a door comin' my way, I'm knockin' it down. And if I can't knock down the door, I'm sliding through the window.
>
> Rosie Perez

Martin Luther King Jr. dreamed of a future when children would be judged "by the content of their character rather than the color of their skin." Forty years later, King's character was questioned in the comedic film *Barbershop*. Black leaders such as the Rev. Jesse Jackson, who marched alongside King in the Civil Rights era, were outraged. Yet the Rev. Al Sharpton's call to boycott the film or at least edit the offending remarks from the home video version were roundly rejected. Patrons at real-life black barbershops found no problem with the movie, only with Jackson and Sharpton.[52] The traditional black leadership failed to recognize the progress evident when King, his essential place in history firmly secured, is judged (or satirized) based on his character.

We recognize how politically incorrect the announcement by two white men that we're living in a post-racial world may appear. Certainly, due diligence will always be essential to uphold civil rights and oppose all forms of racism. A quick survey of high school cafeterias would reveal that many kids still segregate themselves by skin tone.[53] Yet a post-racial era has moved beyond the old either/or understanding of race. For the first time in history, the 2000 U.S. census allowed people to check more than one box when responding to the question of race. Seven million Americans, more than half of them under age eighteen, considered themselves multi-racial.[54] This means, from now on, U.S. racial statistics will add up to more than 100 percent. This also undercuts our traditional categories of race and ethnicity. One of the authors of *Ego Trip's Big Book of Racism!* declares, "Race isn't race, it's culture. We have to acknowledge that one culture is different from another. And then we need to respect that. . . . We've gotta redefine racism."[55]

Different leaders have arisen alongside these changing definitions of race. University of Southern California film professor Todd Boyd notes, "Thurgood Marshall, Medgar Evans, James Meredith, and Fannie Lou Hamer have morphed into Sean 'P. Diddy' Combs, Russell Simmons, Master P, Queen Latifah, and Missy Elliott. These leaders of the new school understand that power in this society is consistent with the size of your bankroll."[56] While affirmative action is debated on college campuses, statistics indicate that the most underrepresented group of Americans at universities is not Latinos or blacks but students from low-income families. In the 1980s, Chuck D. of Public Enemy repeatedly called rap music "black people's C.N.N." In the new world, rap music serves as white, Latino, Asian, and Native American people's C.N.N. too.

Marketing consultant Santiago Pozo says, "What we're seeing is the browning of America."[57] Inner-city black kids wear uniforms to school, while suburban kids don Sean Paul and Enyce, trying to emulate rappers. Universal Studios vice chairman Marc Shmuger cast Vin Diesel in *The Fast and the Furious* and the Rock in *The Scorpion King*. He says, "All my 9-year-old boy does is imitate black culture. To him, that's what is cool. He wants to walk like Kobe Bryant and dress like Lil' Bow Wow. We'd be crazy if we didn't try to reflect that in our movies."[58] *The Matrix* trilogy previews this color-blind future. "As the rapper Jay-Z has said: 'We didn't cross over, we brought the suburbs to the 'hood.'"[59]

In the 1980s, Spike Lee's groundbreaking films, such as *Do the Right Thing*, defined everything by race. He exposed the racism lurking behind the counter of convenience stores and inside neighborhood pizzerias. He explored the *Jungle Fever* that attracts black men to white women. Yet he's failed to find an audience for subsequent films, even when casting white stars such as Edward Norton in *25th Hour.*

The next generation of filmgoers has embraced the reverse roles of race presented in *Save the Last Dance* and *Crazy/Beautiful.* Sara mourns the death of her mother in *Save the Last Dance* and is forced to move to the south side of Chicago to live with her estranged father, a jazz musician. Her dreams of becoming a ballerina die alongside her mother. As a white woman in an overwhelmingly black school, Sara struggles until Chenille, a smart, sassy black student (and unwed mother) reaches out to her. Chenille's brother Derek becomes Sara's role model, coach, and boyfriend. Within their complicated but successful interracial romance, Sara finds the support and encouragement she needs to renew her dream.

In *Crazy/Beautiful,* Nicole's falling grades and casual drug use stand in marked contrast to the lifestyle of her upstanding Hispanic boyfriend, Carlos. The film clearly condemns disinterested, affluent parents who are too wrapped up in their own issues to worry about their children's needs. The Mexican family demonstrates love and support, while the white family needs much more than counseling to heal their fractured relationships. In the end, Carlos's love and compassion save Nicole and secure him an appointment to the college of his dreams.

George Washington stands out as the most mature, poetic, and insightful film about post-racial America. Twenty-five-year-old director David Gordon Green cast unknown, nonprofessional actors. He shot his low-budget film on location, in the poor neighborhoods around the North Carolina School of the Arts. It is a slow, poignant study of kids who have been cast out by the system, left to fend for themselves. The majority of the characters are black, but the film is more about class than skin color. No one in the movie is named George Washington, but the title and the film raise unspoken questions about unequal opportunities. Can anyone truly grow up to be president in America? The shockingly hopeful ending suggests that even the poorest black kid with a father in prison can demonstrate the character and resolve essential for greatness. Such grand dreams can be realized only in a post-racial culture. The fact that the most popular rapper is white and the top golfer is black shows that we've definitely flipped the script on race.

Post-human

> The only *ism* Hollywood believes in is plagiarism.
>
> Dorothy Parker

Digital technology allows us to make perfect copies of original material. MP3s can be downloaded from the computers of people we've never met. Adobe Photoshop enables us to alter photographs, from taking the red out of eyes to changing backgrounds, shapes, and colors. *Jurassic Park* brought extinct dinosaurs back to life. *Titanic* resunk a long-buried ocean liner. Agent Smith replicates himself a hundred times over in *The Matrix Reloaded.* Milli Vanilli lip-synched their way to a Grammy for best new artist. French postmodern theorist Jean Beaudrillard calls this "an age of simulacrum," in which the differences between the original and the copies have vanished.[60]

The success of robotic cyber pets such as Sony's Aibo spawned imitators Tekno Kitty, Chirpy-Chi, and Shelby the Clam. In "innocent" films such as *Babe* and *Snow Dogs,* animals appear to talk. Scientists at the Massachusetts Institute of Technology have developed video technology that can put words in people's mouths, and viewers can't tell that it isn't real. Such technology could be misused to discredit politicians, to embarrass people on the web, or to illegally use trusted figures to endorse products.[61]

The ground between the real and the manufactured shifted when British scientists introduced Dolly, the first cloned sheep. A French cult announced the cloning of the first baby, named Eve, right after Christmas 2002. Technology has brought us to the brink of what Francis Fukuyama calls "our posthuman future." He warns, "The single greatest danger will come when genetic engineering for human beings—so-called germline engineering—becomes possible, and then you are talking about a period completely unprecedented in human history, where human beings will consciously be able to take over the evolutionary process."[62]

Bill McKibben considers the promises and dangers of such biotechnology in his book *Enough: Staying Human in an Engineered Age.*[63] He accepts the positive applications of somatic gene therapy, in which doctors try to cure diseases by grafting new genetic material into an existing patient. But the debate rages around the addition or removal of genes within developing embryos. Those who support therapeutic cloning and stem cell research trumpet the potential to end genetically linked diseases and disorders such as diabetes and cystic fibrosis. But McKibben worries about the short ethical leap from eliminating a condition to enhancing positive traits. The possibility of designer babies could prove too tempting for affluent parents, driving the gap between rich and poor, powerful and powerless into our very biology. McKibben urges us to reject these technological paths, to consider being human "enough."

The potential to play God, to pursue immortality, pushes these issues beyond the ethical into the theological. While people of faith will undoubtedly argue against human cloning by saying, "Humans were created in the image of God," the public debate will undoubtedly range much farther. Fukuyama states, "My own preference would be a slogan like 'Hands off human nature.' You don't want to do things that really change core human behaviors, that turn people into gods or subhumans, in effect."[64] Will we devolve into a culture in which people can't distinguish the real from the surreal? Without a shared, biblical ethic about our humanity, are we doomed to a world of simulacra?

Pop culture raised these prescient issues long ago. Mary Shelley's *Frankenstein* dealt with scientific experimentation's dark side. Science fiction films such as *2001: A Space Odyssey, Blade Runner, The Terminator,* and *The Matrix* have raised serious questions about the dangerous results of scientific "progress." Japanese anime dealt with the blurring of man and machine in *Akira* and *Ghost in the Shell.* Radiohead's *OK Computer* deals poignantly with the alienating aspects of technology. The blurring boundaries of what's human inspired haunting and disturbing films such as *The Stepford Wives, Gattaca,* and *AI: Artificial Intelligence.* Instead of blaming pop culture for dehumanizing us, perhaps we should learn from its most prophetic expressions.

Hollywood also needs to pay attention to the lessons these products deliver. In a post-human world, people desperately long for something real, genuine, and authentic. Audiences rejected studios' efforts to recycle old television series into forgettable movies such as *The Flintstones, The Beverly Hillbillies,* and *The Mod Squad.* One of my students, Colin Ryan, admitted, "I used to get excited when I heard that an old movie or story was being redone. I do not think that anymore. I am offended more and more each time I see a pop remake of a historically significant movie—*Planet of the Apes, Shaft, The Time Machine, Rollerball.*"[65] He looks beyond the veneer that digital effects and Dolby Digital surround sound offer. Ryan says:

> I know that the powers that be have no faith in me as a moviegoer. They bear for me no esteem, no appreciation, no respect. And it is this feeling which will change the

art of our generation. . . . New technology is a drug, a temporary drug which can only fuel our lust for more new technology. I believe that we as a generation will get so full of force-fed pop movies that we will create something altogether new merely to satisfy our need for real sustenance.[66]

The millennial consumers have just begun to sing their own songs, to direct their own scripts, to make their own statements.[67] The Backstreet Boys and Britney Spears sang songs crafted by older producers in studios as far away as Sweden. But their manufactured sounds resulted in an incredibly desperate, unvarnished cry for authenticity. John Mayer and Ryan Adams brought back the folky sounds of James Taylor and Neil Young. The soundtrack to *O Brother, Where Art Thou?* confounded all expectations, as a rootless culture embraced the ultimate roots of music, bluegrass. MTV's *Unplugged* took musicians out of the studio, away from the overdubs. Nirvana, Eric Clapton, R.E.M., Lauryn Hill, Staind, and Jay-Z rose to the occasion with poignant, unplugged performances. VH1's *Storyteller* goes back to the genesis of rock 'n' roll, to the songwriters' sources and inspirations. *The Blair Witch Project* proved what a collective of filmmakers outside the Hollywood system can pull off without special effects. While employing far too many fledgling actors, reality TV series aspire to offer an authentic portrayal of normal people engaged in challenging situations and relationships. Dating shows proliferate because eighteen year olds desperately need help negotiating *the eighteen years* between puberty and marriage. In an era of role-playing, online gaming, eddresses, and identity theft, "keeping it real" is a prayer for the twenty-first century.

Post-traumatic/therapeutic

> The first murder recorded in the history of man was when Cain killed his brother Abel. No doubt people wrote and sang songs about it, and we've been doing it ever since.
>
> Johnny Cash, liner notes to "Murder"

> I've often wondered if gangsta rappers know how little separates their tales of ghetto thug life from Johnny Cash's tales of backwoods thug life.
>
> Quentin Tarantino

Science cannot explain the events of September 11, 2001. A rational religion in which people adhere to strict moral codes cannot be squared with the collapse of the Twin Towers. Such an event raises timeless questions about a good

God in a world of evil. Psychology, whether seeking to analyze the perpetrators or comfort the victims, comes up empty. Teen anxiety will not be arrested by additional antidepressants. Scott Young, director of the City of the Angels Film Festival, believes, "People are giving up their therapists and turning to their philosophers instead,"[68] or to their psychics! Yet these new philosophers aren't rationalists. Increasingly, they're artists throwing ideas on a movie screen. Craig's entering class at the University of Southern California's School of Cinema-Television featured graduates of Harvard, Brown, Stanford, the University of Chicago, and the Sorbonne.[69] The most intellectual students from around the world desperately want to "waste" their education making movies. Philosophy majors such as Wes Anderson choose to express their thoughts through quiet, gentle, and comedic moments in *Rushmore* and *The Royal Tenenbaums*. Richard Kelly's metaphysical coming-of-age story *Donnie Darko* serves as a cannon shot for a generation tired of being medicated. Drugs don't work; therapy doesn't work. *Donnie* needs much stronger stuff to alleviate his suffering.

In *Magnolia,* Paul Thomas Anderson pushes psychological realism to its limits but reaches a therapeutic dead end. What do the tortured characters in *Magnolia* do to snap out of their cycle of familial dysfunction? They sing! Aimee Mann's song "Wise Up" serves as the emotional centerpiece, the place where everyone comes to their senses. They join her in singing, "It's not going to stop, til you wise up." Moments later, they do. Where do characters trapped in destructive habits find grace and forgiveness? In an utterly illogical, utterly biblical rain of frogs. Absurd, unexpected, divine intervention offers scary and humorous relief from the pain of molestations, drug addiction, and megalomania. *Magnolia's* ending cannot be explained in any traditional sense of plot development or psychological payoff. It's beyond therapy. Anderson offers audiences an experience, a deeply spiritual, open ending full of hope, possibility, and promise. In a world in which terrorists bring down skyscrapers and architects design "chaos," a rain of frogs makes perfect sense.

Casting about for a theme for the eighth annual City of the Angels Film Festival, the planning committee felt haunted by the image of Timothy McVeigh on *Newsweek* magazine, a literal "Face of Evil." So Fuller Theological Seminary, Catholics in Media, Family Theater Productions, and a host of other faith-based organizations sponsored a pre-Halloween retrospective of horror films entitled "Touches of Evil."[70] We (Craig produces the event) invited the greatest "name brand" horror director to talk about his life and work. He agreed to return to his "scary" roots. Guess where the director of *Nightmare on Elm Street* went to college. Wes Craven's conservative Baptist roots took him to Wheaton College in Illinois, Billy Graham's alma mater.

Craven accepted our invitation to talk about his Christian origins at the City of the Angels Film Festival well before the events of September 11, 2001. When asked, "What's the scariest movie you've ever seen?" Craven answered, "It wouldn't be a movie from Hollywood." Instead, Craven cited footage of

World War II; atomic bombs; the assassinations of John F. Kennedy, Martin Luther King Jr., and Robert F. Kennedy; and Vietnam. He added all "sorts of images seared into our being from Little Rock to Cambodia, Jonestown, Rwanda, and Bosnia." Craven's point? "I mention all this unpleasantness for a reason. Modern horror films, of which I am admittedly a practitioner, are to me simply post-traumatic nightmares of a world that has seen horror, more horror, than it can handle alone. When we go into a theater, it's to have the terror of real life marshaled into some sort of order, so it can be dealt with. The chaos is caged for a few hours in a graspable narrative."[71]

As a sidebar event, Reel Spirituality, an Institute for Moving Images at Fuller Seminary's Brehm Center for Worship, Theology, and the Arts, hosted "Wrestling with Judas." We discussed a provocative horror film produced by Wes Craven, *Dracula 2000,* which makes the daring suggestion that Dracula may actually be Judas, condemned to wander the earth in search of absolution. Finally, there is an explanation as to why Dracula fears the Bible, hates the cross, and flees holy water (not to mention an explanation for those deadly silver bullets—Judas sold out Jesus for thirty pieces of silver)! Dallas Willard, philosophy professor at the University of Southern California, railed against a therapeutic culture that would assign Judas "reasons" for his betrayal. Willard spoke as someone tired of watching Christians explain evil and justify sin. Fuller Seminary professor emeritus Ray Anderson argued on behalf of the psychological, drawing on his book *The Gospel according to Judas.* Was Judas inherently evil, responsible for his choices, rightly condemned? Or was Judas a victim, painted as the devil when his actions were essential to God's plans for Jesus? While *Dracula 2000* may appeal only to hardcore horror fans, the spiritual undercurrent coursing through horror films must be acknowledged. While the church has tended to shy away from uncomfortable questions about the nature of good and evil, Hollywood has stepped into the gap.

Every semester, I (Craig) ask my students at the Los Angeles Film Studies Center to name a favorite film. Invariably, students from a cross section of small Christian colleges will praise *Se7en* (Seven). Directed by David Fincher from a script by Andrew Kevin Walker, *Se7en* offers the most unflinching portrait of postmodern life as literal hell. A serial killer borrows from Chaucer and Dante, turning each murder into a graphic "sermon" on the seven deadly sins. Shot in a steady rain of desaturated colors on film stock that looks as though it were processed in a coffeepot, *Se7en* drains almost every shred of hope from the on-screen cops and the audience. *Se7en*'s devout murderer John Doe leaves a quote from Christian poet John Milton at a crime scene: "Long is the way and hard that out of hell leads up to light." *Se7en* never approaches anything resembling light. Philosophy professor Thomas Hibbs writes eloquently about *Se7en* in *Shows about Nothing* and correctly concludes that "*Seven* suffers modernity's chief affliction—the silence of God. . . . The Hell of *Seven* is one without prospect of purgatory or paradise . . . without a providence to bring good out of evil, evil endlessly begets evil. . . . The only hope available to us consists not in succumbing to the meaninglessness of it all, but in keeping alive our sense of injustice and disorder of contemporary life."[72] Given the film's incredibly dark ending, Hibbs finds himself surprised by "a residue of goodness . . . an unquenched thirst for justice" that drives detective Somerset, the film's survivor. *Se7en* communicates plenty about how much hell postmodern audiences willingly endure. Easy answers and quick fixes are vanquished by the overwhelming evil in *Se7en* (and our recent history). Does that explain why the film is a surprising favorite among Christian college students?

When the safe, conservative TV industry starts to deal directly with death, then surely it's time for people of faith to wake from their slumber and tackle nitty-gritty, grisly subjects. NBC borrowed elements of *The Silence of the Lambs* for their woman-cop-battles-serial-killer series *Profiler.* By 2002, CBS's breakout hit series *CSI: Crime Scene Investigation* followed forensic experts in Vegas and Miami, NBC's *Crossing Jordan* tracked a female medical examiner, and WB's *Glory Days* included a coroner who runs a body farm out of her house.[73] HBO's edgy *Six Feet Under* begins with a different death each week. Instead of solving a crime, *Six Feet Under* deals with the death industry as a family business. Created and produced by Alan Ball (Academy Award–winning screenwriter of *American Beauty*), *Six Feet Under* "brings the same idiosyncratic voice to his TV show—satirical, philosophical and disturbing, often all at the same time."[74] *Newsweek* TV critic Mark Peyser suggests, "No TV program has ever focused so squarely on the barest of existential questions while still feeling like popular entertainment."[75] Actress Rachel Griffiths marvels, "Somehow Alan is able to put the darkest, bitterest, most complex things into a meal that people are not afraid of eating. There's a whole level of spiritual inquiry that no other TV show has."[76] She notes the show's post 9/11 relevance: "In America now, there's the sense that death is a character who is in the room."[77] Ball acknowledges the show's ambivalence toward death: "I realized I don't have to explain everything. I don't have to spoon-feed the audience. It's OK for things to be a little weird and upsetting."[78]

For postmoderns (and Dante's *Divine Comedy*), the road to heaven must go through hell.

Post-ethical/institutional

Businesses have reported a surprising byproduct of the prosperity of the new economy of the nineties: cheating.

J. Walker Smith, marketing expert,
quoted in *Life Is Not Work, Work Is Not Life*

> Bless the grocer for this wonderful meat, the middleman who jacked up the price, and let's not forget about the humane but determined boys at the slaughterhouse.
>
> Ned Flanders, blessing dinner on *The Simpsons*

While democratic capitalism has triumphed, our most hallowed institutions have become a joke. The Republicans gave us Watergate. The Democrats spawned Monicagate. The legal system gave us the O. J. Simpson trial. Companies touted as role models for the new economy such as Enron were exposed as bankrupt frauds. A rogue reporter undermined the integrity of the *New York Times.* The home run records of baseball slugger Sammy Sosa were uncorked by a questionable bat. Trust in religious institutions has also plummeted. Catholic priests and bishops seemed more concerned about potential lawsuits than protecting victims of sexual abuse. In our post-ethical world, *Time* named three women who blew the whistle on scandalous institutions "Persons of the Year."[79]

Yet pop culture has also become institutionalized, characterized by greed and focused on plunging profits. Record companies that bilked artists for years through deceptive accounting practices now decry CD burning as stealing from starving artists. Baseball has been tainted by strikes, as millionaire players protest the practices of even greedier owners. Attendance has fallen in each of the big four professional sports, as fans resist rising ticket prices.

The next generation has responded to institutional corruption with a sneer and a smile. Action sports such as snowboarding and skateboarding exploded among kids eager to break the rules. They respond to police codes banning them from schools and shopping malls with the slogan, "Skateboarding is not a crime." Finally aware of the unfair prices of compact discs, teens in the post-ethical world created file sharing. The music companies sued Napster out of existence, but a second wave of share-ware followed that genie out of the bottle. The songs kids have stolen urge them to "rage against the machine" and "break stuff." Efforts to recreate Woodstock '69's "three days of peace, love, and music" were greeted by Green Day's mudslinging and Limp Bizkit–inspired riots and sexual assaults.

With the authority of political, judicial, financial, and religious institutions undercut, the next generation has grown increasingly cynical. Earnest magicians like David Copperfield look ridiculous when compared to caustic prestidigitators Penn and Teller. Ads for Penn and Teller's stage show warn fans to "Lock Up Your Bunnies." Penn Jillette explains: "We tell the audience at the top that it's all fake, so there's an underlying moral foundation and they can explore the notion that if these losers are able to distort information so skillfully, what can other people do?"[80] Twenty-first-century magicians reveal how the old tricks are done while simultaneously performing another unexpected trick—raising audience consciousness.

The most innocent and innocuous of art forms, animated television shows, demonstrate even more bite. *The Simpsons* started the harangue, making fun of the ideal nuclear family. MTV's *Beavis and Butthead* made Bart Simpson look like a role model. Fox's *Family Guy* and *King of the Hill* continued the satirical slant. Comedy Central's *South Park* introduced kids who cuss and Mr. Hanky, a literal, walking, talking piece of crap. Yet *South Park* consistently deals with substantive issues such as free trade and stem cell research.

The most celebrated artists proved that in a post-ethical world, nothing is sacred. Andres Serrano stirred up controversy with a photograph of a crucifix dropped in his urine entitled *Piss Christ*. In the "Sensation" exhibit, the pope was struck down by a meteor. Chris Ofili threw cow dung at the canvas to complete his portrait of a black virgin Mary. Yet many in the next generation seem unmoved by either side in these controversies.

Evangelical Christian leaders have certainly offered artists, comedians, and political cartoonists an endless supply of material. The scandals arising from the ministries of Jim Bakker and Jimmy Swaggart made *televangelist* a permanently dirty word. Thankfully, some of the most biting and critical voices have arisen (appropriately) from within the faith community. Harvard Divinity School grad John D. Spalding chronicles our hilariously flawed search for God in his Beliefnet column, "A Sick Soul." After thirty years of irregular publication, *The (Wittenburg) Door* still serves as "the world's pretty much only religious satire magazine." Much of its humor comes from "found objects," the kitsch art often found in Christian bookstores. It paved the way for at least two outrageous web sites.

Landover Baptist began as a student radio broadcast at Jerry Falwell's Liberty University in 1989. Chris Harper and Mike Allen were eventually expelled. Allen went on to write for *Beavis and Butthead* and *King of the Hill,* but Harper saw the world wide web as a perfect opportunity to resurrect Landover. At www.landoverbaptist.org, Harper created a complete megachurch, full of staff biographies, news, and advice. Articles include, "Effeminate Man Asked to Leave 11 A.M. Service" and "Homosexuals Featured in Oxygen Ad: Church Members Encouraged to Stop Breathing." Harper figures 75 percent of the people who visit the site think it's a real church. He notes, "It's been said that Landover is unique in that it's a litmus test for human behavior." He revels in the apparent contradictions. "How can you say this about the church and yet be a Christian at the same time?" Harper affirms religious satire by borrowing from Søren Kierkegaard: "If Christianity is to be introduced, one must first expose the illusion." He states, "Once the illusion is gone of what people think Christianity is supposed to be, I think a person's heart becomes more open to see the truth."[81]

British web site www.ship-of-fools.com bills itself as "The Magazine of Christian Unrest." Cofounder Simon Jenkins asserts, "We think Christians should be restless about the state of the church today, and stirring up unrest in the wider world as well."[82] Ship of Fools points out the humor in "gadgets for God," such as a 110-foot-tall Jesus hot air balloon, a talking tombstone, and WWJD? boxer shorts (complete with false fly—access denied!). They also send out "the mystery worshiper" to visit churches and answer questions such as, "How hard was the pew?" and "How hot was the coffee?" Jenkins explains his basic goal: "It's like holding up a mirror to churches and saying, 'Is this how you expected to look? Are you happy looking like this?'"[83] He revels in "the sheer power of laughter, which is deadly dangerous for people in authority. Hitler and Stalin hated and banned laughter, because they feared its power to cut them down to size, and the same has been true for Popes and bishops, elders and deacons, and all the other Christian prima donnas who take themselves more seriously than God."[84] He recalls the story of a bishop who attended a children's Sunday school party in Uganda. When he arrived in full robes and pointy hat, a little child cried, "Oh, are there going to be clowns as well?"[85] Those who regularly visit the web site include "people who like their religion disorganized, people who feel alienated from the church, people who are on the fringes of the faith and who are on their way in or on their way out."[86] Perhaps the twenty-first-century church's ability to laugh at itself will determine which way people will head. Laugh and the world laughs with you. Fail to laugh and the world simply laughs at you.

Philosopher Paul Ricoeur suggests that people are changed not by ethical urging but by transformed imagination. Kevin Smith's imaginative 1999 film *Dogma* certainly proves that Christ will survive our sincere efforts to update him. Smith lampoons the church's rollout of a new campaign, "Catholicism Wow!" Famed, profane comic George Carlin plays Cardinal Glick, who unveils a new statue of the Buddy Christ. In reducing God almighty to a Buddy Christ action figure, Smith serves notice that the marketing of Jesus deserves to be satirized, lampooned, and destroyed. In *Virtual Faith,* Tom Beaudoin concurs: "The Jesus, which Xers and their popular culture justly mock and ironize, has been domesticated and drained of any spiritual energy."[87] He lacks humor, vitality, and personality. Smith follows the example of Jesus, using humor to make his audiences laugh until it hurts (and more importantly, to laugh until we change). Patrick Henry summarizes the tension: "To be both ironic and Christian is to know, with a knowing deeper than doctrine, the simple, unnerving truth that the visage of faith is not the happy face but the masks of comedy and tragedy, alternating, unpredictably, between laughter and tears . . . crying because it's so funny and laughing because it hurts so much."[88] Smith calls it "reverence through irreverence." In the liner notes to *Dogma's* Special Edition DVD, Smith acknowledges the challenge of mixing religion and comedy: "I hope God's got a sense of humor. If not, I'm really screwed."[89] Aren't we all?

Post-Christian

One cannot have God for one's Father who has not the Church for one's Mother.

Cyprian, ancient Bishop of Carthage

If the current trend continues, we're going to be a heathen nation.

Coach Bill McCartney, founder of Promise Keepers[90]

On November 13, 2002, Alan Roxburgh delivered one of the most insightful and haunting lectures we've ever heard at Fuller Seminary. Addressing the crisis of the church in North America, he pointed out the cultural blindness that has caused Christians in the West to view themselves as "exodus people" marching toward a triumphant future in the Promised Land. Consequently, we approach our culture as conquerors, warriors, with an arrogance that suggests it belongs to us. But Roxburgh more accurately described our status as "people in exile" who have lost our power, our authority, our central place in the cultural landscape. Exodus people write marching songs. Exile people must learn to grieve, to weep, and to accept their loss. Yet the post-exilic message of grief given by prophets such as Isaiah, Jeremiah, and Ezekiel was rejected by their contemporaries who wanted to hold on to the past, to celebrate the glory days, to deny the painful present. But only after fully mourning their loss could God's exiled people receive the new hearts and spirits promised in Ezekiel 36:26.

Cyprian's sentiments about mother church sum up how things used to be. Through the end of World War II, being part of the Christian church was utterly natural and essential. To stay away from the church was to stay away from God. But things have changed. We live out our faith in entirely new environments and do our theology in a world not known before.

The 2001 American Religious Identification Survey reported that more than 29.4 million Americans said they have no religion, more than double the number in 1990 and more than the total number of Methodists, Lutherans, and Episcopalians in the United States.[91] Sociologists from the University of California also found that the number of Americans who claim to have no religion has doubled in the last decade. But that increase does not correspond to a loss of faith. Researcher Michael Hout discovered that "most people who have no church still are likely to say things like, 'God is real.'"[92] Religion has been exchanged for "spirituality"—which can mean any number of things depending on who is asked.

Names matter. Staid financial firm Andersen Consulting entered the new century as Accenture. Rising inner-city violence prompted basketball's Washington Bullets to change their nickname to the Wizards. Tobacco company

Philip Morris gave up trying to change the public's negative perceptions. They renamed themselves the Altria Group.

To much of the Western world, religion often connotes judgment, ignorance, hypocrisy, and intolerance. One hundred years ago, the term *fundamentalist* arose from pamphlets that defined the fundamentals of the Christian faith.[93] Fifty years later, evangelicals sought to shed the baggage associated with the name. Now, even Bob Jones University wants to shed its fundamentalist label. President Bob Jones III wrote, "Instead of 'Fundamentalism' defining us as steadfast Bible believers, the term now carries overtones of radicalism and terrorism." Jones suggested using the word *preservationist* to describe "Christians with a fierce belief in the Bible's literal, inerrant truth."[94] Whatever you call it, "Christianity" needs much more than a name change. It needs open heart surgery.[95]

In 2002, researchers found that college students associate religion with institutions or organizations but spirituality with a direct personal experience of God.[96] University of Washington sociologist Rodney Stark states, "People aren't really saying, 'I have no religion.' They are saying, 'None of the above.' . . . People who believe in God—and they do—who pray—and they do—are not secular, they are just unchurched. They've never been to church and in many cases, their parents didn't go either."[97] Spirituality definitely signifies a discarding of hierarchical thinking carried over from historic religions of an earlier age, an abandonment of authoritarian concepts of reality and dualistic concepts.[98] But we should fear this. As Thomas Oden writes, "Spirituality in the New Testament sense is not a moral program, not a set of rules, not a level of ethical achievement, not a philosophy, not a rhetoric, not an idea, not a strategy, not a theory of meditation, but rather simple *life lived in Christ*."[99]

The next generation may connect with the journey of Tom Beaudoin, author of *Virtual Faith:*

> I was awash in popular culture and alienated from official religion. Despite all this, I still considered myself unmistakably "spiritual." By this, I meant that I thought about religion, I thought there was more to life than materialism, and I pieced together a set of beliefs from whatever religious traditions I was exposed to at the time. I considered myself a little Jewish, Protestant, and Catholic all at once.[100]

On their web site, chart-topping rock band Creed goes to great lengths to distance themselves from the "Christian" label. "No, we are not a Christian band. A Christian band has an agenda to lead others to believe in their specific religious beliefs. We have no agenda!"[101] Ask Creed about their beliefs and lead singer-songwriter Scott Stapp will say, "There's always a spiritual thrust to what I'm writing. Spiritual, not religious. For me, religion was about 'what not to do.' Spirituality opens you up, sets you free."[102] Even harder rocking band P.O.D. echoes the same discomfort with religious labels. Lead singer Sonny

Sandoval says, "We realized pretty quickly that this 'Christian band' stuff is a box." Drummer Noah "Wuv" Bernardo agrees: "We're not going out there with a cause. We're going out there to tell our life story—who we love, and what makes us people."[103]

Dave Thomlinson addressed this reality in his influential book *The Post-Evangelical*. He says, "At the time of writing [1995], the term 'post-evangelical' has no formal definition, there is no body of theology behind it, no published agenda and certainly no organization, and yet it is surprising how many people on hearing the word for the first time immediately understand its significance and have a rough idea of what it might imply."[104] Outspoken techno superstar Moby has tried to define his faith in a post-Christian culture. He told Q magazine, "I'm a Christian in a very unconventional, idiosyncratic sense of the word. I don't go to church, I'm not a member of any denomination, I would never argue about religion with anyone. I love Christ, I love the teachings of Christ, but I don't think I'm right."[105] To some, Moby's "statement of faith" contains irreconcilable contradictions. To others, he expresses a painful, lived paradox—love for Christ, estrangement from institutionalized religion.

The spiritual search is on in our post-Christian Western world. Pop culture offers abundant proof. But we fear that misunderstandings of the signs will only lead to further estrangement. We must not approach the culture with the exodus attitude of "more than conquerors." Instead, we must learn the humble and broken posture of an exile people eager to discover God's plans for them. This book enters into the paradox of pop culture, hoping to discover a matrix of meaning. We write in an effort to inspire a statement of faith we can affirm, a community of faith we can join, and a demonstration of faith we can be proud of. We hope to spark much more than a name change.

Walter Brueggemann finds reasons for hope amid Israel's time of exile in *Hopeful Imagination*. He identifies grieving as a mandatory precursor to the future of God's exiled people. Only when they relinquished the known world could they receive a new world given by God through his post-exilic poets, Jeremiah, Ezekiel, and Isaiah. Brueggemann points out that "poets have no advice to give people. . . . They only want people to see differently, to re-vision life."[106] This is the role that pop culture's finest poets play today. But poets like Jeremiah will often encounter massive resistance. "The ideology of our age does not believe in a God who can work a real newness at a zero point and so it must defend, guard, and protect at all costs the old, which is thought to be the only source of life. It urges to keep the wagons tightly in a circle. . . . Jeremiah believes that God is able to do an utterly new thing which violates our reason, our control, our despair. Jeremiah bears witness to the work of God, the capacity to bring a newness *ex nihilo*."[107] Jeremiah's letter to the exiles announces, "'For I know the plans I have for you,' declares the LORD, 'plans to prosper you and not to harm you, plans to give you hope and a future'" (29:11). But that future can begin only by accepting and grieving our painful place in exile.

This book will offer plenty of reasons to grieve, but hopefully they will shock us into self-recognition and allow us to see and hear the new thing that God is ushering in, with or without us. We want the hopeful imagination found in Isaiah 43:18–19, where God challenges his people to "forget the former things; do not dwell on the past. See, I am doing a new thing!"

We are eager to see what the emerging generation will reconstruct out of ashes found in exile. The biblical role model Nehemiah learned how to cooperate with his captors, to curry the favor of those in power. Nehemiah acknowledged the painful parts of the past while focusing on rebuilding. For people of faith today, the time for marching in triumph may be over. The time for weeping and remorse may be at hand. Yet out of exile will arise a return to the Lord, propelled by humility, focused on rebuilding the fallen temple of God. May we get on with the grieving so that the humble rebuilding may commence.

"CREATIVITY SERVES ONLY ONE PURPOSE,
TO DELIVER THE MESSAGE SAFELY. WORRY NOT
ABOUT MAXIMIZING LEARNING, OR GENERATING
SUPERIOR AWARENESS, THAT TOO SMALL BUDGET IS DEVIL ENOUGH."

2

advertising

The Air That We Breathe

The Coke sign does not simply mean a refreshing drink; it means America got there first.

Humphrey McQueen

Buying is much more American than thinking.
Andy Warhol

Advertising ministers to the spiritual side of trade. It is a great power that has been trusted to your keeping which charges you with the high responsibility of inspiring and ennobling the commercial world. It is all part of the greater work of the regeneration and redemption of mankind.

Calvin Coolidge, speech to the American Association
of Advertising Agencies, 1926

Advertising might seem like a slight subject to tackle in a book about theology and popular culture. We understand the need to discuss film or music, even art, but advertising? It seems so immediately forgettable, so worthless in the grand scheme of things. This would perhaps be the first mistake. Madonna calls pop music an "absolute reflection of the world we live in,"[1] but advertising surrounds us subtly and completely. Of course, much of advertising can be brain-numbing, devoid of any real creativity. But it captures the national psyche in amazing ways (think of Nike ads). The average television viewer watches roughly forty thousand commercials a year! In our global marketplace, advertising creates the air that we breathe.

President Coolidge's speech seems prophetic in light of the massive influence that advertising and branding now impose on our world. When he spoke those words, a clearer delineation existed between the purposes of advertising and religion. Religion spoke about the afterlife, prepared the soul for the next world, while advertising addressed the here and now. But things have changed. Now ads do so much more than inform. They help us make decisions, develop values, take risks—treading on religion's traditional territory. In our consumer-driven society, advertising often serves as our language. Theology must engage this meaning-making, soul-defining medium.

Branding Will Save the World: The Power of Advertising

> We are no longer eating food or drinking drinks; we practice "body management" and are buying convenience, escape, energy.
>
> Marc Gobé, *Emotional Branding*

ADVERTISING DRIVES THE GLOBAL ECONOMY

Advertisers spend more than four hundred billion dollars a year getting their messages out. Enough said. That much money can generate an awful lot of influence. Yet how rarely do we reflect on who creates the commercials, billboards, and ads that surround us? In 1986, Batten, Barton, Durstine, and Osborne (BBDO) merged with Doyle, Dane, Bernbach and Needham, Harper, and Steers to create a massive, multinational holding company. London-based Saatchi and Saatchi took over Ted Bates's agency in the United States. In 1988, the French company Publicis traded equity shares with Foote, Cone, and Belding. Between 1987 and 1989, London's WPP group absorbed American stalwarts such as the J. Walter Thompson Agency and Ogilvy and Mather, becoming the world's biggest marketing communications company. This is not a book about economics, so I will leave the financial aspect of this industry to those better informed to deal with it. But the economic element cannot be avoided. Fewer and fewer corporations control more and more of what we see on billboards, buses, and commercials. As advertising's influence expanded, the key players contracted.

ADVERTISING SHAPES POPULAR CULTURE

"Old Navy, Old Navy performance fleece . . ." Remember those wacky ads featuring fashion critic Carrie Donovan, Morgan Fairchild, and a host of other minor celebrities hawking cheap clothing in a hip way? Or how about the Gap khaki ads that featured bright-faced, multiethnic dancers dancing to swing music? Or how about Taco Bell's talking Chihuahua? The list goes on and on. Catch phrases on everyone's lips and T-shirts include: "Where's the beef?" "Wassup!" "Just do it." Advertising stands as the last vestige of common culture in an increasingly fragmented society. Perhaps that's why certain ads generate so much conversation. Advertising doesn't just sponsor television programs today; it shapes and creates them. Consider the premiere of the action series *Alias*. Nokia sponsored the first episode without commercial interruption. The publicity surrounding this new approach to advertising and television generated huge interest in the company and consequently lifted its product profile in the public mind. Ford brought television back to its roots by underwriting a reality game show on the WB called *No Boundaries*. Ford cars take the contestants on every adventure. All Fords, all the time.

Advertising Reflects Our Culture

An examination of advertising tells us plenty about our society. Marshall McLuhan said that advertisements are the "richest and most faithful daily reflections that any society ever made of its entire range of activities."[2] Questions of influence, "Who is shaping whom?" cannot be easily answered. The uneasy, mutual journey between advertising and culture can hardly be separated. At times advertising can appear to, and perhaps does, tell us what to think or what to do, but more often it reflects trends and ideas that have already begun to take hold in culture. If the opposite were true, then the success rate of the various segments of the entertainment industry and the products sold through advertising would be even greater.

The style of television ads in particular gives insight into the way we live. The current trend in advertising is to focus on the "real world." The wholesome, all-American family approach to advertising has largely given way to more realistic views of modern life. Gritty beer commercials and a new kind of aggression in ads that reflect the tough competitiveness in life have replaced the sanitized view of life as "it should be," which used to characterize advertising.

Advertising Is an Incredibly Powerful Art Form

Calling advertising the most advanced art form[3] may seem silly given the poor quality of many ads. But there are moments when advertising captures the human spirit in deep and profound ways. Many of the world's great art museums now regularly feature commercial advertising in shows. I visited an amazing show on consumerism and branding called "Brand.new" at the prestigious and very old-school Victoria and Albert Museum in London. Absolut Vodka commissions many of the world's most famous artists to create art around the shape of their vodka bottle. Mark Fenske, a copywriter famous for his groundbreaking work for Nike, says that because "advertising deals with the minutiae of everyday life, any art that comes out of it is going to be particularly relevant and powerful."[4] Much of the art world seems to be consumed with ever increasing movements away from reality. Perhaps that is why commercial art can speak so powerfully at times; it gives people something to hold on to, to help them make sense of their life, their world.

ADVERTISING CREATES AWARENESS AND INSPIRES

Nike's "just do it" ads reflect the increasing role advertising plays in the world. These ads got people all over the world to be more active, more aware of the need to take care of their health (and, of course, to wear expensive clothing and sports shoes!). In recent years, advertising has become a forum for inspirational and enlightening ideas. Of course, advertising still encourages drinking and smoking, but ads have also challenged us to lay down our cigarettes (the "truth" campaign), drive more carefully, and abolish apartheid in South Africa. Not all advertising brings out the best in people, but the best ads certainly change lives and minds.

Such reasons make advertising a compelling arena for discussion and theological reflection.

Spirituality in an Age of Consumerism: The Hereafter Becomes the Here and Now

> They rage against materialism, as they call it, forgetting that there has been no material improvement that has not spiritualized the world.
>
> Oscar Wilde, *The Critic as Artist*

> When the historian of the Twentieth Century shall have finished his narrative and comes searching for the sub-title which shall best express the spirit of the period, we think it is not at all unlikely that he may select "The Age of Advertising" for the purpose.
>
> *Printers' Ink*, May 1915

In his compelling book *Lead Us into Temptation*, James Twitchell writes, "When we have few things, we make the next world holy. When we have plenty, we enchant the objects around us."[5] He discusses the battle between materialism and spirituality, arguing, quite convincingly, that materialism does not simply meet material needs but allows people access to meaning, to transcendence.

Materialism and consumerism are part of what it means to be human. The industrial revolution did not produce materialism; rather, a desire for products produced the revolution. Humans have always produced and exchanged things. But a highly materialist age challenges us to find a place for the spiritual.

Many in the advertising business regard creativity as God-given. Industry giant and maverick commercial director Joe Pytka regards his craft as a God-given gift rather than simply an intellectual pursuit. "It's a high craftsmanship as is music. And the inspiration in it comes from God."[6] When surveyed about creative writing, communication industry members considered the Bible the most creative book ever written.[7] We're not suggesting that such beliefs extend beyond surface admiration. Certainly, advertising can supplant older, more religious worldviews with new and shallower ways by which to frame one's life.

We all have stories by which we live—family stories and larger cultural stories that tell us who we are as a nation or a people. These stories give us our identities. In the past (and in many traditional cultures still today), these shaping stories were religious in nature. They were the creation stories, nature stories, god stories that every culture possesses. Every culture seeks to explain its existence, to answer questions of ultimate meaning. While less dependent on "old stories," Western culture still clings to its "mythology." The resurgence of interest in spirituality that marked the end of the twentieth century surprised many modernists who were convinced that science and reason had rid the world of the mythic or the divine. Philosophers proclaimed the death of God, but someone forgot to tell the broader population! Access to more material goods has not dimmed interest in the divine. Surprisingly, advertising fills the void where the old shaping stories used to function, creating new possibilities for who we can become as individuals. These stories continually mutate, offering more and more options.

This chapter suggests that: (1) advertising has replaced spirituality as our shaping story. The stories that give us our identity and shape our sense of self are more likely to come through advertising than religion. James Twitchell notes, "You can still see the religious roots of commercialism in advertising. Buy this object and you'll be saved. You deserve a break today. You, you're the one. We are the company that cares about you. You are in good hands. We care. Trust in us. Buy now."[8] (2) People are not as naive or as gullible as we sometimes think they are. As a consumer, I recognize the unspoken messages of ads. I recognize that I often buy the idea, the *grand idea,* being advanced rather than the product. I am often more interested in the vibe, the feel, the meaning than the product. I buy things because I can, because I want to, and sometimes for what I think they can bring me or give me. I want what surrounds the product, the idea behind it, usually because it speaks to my life more than much of the religion I have been exposed to. And (3) we should take seriously the religious function of both advertising and consumerism. Jesus himself raised issue with the relationship between faith and materialism in his oft-quoted maxim, "You cannot serve both God and Money" (Matt. 6:24). What do you do when money gets enchanted, gets "spiritualized," and products become tools for the appropriation of larger ideas and values?

Think Small, Just Do It, Think Different: The New Trinity

> Corporate identity programs need to be visionary, integrated, visceral, and reflective of a true commitment from corporations to share their values with the consumers.
>
> Marc Gobé, *Emotional Branding*

In 1960, advertising experienced a quantum leap. As with many shifts, its influence sharpened in hindsight, with time clarifying how significant this event was to advertising and to society in general. In the post–World War II economic boom, everything in America was big and colorful. Before the tumultuous events of the hippie revolution, Cadillacs and Chevrolets were brash and bold. Then a magazine ad for a Volkswagen Beetle appeared. The ad was black-and-white. The page was bare, except for a small photo of the car. A line at the bottom read, "Think small." Hardly the stuff of revolutions. But this ad marked a revolution in advertising with long-term reverberations. The ad caused people to rethink the way they viewed the automobile. The ad challenged readers to shift perspective, to challenge ideas of social conformity. "Everyone else drives big luxurious cars, but you are different. You live differently, so you should buy a Beetle." In a highly individuated modern society in which mass production and consumption were the order of the day, this appeal to uniqueness and free thinking prompted revolution. It marked the moment when advertising moved from simply telling us what to buy to offering ideas on how to live. Instead of simply selling a product, the Beetle ad introduced a new way of looking at the world. We are now so used to this approach that we seldom realize the significance of such a "subtle" shift. The Volkswagen campaign established a new standard, becoming the father of advertising's enduring "trinity."

Just do it. Words we've lived by. Nike's ubiquitous campaign became advertising's favorite son. A Nike ad for the 2000 Summer Olympics put the just do it philosophy in context. As a basketball player dribbles and shoots, title cards proclaim, "Everyone Practices . . . Some Sort of . . . Religion." Nike's religion features the world's greatest athletes, especially the dizzying heights of Michael "Air" Jordan.

James Twitchell is rapturous in his examination of a Nike ad featuring Jordan:

The man who flies. . . . Mr. Jordan is hanging there in the sublime—if you look at Renaissance church paintings, or Impressionistic landscape paintings, you realize that whatever there is in this ethereal band of air is graced with transcendental meaning. The golden halo of a hovering Giotto angel . . . is a signifier of man's ancient yearning for life above the limen (the edge), at the edge of transcendence.[9]

All of this poetry and religious rapture in response to an ad for shoes! Not so long ago perfectionism ruled advertising. But Nike initiated a cultural shift by also discussing failure. When athletes talked about their faults, their weaknesses, and their humanity, audiences listened even more intently. Nike presented Air Jordan as fully god, fully man.

The spirit of advertising moved me on Santa Monica Boulevard. A huge billboard featured a black-and-white photo of Gandhi, and in the bottom right-hand corner of the photo there was a little logo of an apple and a tag line: "Think different." Macintosh's "think different" campaign is quite simple: Take a culturally familiar figure who needs no identification, such as Martin Luther King Jr., Picasso, or Einstein, and add two simple words. "Think different" reveals the power beyond these pioneers and, by association, the company whose product is being hawked. The slogan brilliantly appealed to our cultural mind-set, our desperation to feel some sort of uniqueness. The "best" products make us feel both a part of the crowd and set apart from the crowd at the same time. Advertising promised definition and distinction. Such simultaneity highlights advertising's meaning-making power and consumerism's broad appeal.

The Ten Commandments of Advertising

Fulfilling the vocation of the consumer means more choosing, whether or not this results in more consumption. To embrace the modality of the consumer means first and foremost falling in love with choice; only in the second, and not at all indispensable place, does it mean consuming more.

Zygmunt Bauman, *Work, Consumerism, and the New Poor*

The "big three" just discussed reveal only the tip of the iceberg. The bulk of today's advertising urges us to do much more than simply buy a product. Advertisers connect their products to a certain lifestyle or worldview, appealing to seekers of that particular perspective. The following ten commandments of advertising represent ten shaping stories, adopted by many in our culture as a way of focusing their lives. As with much of postmodern culture, it is not an either/or situation. A cut-and-paste approach dominates product appropriation.

www.defytherules.com

Adobe® software lets you
do the impossible on the
Web. Go. See for yourself.
Inspiration becomes reality. **Adobe**

A culture that prizes individuality naturally views itself as a rebel culture. Breaking the status quo is a huge factor in advertising. Many ads and products aimed at the youth culture focus on acts of rebellion and invite the recipient to break the rules. An ad for software maker Adobe plays on this theme. The view is from the top of the Golden Gate Bridge, a place where ordinary people are not allowed to go. The copy line of the ad offers a web site address: www.defytherules.com. And below it is a little information about the product. Although the company wants the viewer to purchase its product, the ad is also about generating a particular worldview, which transcends any product. The shaping story suggests that one can become an iconoclast by purchasing certain products infused, if you will, with the energy behind the idea.

The theological challenge raised by this particular ad is that iconoclasm can be achieved simply by ignoring society's norms and buying into the "spirit" of Adobe software. True iconoclasm is achieved not through the purchase of products but the development of character.

PAIN IS GOOD

BATCH #37. A new hot sauce from CALIDO CHILE TRADERS.

Calido Hot Sauce is a small company attempting to take a big bite out of the large and lucrative food market. How does it compete with the larger, more affluent companies whose budgets probably outweigh its profits? By niche marketing its product to a certain portion of the public. "Pain is good," a play on the old maxim "No pain, no gain," serves as the tag line. To sell its hot sauce, the company directs its product toward the segment of the population who will most identify with the tag line. Surprisingly, it goes after young people rather than war veterans. It aims to identify with the general pain of a post-traumatic life rather than with specific events such as war.

Pain comes from being from the underside of an affluent culture, rooted in a lack of resources or access to certain things expected from life in the West. Pain is a hot commodity in our culture. Not pain as we have traditionally understood it. After all, we have not experienced much hardship or deprivation by the standards of prior generations. But there is pain nonetheless, and it has become a familiar marketing tool for everything from hot sauce to extreme sports equipment. Advertising offers more about how to live than what to buy. In this case, we are offered a way of living, living with and through pain. The message suggests that there is something to be gained from the pain of life. Finding strength through pain is a better way of living than avoiding it.

Tom Beaudoin notes that suffering is a sort of "boundary experience that forces us to confront questions about our own human limits."[10] He also suggests that "self-consciousness about suffering"[11] is a distinguishing characteristic of young people today—one that marks a significant cultural shift in societal attitudes toward pain and suffering. The theological challenge raised here deals with how we incorporate ideas about pain and suffering into our spiritual lives. There has been a strong thread of avoidance, if not downright denial, in regard to suffering in much of the church's theological perspectives. Rather than focusing on only the triumphal aspects of Christ's life, we might do well to reconsider and emphasize the role of suffering in Christ's life—he was, after all, the Suffering Servant, as Isaiah called him.

8. BE YOURSELF

Find yourself, know yourself, be yourself, lose yourself—philosophy has toyed with the idea of the self over the centuries. Now comes advertising's contribution. An ad for Avia sports shoes aims at women and features the athletic, self-assured figure of a woman idealized by late-twentieth-century culture.

The last decades of the twentieth century saw women emerge in remarkable ways. As men lost their way at the end of the century, particularly in terms of male identity and traditionally defined male roles and functions, women found theirs. The twentieth century may be remembered as the century of the woman. While not all was good for the female sex, huge advances were made. In popular culture, women progressed in leaps and bounds. Women moved boldly into previously exclusive male domains. Female action heroes (such as Linda Hamilton in *The Terminator* or Angelina Jolie in *Lara Croft: Tomb Raider*) lit up movie screens. Singers from Whitney Houston to Mariah Carey topped the charts. Sarah McLachlan founded Lilith Fair, an all-female celebration of music and womanhood.

By using the tag line "The only competition is you," the Avia ad appeals to women by playing against a couple of unspoken but widely accepted views—first, that sport is not competitive. The larger idea behind the ad is aimed at female empowerment, which is an idea that often goes hand in hand with female solidarity. In that light, sport becomes a communal activity, an environment of mutual support in which individuals are liberated from the pressure of external competition and are free to focus on challenging themselves. Instead of concentrating on other participants, "true" athletes perform as individuals. Push yourself, ignore all outside forces, and concentrate on yourself. You may be in a room full of other bodies, but the only one that counts is your own. You don't have to compete with others, so push yourself. By emphasizing "is," this ad seeks to impart the "great truth" that only the individual counts. The ad is more about self-realization than self-improvement. Being true to oneself is paramount—and, of course, this particular sports shoe will aid in that process!

This ad also brings up a major theological challenge by highlighting the postmodern emphasis on physicality. Humanity has always been fascinated with the physical. Ancient Greek athletic clubs, which focused on body beauty, left an indelible mark on Western culture. The modern age elevated Western fascination with the body in terms of exercise and body shape. The sexualizing of society through advertising coupled with the individuation and advancements of the modern age has resulted in new body relationships. These new relationships involve changed perspectives regarding gender and sexual norms, prolonged and improved physical lives, and, of course, a much more open view toward sex and sexuality in general. The postmodern loss of faith in the future has left people with a new hunger for the physical. Physical exercise has also undergone a major transition, shifting from a rootedness in the duality of the modern age to an integration of body and soul. Consider the rise of interest in yoga and meditation, not merely as means for peace of mind but for strengthening the body. The aerobics revolution has been replaced by ashtanga and other physical forms of yoga that combine physical fitness with spirituality. Spirituality must be grounded in the earth to appeal to seekers today. Part of the cultural fascination with Eastern forms of religious practice stems from their tendency to emphasize living in this world rather than focusing on the afterlife.

Conflicting ideas and stories exist side by side in our post-rational, pluralistic culture, and people often hold conflicting ideas with apparent ease. While some ads promote being oneself, others recommend reinventing oneself. Reinvention of oneself consumes a large part of post-human life. Levels of unparalleled anonymity offered by the Internet allow us to present ourselves in myriad, and in generally anonymous, ways. A European web site called Cycosmos.com allows subscribers to adopt new physiques, personalities, and genders and to enter a world of their choosing that is inhabited by other compatible creations. The highly successful video game *The Sims* allows players to create new environments—homes, towns, restaurants—filled with people. Many people have multiple user names for their web activities, allowing role-playing and exploration.

Fashion has become a large part of identity making in the post-human world. People play dress-up with their clothing in order to present a particular persona to the larger world. An ad from Nordstrom department stores plays on the idea of reinventing the self with the underlying assumption that shopping purchases can help with the transformation. The ad features a pair of sexy high-heeled women's boots overlaid with a simple slogan: "Reinvent the girl next door." The suggestion is that times have changed and that the girl next door no longer has to be the quiet, stay-at-home type of the 1950s. She can be sexual, liberated, and desirable. It seems obvious that purchases cannot really affect change. But in a culture in which products are more than products and are in fact ways of being, a connection can easily be made.

Living in a consumer culture, we all experience on some level the tendency to connect personal change and transformation with the purchase of certain products, even "buying" the concept of simplicity rather than opting for a simple lifestyle as an alternative life choice. We understand that we expect certain things from our purchases such as durability, reliability, quality, and value for the money. Consider the amount of trouble people go through to purchase fake designer products. Why do we buy fake Chanel bags or Nike clothing? Because their powerful brand images offer subtle reassurances. These brand identities and logos are so powerful that we attribute similar ideas to what we know are fake brands. Why engage in such self-deception? Because we recognize that these brands grant us certain feelings of status and fashion value. So why shouldn't a pair of shoes contribute to the reinvention of self? Nordstrom has turned this cultural perception into a permanent niche.

Again we face theological challenges related to the construction of the self and identity in consumer culture. How does theology address a culture in which people derive their sense of identity from products? Merely invoking God versus mammon ideas does not work. These are complex cultural realities, not minor side issues. A theology of shopping and consumerism is no laughing matter.

Marc Gobé, in his incredibly insightful book *Emotional Branding,* points out that shopping today is an all-sensory activity. Merchandisers use scents to create familiarity, color theory to attract consumers. They use symbols (the iconry of the postmodern world) to captivate the imagination and create environments. Take a walk around your local shopping mall. Note the differences in each store's smells, the colors they employ, and the visual environments they create. Pay particular attention to their use of lighting and the kind of music being played. According to Gobé, all these things and more contribute to the sensorial branding experience.[12] The products themselves are also approached in different ways. Remember, we are being offered ways to live as much as products to buy. This change in focus requires a change in marketing approach. Brands are now imbued with concept and personality, designed to create an emotional bond with consumers. Gobé points out that corporate identities are "transforming from the '*dictated*' visual identities of the past . . . to 'personal' visual identities"[13] (a more fluid branding process that allows a product to be perceived in a variety of ways, often differing from consumer to consumer, which in turn allows consumers to reinvent themselves).

This shift from dictatorial to a more fluid consumer-oriented interpretation transcends the advertising/consumer world. The postmodern shift rejects authoritarian values. Many once powerful voices have lost their right to speak in the marketplace because of their unwillingness to listen to their audience and change their approaches. The post-institutional corporations allow greater interaction between both sides. That's why Philip Morris adopted a new name. It was trying to position itself as a different kind of company.

Theology needs to adopt a similar listening posture, allowing for a more personal engagement with its audience. Jesus often engaged in dialogue by asking questions of his audience: "What do you say?" or "How do you see . . . ?"

Religious authorities have been notoriously authoritative about most things, rarely allowing room for dialogue. In a post-institutional world, a theology out of popular culture must be rooted in dialogue and engagement.

6. BE PROUD OF WHO YOU ARE

Ads that emphasize being proud of who you are represent tribal advertising. Such advertising focuses on a particular group of consumers who think, look, and act a certain way. Advertisers have become very adept at targeting consumers according to gender, race, age, and so on. They acknowledge the diversification of the market and understand that the days of mass marketing are gone. They adopt and celebrate cultural diversity and invite us to identify with our particular affinities.

An ad for Budweiser revolves around a group

of guys who make up a word that develops a meaning and personality beyond comprehension. The word "Whassup!" serves as a greeting, an exclamation, an expletive, anything you want it to be. It creates immediacy and intimacy within a certain group.

Some people love these ads, and others hate them. Some see them as juvenile and demeaning; others see them as funny. As with all contemporary advertising, these ads and their creators must walk a fine line. McDonald's pioneered the use of African-American slang in its commercials, the innocuous Mickey D's. The Budweiser commercial employs another slang word, but its success goes beyond the cultural boundaries it addresses. This ad became a favorite in Great Britain, achieving cultural breakthrough. T-shirts emblazoned with the word were everywhere. "Whassup!" was used by celebrities, newspapers, and people on the street. The underlying message is one of pride, of satisfaction with oneself and one's position or station in life. There are also class implications. Many of these ads are directed toward the blue-collar segment of the population, people who do not have either the aspiration or the means for cultural advancement. These ads invite consumers to celebrate who they are with unabashed glee. In an age of athleticism, plastic surgery, and expensive fashion clothing, these ads often feature overweight, beer-bellied throwbacks to another age. They are examples of niche marketing and advertising.

What a prime theological invitation to explore Jesus' inclusive message. These ads are driven by the idea that society has misfits who are ignored and overlooked by the larger society. These ads play on that rejection and offer alternative means for a sense of inclusion and community. Advertising that highlights inclusion and exclusion offers a prime arena for the gospel message of a banquet table prepared for all.

5. GET REAL

A successful brand is ultimately a question of authenticity. The quest for authenticity drives both sides of consumerism, buyers and sellers. A successful brand achieves a level of authenticity in the minds and experience of consumers. At the same time, a brand must reflect the values of the company behind it. We call our own failings at personal authenticity behaving out of character. We are composed of a number of values that determine our ethical framework as a person, and when those values govern our lives, we are acting authentically. Conversely, when something else takes precedence, we feel out of balance, not ourselves. Brands face the same challenge. Brands that advertise their wares through appeals to authenticity must make sure that all they present relates to the core values behind their products. Levi invented denim jeans, and its ads appeal to the authenticity of the product. Other products may use the term *jeans,* but Levi is the originator. One ad appeals to the longevity of the company and relies heavily on retro-looking artwork to underscore the authenticity of the jeans. Behind the ad lies the claim that authenticity counts for something. It should be pursued and accepted.

Authenticity surfaces in contemporary religious preferences. Being real is a key factor in understanding the dynamics of post-human spirituality. While the modern age placed a high premium on theories of faith, the postmodern era searches for authentic practices of faith—showing rather than telling. Experimentation and innovation run throughout contemporary spirituality. The word *spirituality* no longer refers to an already-held theological standpoint but to a search for meaning via experimentation, questioning, and exploration. Advertising co-opts religious language because spirituality does not require a specific a priori theological view. Words such as *soul* and *salvation* dot the advertising landscape. The salvific power of a Volvo or a pair of jeans may seem ridiculous. But consumerism offers alternative routes to salvation outside religion. Central to all of this is authenticity—whether or not a product delivers on its claims. Companies that appeal to authenticity must take great care in building their core values into their products.

In 1942, Coca-Cola launched an ad campaign called "The only thing like Coca-Cola is Coca-Cola itself. It's the real thing." The company brought this campaign back successfully in the 1970s. The claim to be the real thing, the claim to authenticity, elevates one brand over another. Most ads carry claims of some sort; it tastes good, smells good, whitens teeth, and so on. These claims sound meaningless compared to authenticity. Savvy consumers tend to disbelieve most promises, so advertisers must carefully support their claims. As a European, I have always been taken aback when driving through a small American town whose local burger joint claims to have the world's best burger or the number one french fries in the world. I have tried some. Believe me, they were usually empty claims that I didn't believe in the first place! When a company declares that its product is the real thing, the authentic one, and that all others are mere imitations, it must back it up. Customers will verify the claim via their experience. Packaged claims that Christianity is the real thing have not always withstood customer scrutiny, and Christ has suffered greatly for it.

A campaign from innovative European clothing company Diesel takes topical cultural ideas and inverts them. It juxtaposes the irony of a cynical world with the need to be authentic. The ads attack the very claims that ads like to make by attacking products that promise too much. "Don't believe the hype—these are just clothes!" The ad plays on the very idea it propagates, namely, that it cannot "sell" anyone a particular lifestyle, just clothing.

Other lines such as Sprite's "Obey your thirst" take on those nauseating oh-so-happy-singing-and-dancing-around-the-breakfast-table-orange-juice commercials by using a tag line that says, "It's just a drink!"

This form of advertising has been used successfully to take on larger social issues such as the effects of drugs, alcohol, and smoking. Consider an elaborate spoof mocking the claims of a cigarette company. A cowboy looks eerily familiar as the brand identity of Marlboro cigarettes. The font resembles the company's well-known logo, but instead of using the company's name, the ad uses the word *impotence*—one of the side effects of smoking that is not found on cigarette packaging.

3. GET CONNECTED

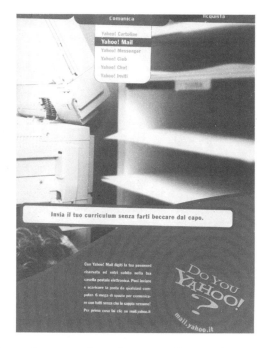

In a borderless culture, words such as *networking* and *connected* have cultural credibility. Traditional means of social relationships have fragmented or been discarded. The postmodern person yearns for community and connectedness. But how and what makes a person feel connected is the issue.

Consider an Italian ad for the American-based Internet company Yahoo. It follows a trend among new technology companies in using connectedness as a means to generate interest in its product, in this case global Internet access. You may not know anyone in your apartment building, but that doesn't mean you're not connected. Many Internet companies portray the world-saving capabilities of their services (a reality that has been greatly undermined by the recent collapse of Internet technology futures on the world's stock exchanges): They can connect you to the universe. You want movies? music videos? banking? They're all right here at the touch of a fingertip. These ads imply that new technologies improve our relationships, infusing them with things that up until now were lacking—and who wouldn't want that kind of connection?

Of course, to take advantage of this connectedness one must get connected to the products first—purchase computers, software, and so on. Behind many of these ads lies the unspoken threat that you need to move fast or you will be left behind. It is a surprisingly old-fashioned hard sell by proponents of new ways of engaging life. Yet the ads are successful because borderless people often feel disconnected and are attempting to find ways to feel a new sense of community.

Getting connected is a central theme of the Christian faith—getting connected to God, to a community. The postmodern hunger for connectedness, for networks, for community provides ample opportunity for renewed mission. There is also a challenge involved with a culture obsessed with the future and all things new. The next thing is not always the best thing; sometimes we need to connect with something other than the latest craze. Products don't really allow for the real connections we seek. They are pseudo-connections at best.

2. Prioritize Your Life

We turn now from technology ads to that mainstay of contemporary urban life—coffee. Where would we be without our daily caffeine infusions? Coffee shops have become the new meeting places of the twenty-first century. They foster community (warm, friendly staff), encourage interaction among strangers as well as friends (soft furnishings in small, intimate environments that encourage conversation), and get us to work wide awake and ready to go! These stores offer a designer approach to coffee—lattes, cappuccinos, and frappuccinos made individually, anyway you want them. Starbucks supplanted more old-school coffee companies such as Maxwell House. So Maxwell House fought back by connecting its product to the basics of life. One ad focuses on drinking coffee at home, challenging people to remember important things such as home and family. While Starbucks offers hip coffee, Maxwell House returns us to a more simple time—by purchasing its coffee instead!

The ad is highly personal—no big, artsy logo—just a handwritten text focusing on a commitment to self-improvement and a tag line urging us to make every day count. Urban life can become overwhelming because of the high pressure world we live in. Burnout abounds. These ads advocate a return to simplicity and a reprioritizing of life (much as religion desires).

Consider the recent Mastercard campaign that puts price tags on life experiences. Want to know the value of things? Tickets to a ballgame? That has a price. Your son's first hot dog? Again a value. At the end, what is it worth to see your child enjoy his first big-league game? Priceless. For everything else—Mastercard. These ads list priorities for us. In the Maxwell House ad, the woman lists "forgive my husband for snoring," "stop finishing other people's sentences," and so on. Life has grown so complex that advertising even tells us what our priorities should be. Maxwell House reminds us to have a cup of coffee before we get on with our newly re-prioritized lives!

Advertising plays to the need we all have for some kind of purpose and structure. It would be a mistake to view our post-rational life as disorganized and free-form simply because institutional suspicion rages. Many people today, particularly critics of all things postmodern, bemoan the seeming lack of organization in postmodern culture and the deep suspicion of authority and established structures. But this doesn't mean that everything is without form. Things are being reconfigured, recontextualized, a point often missed by those who see only the dismantling and deconstruction of postmodernity. There is a big difference between institutions and organization. People eschew institutions but not necessarily organization in life. As God's people, we must get our priorities straight, beginning with that difference.

The challenge associated with a culture engaged in re-prioritizing is that much of the "old world" gets left behind. Much of the cultural animosity toward or disregard for the Christian faith is related to antiauthoritarian, antiestablishment sentiments and a pervasive view that the church is a remnant of another age and part of the "establishment." The church's wholehearted embrace of modernity has left it vulnerable and often rejected in contemporary culture. We would do well to re-prioritize the nature of our ecclesiology and rethink the role the church has as an institution in the postmodern world.

1. CONTROL YOUR OWN DESTINY

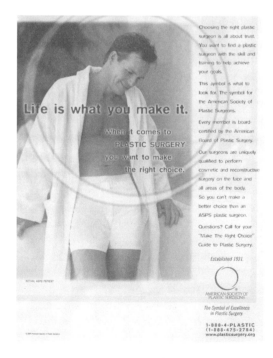

An ad for the American Society of Plastic Surgeons promotes male cosmetic surgery and features the tag line "Life is what you make it." Restructuring our body image is a means of bettering ourselves. The ad also highlights the belief that in our fragmented, deconstructed, every-man-for-himself society, we can't rely on anyone but ourselves. Look out for No. 1. In a post-institutional setting, we can no longer count on friends, family, or the government to help us. So we must help ourselves. This ad trades on the "empowering" aspect of a product. Plastic surgery appeals to this dynamic.

There is a deep mistrust of institutions and ideology in contemporary society. Early twenty-first-century society finds itself in the twilight of modernity's ideals—the future has not realized its potential, and there is a sense that we are on our own. We can no longer trust in institutions, be they political, social, or religious, to protect us and meet our needs. We "exist in a state of continuous construction and reconstruction; it is a world where anything goes that can be negotiated. Each reality of self gives way to reflexive questioning, irony, and ultimately the playful probing of yet another reality. The center fails to hold."[14] This lack of a center has led to an increasingly isolated society in which individuals must fend for themselves.

Our sense of isolation also arises out of society's extreme commitment to individual freedom. Religion too became a private affair in the modern era. Evangelicals promoted individuality through the language of personal salvation. By promoting a singular and personalized initiation process, Christians in the past century often neglected the larger communal claims of the New Testament.

Contemporary advertising encourages Christians to rediscover a communitarian theology. In the postmodern world, there is a growing desire for community. The success of online communities of all kinds demonstrates this. Even the virtual communities of CD-ROM games such as *The Sims* are examples of the hunger for connectedness. How the church can connect with a culture riddled with dysfunctional relationships and highly individuated persons is a challenge, but there are clues and precedents found in the biblical text. In a culture in which people are desperately trying to find their "true selves" and are prepared to experiment with all kinds of things, from plastic surgery to shopping, to do so, it shouldn't be too difficult to introduce the communal nature of the gospel as a starting place. The affirming message of the gospel is that God wants to aid and guide us in the struggle to be human and invites us into a relationship with him. The Bible also teaches us that we find ourselves and true fulfillment not in isolation, not even as we engage with one another, but rather when we relate to God through one another. The challenge for the church is to emphasize the communal nature of the Christian faith and to commit to authentic expressions of that nature.

The New Priesthood

> Mass production demands the education of the masses; the masses must learn to behave like human beings in a mass production world. . . . They must achieve, not mere literacy, but culture.
>
> department store magnet Edward A. Filene

We have looked at the new trinity: Volkswagen, Apple, and Nike. We have examined the ten commandments of advertising. To continue this slightly tongue-in-cheek critique of advertising as religious substitute, we must consider how these shaping stories are mediated to us via the new priesthood.

If advertising shapes our fantasies, then celebrities demonstrate how to fulfill them. They teach us what to wear and where to buy it. In a nation of shopping malls, celebrities are the arbiters of taste, the signifiers of cool, the people telling us how we should live. James Twitchell says, "Celebrities are the priests in the empire of things."[15] Celebrities serve as our spirit guides steering us toward the new sacraments—shoes, sunglasses, and designer jeans. Kenneth Gergen attributes our willingness to reconstruct ourselves based on celebrity styles and fashion to our "ersatz being." "If identities are essentially forms of social construction, then one can be anything at any time so long as the roles, costumes, and settings have been commodiously arranged."[16] Celebrities serve as the models for whatever persona we may want to try on. In an ironic twist, the richer and more powerful the celebrity, the more likely it is that he or she never has to buy anything. Fashion designers woo stars in the annual Oscar derby, trying to get stars to wear their gowns down the world's most visible fashion runway. The competition is just as fierce backstage, as Oscar presenters receive twenty thousand dollars' worth of free products in gift baskets. Shampoos, fragrances, jewelry, handbags, sunglasses, and cell phones jostle for position. Gift baskets are considered cost-effective marketing because "there's so much value in saying Cher uses this product, Bono has these glasses."[17]

Christopher Lasch thinks advertising uses celebrities to institutionalize envy. Consumption becomes the answer to loneliness, sickness, weariness, lack of sexual satisfaction. "Advertising . . . manufactures a product of its own: the consumer, perpetually unsatisfied, restless, anxious and bored."[18] He finds it suspicious that the decline in organized religion coincided with the rising commodification of everyday life. But Twitchell argues from another angle. Rather than simply bemoaning the decline in organized religion and the rising commodification of everyday life, he suggests that we are not materialistic enough. We have bought the celebrity aura that surrounds a product, but we need to push through to identify the deeper needs inside us that propel our shopping sprees. We add most of the true value to products.

Sure, the celebrity adds a cool cachet, but we perform the actual magic of making ourselves feel sexier in those Diesel jeans. We buy the image they project, but our imagination does far more work, allowing us to picture ourselves as somehow smarter, sexier, or both. Twitchell inverts the popular notion that advertisers dupe the public. We dupe ourselves into believing we don't like to be deceived. Advertisers appeal to our desperate need to be noticed, making us feel important, allowing us to feel seduced, loved, wooed. Just like a celebrity![19]

Now, you can purchase goods directly from celebrities themselves. Home Shopping has taken "selling of lifestyles" to a new level. TV and studio executive Barry Diller supposedly saw the potential when his friend Diane Von Furstenburg moved $1.2 million worth of her designs in ninety minutes. He paid $25 million to buy QVC, expanding its commitment to Quality, Value, and Convenience (or is that credit cards?).[20] Scads of second-tier celebrities lined up to hock their wares. Former TV stars such as Meredith Baxter, Fran Tarkenton, and Victoria Principal gave up their slots on Hollywood Squares for the far more rewarding sets of HSN and QVC. Lest you consider home shopping the exclusive province of nimwits and blue-haired grandmas, consider the highbrow campaign of American Express. What began as an effort to identify celebrity card members eventually became "famous people and their stuff." They captured Jerry Seinfeld (comedian, author, cereal lover) on a Manhattan street surrounded by a few of his "favorite things." Twenty-one items are listed, from his Pez collection to a shoe polisher, along with the places where you can find "items like Jerry's": Radio Shack, Hammacher Schlemmer, and Crate & Barrel.[21] Whether the situation is highbrow or lowbrow, ironic or obvious, celebrities increasingly sell us stuff.

Martha Stewart tapped into this zeitgeist, creating an entirely new type of celebrity—"lifestyle advisor."[22] She told us how to use beautiful stuff to create beautiful lives. But a generation looking for something authentic has engaged in Martha bashing. By the time her products reached K-Mart's shelves, savvy shoppers bailed on "Martha Stewart Living." With her Wall Street scandal, Martha proved that the only threat to celebrity salesmanship is celebrities.

Consumption, Culture, and the Pursuit of Happiness

A good ad should be like a good sermon: it must not only comfort the afflicted—it also must afflict the comfortable.

Bernice Fitz-Gibbon, quoted in *AdCult USA*

Defy the rules. Recognize pain rather than deny its existence. Be yourself. Accept yourself as body and spirit. Shun authority. Seek engagement. Be proud of who you are. Beware of the hype. Get connected. Re-prioritize your life. Take control of your destiny. Here is a theological anthropology worthy of the best reflection by the church. What is it to be fully human? This is the question that advertising seeks to answer, a question that was once the pursuit of philosophers and theologians. Advertising is an incredibly powerful form of pop culture that influences us on levels far deeper than getting us to choose certain products. Life choices are part of today's world of advertising and consumption.

"The glory of God," Irenaeus wrote, "is a human being fully alive." In contemporary society, to be fully alive is to shop. Advertising offers us ways to be alive, ways to be human. A theology out of popular culture, drawing from the world of advertising, must grapple with what it means to be fully human. Such an embodied theology must address issues of the whole self—spirit, soul, and body—and respond to ideas and values about how religion helps shape identity. This lived theology must deal with the transformation of an entire way of being rather than settle for intellectual consent as conversion. This real theology must demonstrate authenticity and praxis rather than propositions and theories. It must appeal to tradition and rootedness without getting caught in legalism and mere traditionalism. Finally, it needs to be communal in focus, helping individuals discover their sense of self and identity within the context of a communal religious approach. People want to belong. Theology and ecclesiology should reflect that desire and offer a sense of belonging.

Before I leave this topic, I offer one last thought. What about God? Does he need a new advertising campaign? I was given an article entitled "Does God Need a Rebrand?" from the web site brandchannel.com.[23] The article assumes the existence of God, but it questions whether God is delivering on his "brand promise." If not, does the divine need a repositioning strategy for the new millennium? Despite the obvious tongue-in-cheek approach taken in the article, as a follower of God, I took the challenge quite seriously. The debate centered around "God's marketing campaign" and assessed the Creator's relevance, credibility, differentiation, and stretch.

The article declares, "God is like an Oldsmobile—once great, now no longer relevant." Oldsmobile is out of business—relegated to classic car shows. The heady days of Christianity's ascendance in Western culture have passed. Despite pop culture's strong spiritual search, a general apathy greets both the Christian message and its practice. This is because the message is simply not connecting with people. The great theological task today is to re-think the "message"—to contextualize the gospel for the postmodern world. To some it may seem threatening if not somewhat heretical to say that we need a new message, but we do. The bulk of our theological and apologetic outlines are modern and no longer speak to today's culture. Somehow we have become bogged down in a myopic view of Scripture and the gospel story. We have to find ways to reread and reconnect the gospel message to this culture and to provide answers to questions being asked today. For instance, much of contemporary apologetics is centered around the idea of proving the existence of God. That may well have been necessary in the modern era, but the existence of God is not much of a question today. A bigger issue might be which god and why. The postmodern era is inherently religious, which leads to different implications theologically. India.Arie had a hit with a song titled "God Is Real." The need is not to argue God's existence but to challenge the kind of god India.Arie and others believe in.

Public confidence in organized religion plummeted following the Roman Catholic Church's sexual abuse scandal.[24] For some, the events of September 11, 2001, dented God's credibility. When brands lose the public's trust, recovering credibility can be difficult. Consider the ongoing problems of Firestone tires. Reports of exploding tires and fatalities were exacerbated by cover-up and blame-shifting. Was God's credibility undercut by the numbing violence of two world wars? Some would say yes. Appeals to the omnipotence and omniscience of God seem to come up short in the face of death camps, killing fields, ethnic cleansing, dictatorship, terrorism, continental starvation, and ravaging diseases. What can be done to repair the damage and restore public confidence? Perhaps we need to reexamine the claims we've made for God and rediscover the nature of the divine amid such harsh realities. We need a new position on God's relationship to human tragedy. The world we live in demands that those who claim to speak for God rethink their understanding of both the nature of evil and God's character. The task before us is not cosmetic adjustments to our theology or slight style shifts in our worship but rather radical rethinking of the very nature of theology (something we address in the conclusion to this book). God has taken some hard knocks, and our "easy answers" will not do. We no longer live in a largely Christianized society; many are unfamiliar with the Christian faith, and our pat answers often fail to strike a chord. As Roger Haight says, the "theologian still must interpret Jesus for our time."[25] The question of suffering and evil is one that must be revisited in and for *our* time. Bono and U2 addressed the tension between God and evil in song: "God is good, but will he listen?" God's seeming reticence in a world of pain and despair caused Bono to shout, "Wake Up Dead Man." In a post-traumatic world, we can no longer avoid evil. How does following God address the questions of ultimate meaning that haunt our lives?

On the subject of differentiation, the article raises questions about religious pluralism. Perhaps the Christian God's distinction has been lost in a sea of differing ideas and opinions about the divine. A couple of options present themselves in this category. We can entrench, dig in, and affirm, as many do, that Christianity is the only way. This would be a Coca-Cola–like approach: "We are the real thing—the others are mere imitations." However, this valid approach tends to limit the reception of the message, for many people resist dogmatic and seemingly arrogant assertions of one idea as superior to all. These blended times are marked by a willingness to embrace any idea, putting it on a level playing field with all other ideas. The other option is to expand our view of the nature of religion itself, broadening and embracing the complexities of religious beliefs and ideas while retaining the uniqueness of the Christian faith. This delicate and challenging option offers more promise in the present social climate. "There is also a positive side to postmodernity and its reception of religious pluralism. Theologians and others who allow religious pluralism to germinate in their thinking have passed beyond tolerance of other religions to a positive appreciation of the religious traditions they contain."[26] Many people seem to think that one must polarize at one end or the other in the universal/pluralist debate. We must move the issue of religious pluralism out of the realm of debate over whether one religion is better than another and into a more meaningful conversation about the very nature of religion itself. Only then can we develop a fresh understanding of the nature of Christian mission and its role in the globalized world.

The final category the article discusses is what it calls stretch. We might use the word *maturity*. Has God been trapped in a sort of prolonged pre-adolescence? Is the Creator now being challenged to finally grow up and face the world squarely? "God is frozen in time and place, serving only a limited number of people," the article declares. It also emphasizes that very few brands cross generational boundaries successfully—thus the struggle of the present incarnation of Christianity to appeal to vast segments of young people across the Western world. We live in an age in which generational theory has been developed into a fine art. Advertising aims specifically at the different demographics. How does Christianity cross cultural and social boundaries and appeal to young and old, rich and poor? We must diversify—offer different things to different people. We must uncover the particular needs of individuals and attempt to meet them rather than simply offer a broad, generic, sanitized version of the truth.

I realize I am speaking broadly and therefore am opening myself up to charges of ignoring the vibrancy of Christian faith where it is "working." But I am interested in where and why Christianity is *not* working in the West. Coca-Cola markets itself to a number of demographics and cultures. While it retains overall brand identity, it readily adopts new approaches and forms to appeal to new markets. Twenty-first-century Christianity should not look like the twentieth-century version.

The article ends with a question: "So tell us, is God driving an Oldsmobile with Firestone tires, or is God watching MTV while making transactions through Deutsche Bank on an IBM computer?" Some people love Oldsmobiles and associate with a small group of mutual Oldsmobile admirers. Others watch MTV and dream of the car of the future—then go out and build it. The debate is archived online. Advertising and theologizing carried out on the Internet. Who would have imagined such a thing?

The Saint of Celebrity

3

celebrities

Ancient and Future Saints

The entire American people seem to have gone goofola about celebrities.

Steve Allen[1]

Circus freaks, celebrities, it's all the same thing.

Roseanne[2]

Whenever friends come to visit me in Southern California, I (Craig) ask what they want to see. Answers range from Disneyland to the Hollywood sign. We also usually visit Sunset Boulevard, Venice Beach, and the Santa Monica Pier. And no tour would feel complete without a stroll down Hollywood Boulevard's Walk of Fame. I love the strange juxtaposition of current "megastars" beside "wanna bes" and "never really weres." Most people don't realize that the stars on Hollywood Boulevard are for sale (not that *anyone* can buy a star). Celebrities who want to be walked on must cover the basic expenses for the construction, installation, and ceremony. The celebrity hand- and footprints outside the Chinese Theater always offer a kitschy charm. Tourists love "sizing up" the stars, noting Judy Garland's petite feet or how easy it is to fill Sylvester Stallone's shoes.

If stepping in Frank Sinatra's shoes fails to suffice, roadside vendors offer "Star Maps."[3] Tourists can drive through Beverly Hills and Bel Air on a self-guided search for homes of the rich and famous. Roxbury Drive provides the highest star to mailbox ratio. The former homes of Jack Benny, Lucille Ball, and Jimmy Stewart rest ungated and unguarded for all to photograph. The

Osbournes live nearby, joyously launching profane tirades and refrigerated hams for MTV's cameras. But be careful—after their meteoric rise to fame they installed water jets to blast the overly curious.

If visiting friends want a close encounter with a live celebrity, I take them shopping along Melrose Avenue. I took two tourists from North Carolina down the street with eyes open and cameras ready. Within minutes, Jerry Seinfeld strolled toward us in his standard uniform—jeans, button-down shirt, white sneakers. Casually, under my breath, I murmured to my friends, "There's Seinfeld." They said, "What?" Jerry got closer. I whispered, "Seinfeld." My friends asked, "Who?" As Jerry passed us I blurted out, "Seinfeld!" Like many tourists, they failed to recognize a real live celebrity when they saw one. They ran down the street to recapture the moment. But their close encounter had passed. A photo of the back of Jerry Seinfeld's head is the only physical evidence of their treasured superstar sighting. How could they have missed him? Did they expect to see stagelights following him down the sidewalk? Where was his entourage, his bodyguard, his legion of fans? Jerry seemed so plain, so ordinary, so normal.

Living in Los Angeles and working in the entertainment industry provide me with almost everyday access to celebrities.[4] I've strolled down red carpets past a phalanx of photographers. I've been inside the velvet rope. I've experienced backstage passes, VIP seats, and private after-parties. I'm familiar with the aura of celebrity and the machinery that creates it. I can join film critic Richard Corliss in calling celebrity "possibly *the* most vital shaping (that is to say, distorting) force in our society."[5] But I want to dig deeper, to figure out what stars reveal about our culture, our values, and our God.

Idols have been created and destroyed for centuries. Are they helpful role models, embodying our highest aspirations? Or do they compete with God, turning our attention from the Creator to the creation? Should we join a long line of iconoclasts in smashing such false gods? I choose to resist the temptation to dismiss celebrities as idols. Celebrities perform a valuable social and theological function. Celebrities sharpen our ideals, bear our disappointments, and promote our hopes of immortality. The problem does not reside in celebrity itself but in the shifting sands of our criteria for fame. Rather than labeling stars as idols to be resisted, I consider some stars secular saints that deserve to be celebrated, maybe even venerated.

This chapter traces the ancient roots of today's stars, identifies the competing biblical takes on fame and idols, and points out how American democracy provided the crucible for the invention of celebrities. What aspects of twentieth-century America allowed for the explosion of star-making machinery? What spiritual needs fueled the rise of publicists, the creation of *People* magazine, the birth of *Entertainment Tonight*? Has a Protestant church intent on idol smashing actually encouraged the proliferation of even more celebrity obsessions? What's the proper function of celebrities in our everyday lives? Cultural historian Neal Gabler outlines our confusion:

> The spirituality, the alternative reality, the easy transcendence, the celebrity homilies, the gospels inspired by celebrities' deaths, the icons on their way to apotheosis—all these edged entertainment, as incarnated by celebrities, ever closer to theology, in a way, turning the tables. If religion had become entertainment, entertainment was now becoming a religion.[6]

How should we respond to this seemingly irreconcilable paradox?

The Original Stars

> Man is the measure of all things.
>
> Greek philosopher Protagoras, fifth century B.C.

> Those of us who are fans, we use these celebrity lives in ways that transform our own. I sometimes think that these are our gods and goddesses, these are our icons, and their stories become kind of parables for how to lead our lives.
>
> Amanda Parsons[7]

What can ancient mythology tell us about our current obsession with celebrity? What was the original purpose of astrology, mythology, and storytelling? Was it to humanize the gods? Or deify humans? When the gods exhibit human behavior, is that an attack on the divine or a complement to the Creator? Do we have a built-in need for heroes and role models that celebrities satisfy? If we were created to worship something, who or what deserves our adulation?

In ancient B.T. (before television), people still tuned in to nightly shows. They simply looked up. The constellations told a different story every evening. The cast and shows changed with the seasons. Imagine the joy a shifting of the sky would provoke. New stars meant new characters, new conflicts, new stories. Life's most troubling questions found expression on the biggest canvas. The first "stars" included Taurus the Bull, Cassiopeia, and Orion. They acted out tales of dysfunctional families, fatal attractions, and calculated revenge. Audiences worried about the insignificance of their "little lives" looked up to eternal role models. Yet the stars also demonstrated lamentable behavior that made the viewers' follies comforting and familiar. From the beginning, the stars offered role models to follow and mistakes to avoid.

Most early art and writing had a sacred purpose. Egyptian temples, columns, and stone carvings commemorate Egyptian "celebrities." Yet their rigid deities (usually pictured standing, sitting, or lying down) rarely took an exclusively human form. Divine kings (called Pharaohs in the Bible) were often flanked by a cow goddess or the hawk god. King Chephren's head was saddled to a feline body to form the Great Sphinx. Ancient Mesopotamians crafted bas-relief sculptures of winged men with bird's heads or winged lions with bull's heads.[8] The first gods, crafted in Egyptian and Mesopotamian culture, were fanciful, unnatural hybrids that looked nothing like us.

Greek mythology shifted the focus from how different gods are to how human divinity can be. Homer's *Iliad* endures as the first written product of Greek pop culture. In her definitive study of mythology, Edith Hamilton declares, "The Greeks made gods in their own image."[9] That may serve as a definition of idolatry or as a desperate, creative hunger for the divine. The Greeks were preoccupied with the visible, with the world around them. Their art celebrated the beauty of human beings, with statues that looked like us. Greek gods such as Hercules didn't descend from the stars; they could be traced to actual cities such as Thebes and Corinth. Real-life peaks such as Mount Olympus served as home to legendary gods such as Zeus, Apollo, and Aphrodite. Like most mythologies, the Greek version tackled questions such as how the world came into being and what caused thunder and lightning.

But the Greeks also introduced a unique element to mythology: entertainment. The quest for the golden fleece was a great yarn, Orpheus and Eurydice a tragic character study. Art historian Frederick Hartt concludes, "The Greeks peopled their world with gods who, like themselves, lived in a state of constant rivalry and even conflict, often possessed ungovernable appetites on a glorified human scale, took sides in human wars, and even coupled with human beings to produce a race of demigods known as heroes."[10]

The Romans fused Greek mythology with their own gods, so Zeus became Jupiter, Ares turned to Mars, Aphrodite was renamed Venus. As a practical, conquering people, the Romans had little use for storytelling. Their gods were useful, connected to "the simple acts of everyday life."[11] Household gods Lars and Penates were connected to ancestors, expected to guard hearth and home. The Romans reserved their public acts of adoration for their emperors. Roman rulers were immortalized in marble statues, often rendered as just heads or busts. For the Greeks, such separation of the head from the body seemed unnatural. Romans interested in preserving and worshiping their ancestors made the scale of their statues "convenient." Greek mythology may be read as a sincere effort to reach God. Roman mythology looks more like a calculated effort to deify humans.

Famed folklorist Joseph Campbell compared the mythologies of ancient civilizations to develop his concept of the mono-myth. Heroes "venture forth from the world of common day into a region of supernatural wonder: fabulous forces are there encountered and a decisive victory is won: the hero comes back from this mysterious adventure with the power to bestow boons on his fellow man."[12] Heroes serve as go-betweens, mediators between humans and the divine. George Lucas built on Campbell's ideas to form the basis of *Star Wars,* Obi Wan Kenobi, and the force. Jedi knights must learn to tap into a supernatural power, the force. But they must also be careful not to co-opt that power for their own purposes.

Campbell affirmed the power of myths during an era in which they were dismissed as faded lies. He longed for a return to an era in which meaning was found in shared stories. Campbell found the modern emphasis on the individual distressing, the source of our fractured human psyche.[13] Yet the recent success of big screen mythologies such as *The Lord of the Rings, The Matrix,* and *Harry Potter* suggests that we have entered a postmodern world desperate for stories of heroic virtue. The moral clarity of these epic stories offers comfort in a time of fewer absolutes.[14] Heroism arises from resisting temptation, renouncing power, choosing goodness. Those who make the right and wrong choices may find their actions etched in eternal stories, written in the stars (or in the movies).

Questioning the King

> Those who make them will be like them, and so will all who trust in them.
>
> Psalm 115:8

> The idol is the measure of the worshipper.
>
> James Russell Lowell, quoted in *The Image*

The history of art can also be seen as the history of royalty. Court painters and court biographers were paid to record the accomplishments of god-like emperors. Coronations, war victories, and family portraits tell us all the rulers wanted us to know. Literature fills in the details of battles, from tribal clashes to family feuds. Royalty's special status found reinforcement in those written and painted histories.

Divine emperors were born to rule, backed by impeccable bloodlines. Japanese emperors preserved their enlightened status by outlawing critical biographers (and allowing emperor worship to continue in Japan until World War II). Yet current British tabloids such as *Hello* and *OK!* celebrate and debunk the royals at the same time. The first celebrities were born famous, blessed at birth. So what took the luster off royal crowns? It wasn't only an insatiable desire for behind-the-scenes dirt.

Thousands of years ago, Yahweh, the God of the Old Testament, challenged emperor worship. Commandments handed down to Moses on Mount Sinai sounded simple and direct: "Thou shalt have no other gods before me." Who deserved the Hebrews' loyalty and devotion? Not rulers like Pharaoh or idols like Baal, but the true deliverer, the one behind and before the exodus out of Egypt, Yahweh. The Bible undercut the Egyptian monarchy with a theocracy, one nation under God. Yahweh steered Moses and his people toward the Promised Land. After plenty of bloody battles, Joshua ushered them into a land flowing with milk and honey. The Lord continued to fight for Israel, calling them to monotheism and delivering them from enemies such as the Philistines. But the Israelites eventually tired of the arrangement, becoming eager to emulate their neighbors' form of government, monarchies.

The Bible offers competing views on what kingship meant for Israel (and how God's people should respond to outside cultural influences). In 1 Samuel 8, the elders of Israel demand a king, a visible symbol to follow, "such as all the other nations have" (v. 5). Yahweh gives Samuel a long list of reasons why they will regret having a king, from military service to exorbitant taxes (vv. 11–18). But the people insist. We want "a king to lead us and to go out before us and fight our battles" (v. 20). God eventually capitulates, giving the people what they want in Saul (even if he's not what they truly *need*). Old Testament scholar Walter Brueggemann notes, "There is for Yahweh, as for Samuel, a wistfulness and deep sadness. Something precious is being forfeited in Israel, and Israel seems not even to notice."[15] The old purity has been lost, a sacred tradition compromised.

Some biblical scholars see 1 Samuel 9–10:16 as an abrupt shift to a positive, alternative view of kingship.[16] Saul is singled out for anointing. He is a highly respected leader, chosen by God to deliver his people from the Philistines. God speaks to Israel through the example of other nations (and a king!). How surprising to see the emperor-worshiping culture around God's people affirmed, teaching Israel how to be a better nation. The wisdom of Saul's kingship is demonstrated in his first royal action, a decisive military victory (1 Samuel 11).

Yet before Samuel retires, he reminds Israel of God's action in the exodus and the continuing need for Israel's monotheism (1 Samuel 12). He lays out the requirements: "If both you and the king who reigns over you follow the LORD your God—good!" (v. 14). But he closes with a warning not to follow idols. "They can do you no good, nor can they rescue you, because they are useless" (v. 21).

Israel's conflicted feelings expressed in 1 Samuel—"Give us a king!" "Why do we have a king?"—surface in competing notions of celebrities, saints, and idols. Sometimes we worship our kings; sometimes we knock them off their thrones. We look to our leaders as role models of civic virtue. Yet when they stumble, we're reminded how human they (and we) are. We know celebrities do not deserve to be worshiped. We recognize that talent and blessings, such as Michael Jordan's jumping ability, can come only from God. Yet we desperately want to "be like Mike," to bask in his legendary greatness.

The same tension can be found in Catholic and Protestant theology. Catholics look to saints as a blessing, a God-given intermediary pointing to the divine. Protestants adopted Samuel's approach, smashing idols, taking down images, challenging people to return to pure, unadulterated monotheism. Both schools can trace the roots of their beliefs to 1 Samuel 8–12. Kings (and popes) can be God's plan or an occasion for idolatry and injustice.

By Samuel 13, with Saul's kingship already undermined, the Lord seeks a replacement, "a man after his own heart." Samuel's warnings about kings seem to come tragically true. Yet the celebrated reign of King David suggests that kingship was a great thing for Israel, a blessing from God that ushered in a golden era. Those who considered the monarchy an assault on Yahweh's primacy were proven wrong. Monarchy is not evil in and of itself. What matters are the choices made by people in power.

While Israel's experimental theocracy eventually capitulated to monarchy, the Greeks created their own experiment with individual choice—democracy. The Greek city-states governed themselves via representatives in Athens. While the playing field was hardly leveled (not a lot of women served in those early Senates), the Greek notion was revolutionary. All men were created equal, with no one accorded special status. Representatives were elected by the people based on their deeds, not their birthright. Sure, the election could become a popularity contest, but government starting from the bottom up seemed preferable to the traditional top down monarchies. When America's founding fathers adopted the Greek ideal, they inadvertently paved the way for a merit-based system, for the will of the masses. They also paved the way for our current obsession with (and need for) celebrity.

Earning It

> Shakespeare divided great men into three classes: those born great, those who achieved greatness, those who had greatness thrust upon them. It never occurred to him to mention those who hired public relations experts and press secretaries to make themselves look great.
>
> Daniel Boorstin, *The Image*

In Steven Spielberg's harrowing World War II drama *Saving Private Ryan,* a dying soldier utters a simple phrase: "Earn it." What is "it," and why does it need to be earned? Words such as *fame* and *famous* come from *fama,* the Latin root roughly translated as "manifest deeds."[17] In ancient Greco-Roman culture, fame was reserved for only a few celebrated conquerors, and it was based on deeds, actions, accomplishments. Fame eventually became linked to military might and was spread through myths and stories, which Herodotus drew on to write the first official history. Subsequent historians, biographers, and hagiographers earned warriors such as Hannibal and Alexander the Great a permanent place in the military hall of fame. Alexander used Callisthenes as a spin doctor to link his deeds to the gods of Homeric origins. Julius Caesar and Marc Antony found fame via their noble actions, ensuring their divinity by connecting themselves to gods such as Apollo, Neptune, and Mars. When the Roman Senate gave Octavian the title Augustus, it meant much more than army commander. Emperors were often deified after death, worshiped because they had "earned it."

Augustus's abusive successors demanded allegiance, obedience, and worship irrespective of their behavior. Nero led the shift from "worship me because I was a great king" to "worship me because I am king." Caligula and Domitian carved out a notorious place in history via incompetence, indifference, and particularly heinous crimes. By trying to elevate themselves above ancient Rome, Caligula and Nero earned eternal revulsion.[18] "Good emperors" Trajan and Hadrian restored Roman glory, solidifying the empire through brilliant maneuvers and sound fiscal policies.

The Bible records a similar pattern, alternately praising or denigrating Israel's various kings. Foolish rulers Rehoboam and Jeroboam split the kingdom solidified by their much wiser father, Solomon. Rather than being judged solely by their conquests or military prowess, Israel's kings were evaluated according to their sense of justice and righteousness. Josiah got high marks for upholding the law, while Manasseh earned condemnation for his association with idolatry and corruption.

The biblical account of conflicted King David provides a fascinating case study. His athletic and military exploits started early, with his unexpected upset of Goliath. David also demonstrated considerable talent as a prolific singer-songwriter. The Psalms endure as a collection of his greatest hits. The Bible also records a legendary celebration at which David the dancer got a little too naked for some people's tastes. And shockingly, the writers of Scripture side with David, not his critics. But Scripture is also critical of David, especially when in his lust for Bathsheba he used his position to send her husband, Uriah, to certain death. As far back as the Bible, we find sullied heroes, role models who disappoint, saints who act like sinners. Yet despite his public scandals, David is still credited with having a "heart for God." Bible heroes may exhibit lapses in judgment, but in the divine economy, their good deeds can still outweigh their questionable activities. In fact, their failings often make them even more lovable and approachable. Perhaps the flawed celebrities who dominate our headlines can still serve as important role models, especially in their fallenness.

Almost every culture has had good rulers and bad rulers, those who reflected the divine and those who considered themselves divine. From Charlemagne to Henry VIII, the legends of European kings rose and fell and were rooted in their performance. Asian rulers' reputations varied, from Kubla Khan to Genghis Khan. A vigorous oral tradition assigned African rulers to halls of fame or shame. When democracy reemerged with the French Revolution, royalty's fame (and wealth) took a big hit. Commoners brought down the old gods. A famous painting shows Napoleon crowning himself, while church officials stand idly by, powerless. Napoleon understood where his true "competition" resided. He did everything but anoint himself a god.

Tired of the taxation of British King George III, American colonists fused the theocratic warnings of 1 Samuel with Greek democracy. The early American heroes were primarily warrior-politicians. Tales of cherry trees and crossing the Delaware secured George Washington's place as a founding father. War heroes often became instant celebrities whom voters found hard to resist. Andrew Jackson, Ulysses S. Grant, Theodore Roosevelt, and Dwight Eisenhower all started their presidencies in the battlefield. Even John F. Kennedy sailed to early fame via his PT 109 exploits.

The British royals held on, as figureheads—until Lady Diana Spencer joined the family. Diana became "the people's princess," set apart by her style, her deeds, her vulnerability. When her storybook marriage fell apart, Diana's legend only grew. She become more sympathetic, more common, more like one of us. *People* magazine returned to her story again and again, making Princess Di its most frequent cover girl. She combined the best of Shakespeare's categories. She was born a lady, married into royalty, was a devoted mother to William and Harry, was committed to good deeds, and suffered from our same problems of divorce, anorexia, and what to wear. She ushered in a new era in Britain's celebrity coverage as the endearing, flawed, "common" monarch. Her humanness undercut royal pretension. Consequently, Mark Frith, editor of the British tabloid *Heat,* states, "We don't cover royalty at all. You could argue that William and Harry are huge celebrities, but we've decided that the word celebrity doesn't include people with titles."[19] Although still dogged by an old-class system, Britain is slowly shifting from a monarchy to a meritocracy—a place where you earn what you get.

Our Star-Making System—Democracy

The United States began as an experiment, a place where individualism and achievement—"American exceptionalism"—could triumph. Anyone could become president. Anyone could make a million dollars. We exercised our right to vote in everything from presidential elections to the choosing of the next "American idol." We created our own royalty out of achievers based on the fundamental belief that talent and hard work are rewarded. But when we began to reward people for something less than talent and hard work, these ideals became endangered.

If America was originally a meritocracy, founded on the belief that the cream will rise to the top, why are we inundated by examples of people who are famous for being famous? The music video for Moby's song "We Are All Made of Stars" takes viewers on a glossy trip through Hollywood. Moby, dressed in an astronaut's space suit, encounters a passel of people famous for everything but talent. The caretaker of O. J. Simpson's house, Kato Kaelin, makes an appearance. Ron Jeremy, a former porn star whose hairy body earned him the nickname Hedgehog shows up. Washed-up child stars such as Todd Bridges, Gary Coleman, and Corey Feldman age anything but gracefully. Moby cruises the Sunset Strip with the ultimate self-promoter Angelyne. By surrounding himself with the most mundane "celebrities" possible, Moby drives home the theme "We are all made of stars." Is that a sign of progress or devolving standards? Zsa Zsa Gabor, Jenny McCarthy, and Fabio are celebrities who exhibit no apparent talent, occupying no defined role. Now, even malefactors such as Gary Condit, Heidi Fleiss, and Monica Lewinsky have ascended to celebrity status.[20] How did fame shift from role models who performed great deeds to celebrities who are known for their well-knownness?

Forty years ago, historian Daniel Boorstin described America's shift from a nation of "ideals" to "images." He explained, "An ideal has a claim on us. It does not serve us. We serve it. If we have trouble striving toward it, we assume the matter is with us, and not with the ideal. . . . An image is something we have a claim on. It must serve our purpose."[21] The shift from seeing images as pale imitations of our ideals to considering ideals unrealistic projections of images cannot be overestimated. Heroes who used to fill us with purpose have been replaced by celebrity "receptacles into which we pour our own purposelessness. They are nothing but ourselves seen in a magnifying mirror."[22] Boorstin found that "the hero was distinguished by his achievement; the celebrity by his image or trademark. The hero created himself; the celebrity is created by the media. The hero was a big man; the celebrity is a big name."[23] Use of the term *fame* peaked with the start of the 1900s. The word *celebrity* grew in the 1920s with the rise of talking pictures, dropped during the thirties and forties (perhaps because heroism seemed especially essential during World War II), grew in the sixties alongside the Beatles invasion, took off in the mid-seventies (alongside the birth of the blockbuster with *Jaws* and *Star Wars*), and exploded in the affluent eighties and nineties.[24] The decline of deeds and the rise of celebrity coincided with the rise of the means to promote fame for fame's sake—the mass media.

Our Celebrity Engine—The Mass Media

If newspapers are useful in overthrowing tyrants, it is only to establish a tyranny of their own.

James Fenimore Cooper

Two of the most important early inventions that created mass media were the photograph and the rotary printing press. In 1802, Madame Tussaud's famous French wax museum arrived in England. In the pre-photographic era, audiences flocked to her wax museum, a cheap, accessible way to see images of acclaimed leaders and infamous criminals.[25] A best-selling author such as Charles Dickens may have been widely read and celebrated, but he never would have been mobbed on London's streets. Not enough people would have recognized him. The rise of photos and newspapers coincided with the rise of "pre-celebrities." Newspaper reporter Mark Twain constructed an enduring persona out of a white suit, scruffy mustache, and bad attitude. Matthew Brady's photographs of Abraham Lincoln added to his legend. Photography and mass-produced handbills created outlaws in America's wild west. Widespread distribution of "wanted" posters secured a permanent place in western lore for Jesse James, Billy the Kid, and Buffalo Bill.

The rotary printing press allowed newspaper circulation to explode. In 1895, Joseph Pulitzer was selling five hundred thousand copies of the *New York World* every Sunday. William Randolph Hearst undermined Pulitzer's dominance by inventing rather than reporting the news. Critics could question Hearst's ethics, but none could argue with the rising circulation numbers of his *New York Journal.* Hearst understood that the public cared about issues and events only when the stories became "personal."[26] In other words, personalities, not positions, sold papers. If he had to manufacture or fictionalize a few heroes, so be it.

One of Hearst's most surprising and enduring stars remains beloved evangelist Billy Graham.[27] Graham's fame skyrocketed following his "Christ for

Greater Los Angeles" campaign in 1949. Hearst encouraged his papers to "puff Graham," and America soon had their most famous preacher. Subsequent, high-profile celebrity conversions heightened interest and sold even more papers. Undoubtedly, God gifted Graham to spread the gospel, but God also used Hearst's media empire to raise Billy's profile.

America's first "celebrities" also included star preachers such as Charles Finney, Henry Ward Beecher, Dwight L. Moody, and Billy Sunday.[28] They transfixed audiences with dramatic stories and theatrical timing. Traveling evangelists attracted huge crowds, taking their tours on the road and under a tent. They offered thrills and spills beyond any circus. The use of music, the dramatic pauses, the special seating for those particularly worried about their salvation created a uniquely American merging of entertainment and religion. Walt Whitman called revival meetings of the 1830s "our amusements." Frances Trollope commented that a "stranger from the continent of Europe would be inclined on first reconnoitering the city, to suppose that the places of worship were the theatres and cafes of the place."[29] Catholic priests such as Father Coughlin and Bishop Fulton Sheen pioneered radio and television broadcasting. Early televangelists Reverend Ike and Rex Humbard blazed trails for Jerry Falwell and Jimmy Swaggart. Sister Aimee Semple MacPherson staged her kidnapping in an effort to boost interest and attendance at her Angelus Temple, the mother church for the Four Square denomination. Marginalization by the broader culture has only increased the faithfuls' hunger for celebrities to call their own. When Bob Dylan, Gary Busey, Charlie Sheen, and Jane Fonda experienced some form of conversion, the news spread rapidly through the Christian grapevine.

Critics of our celebrity culture believe "that highly visible people [should] not receive disproportionate reward in relation to their real contributions, that society should nurture real talent, and that society's image-makers should restrain their distortions and manipulations of reality."[30] Yet how does such an important message get out? The most vocal critics of Hollywood resort to press conferences, P.R. events, and publicity stunts to raise money and generate coverage for their complaints. Christians use radio and TV to lambaste the slanted media then get upset when their public misstatements are used against them. Former baseball player Darryl Strawberry's drug problems could teach celebrity Christians that they can't afford to make mistakes in public. That's the price of their high-profile calling.

Artistic efforts to expose this confusing "reality" often get trapped in the same house of mirrors. Movies such as *The Truman Show, EdTV,* and *Showtime* wrestle with the invasion of cameras, the loss of privacy, the confusion created by an omnipresent media. Yet for all their earnestness, such efforts to critique the media by creating more media ultimately only reveal the enduring power (and limits) of the media. We can't complain about the air we breathe without inhaling. Instead of complaining about how the media manipulates us, we should address the enduring questions that emerge when we stare in the media mirror. What's real? Am I really alive? Or just caught in a matrix of illusions? The search for authenticity is on. Can people of conscience use the media without being consumed by its illusions?

It's almost impossible to use the media to comment on the media without becoming another cog in the same machine. Malcolm Muggeridge calls the Christian use of mass media "the fourth temptation." Would Jesus, tempted by Satan to expand his influence in the widest, fastest, most powerful way possible, have employed the mass media to spread his message? "How could he possibly refuse what would enable him to reach a huge public, right across the Roman Empire, instead of the rag, tag and bobtail lot following him around in Galilee?"[31] Having long ago embraced nearly any means necessary to spread the word, evangelical Christians found themselves too committed to celebrity to resist the third most powerful wave of mass media—the movies.

Our Greatest Invention—The Close-up

We've no control over our conception, only over our creation.

Tony Curtis

I pretended to be somebody I wanted to be until finally I became that person. Or he became me.

Cary Grant

Pulitzer and Hearst could not have predicted the personality-generating power of an 1895 invention: the close-up. Richard Corliss contends that celebrities are a twentieth-century phenomena, created by unexpected innovations in technology. The industrial era produced legendary rags to riches biographies of Andrew Carnegie, Henry Ford, and Thomas Edison. Americans respected their deeds, their ability to create or at least "perfect" processes. As scientific advances allowed astronomers to discover hidden galaxies and distant constellations, so advances in mass media allowed the discovery of even more barely flickering "stars."

The first movie stars didn't have names. They were known, for example, as "the Biograph Girl," a tribute to a studio rather than personal fame. The movie close-up changed all that. D. W. Griffith's cinematic innovation "had the effect of isolating the actor in the sequence, separating him or her from the rest of the ensemble for close individual scrutiny by the audience."[32] Close-ups directed attention away from the role being played, past the story, onto the individual playing the part. "Inevitably one begins to wonder about him or her, what he or she is really like off the screen."[33] The close-up allowed audiences to get closer to stars.

Audiences soon created the star system, demanding that their idols be named. The Biograph Girl, Florence Lawrence, became the first "named star" thanks to some strategic lying on the part of her new home, Imp Studios. Movie mogul Carl Laemmle planted a story in the St. Louis newspapers that the Biograph Girl had died in a streetcar accident. Laemmle then blamed Biograph for faking her death in an effort to cover up her transfer to his Imp Studios.[34] Laemmle found a brilliant way to generate free publicity, announcing that Florence Lawrence no longer worked for Biograph. He sent her to St. Louis accompanied by the costar of her first Imp film, King Baggott. Thanks to audience interest and Laemmle's understanding of the mass media, Florence Lawrence became a "name." Within a year, the movie-obsessed magazine *Photoplay* premiered. Stars' salaries rose from five dollars a week to twenty-five hundred dollars a week, just as the Biograph studio had feared.[35] Anonymity had been much cheaper, even for Laemmle.

Studios soon discovered that stars, not writers or directors or producers, sold movies. More fan magazines soon followed, loaded with images manufactured by studio publicity departments.

> What happened in this period is that the public ceased to insist that there be an obvious correlation between achievement and fame. . . . Beginning with the star system in Hollywood, it was possible to achieve "celebrity" through attainments in the realms of play—spectator sports, acting—and almost immediately thereafter it became possible to become a celebrity (a new coinage describing a new phenomenon) simply by becoming . . . a celebrity.[36]

When "America's sweetheart," Mary Pickford, signed a million-dollar contract with Adolph Zukor's Famous Players on June 24, 1916, a civilization founded on heroism and deeds came tumbling down. "Reward began to detach itself from effort and from intrinsic merit. . . . The old, reasonable correlation between what (and how) one did and what one received for doing it became tenuous (and in the upper reaches of show biz, invisible). . . . One of the bases for morality began to disappear."[37]

Actors became valuable commodities, hot properties. Movie moguls discovered, "A celebrity is a person whose name has attention-getting, interest-riveting, profit-generating value."[38] Studios taught potential stars how to walk, talk, and smile, turning Hollywood into a dream factory, a high-stakes finishing school. Teeth were fixed, breasts heightened, hair and eye color adjusted. Actors' names were changed from Bette Joan Perske to Lauren Bacall, Issur Demsky to Kirk Douglas, Norma Jean Baker to Marilyn Monroe.[39] Publicists, agents, marketing departments, cinematographers, and the Hollywood Press joined together to create the celebrity industry. To disguise the star-making machinery, Hollywood created the myth of "the natural." Stars were "discovered" at soda shops and street corners. They had "something special," a certain star quality that put them a cut above ordinary people. Looks and appearance became the new heroic standards. Stars weren't made—they were born.

Yet when stars veered from the image that the studios created, fans rejected the real persona. Comedian Fatty Arbuckle saw his career collapse in a series of trials surrounding the death of an actress in his San Francisco hotel room. Douglas Fairbanks, Mary Pickford, and Charlie Chaplin took their fame to the bank. Joining forces with director D. W. Griffith (the Spielberg of his era), they created their own studio, United Artists. Yet through artistic and commercial independence, these stars learned some hard lessons. Mary Pickford couldn't cut her curls. She continued to play innocent ingénues into her thirties. When Fairbanks and Pickford got divorced, America's sweethearts were dethroned. Private lives had to conform to the adoring public's expectations. Chaplin tried to shake his cute, heartwarming tramp. When his communist impulses surfaced, Chaplin discovered his fans' loyalty was quite limited. Even today, whenever Tom Cruise, Harrison Ford, or John Travolta step outside their standard, heroic characters, they risk audience rejection. Moviegoers love the swashbuckling Harrison Ford as Han Solo or Indiana Jones, but make him a serious, romantic lead in *Hanover Square*, *Regarding Henry*, or *Sabrina*, and audiences stay away—in droves. When Travolta let his faith in Scientology drive his decision to make *Battlefield Earth*, box office poison resulted.

So why did we invent the movie star? Peter Jennings, anchor of ABC's *World News Tonight* (and a native of Canada), observed, "No country in the world is so driven by personality, has such a hunger to identify with personalities, larger-than-life personalities especially . . . as this one."[40] Neal Gabler agrees: "No society has ever had as many celebrities as ours or has revered them as intensely."[41] The celebrity industry actually manufactures our primary culture-shaping export—movie stars.[42] Graydon Carter, editor of celebrity-friendly *Vanity Fair*, explains his dependence on stars for cover stories: "This magazine goes around the world. Movie stars have been a common currency around the world. Each country has its own television and music stars, but movie stars are global."[43] How interesting that America, the democratic ideal, would serve as the incubator of modern celebrity. With no king or queen to idolize, Americans manufactured their own royalty—homegrown Hollywood stars. A historic exaltation of the individual has resulted in a deification of "ordinary people." Celebrities are "just like us" but also possess a certain magic, an otherness that allegedly can't be manufactured or duplicated.

Was there only one Marilyn Monroe? Will there never be another James Dean? What is charisma, magic, star quality, presence? The authors of *High*

Visibility call these recurring concepts myths that are carefully designed to hide the celebrity industry. Legends of star presence tell us what we want to believe—that every person is unique, that artists are geniuses, that talent wins out.[44] All we need is one lucky break to become an overnight success. We don't think of stars as manufactured because they're people, not products, right? Aren't they born to act? Time serves as a leveler, a way to sort out talent from hype. Seen any good Tom Arnold films lately? Heard anything from *Vanity Fair* cover girl Gretchen Mol? "The passage of time, which creates and establishes the hero, destroys the celebrity. One is made, the other unmade by repetition."[45] Be encouraged that the celebrity industry doesn't always work. Posters and advertising featuring the next big star (Josh Hartnett? Jonathan Taylor Thomas? Ralph Macchio?) do not always guarantee box office success. Despite the celebrity industry's best efforts, sometimes the moviegoing public refuses what they've been force-fed. Even a high-profile fling with Tom Cruise failed to give Penelope Cruz superstar status. Stars may be made, but the public is not always sold.

Our Idol Makers—Publicists

> Though stardom in any form automatically confers celebrity, it is just as likely now to be granted to diet gurus, fashion designers, and their so-called supermodels, lawyers, political pundits, hairdressers, intellectuals, businessmen, journalists, criminals—anyone who happens to appear, however fleetingly, on the radar of the traditional media and is thus sprung from the anonymous mass. The only prerequisite is publicity.
>
> Neal Gabler, *Life the Movie*

At a dinner party a few years ago, I asked the ten people present, "If you could have dinner with any person, living or dead, who would you choose?" The first choices were Jesus Christ, Abraham Lincoln, Mohandas Gandhi, and Martin Luther King Jr. Imagine my surprise when one guest followed the lists of saints and statesmen with Julia Roberts. Why out of all the people in the history of the planet did she want to have dinner with Julia Roberts? "She seems like a neat person." This is what a steady diet of *People, InStyle,* and *Us* produces.

What makes Julia Roberts a celebrity? Her hair? Her smile? Her acting? What makes Julia Roberts seem so cool, so approachable, so neat? Like most celebrities, Julia Roberts has a passel of agents, managers, and public relations firms who make sure she's neat. They manage the timing of her cover stories, her interviews, the photo spreads of her home(s). They carefully avoid too much exposure but coordinate her media blitzes to coincide with film openings and pre-Oscar promotions.

Halle Berry and Will Smith (and their handlers) worked this to perfection in their race for 2002 Oscar nominations. Smith and Berry shared the cover of *Entertainment Weekly* during the anxious weeks when Academy voters held their ballots. They also happened to share the same publicist and talent agency.[46] When the magazine outlined the Academy's atrocious record in nominating actors of color, the intended effect was to shout, "Here's your chance." Smith got his nomination despite the box office disappointment of *Ali*. Berry's nomination came despite (or perhaps because of) her headline-grabbing nude scene with Billy Bob Thornton in *Monster's Ball*. Berry's unprecedented, overdue Oscar win came through a combination of performances—hers and her publicist's. Denzel Washington's concerted efforts not to campaign made his Academy Award for *Training Day* (2001) all the more remarkable—an Oscar earned rather than "managed."

My close encounter with hotel heiress Paris Hilton stands out as the best (worst) example of the power of P.R. I first encountered Paris and her younger sister at the 2000 Sundance Film Festival. At virtually every party I waited to enter, the Hiltons arrived with an entourage and immediately were whisked inside, past security, beyond the velvet rope. "Who are these girls? Why are they getting preferential treatment?" I found out when a photo of Paris, showing off her furry little halter top, popped up in *Entertainment Weekly's* coverage of Sundance. Was she an actress appearing in one of the films? A jury member handing out awards? No, just a hotel heiress with sufficient funds to retain an effective P.R. firm. The *Los Angeles Times* ran another picture of Paris on the occasion of her twenty-first birthday. The paper chronicled a month of party plans, beginning with a pre-birthday pajama party at the club Lotus in New York. She celebrated her actual birthday with dinner at Studio 54 in New York and a late-night bash at the club Light in Las Vegas's Bellagio Hotel. Two weeks later, Paris threw a party in L.A. at the GQ Lounge inside the Sunset Room.[47] How do I know this? The power of a publicist.

Larry Tye chronicles the birth of public relations in a biography of Edward Bernays entitled *The Father of Spin*. Back in the 1920s, the American Tobacco Company hired Bernays to promote Lucky Strike Cigarettes, especially among women. Bernays enlisted "experts" to suggest that "thin is in." Photographers and fashion editors were soon shooting "slender Parisian models in haute couture dresses." A British medical officer advised, "The correct way to finish a meal is with fruit, coffee, and a cigarette . . . to disinfect the mouth and soothe the nerves."[48] Arthur Murray signed a letter asserting, "Dancers today, when tempted to overindulge at the punch bowl or the buffet, reach for a cigarette instead."[49] The campaign worked, but American Tobacco asked Bernays, "How can we get women to smoke on the street?" To overcome a social stigma that only "loose" women smoke outside, Bernays enlisted the help of a psychoanalyst, a friend of his famous uncle, Dr. Sigmund Freud. Bernays was encouraged to link smoking to emancipation, to turn cigarettes into "torches of freedom." Bernays rallied New York debutantes, "in the interests of equality of the sexes," to light "another torch of freedom by smoking cigarettes while strolling on Fifth Avenue Easter Sunday." Churches along the parade route were invited to participate. On March 31, 1929, ten elegant ladies, "with floppy hats and fur trimmed coats," strolled down the avenue, cigarettes self-consciously by their sides.[50] It was front-page news, complete with photos, from Nebraska to Oregon. Mission accomplished through the creation of the first pseudo-event.

Historian Daniel Boorstin coined the term *pseudo-event* to describe the art of public relations. To get press coverage for their clients, publicists create movie premieres, award ceremonies, sponsored sporting events, demonstrations, even hunger strikes.[51] These "media handlers" create press kits, write speeches, plan tours, schedule interviews, broker cover stories, and coordinate marketing plans. Magazine editors allow publicists "to dictate when and where a story will run, which photographer and writer will be hired, which quotes from the star can be used, which of the star's friends can be interviewed, and which questions or subjects will not be allowed."[52] Also known as handholders, publicists accompany stars down the red carpets—offering assurance, boosting confidence, and steering them strategically through the voracious press.

Yet the best publicist is an invisible publicist, coordinating everything with a firm but imperceptible (to the public) grip. Pat Kingsley may be the most powerful woman in Hollywood, publicizing the most recognizable stars on the planet, such as Tom Cruise and Tom Hanks. Yet how many people (outside Hollywood) recognize Pat Kingsley?

Publicists are also paid to keep their clients out of the news. When a problem arises, such as Hugh Grant's arrest for soliciting prostitute Divine Brown on Sunset Boulevard or Eddie Murphy's arrest for picking up a cross-dressing prostitute on Santa Monica Boulevard, publicists quickly become spin doctors. Whether in promotion mode or damage control, publicists serve as a celebrity's voice, refining and redefining a star's relationship to his or her adoring public.

Neal Gabler suggests that pseudo-events have become so ubiquitous that we can no longer separate the pseudo from the authentic. The media no longer report what people do; they report what people do to get attention via the media. "As life was increasingly being lived for the media, so the media were increasingly covering themselves [the media] and their impact on life."[53] Public relations now provides more than 70 percent of all information that is published as "news."[54] Yesterday's blatant fanzine *Photoplay* became today's "respectable" *Premiere* magazine. The reputable Time/Life corporation introduced *People* magazine in 1975. Sony Studios made headlines by using fake critics to promote otherwise unexciting features. A studio head acknowledged, "I think of the Hollywood press as an extension of my marketing department, but because I don't actually pay them, I can't always tell them what to write."[55] The E! network began as an arm of the Fox marketing department, a well-oiled publicity machine. E! still amounts to a twenty-four-hour ad for the entertainment industry.

Yet efforts to illumine the massive game of favors, trades, and media manipulation fall on mostly deaf ears. In fact, shows about the star-making process have become an industry unto themselves. The behind-the-scenes creation of music acts such as the Backstreet Boys and *NSYNC went public in television programs such as *Pop Stars* and *Making the Band*. Top 40 hits from made-for-TV bands such as O-Town resulted. The British television program *Pop Idol* invited viewers into the process, allowing them to vote for the winner. More than ninety-one million people called in on the final night. Producer Nigel Lythgoe noted, "In the U.K., it became a moral obligation to vote."[56] *American Idol* spawned similar mania, turning Texas cocktail waitress Kelly Clarkson and the song "A Moment Like This" into top-of-the-chart sensations.[57] Such democratic programming illustrates the public's ongoing stake in the creation of stars and the futility of attacking the celebrity industry. Of course, Tom Cruise is promoting his new film. Of course, he'll make the rounds from *Oprah* to *Letterman* to *Leno*. As with advertising, most people know they're being manipulated but could care less. The not-so-disguised sales pitch is part of a much larger social contract. We want our brush with greatness, our taste of immortality. Skip the sermonizing—give me my celebrity fix!

So why do we insist on believing that stars have something special, something magical about them? Our ability to ignore the ethical implications of the star-making machinery could be evidence of massive self-interest. Christopher Lasch called us "the culture of narcissism."[58] But our endless fascination with celebrity could also demonstrate the depth of our spiritual hunger. We create celebrities in our image (like us but not us) as an ideal, an elusive bundle of heroism, beauty, humor, and perfection. In a nation in which anyone can become king or president, we need people to show us the way, to set our standards. Celebrities serve as our vicarious heroes, going before us on the ultimate journey we all desperately want to take. They give us a taste of immortality, a preview of eternity. Daniel Boorstin suggests, "Having made celebrities, we have a duty to worship them."[59] Our need for celebrities to be real and true yet wholly other is in direct proportion to the "transcendence gap" in our lives.

In a post-Christian culture, celebrities stand in as our high priests, our conduits to the divine. We want them to be perfect, to suggest what's possible, to offer an image of eternal beauty, the *imago Dei*. But what happens if they fail to live up to our lofty expectations? What if they turn out to be false gods, manufactured idols? We need someone to smash these graven images. We call in the tabloids.

Our Iconoclasts—The Tabloids

> The higher the I.Q. the greater the need for gossip.
>
> ad campaign for British tabloid *Heat*

> You have to remember, whenever there's a spotlight, there's always a cross hair built in, and notches in the barrel filed for luminaries.
>
> Ken Kesey

The first Hollywood publicists kept the stars' private lives under wraps. Joan Crawford's horrendous parenting, Rock Hudson's homosexuality, and Spencer Tracy's lifelong affair with Katharine Hepburn remained hidden until after they had died. Judy Garland's enduring battle with addiction slipped out, tainting earlier images of Dorothy following the yellow brick road to Oz. Gradually, the studios came to realize their stars' backstage traumas could generate even more fan interest. Elizabeth Taylor's multiple marriages and public divorces turned her offscreen life into an ongoing soap opera. Suddenly fans could follow their favorite stars' unfolding personal dramas. Their "real" ups and downs superseded their movie roles. Hollywood followed public sympathy in rewarding Elizabeth Taylor with an Oscar for *Butterfield 8* after a very public illness. Her life became an open book, full of twists, turns, and reversals, especially in her on-again/off-again relationship with Richard Burton. Their tempestuous offscreen romance generated more sparks (and interest) than their roles in *Cleopatra* or *The Taming of the Shrew*. Tom Cruise and Nicole Kidman submitted themselves to the same verisimilitude in Stanley Kubrick's final film, *Eyes Wide Shut*. Despite their repeated hunger for privacy, stars continue to reveal their secrets to Barbara Walters on national TV. Why do we care about stars' private lives?

Mark Frith, editor of *Heat* magazine, believes, "We all pretend we're not interested in gossip, but it comes down to how you do it. . . . We give it to people in a magazine that they're not ashamed to read."[60] London fashion designer Matthew Williamson admits, "I love it, but it's like candy—you need a fix."[61] Gossip fuels the celebrity machine. Only the biggest stars inspire public fascination with their private lives. While tabloid journalism has inspired lawsuits and damaged psyches, scandal sheets such as the *National Enquirer* have created a twisted but definite sense of community. They treat celebrities as our national (or international) cast of characters. Shoppers can follow the ongoing "real-life" sagas of Oprah's weight loss or Robert Downey Jr.'s drug addiction in the checkout lines at the grocery store. Their real stories are better than television, because the ending is always a cliff-hanger. "Will Liz find permanent happiness with some husband or other? Will X win his fight against booze? Will Y get off drugs for good?"[62] The biggest tabloid stars skip acting altogether. Their "storybook" lives provide sufficient and ongoing interest. Jacqueline Kennedy Onassis and Princess Diana simply played themselves. Their fairy-tale marriages and personal styles turned them into fashion icons. As their honeymoons ended, their lives became public dramas, Greek tragedies full of early wealth, idyllic children, disintegrating marriages, and tragic deaths. They served as our constellations, providing suspense as we wondered how their cliff-hanger stories would end.[63] Neal Gabler suggests, "Not only are celebrities the protagonists of our news, the subjects of our daily discourse and the repositories of our values, but they have also embedded themselves so deeply in our consciousness that many individuals profess feeling closer to, and more passionate about, them than about their own primary relationships."[64]

Tabloid journalism eventually gave rise to tabloid television, with the innocuous *Entertainment Tonight* inspiring the savage *Hard Copy.* Such programs appeal to our need for constant info and celebrity dirt. The latest gossip about Whitney Houston or Rob Lowe became the new news. While viewers knew what to expect on *Hard Copy,* "serious" reporters such as Barbara Walters went farther in legitimizing tabloid television.[65] Forced to compete with sitcoms and dramas, news magazines such as *20/20* replaced hard news with celebrity confessions. Competing for exclusive interviews with Michael Jackson or O. J. Simpson, news reporters agreed to keep the questions soft and the profile positive. The reporters became famous in the process, commanding celebrity salaries themselves. Their subjects asked for them by name. Would Barbara Walters, Connie Chung, or Katie Couric offer the best confessional, the easiest absolution? Talk show host Rosie O'Donnell entrusted her secret to Diane Sawyer, coming out as a lesbian eager to challenge adoption laws on ABC's *Primetime.* Art critic Robert Hughes lasted only a single broadcast at *20/20,* perhaps because he summarized news magazines so accurately:

> There was a voyeuristic interest in confession of sins. There was the fixation on celebrity. There was the almost total absence of any serious news. . . . There was the phony sentimentality, the mock humanism. Above all, there was the belief that reality must always take a back seat to entertainment, so that the audience must not be overtaxed, so that they will come back for more of the same twinkle.[66]

Yet to criticize television for being shallow and star driven seems utterly pointless. Daniel Boorstin anticipated our rising obsession with tattletale shows back in 1961. He understood how even the story behind the story created its own news. "Our efforts to get behind the scenes, to expose celebrities as fakes or phonies, end up self-defeating. It only heightens interest in the process. Raises another layer of news about the fabrication. Arouses curiosity about how the magic trick was performed."[67] Anne Heche began her relationship with Ellen DeGeneres as a rising young actress without a box office hit. Their offscreen romance turned Heche into the second most famous lesbian in America (just behind Ellen!). Exposing celebrity secrets only increases their fame.

Richard Corliss also considers criticism of tabloid journalism misguided. "One might argue that the tabloid is a truer portrait of life in our times than one finds in the *New York Times* or any other publication that attempts to impose order and meaning on the day's events. Maybe love nests and axe murderers are a truer projection of our times, our inner lives."[68] Celebrity mistakes offer an important reminder of our fallenness and fallibility. In fact, celebrities stand in our place, acting out and strapping on our cumulative, cultural sins.

Our Scapegoats—Fallen Stars

> If it gets to the point where you can't put a large-mouth bass on the cover of *Field and Stream* unless you've got Jenna Elfman holding that large-mouth bass, then you've gone too far.
>
> Joe Levy, senior editor at *Rolling Stone*[69]

> I don't care what is written about me so long as it isn't true.
>
> Katharine Hepburn

I saw Gary Coleman pumping gas. The diminutive star of the eighties sitcom *Different Strokes* now works as a security guard at my neighborhood mall. A woman shouted, "Hey, you're Gary Coleman!" He snapped back, "That's not my real name. That's not how I live." He opened the back door on his ragged Toyota and pulled a baseball cap over his head. The piles of money he earned as a child star are long gone. The only headlines he now makes involve lawsuits to reclaim his lost earnings and fights he breaks up at the mall. The public is finished with Gary Coleman even though he's still a young man with many potentially painful years ahead of him. What happens to former celebrities? Why do we enjoy knocking down the idols we once celebrated? Why are old sitcom stars sent into the wilderness, branded as washed up for life?

YOU THINK THERE'S ANY CHANCE OF R. KELLY AND MARTHA STEWART BEING CELL MATES?

IF THERE IS A GOD, I DON'T THINK HE'S GOT **THAT** GOOD OF A SENSE OF HUMOR.

The rise and fall of their careers follow an ancient pattern connected to religious rites. The creation, adulation, and destruction of human idols can be found as far back as the Aztecs. Writer Ron Austin found, "The Aztecs chose a young man on the basis of his personal beauty, and honored him for a season before ripping his heart from his body. The ancient Greeks picked a poor man or an ugly or deformed person to be wined and dined and then stoned to death. By the time of the medieval carnival days, the sacrifice of humans had evolved into the mock crowning of pretend 'kings.'"[70] Quasimodo performs this function in *The Hunchback of Notre Dame*. The last week in Jesus' life goes from the dizzying heights of a triumphant Palm Sunday to the mockery of a crown of thorns. The demand for a sacrifice, a cleansing substitute, can also be traced to the Old Testament.

Yom Kippur is the holiest day in the Jewish year. The annual Day of Atonement began in Leviticus 16, when God offered Moses specific instructions on how to make a sacrifice. Aaron, the high priest, served as an intermediary between the holy God and the sinful people. After making atonement for himself and his house (v. 6), Aaron was to slaughter a goat as a sin offering for the people (v. 15). He sprinkled the blood on the mercy seat in the Holy of Holies, purifying the temple. Then a second goat was brought forward. Aaron was to "lay both hands on the head of the live goat and confess over it all the wickedness and rebellion of the Israelites—all their sins—and put them on the goat's head. He shall send the goat away into the desert. . . . The goat will carry on itself all their sins to a solitary place" (vv. 21–22).

Like Old Testament scapegoats, celebrities bear the community's weaknesses. Having risen to great heights, they often end up cast out for our collective sins. They embody the tension outlined in 1 Samuel. As our "kings," they are held to higher standards. But the smallest mistake can also bring down the wrath of God or, even worse, the rejection of the public. Richard Corliss admits that the famous can get preferential treatment. "The new celebrities had . . . plugged into the most basic of American fantasies, the dream of reward without apparent effort, the dream of being uplifted overnight. No wonder there was a well of forgiveness, which over the years ahead would wash away many sins."[71] Yet celebrities also carry the burden of our shame. Over the course of their careers, they experience almost every sacrament, from the baptism of fame to enforced public confessions to the absolution of sins. Stars travel a well-paid road from idol to scapegoat.

Many end up in court, in jail, or in an early grave. Why do celebrities so often unravel? Many end up separated from themselves, unsure where their public persona ends and their private life begins. That dangerous personality gap can lead to addictions, arrests, and suicides. *Saturday Night Live* star Chris Farley overdosed trying to live up to John Belushi's legendary excesses. From Janis Joplin to Kurt Cobain, the litany of celebrity suicides grows annually. But the predictable pattern traced on every episode of VH1's *Behind the Music* cannot be blamed solely on the celebrities themselves.

In *The Frenzy of Renown,* Leo Braudy charts the way in which the media always destroys what it creates. The inevitable backlash comes with a painful second film or the follow-up to a platinum-selling compact disc. MTV's claymation *Celebrity Deathmatch* takes our scapegoating to a comedic extreme. Forced by the mass media to follow the minutia in Celine Dion's career (from her humble Canadian beginnings to her retirement to have a baby through her "triumphant" comeback as a one-hundred-million-dollar-a-year Vegas lounge singer), we naturally want to see her pummeled in a grudge match against *Titanic* star Leonardo DiCaprio. Who cares whether their "hearts will go on"? We created them; we can destroy them.

In a bizarre example of life imitating art, the Fox Network created *Celebrity Boxing.* Danny Bonaduce of *The Partridge Family* knocked out Barry Williams from *The Brady Bunch;* Todd Bridges from *Different Strokes* pummeled white rapper Vanilla Ice; and scandalous ice-skater Tonya Harding took out scandalous Clinton dater Paula Jones more effectively than she did Nancy Kerrigan. These pairings of celebrity has-beens brought the Fox Network their highest ratings in a year, topping CBS's *Survivor.*[72]

When genuine, washed-up stars boxed one another in a made-for-television event, some people concluded that celebrity culture couldn't sink any lower. Mitch Albom, author of the inspiring *Tuesdays with Morrie,* gave up: "I have written endlessly about our trash culture society, fiddling while the rest of the world burns. I have encouraged reading, listening to music, talking to family, exercising, even chanting at the edge of a riverbed—anything as an alternative to the E! Channel, 'Access Hollywood,' or the Psychic Friends Network. And what happens? Fox puts six has-beens in a ring and has a ratings smash."[73] Cultural commentator Robert Thompson considered the event a by-product of American journalism. "Fox simply exploited the monsters created by the news cycle. News managed to create equity in Tonya, Paula, Danny, and Todd, and Fox has managed to find a way to cash in on that celebrity now that the news cycle is finished with them."[74] Fox vice president Mike Darnell welcomes negative publicity, defending his program: "All we do is put together what we think has great entertainment value. I'm amazed at how many people look at what we do with a philosophical bent."[75]

Neal Gabler took *Celebrity Boxing* as a commentary on how we feel about celebrity: "People like low grade entertainment, and have for a long time, not because they are stupid, but because they realize this kind of behavior is transgressive. There is a real thrill to sticking it to the custodians of culture"[76] (and to celebrities!). Albom spells it out: "I'm thinking 'Gladiator' here. We grab all these desperately-clinging-to-the-last-rung-of-celebrity types and let them battle to the death. That way, when it's over, we only have one annoying, low-talent person on our hands. And we drop a safe on him."[77]

What fuels such hatred and contempt? Why do former stars no longer seem human? Constant overexposure has turned them into commodities, equally suitable for a makeover in *Seventeen* or a tumble on *Celebrity Deathmatch*. Artistic efforts to comment on the superficiality of celebrity and tabloid TV are self-defeating because they serve an important function. Celebrities not only bear our highest aspirations but also carry our greatest disappointments. They remind us how fleeting fame is, how foolish our efforts to generate immortality in and of ourselves can be. Former celebrities remind us how silly and toothless our idols actually are. Iconoclasts need washed-up stars to serve as human sacrifices, carrying our culture's many sins—especially our misplaced faith in celebrities.

Our Pantheon—Dead Celebrities

> Young is better than old. Pretty is better than ugly. Rich is better than poor. TV is better than music. Music is better than movies. Movies are better than sports. Anything is better than politics. And nothing is better than a celebrity who has just died.
>
> Richard Stolley, *People* magazine editor, quoted in *Life the Movie*

John Wayne and Humphrey Bogart sell beer. Fred Astaire dances with a vacuum cleaner. Frank Capra and Jim Henson encourage Apple Computer buyers to "think different." Digital technology turned dead celebrities into big business. Control of the Three Stooges has landed in court. Martin Luther King Jr.'s children expect to be paid whenever excerpts from "I Have a Dream" are played. Guerrilla artist Shepard Fairey slapped "Andre the Giant Has a Posse—Obey" on posters and decals as a joke.[78] He never expected to inspire lawsuits from the WWF.

The dead celebrity business thrives along Hollywood Boulevard. Graveline Tours piles visitors into the back of a hearse for a journey past celebrity death sites. From the site of John Belushi's overdose in a cabana behind the Chateau Marmont to the spot where River Phoenix had a seizure on the sidewalk outside the Viper Room, Graveline hits all the lowlights along the Sunset Strip. The legend of James Dean lives in a statue outside Griffith Observatory. "Forever Hollywood" cemetery charges a premium to be buried near such luminaries as Tyrone Power, Cecil B. DeMille, Douglas Fairbanks, and Rudolph Valentino. Yet dead celebrities transcend the borders of Hollywood. Jim Morrison's Parisian resting place attracts perpetual pilgrims. Highgate Cemetery in London charges admission to view the graves of George Eliot and Karl Marx.[79] When Elvis fans make pilgrimages to Graceland, do they come to remember a singer or to claim a touch of his immortality?

The international outpouring of grief following Diana's death in a Paris tunnel on August 31, 1997, caught many commentators by surprise. Why did Diana's shocking accident cause the famous stiff upper lip of Britons to quiver so uncontrollably? The spontaneous shrines that arose in the streets (even outside the British embassy in west Los Angeles) suggest an air of pilgrimage. Flowers bombarded Diana's casket, signs of a desperate longing to connect with the people's princess. Many blamed the media for her death, especially when a trail of paparazzi led to the crash sight. Elton John's poignant musical tribute "Candle in the Wind" suggested that Princess Di, like Marilyn Monroe, was a victim of a voracious press—"even when you died, the press still hounded you." We both created and destroyed Diana, serving her up as a sacrifice to our insatiable desire for news, for gossip, for role models, for fame, for immortality. Her death seemed a far too fitting end, the fifth act in a Shakespearean tragedy. Diana was sacrificed for our sins, taking on all the vicarious suffering and glorification we long to experience (from afar).

The concurrent death of Mother Teresa added an interesting complement and counterpoint to Di's demise. Mother Teresa's actions on behalf of Calcutta's poorest citizens demonstrated clear, biblical virtues. Her Missionaries of Charity hospitals nurse, clothe, feed, and comfort societal outcasts. A case could be made that Diana practiced the same virtues. She lobbied for the poor, bringing publicity to the victims of AIDS, land mines, and civil war. Elton John sang, "You were the grace that placed itself where lives were torn apart," while wondering, "who'll miss the wings of your compassion?" While Mother Teresa went farther in selling all she had, Diana still offered her gowns and star power to charity auctions. Her life serves as a study in Proverbs, an illustration of the fleeting nature of riches and the enduring power of benevolence. Do they represent different expressions of the same core values? Is Diana a secular saint?

British theologian John Drane pushed the possibilities even farther, finding surprising parallels between Diana and Christ.[80] Both came from obscure origins, operating as outsiders in a rarefied world. Both demonstrated compassion toward the oppressed with a special softness for children. In his eulogy, Diana's brother, the Earl of Spencer, called her "a symbol of selfless humanity . . . standard bearer for the rights of the truly downtrodden." He celebrated "her innermost feelings of suffering that made it possible for her to connect with her constituency of the rejected." Jesus and Diana were opposed by particular power brokers, hunted down by agents of authority. Her brother noted that her "genuinely good intentions [were] sneered at by the media," and he called Diana "the most hunted person of the modern age." Both died a very public, very cruel, lingering death that left their beauty disfigured and their bodies broken. Both were laid to rest in a brand-new grave. The only thing missing from Diana's "Christlike" life—a resurrection. Yet her memory definitely lives on at Althorp Estate, where visitors pass through a neoclassical lakeside temple. Etched beside a portrait of the princess is a phrase taken from one of her speeches: "Whenever you are in need, call for me, and I will answer." Her sainthood seems assured, with or without the church's blessing.

Our Canonizer—St. Andy Warhol

A career is born in public—talent in privacy.

Marilyn Monroe

Painter Andy Warhol, a lifelong Catholic, "canonized" celebrities such as Elvis Presley, Marilyn Monroe, and Jacqueline Kennedy. His huge, silk-screened portraits of stars raised them to the level of icon. Borrowing from Byzantine art, Warhol presented his subjects in a straightforward manner, looking outward at viewers, inviting them to commune with the subjects' "eternal" fame. In Pittsburgh's Andy Warhol Museum, these totemic paintings from the sixties dominate an entire room.[81] Liz Taylor occupies a wall beside a silk-screened photo of Marlon Brando from *The Wild One*. Portraits of Jackie Kennedy in joy and in mourning add a poignant note of regret. Marilyn Monroe is rendered three times. The same image of a young Elvis Presley confronts viewers eleven times. The repetition of Warhol's images confirms what the celebrity industry suggested. The human product, "celebrity," can be manufactured, sampled, reproduced hundreds of times, burned into our collective memory through constant repetition and vigorous (self-) promotion.[82]

But Warhol created much more than pop art. His taste and persona captured a culture zeitgeist, the celebrity industry in all its absurd glory. Once stars became "common," the need for even grander stars, gradations within the pantheon, became necessary. Warhol coined the term *superstar*.[83] In his 1966 film *The Chelsea Girls,* Warhol renamed actress Ingrid Von Scheven, Ingrid Superstar. Warhol compressed the name change–makeover process into a single event by naming Ingrid a superstar. Warhol also legitimized celebrity by founding *Interview* magazine in 1969, well before *People* hit newsstands in 1975. *Interview* was originally a film journal, rooted in the fan magazines of Andy's Pittsburgh youth. *Interview*'s groundbreaking but simple format was contained in the title. Warhol anticipated our era, when celebrities would generate news whenever they spoke. No editorial changes or spin needed. Just turn on the tape recorder and let celebrities pass on their wisdom.

Ultimately, Warhol's most surprising work of art may have been his own persona. A poor, immigrant kid from Pittsburgh proved that America is the land of opportunity, a place where people like Andrew Warhola can change their names and repeatedly reinvent themselves. He said, "I'd prefer to remain a mystery. I never like to give my background and, anyway, I make it all up different every time I'm asked."[84] An associate called him "a promoter who creates—and his greatest creation is himself."[85] Warhol turned his life into an art form, demonstrating that artists can become celebrities. His "disciples," who learned the art of self-promotion, include Keith Haring, Jean-Michel Basquiat, Julian Schnabel, Kenny Scharf, and Jeff Koons. Haring said that Warhol "reinvented the idea of the life of the artist being Art itself. . . . He blurred the boundaries between art and life so much that they were practically indistinguishable."[86] Warhol himself suggested, "If you want to know all about Andy Warhol, just look at the surface of my paintings and films and me, and there I am. There's nothing behind it."[87] He became the ultimate void, a blank canvas on which we could paint any wishes, dreams, or hopes. In 1987, Warhol ascended through death to the celebrity pantheon, assured immortal, iconic status between Marilyn and Elvis.

At a memorial mass at St. Patrick's Cathedral on April Fools' Day, John Richardson revealed Warhol's greatest secret, his spiritual side. In his eulogy, Richardson suggested, "The knowledge of [his] secret piety inevitably changes our perception of an artist who fooled the world into believing that his only obsessions were money, fame, glamour."[88] Did Andy hide his faith amid celebrity portraits and Studio 54? Or did Warhol express what we now understand—that celebrities are our new icons, shallow substitutes in an era of endless commodification? Art historian Jane Daggett Dillenberger traces the repetition in Warhol's work to the iconostasis screen of Andy's Byzantine Orthodox Church roots. "From the time that he would have been carried there in the arms of [his faithful mother] Julia as a baby, he was exposed to long hours of sitting in front of the iconostasis screen with that flickering candle light and that repetition of images, as well as the repetition that occurs in liturgy."[89] A closer look at Warhol's repetitive images of Elvis and Marilyn suggests that he was trying to create a holy space, to carve out a transcendent moment for jaded museum-goers. Warhol reproduced images from the halcyon days of Elvis and Marilyn, our secular saints. These images served as the cornerstones for a 1994–95 touring exhibition entitled "Elvis + Marilyn: 2 X Immortal." Warhol ensured that a single name (and image!) identifies them—now and forever. They are fixed in time as eternally youthful icons.

Who stands between us and God throughout church history? Saints and martyrs serve as mediaries, examples, virtuous role models. Perhaps they started as a concession, an acknowledgment rooted in 1 Samuel that although worship of God alone is preferable, a fallen flesh-and-blood role model often helps us understand what we should be doing. Some Protestants question Catholics' veneration of saints as a form of idolatry, yet evangelical saints have ranged from C. S. Lewis to Amy Grant. In fact, Protestant skepticism regarding "religious saints" may have encouraged the rampant canonization of secular saints instead. Which is preferable? An array of time-tested saints connected to particular questions and needs or a constellation of freshly minted stars popping up on sitcoms, advertisements, and talk shows?

The Catholic Church still follows a strict canonization process, initiated only *after* someone dies, involving petitions, dossiers, and an investigation conducted by a devil's advocate. The passage of time tests both celebrities and saints. Who will be forgotten? Whose legend will grow? The underappreciated 1999 film *The Third Miracle* highlights the canonization process in humane, uplifting ways. Ed Harris plays a doubt-ridden priest investigating an unlikely potential saint. (For a more postmodern take on sainthood, check out Lars von Trier's poignant film *Breaking the Waves,* discussed in the movie chapter.) Poet Phyllis McGinley calls sainthood "haloes for heroic virtue." She points out that "in times of crisis we need saints. They appeared by the hundreds in the first centuries of Christianity when Europe was struggling out of nearly universal darkness into what then passed for the light of civilization. . . . Whenever and wherever an evil has existed, from slave-trading to the miseries of famine and war, saints have sprung up to mitigate those evils."[90]

Saints take the Gospels seriously. Despite the fashion, the trends, or the economics, they dare to nurse the sick, clothe the naked, feed the hungry, comfort the afflicted. They don't consider "Sell all you have and give to the poor" a pie-in-the-sky ideal. In the face of war or aggression, they turn the other cheek, returning good for evil. Pope John Paul II has initiated a canonization boom, approving more people for beatification and sainthood than all the other twentieth-century popes combined.[91] His canonization of 276 saints and beautification of 768 people demonstrate our hunger for goodness in an era of evil. His actions stand as a brilliant, subversive, and enduring response to celebrity culture. We must recognize the value of role models, of mere humans who dare to live Christlike lives.[92] If not, what values will be provided by our secular saints?

Our Highest Virtue—Cool

> Celebrities have become, in recent decades, the chief agents of moral change in the United States.
>
> Richard Corliss, *Intimate Strangers*

By now, Andy Warhol's oft-repeated dictum "In the future, everybody will be world famous for fifteen minutes" has become passé. We can look back and laugh, because the actual time frame is more like fifteen seconds. The explosion of media outlets guarantees that almost everyone in the Western world gets a moment in some spotlight. TV cameras scan sports stadiums in search of scantily clad babes or beer-bellied brutes showing skin in subzero temperatures. Tourists gather outside NBC's *Today Show,* flashing signs for loved ones back home. MTV's *Total Request Live* updates a formula established by Dick Clark on 1950s *American Bandstand,* making teen audiences "the star." Adolescent fans surround host Carson Daly, hoping to introduce the next song or have their dedication aired. Outside the studio, teens jam Times Square, mugging for the cameras. Neal Gabler has come closest to describing this "Hi, Mom, I'm on TV" phenomenon.

> It's one thing to say that life is *like* a movie. . . . I'm saying that we've crossed a threshold—that life *is* a movie and we're all to a greater or lesser extent performance artists in and an audience for this ongoing show.[93]

According to Gabler, from the clothes we wear to the cars we drive, our entire lives have become a movie (or rather a "lifie"), staged for the approval of others. Celebrities set the standards we try desperately to fulfill, whether as CEOs or seventh graders.

PBS attempted to address this vicious circle in a *Frontline* report called *The Merchants of Cool.* Reporters interviewed executives from advertising firms and MTV to uncover the marketing machinery behind youth culture. Covering a talent scouting competition, *Frontline* trained their cameras on the aspiring teens while they were dancing. Soon, the teenagers ramped up the sexuality of their dancing, performing for the cameras. Why did the teens turn to sexual moves, bumping and grinding? Because they had seen it on TV. Host Douglas Rushkoff concluded that the teens were doing what they thought was expected of them based on what they had seen of teenagers on TV. Real teens were acting like TV teens in a show about the marketing of what it means to be a teenager. Of course, adolescents come away with an identity crisis, trying to figure out who they are.

What are dancing teens desperately trying to achieve? The clothes, the poses, the ironic detachment that has practically defined teenagers stem from the desperate pursuit of the highest virtue in celebrity culture—cool. Jazz trumpeter Miles Davis played it. James Dean embodied it. Michael Jackson had it and lost it. In their brilliant book *Cool Rules: Anatomy of an Attitude,* Dick Pountain and David Robins dare to define the ever allusive, ever attractive notion of cool. They see cool as "a permanent state of private rebellion . . . concealing its rebellion behind a mask of ironic impassivity."[94] They trace the roots of cool back to Africa, to Yoruba civilizations that valued composure or cool as a spiritual virtue. They suggest that Africans, forced into slavery on American shores, preserved cool in an effort to retain their spiritual integrity. "All that white owners were allowed to see were caricatures of subservience, heavy with irony, behind a Cool mask that concealed the contempt and rage that the slaves felt."[95] The concept of cool crossed over to white audiences via jazz and blues musicians. While white audiences embraced rebels such as Little Richard and Chuck Berry, it took Elvis Presley to confirm the new "cool rules." Today's coolest rappers, from Jay-Z to Snoop Dogg, continue the Yoruba tradition of understated rebellion, while Eminem is the more popular lightning rod for protestors. Eminem embodies "an oppositional attitude adopted by individuals or small groups to express defiance to authority—whether that of the parent, the teacher, the boss, or the prison warden."[96] Pountain and Robins explain why the church often perceives pop culture as the enemy:

> It is no coincidence that we have described Cool as almost the antithesis of the Christian virtues of faith, hope, and charity. Nor does Cool have much in common with the more specifically Protestant virtues of hard work, thrift, and self-discipline. . . . Cool is a new mode of individualism, flexible enough to cope with the pace of transformation of work in the deregulated global economy. . . . Cool enables people to live with uncertainty and lowered expectations by concentrating on present pleasures. In short, when the going gets tough, the Cool go shopping.[97]

To the degree that the church has aligned itself with the powers-that-be, it has adopted a state of permanent uncoolness. Youth ministers spend hours trying to cook up creative stunts to make Jesus cool. Kevin Smith satirized Roman Catholic efforts to dress up Jesus in his 1999 film *Dogma*. Audiences laugh at the unveiling of "the Buddy Christ." Jesus Christ, defender of dogma, property of a fallen institution, will likely be viewed as permanently uncool, because cool is a permanent state of private rebellion. Yet Jesus was always antiauthoritarian, defying the religious authorities, redefining who's in and who's out in God's kingdom. We must recover this Jesus who challenged the status quo, defied social conventions, and overturned tables.

Jesus of Nazareth, table turner, joke teller, and rebel leader, is cooler than ever. He shows up on the coolest clothes and the coolest shows. One of the hottest designer labels in L.A. is the Imitation of Christ. T-shirts that announce, "Jesus Hates Your S.U.V." and "Jesus Hates Your Marketing Scam" celebrate Christ's edginess. Jesus boxes and sings on Comedy Central's *South Park,* a perfect complement to the show's satirical bite. The seemingly faithless Marilyn Manson gave the rebel Jesus serious props in connection with his *Holywood* album. The shock-rocker thinks Jesus is the first celebrity. Manson explained:

> I can relate to Christ—he was someone who had ideas that scared people; he eventually became a piece of merchandise to hang on the wall, wear as a necklace, have as a black velvet painting, and ultimately sacrificed himself. He was someone I saw as a revolutionary.[98]

People of faith must follow these cultural leads. We must rediscover that Jesus' parables are "stories that will get you killed."[99] For teens who feel shunned by the system, persecuted for saying something different, the rebel Jesus may be the ultimate inspiration. His suffering and crucifixion only confirm his outlaw status and permanent cool.

Our Purposes—Divine

It's better to be known by six people for something you're proud of than by sixty million for something you're not.

Albert Brooks

At the various award ceremonies, so many celebrities thank God that you realize God is the Ultimate Celebrity. And a forgiving deity at that.

Paul Krassner[100]

Is reading *People* a form of idolatry? Is working in the celebrity industry wrong? Fame offers heady temptations to exploit your position, to believe your own hype, to become the idol the celebrity industry fashioned. When Bob Dylan sang, "You gotta serve somebody," he raised tough questions that the famous must answer. What will I do with my privileged position, my elevated status? Celebrities are not inherently good or evil. They are people faced with high-stakes choices every day—just like us.

The responses to fame have been varied, even positive. Paul Newman sends the profits from his "own" spaghetti sauce and salad dressing to a foundation. Jerry Lewis channeled his celebrity status into a thirty-year crusade to cure muscular dystrophy. Sally Struthers loans her face and name to the Christian Children's Fund. In 1984, Bob Geldof rallied the world's biggest rock stars for a Band Aid single and a Live Aid concert on behalf of Ethiopia. Michael Jackson and Lionel Richie responded by writing "We Are the World." Willie Nelson and

John Cougar Mellencamp started Farm Aid on behalf of struggling farmers. Jay Leno's wife, Mavis, raised awareness about the plight of Afghani women under the Taliban several years before September 11, 2001. Celebrity can be a fabulous platform, the ultimate pulpit. But audiences can also become quite cynical when rich celebrities talk about the plight of the poor. How can stars promote important causes without turning the event into a public relations coup and a valuable photo op?

Vanity Fair declared, "Oprah Winfrey arguably has more influence on the culture than any university president, politician or religious leader, except perhaps the Pope."[101] Oprah's media empire begins with a talk show seen in 112 countries and extends to the Oxygen cable channel, O: The Oprah Magazine, and her Angel Network benevolence fund. In a cover story entitled "The Church of O," Christianity Today noted, "To her audience of more than 22 million mostly female viewers, she has become a post-modern priestess—an icon of church-free spirituality."[102] Oprah acknowledges her strong Christian roots, recalling that at age four, "I knew I was going to help people, that I had a higher calling, so to speak."[103] In 1994, Oprah consciously distanced herself from other "tabloid" or "trashy" talk shows, deciding to clean up her act. Since 1998, Oprah has promoted lofty "change your life TV," complete with practical applications under the lofty rubric "remembering your spirit." The first title proposed for her eponymous magazine? Oprah's Spirit. Anticipating self-important overkill, Oprah shortened the title to O—creating the most successful magazine start-up in history.[104]

What has she done with her wealth and power? Fortune magazine reported that Oprah has donated, mostly anonymously, at least 10 percent of her annual income to charity. Viewers donated $3.5 million to her Angel Network in its first year, funding scholarships and Habitat for Humanity homes. Oprah also sponsors Use Your Life Awards, giving $100,000 to twenty-two individuals whose organizations are engaged in social change. Author Phyllis Tickle concludes, "Anybody who can better the living experience of thousands of people has to be respected. She may not be ordained but she sure is pastoral, and pastoral at a level that has a vast impact."[105]

Bono turned his position as spokesman for U2 into a campaign highlighting third world debt relief. Like many celebrities, Bono rose from humble roots, turning poor Irishman Paul Hewson into Bono Vox, God's second most visible spokesman (hot on the heels of the pope). His appearances at Harvard's 2001 graduation, the World Economic Forum, and the Vatican have raised the biblical notion of jubilee to unparalleled public awareness. He has met with politicians as diverse as Vladimir Putin, Bill Clinton, Jesse Helms, and Kofi Annan. A Time magazine cover story acknowledged the incongruity of this celebrity-lobbyist, asking with utter seriousness, "Can Bono Save the World?" He admits, "I know how absurd it is to have a rock star talk about the World Health Organization or debt relief or HIV/AIDS in Africa."[106] Yet Bono's consistent efforts on behalf of the poor and marginalized make him "the most secular of saints . . . a worldwide symbol of rock 'n' roll activism."[107]

Yet on *The Charlie Rose Show,* Bono shunned the label "role model," believing that his indulgences in alcohol, cigarettes, and profanity disqualify him. But like King David, Bono's failings are central to his music and his mission. Whether discussing his doubts ("I Still Haven't Found What I'm Looking For"), shaking a fist at God ("Wake Up Dead Man"), or taking on the self-important trappings of celebrity ("God Part 2"), Bono's imperfections make him much more lovable and human. He has wrestled with the temptations of fame and power. In *Achtung Baby* and *Pop,* he tackled the irony, the surface, the myth of "the rock star as god."[108] After playing the devil as McPhisto on their Zoo TV tour, Bono entered the Pop Mart concerts in a giant lemon, wearing a superhero T-shirt and singing under a golden arch. He tried everything irony offered, pushing commodification to its absurd and unsatisfying extreme. With *All That You Can't Leave Behind* and their Elevation tour, U2 went back to basics. Bono and the band offered a valentine to fans, couched in (relative) simplicity. Bono knows celebrity can be scary, intoxicating, and absurdly enriching. During an era in which everyone wants to be famous, he's proven that hard work, generosity, faith, and sincerity can still be celebrated, even amid doubt.

The tragic events of 9/11 gave our celebrity culture an unexpected gift. The actions of New York City police and firefighters reminded us what heroism used to look like. Common people, working in mundane jobs, responded with grace under pressure. Hollywood stars pulled together to create *America: A Tribute to Heroes.* On a bare stage, highlighted only by candles, movie and TV stars recounted the stories of firemen, priests, and officers who demonstrated virtues worth celebrating. Writing in *re:generation quarterly,* Andy Crouch welcomed this refreshing alternative to celebrity chic. He challenged people of faith to stop imitating the culture, trying to make Jesus "relevant." For at least a few days, America stopped caring "how hip you are." Heroic criteria shifted to a matter of direction—"which way you were going on the stairs."[109]

After an era of hyper-individualism in which "everyone is a rebel now, no-one is ordinary, no-one wants to be a face in the crowd, everyone wants intense experiences,"[110] we may have turned the corner toward community. The new cool may not be narcissistic, hedonistic, and ironic. At the 2002 Africare dinner, Bono suggested that

history is still making old ideas ridiculous in front of us. Take the idea that the lucky few of us can live in some kind of glass separated from the sufferings of the many. If that idea wasn't demolished already, it shattered on September 11th, 2001.

So what's God working on this year? Two and a half million Africans are going to die of AIDS. I meet the people who tell me it's going to take an act of God to stop this plague. Well, I don't believe that. I think God is waiting for us to act. In fact, I think that God is on His knees to us, to the Church. God is on His knees to us, waiting for us to turn around this supertanker of indifference, our own indifference a lot of the time.

That God Almighty is on His knees to us—I don't know what that means. We should remind ourselves that "love thy neighbor" is not advice. It is a command.[111]

May our lasting tribute to heroes involve a reclamation of celebrity's important theological purpose. We need heroes, we need role models, foretastes of glory divine. May we recover fame—rooted in deeds, tested over time—and imagine a future in which everyone is famous for all the right reasons. Care to join that celebration?

music

4

Al Green Makes Us Cry

The man that hath no music in himself, nor is not moved with the concord of sweet sounds, is fit for treasons, stratagems, and spoils, the motions of his spirit are dull as night and his affections dark as Erebus. Let no such man be trusted. Mark the music.

William Shakespeare, *The Merchant of Venice*

Music helps us to be free; it moves the soul; it may also be the only art that is capable of clearly expressing what we feel about God. . . . Music is an absolute reflection of the world we live in.

Madonna[1]

I (Barry) was having lunch with Al Green. Well, in truth, I was having lunch with about three hundred people at the weekly Gospel Brunch offered at the House of Blues, a theme restaurant and club situated in the heart of Los Angeles's Sunset Strip. A friend told me that legendary soul-singer-turned-preacher Al Green was making an impromptu appearance to sing a couple of songs. Sure enough, halfway through the brunch (which features an "authentic" gospel music presentation, for people who like gospel music without the accompanying church experience), as the singers were encouraging audience participation, out walked Al Green. After huge applause, he launched into song. "I'm so tired of being alone . . ." The opening line from one of his most popular songs rang out over the crowd. I stood there, relishing the moment, and before I knew it tears were rolling down my face. Al Green makes me cry; his music always has, and I don't know why. Perhaps it is the quality of his voice or maybe

125

the signature sound of the Memphis horns. Whatever it is, virtually every time I hear an Al Green song, tears roll—and I am not usually a weepy person!

What is it about music that moves us to tears and laughter and shouts of triumph? Why do fans get obsessed? What makes music lovers create their own personal Top 10 lists, as in Nick Hornby's novel (and subsequent film) *High Fidelity*? Almost all scholarly research or analysis of pop music begins and ends with personal experience. Music invokes specific feelings about where we were when we first heard a song, about a particular tune that defined a summer or a relationship. "People write about rock for love not degrees," wrote Simon Frith in the bibliography of *Sound Effects,* the first book-length academic analysis of pop music.[2] That is not to say that the study of popular music is devoid of critical academic and methodological research. But it's hard to divorce the personal from music analysis. Despite our best efforts to resist music's emotional impact, Al Green still makes us cry.

The relationship between pop music and religion has not been pretty. A 1958 Catholic youth center newsletter urged kids to "smash the records you possess which present a pagan culture and a pagan way of life."[3] Christians have burned records labeled demonic and picketed concerts deemed satanic. While much of this extremism has dissipated, tensions continue. In the world of contemporary Christian music, some people rail against worldliness while others talk about cultural relevance. Pop culture remains a contested arena full of conflicting ideas and concerns.

The approach taken in this chapter moves beyond these exhausting arguments and acknowledges pop music's church roots. The ecstatic songs of rock 'n' roll pioneers such as Jerry Lee Lewis, Little Richard, and Elvis Presley sprang from Pentecostal worship. Resembling an enmeshed family, rock 'n' roll and the American church have battled like kissing cousins. Yet the Reverend Al Green proves that the sacred/secular, gospel/rock split can be healed in a joyous, tear-inducing refrain.

Aural Wallpaper

> I always had my own connection with God, and I prayed every night as long as I can remember. I still do to this day. . . . It is kind of my own personal thing, but it has always been the foundation of my music, too.
>
> Michael Franti, quoted in *Inside the Music*

Pop music is everywhere. When I was young, one had to seek it out in specific places. Now, we live in a world immersed in music. Music surrounds us every time we walk into a store. Banana Republic, Pottery Barn, and Starbucks sell

CDs designed as background music for summer barbecues and beach parties. A genre was even developed for a single form of transport: elevator music.

Identity often starts with music categories: punk, techno, hip-hop, goth, and headbanger. Music, clothes, and attitude are joined together to create personas. English rock star Morrissey remembers listening to a Top 30 show as a six-year-old. After every Tuesday's show, he would run to the typewriter to compile "my own personal Top 30, which totally conflicted with how the world really was."[4] Morrissey joined millions of others who follow the musical charts to work out life.

We approach pop music as fans. We've turned to the radio for comfort, solace, and meaning since early adolescence. We spent hours in local record stores listening to albums and building record collections. Craig bought *Elton John's Greatest Hits* as a ten-year-old. I worked a paper route to earn the money necessary to buy music. Our love of music continues today. We anticipate releases from artists we admire and still delight in searching for new songs, new sounds, new experiences. We go to concerts, play and write pop music, and find that music has deepened our lives in profound ways.

We also approach pop music as followers of Jesus. We want to understand the sociocultural significance of popular music and respond to it in a missional way. What makes pop music so compelling to so many? What are the theological implications of such a phenomenon? This chapter follows two distinct directions. First, it examines the business and ethics of music. What is it selling? Second, it explores the theology of pop music. What is it saying about our world and our God?

For Love or Money?

> There are no bands anymore. . . . There are projects.
>
> Michael Whitaker, director of marketing, A&M Records, quoted in *Global Pop*

In 1941, Theodor Adorno, a member of the Frankfurt School, an institution dedicated to the study of culture, published an influential essay called "On Popular Music."[5] He made three important claims about popular music that may help us grasp the initial concerns about popular music that are still voiced today. They form a challenge for anyone attempting to attach a shred of value to popular music, for while millions around the globe experience music as a pleasure, it also fuels a multibillion-dollar industry. Adorno addressed the ramifications of this strange marriage, this thing called show "business," when pop music was in its gestation period.

Adorno found that popular music is standardized.[6] Once a particular pattern has proven successful, it is exploited to the utmost. For anyone bemoaning pop music's interchangeable boy bands and teenage girl singers, this point rings true. Does it make any difference who sings the songs we hear on the radio today? It could be anyone—the beats are the same, the songs eerily familiar, the names and personalities of the groups redundant. Singers seem to serve merely as the means by which record companies generate income and sell product. Adorno said that to cover up this standardization, the industry engages in pseudo-individualization.[7] In other words, record companies create the illusion of individuality by making minor adjustments to the song structures and sounds, but basically the songs are the same.

Part of this standardization involves the practice of doing the listeners' listening for them, or in modern terminology, "giving them what they want, even if they don't know they want it." Adorno viewed the relationship between commerce and culture as a means by which listeners are subordinated to the capitalist imperative. He saw this as a political way to keep people in line.[8]

The uneasy link between cultural and economic activity under capitalism has always been rampant in pop music, with much discussion about the way in which making music and making money mix. The commercialization of popular culture has been raised time and time again. A long line of critical thought, beginning with Adorno and his peers, presents popular music as irredeemably commercial and subject to the capitalist economic imperatives.

Second, Adorno stated that popular music promotes passive listening. From his Marxist perspective, he viewed life under capitalism as soul-destroying, marked by boredom. This in turn creates a search for escape, for larger meaning, but this halfhearted search is easily met by pop music offerings. Echoing the familiar strains of the high culture-low culture debate, Adorno posited that *serious* music (anything other than pop) plays to the imagination—offering an engagement with the world as it could be. Pop, on the other hand, is passive and repetitive, confirming the world as it is. Pop music can be labeled little more than a pick-me-up, a stimulant. Boredom soon follows, forming a circle that makes escape impossible. The impossibility of escape causes widespread inattention toward popular music. The moment of recognition is that of effortless sensation. The sudden attention attached to this moment burns itself out instantly and relegates the listener to a realm of inattention and distraction.[9] Pop music is a vicious circle, producing distraction and inattention for the distracted and inattentive.

Third, Adorno suggested that pop music acts as a social cement. It helps people make *psychical* adjustments to the mechanisms of everyday life.[10] According to Adorno, although different people respond in different ways to popular music, they fall into two main categories of mass behavior, the rhythmically obedient type and the emotional type. The first type gets distracted from his or her real-life situation by the rhythm. The second type finds emotional release in pop music while remaining unaware of the real state of affairs.

Adorno and those who have come after him have made much of the supposed powerlessness of the consumer—we just blithely consume whatever we are fed by the music industry. This false assumption arises from a rather one-dimensional approach to the subject. Many cultural analysts approach the subject from a Marxist or a neo-Marxist perspective, which automatically necessitates a rather low view of capitalism. This leads to a politicized take on pop culture in general. While the role of economics and the politics of capitalism in popular culture cannot be underestimated, they cannot be considered the whole picture. Too many thinkers in this field miss music's symbolic dimensions. After all, we call musical leaders pop stars, according them mythic status, equating them with heavenly bodies. The symbolism of "guitar gods" should lead our discussion beyond the economic implications of the industry. The powerlessness of the consumer is challenged by a public who bestows divinity on its idols.

The public also removes crowns. Take, for instance, Michael Jackson, the self-proclaimed "King of Pop." Perhaps he had every right to lay claim to that title after the record-shattering success of his genre-defying music in the 1980s. But since then, despite the best efforts of his record company, his press agents, the media, and the theatrics of the man himself, he has been unable to reclaim the public's eye. All the hype and publicity in the world cannot make audiences buy a product if they cannot connect with it. A product does not dictate to a passive market in any realm of popular culture. If it did, there would be far more successful films and CDs. The streets of pop culture are littered with failed attempts to make stars and sell products. For every *Spider-Man* there is a *Battlefield Earth*. Simon Frith notes that only 10 percent of all records released make money.[11]

Today, new ideas and stars emerge from the grass roots. When we speak about pop music, we are talking about a key instrument in the development and identity of people in Western culture today. We locate ourselves in the world through the ideas and values expressed in popular music. Stuart Hall and Paddy Whannel point out that young people identify with these collective musical representations and use them as guiding fictions. Such symbolic fictions are the folklore by means of which a teenager, in part, shapes and composes his or her mental picture of the world.[12] Young people get their ideas from what is in front of them, from their music, their movies, the streets where they live. Jesus practiced his faith and forged his theology in the streets. In the busyness of his ministry, he always managed to stop, to observe, to listen to the children singing in the marketplace (Luke 7:31–32).

The Spiritualization of Pop

> Music, especially sacred music, has a powerful efficacy to soften the heart into tenderness, to harmonize the affections, and to give the mind a relish for objects of a spiritual character.
>
> Jonathan Edwards

If we understand pop music as a key component in the development of identity, a fertile ground for the matrix of meanings that characterize postmodern life, we should not be surprised that pop music has much to say about the shaping of contemporary notions of God and religion. In *Virtual Faith,* Tom Beaudoin argues that pop music has become the amniotic fluid of contemporary society. It is the place where we work out our spirituality.[13] Music embodies society's spiritual ethos. What do we hear? Songs are joyous, sexy, greedy, irreverent, suspicious of institutions, riddled with ambiguity, and bathed in pain.

Conflicted song lyrics mirror the competing beliefs within musicians. Britney Spears espoused a commitment to virginity[14] while at the same time dressing seductively, dancing sensually, and moving in with her boyfriend Justin Timberlake. Beastie Boy Adam Yauch organized the Tibetan Freedom Concerts to raise support for and awareness of the plight of Tibetan Buddhists living under Chinese rule. As a practicing Buddhist, Yauch manages to slip dharmic slogans such as "every thought in the mind is a planted seed" into postadolescent songs about parties, rebellion, and not growing up. Personal tension serves as a great starting point for spiritual journeys.

There are a multitude of spiritual expressions in pop music. Many artists who inhabit the black music genres grew up singing in gospel choirs. While their church attendance may no longer be as steady, their spiritual roots go deep. The influence of the black church on African-American culture continues to spill over into music. But the leaking of spirituality into artists such as the Beastie Boys and Madonna is surprising. Madonna's music has taken a huge turn since motherhood, yoga, and a blend of kabbalah and Hindu mysticism have impacted her life.

The previous decade saw a virtual tidal wave of religious imagery and thought enter the pop music landscape. In the late sixties, Eastern spirituality and mysticism influenced pop culture through bands such as the Mahavishnu Orchestra and the Beatles. George Harrison's forays into the Hare Krishna sect of Hinduism produced "My Sweet Lord." Songs such as "Jesus Is Just Alright" and "Spirit in the Sky" connected with the hippie Jesus People. Today, Fatboy Slim creates the danceable "Praise You," while Moby mixes techno beats and old Negro spirituals. What should we make of it all? Is it trendy, or is it genuine? The answer is both.

Yet many key players in popular music espouse Christian faith without a relationship with organized religion. These players include U2, Moby, Creed, P.O.D., Lifehouse, Lauryn Hill, and Nick Cave. They inhabit various positions in terms of popularity and influence, but each expresses belief in God from a distinctly Christian perspective. Consider the Florida-based rock band Creed. All members of the group come from Christian backgrounds. Their songs and videos draw from their faith tradition. In interviews, lead singer Scott Stapp insists that they do not play "Christian rock." Yet the closing line of their hit song "What's This Life For" proclaims that "we all live under the reign of one king." Lifehouse began as a Friday night youth group band for the Malibu Vineyard Church. They now actively dismiss this connection. They speak of their belief in Jesus but not the organizations that surround him. This pro-Jesus/anti-church phenomenon goes way beyond a fear of rejection by the pop music audience because of an affiliation with the Christian faith, which has largely been consigned to the "uncool" section of culture. It underscores the need for a rethinking of theology and ecclesiology in the postmodern world.

Ireland's U2 remains one of the world's most popular rock bands. Three of the band's four members came to faith together in a nontraditional Pentecostal Christian community in Dublin. They eventually left because of conflict over their involvement in pop music in general and rock music in particular. And yet their music, filled with biblical texts and driven by a commitment to Christ's mission, has found a huge global audience. Lead singer Bono asks, "Can you imagine how it feels to believe in Christ and be so uncomfortable with Christianity? The church is an empty, hollow building. The established church is the edifice of Christianity. It's as if when the Spirit of God leaves a place, the only things that are left are the pillars of rules and regulations to keep its roof on. And we are more and more claustrophobic around organized religion."[15] How sad that he feels that "the new fundamentalists are very, very dangerous. To quote a preacher, I had a sneak look at the back of the book, so I know that the good guys will win in the end. In the meantime, the bad guys are in control and religion has become an industry—something that has more in common with McDonald's than it does with me."[16] Followers of Jesus must deal with the cultural perception that the institutionalized church has reduced religion to hamburgers.

Lauryn Hill, formerly of the New York rap group the Fugees, released an album of "hip-hop-meets-the-Bible," closing with a virtual word-for-word reworking of the famous treatise on love written by Paul to the church at Corinth. Of her own music she says, "People think gospel music is a big choir and people clapping and singing loud. But gospel music is music inspired by the Gospels. In a huge respect, a lot of this music turned out to be like that. During this album, I turned to the Bible and wrote songs that I drew comfort from, because I lost my grandmother, a cousin, a seven-year-old friend—a lot of people close to me."[17]

A cultural dose of "millennium tension" may have allowed for more acceptance of spiritual beliefs. Yet spirituality has inspired artists throughout pop music's brief history. Music always reflects society's search for meaning and transcendence. From the simple folk music of *O Brother, Where Art Thou?* to the gospel hip-hop of Kirk Franklin, God has communicated love, joy, peace, and passion. Theology must learn to listen to artists who sing outside the walls of formal faith. Jesus' followers must tune their ears to desperate wails driven by the Holy Spirit.

Mother Superior

> I took the name Veronica because she wiped the face of Jesus. You weren't supposed to help Jesus Christ while he was on his way to the crucifixion. She was not afraid to step out and wipe the sweat off him and help him. So I liked her for doing that and took her name.
>
> Madonna, on why she added Veronica to her birth name, quoted in *Madonna: An Intimate Biography*

Madonna embodies the tension between espoused spirituality and a lived life. From her debut as the icon of sexualized womanhood to her recent excursions into motherhood and mysticism, Madonna captures a generation (or two) wrestling with the sacred and the profane. Madonna always managed to shock. In her first live appearance on MTV, she dressed as a combination of bride and hooker and writhed her way through "Like a Virgin." In her controversial *Sex* book, she celebrated her commitment to sexual adventure as a fully liberated woman. Madonna demonstrated no respect for authority, no need for convention, and little evidence of any interest in anything remotely spiritual.

Imagine the shock to even her most ardent fans when she suddenly embraced kabbalah and yoga, emerging as a kinder, gentler earth mother. Her 1998 record, *Ray of Light,* touched on the fleeting nature of fame, motherhood, and her newfound spirituality. Prior to this album, Madonna's public relationship with faith involved subversion rather than appreciation. In her video for "Like a Prayer" (it is interesting how Madonna often uses the word *like*—like a virgin but obviously not a virgin, like a prayer but not a prayer), Madonna dances provocatively in a silk night dress before burning crosses. She kisses a wooden saint and brings him to life with her sensuality. Yet she finishes the video by emulating the ecstasies of love and freedom backed by a gospel choir. Hints of things to come?

Madonna's most spiritual album, *Ray of Light,* also became her most successful. Perhaps she simply read the pop cultural zeitgeist and adjusted her music accordingly. But perhaps motherhood tempered her narcissism. The demands of child-raising may have exposed her own need for roots as well as wings. Maybe advancing age brought her face-to-face with a sense of her own mortality. But perhaps even more importantly, maybe she confronted the downside of a life lived in excess and discovered the vital need for a spiritual anchor. Her latest album, *American Life,* is a testament to her newfound spirituality and a critique of both her own and society's obsession with celebrity, fame, and materialism.

Madonna's spiritual practices mirror the burgeoning relationship between non-Western spiritual traditions and a society raised on a steady diet of individuality. Ancient traditions such as yoga and kabbalah have been reconfigured in the hands of new practitioners while still retaining the core of their teachings. This brings to mind the challenge that the Antiochan, non-Jewish converts to Christianity presented to the Jerusalem church. They forced a debate about what was really necessary for their faith to be orthodox. Did they need circumcision? What about food? Or ritual practices? The short reply sent to them by the apostles in Acts 15 highlights an approach similar to the one we might consider taking: "It is my judgment, therefore, that we should not make it difficult for the Gentiles who are turning to God. Instead we should write to them, telling them to abstain from food polluted by idols, from sexual immorality, from the meat of strangled animals and from blood" (vv. 19–20). The gospel has always been a fluid, living entity, and the tensions of that reality have been a challenge from the start.

The Antioch situation is just one example drawn from many in the New Testament in which a faith rooted and nurtured in Judaism recontextualized itself within the more pluralistic cultures of the larger world. There are models for evangelism in which the Hebrew Scriptures remain central (Acts 13:13–43), and other instances in which it seems that the gospel was proclaimed without any mention of traditional source materials (Acts 14:8–18). We seem to have lost something of this fluidity in contemporary mission. Perhaps we are held captive by a perceived orthodoxy in which we see little room for creative ways of telling the gospel story. Contemporary evangelism often appears prepackaged and formulaic, not allowing for contextualizing.

In *Gadfly,* a periodical devoted to the study of popular culture, a recent edition featured a cover article that explored the relationship between contemporary churches and contemporary youth culture. Tyler Thoreson writes, "There's no arguing that Generation X is largely unmoved by the language of traditional Christianity, but you don't see many church leaders wondering if maybe the message itself is the problem. With so few people believing in hell, what's the point in getting so worked up about salvation, whether it's by grace or otherwise?"[18] Thoreson argues that the message of Christianity does not communicate to people who have grown up in a world in which pop culture is amniotic fluid, largely because what religion talks about does not speak to the spiritual needs of today's seeker. The baggage of modern evangelical Christianity makes it difficult for many people to embrace the gospel. It is not a question of compromising truth or even an issue of people not being willing to embrace Christianity's view of transcendence. It may be time to acknowledge the need for changes in the way we articulate and understand the key aspects of faith in order to fulfill the mandate to proclaim the gospel to all creation.

Saint Nick

There is a kingdom.
There is a king.
And He lives without.
And He lives within.
And He is everything.

Nick Cave, *King Ink II*

A final example of someone who uses art as a matrix in which to work out spirituality is London-based, Australian singer-songwriter Nick Cave. While not unknown in the United States, Cave enjoys much more renown outside America. Cave and his band, the Bad Seeds, have a cult-like following of fans who lap up their potent blend of gothic punk rock. A former heroin addict seldom seen not wearing his "uniform" of black suit and tie, Cave cuts a distinctive figure on the music scene. He is distinguished from many of his peers in the punk rock genre by his interest in religion. His songs frequently draw upon the dark imagery of God presented in the Old Testament.

In 1998, a company based in Edinburgh, Scotland, published a new version of the Bible[19] and asked Cave to contribute to the project. This newness came from the Bible's design, not its translation. The company discovered that the sheer size of the Bible discouraged many people from reading it. Canongate designed a new version, selling each of the books of the Bible separately and economically. These pocket-sized Scriptures feature cool covers and an introduction by a figure from the contemporary art field. Bono of U2 wrote the introduction to the Book of Psalms. And Nick Cave wrote the introduction to his favorite Bible book, the Gospel of Mark. His compelling introduction demonstrates Cave's genuine efforts at forming a theological shape for his life.

Art ignited Cave's interest in all things religious. At Caulfield Technical School in Melbourne, Australia, Cave majored in religious art, to the frustration of his instructors who advocated more contemporary art forms.[20] His exploration of Renaissance and Gothic art led him to purchase a Bible so he could identify the religious imagery set before him. And so his lifelong journey with the God of the Bible began.

Cave also developed a fascination for newly emerging punk rock music, whose fiercely anarchistic and antiauthoritarian posturing struck a chord. This rather divergent combination of things sacred and profane provided the context for Cave's ongoing musical and spiritual explorations. Such a rich mine of biblical and theological reflection couched in such an angry music genre demonstrates God's ability to impact and consort with those who find themselves at odds with traditional religious institutions. Theologian Walter Brueggemann writes, "There can be little doubt that we are already in a wholly new interpretive situation."[21]

Cave's approach to spirituality typifies the postmodern world. His reflections are highly individuated and subjective, his relationships to institutional expressions of faith tenuous at best. But while we might bemoan the lack of communal connection in his spiritual life, we should not underestimate the depth of reflection and thought that goes into his work. He says, "It is hard work loathing everything all the time. All that sustained hatred is a painful business, I mean it's so tiring and in the eerie figure that moves through the Gospels, the Man of Sorrows, I felt I was given the chance to reinvent my relationship with the world."[22]

There are two significant themes to follow in Cave's musings about God. The first is the transformation or conversion of his own view of God. The second is Cave's view of the relationship between God and the imagination.

Cave's first encounters with the Bible were firmly rooted in the Old Testament. His study of religious art and iconography drew him to the multitude of Old Testament images most often used by the Old Masters. The Genesis stories were especially rich fodder for the artistic mind. Cave began by coupling these images with the Bible stories that prompted them. He discovered in the pages of the Old Testament a God whom he not only liked but also identified with. "I found there the voice of God and it was brutal and jealous and merciless. For every bilious notion I harbored about myself and the world, and there were a lot of those, there, in the Old Testament was its equivalent leaping off the pages with his teeth bared."[23] Before expressing horror at Cave's "misinterpretation" of God, we do well to remember that this view of God is often used when addressing those we consider in need of judgment and critique.

The images of God that Cave found in the pages of the Bible became perfect fuel for his songwriting ideas and gave a framework for his dark and angry view of the world. Themes of loss, isolation, anger, and despair all found voice in Cave's music and his growing biblical reading. One of his friends said of him, "He was a chaotic character. Nick always had his nose in the Bible. He liked the Old Testament and was obsessed with Jesus. He'd pick up on bits that would interest him, that were controversial in the sense that if he took them out into a different context it would be viewed differently; phrases, lines, words came from the Bible."[24] He took things that he found in the Bible and applied them to his complex world, sometimes using the imagery descriptively and at other times as "fuel for his fire."

In his early writings, Cave exhibited a strong nihilistic bent. Love always failed, people always let one another down, and brutality and violence seemed to be the strongest character traits humans demonstrated. For Cave, love always seemed to be the failed experiment. In "I Let Love In," he voices his feelings about love, the highest of human emotions. He sings, "Despair and Deception / Love's ugly little twins / Came a-knocking on my door / I let them in / Darling, you're the punishment for all my former sins."[25] Cave is suspicious of love. Unlike the first wave of Baby Boomers, he became an adult not in the heady days of idealism and the hippies but in the almost immediate fallout from all the cultural upheaval. It quickly became evident to many of Cave's generation that the promises of the sixties and modernity itself were not going to be realized. Growing up in a working-class Australian environment simply underscored the failure of love as an ethic to live by.

Of course, Cave's ideas about love were complex and often contradictory. Love was primarily the romantic kind, and it was this kind of love that failed. The harsh world of punks and anarchy in which he traveled as a musician had no room for romance or "flowery" philosophy. Life is tough and seems to be growing tougher by the day. Cave's early works are littered with images of barrenness and despair. His favorite Bible reading during this time was the Book of Job. One of Job's friends, Eliphaz, talks to Job and says, "Man is born to trouble as surely as sparks fly upward" (5:7). This became Cave's early assessment of the human condition. "Why wouldn't man be born into trouble, living under the tyranny of such a God?"[26] This dark view of man and God fit his dark stage persona and offstage life. These views fueled Cave's musical career and shaped his view of life. His song "Well of Misery" contains echoes of this sentiment: "O the same God that abandoned her / Has in turn abandoned me / And softening the turf with my tears / I dug a well of misery."[27]

At this time, Cave embodied a person who had rejected any view of God as good. God was cruel, capricious, vindictive, and judgmental, not loving. Yet almost despite himself, Cave allowed slivers of hope into his dark worldview. He was not able to see the possibility of a bright future, perhaps because he was too blinded by his own pain and anger. Yet he waited, he camped, and he watched.

Whatever else his Bible reading may have done, it certainly gave Cave a way to creatively express his rage and anger. It also seems to have, almost unconsciously, taught him that hope does still exist. He certainly picked up on the habits of this God of the Old Testament, but he just as surely picked up on the words of the Old Testament respondents to this God. Though he claimed a delight in this capricious God who makes his followers shudder in consternation, Cave continued to pray and look to God. "Oh, Lord, tell me what I have done / Please don't leave me here on my own," he cried in "I Let

Love In,"[28] the same song that so brutally decried love's redeeming power. While Cave's music continued to be loud, brash, and aggressive, a tidal wave of change occurred in his lyric writing.

As early as 1988, new themes of hope and optimism began to surface in his work, despite a well-documented battle with heroin. What a change for a man who had thrown himself headlong into punk music, gothic-metal musings, and German experimental art theater. A decade before his revelations in the Pocket Canons, changes were well under way. On his album *Tender Prey,* Cave filled almost every song with biblical imagery and themes of mercy. The opening track, "Mercy Seat," tells the story of a man imprisoned and under sentence of death: "It began when they come took me from my home / And put me in Dead Row." Having established that character's plight, Cave introduced larger, eternal themes about mercy and the promise that lies in Christ: "A ragged cup a twisted mop / the face of Jesus in my soup. . . . I hear stories from the chamber / How Christ was born into a manger / And like some ragged stranger / Died upon the Cross." Intertwined with the image of a man awaiting execution is the image of a God who does not judge contrasted with humans who do. "And the Mercy Seat is waiting / And I think my head is burning / And in a way I'm yearning / To be done with all this measuring of truth." There is acknowledgment of God's sovereignty and also his nearness: "In heaven his throne is made of gold / The Ark of the testament is stowed / A throne from which I'm told / All history does unfold / Down here it's made of wood and wire / And my body is on fire / And God is never far away."[29] The song presents a haunting depiction of an execution and an equally stirring movement toward a God who deliberately shows mercy.

Cave matured as a writer and broadened his views of God's relationship with and involvement in human history. The antagonist in the story is not God, who actually seems to care, but humanity, which doesn't. One of the recurring themes in Cave's work is humanity's apparent lack of care for itself and our willingness to overlook the "other" as we selfishly live out our lives. Cave himself was an active participant in this way of life.[30] He immortalized this theme in his pithy song "People Ain't No Good."

Cave's introduction to the Book of Mark reveals the extent of his spiritual journey. After speaking of his fascination with the vengeful God of the Old Testament, he writes, "But you grow up. You do. You mellow out. Buds of compassion push through the cracks in the bitter and black soil. Your rage ceases to need a name. You no longer find comfort watching a whacked-out God tormenting a wretched humanity as you learn to forgive yourself and the world. That God of Old begins to transmute in your heart, base metals become silver and gold and you warm to the world."[31] He reflects on the deep changes taking place inside him that are directly related to his searchings of the Bible. He met an Anglican minister who encouraged him to read the Gospel of Mark (because of its brevity),[32] and in spite of his negative views of Christ, due largely to his religious upbringing, he read. "The Gospel according to Mark has continued to inform my life as the root source of my spirituality, my religiousness."[33] Cave comes to these findings apart from the mediation of the institutional church. In fact, he overcomes his biases toward Christ formed by prior encounters with that church. Far too many people in our society who are interested in spirituality, and even attracted to Jesus, have encounters with religion that push them away.

Once Cave engages Christ, he begins to shape his own spiritual life. Interestingly, what Cave finds attractive about Jesus are not the things on which contemporary evangelism has labored and focused. "The Christ that emerges from Mark, tramping through the haphazard events of His life, had a ringing intensity about Him that I could not resist. Christ spoke to me through His isolation, through the burden of His death, through His rage at the mundane, through His sorrow."[34] The isolation, anger, and sorrow of Christ are hardly the concepts most often tied to evangelistic effort, but they are certainly good calling cards for the alienated elements of contemporary culture. In his book *Communication Theory for Christian Witness,* Charles Kraft writes, "The more we learn about the communication process, the more we become aware of just how crucial the receiver of the communication is to that process. . . . It behooves us to learn as much as we can about what is going on at the receptor's end when we attempt to communicate."[35] Cave and others like him in the realm of popular culture are valuable resources when we consider engaging culture in God's name.

Imagination also permeates Cave's later work. Cave sees the freeing of the imagination as an essential part of what it means when John describes Jesus as the *logos* (John 1:1). Yet he also sees organized religion as an inhibitor of imagination. "What was Christ's great bug bear, and what has sat dung like in the doorway of the Christian Church ever since, was the Pharisee's preoccupation with the law, in preference to the logos."[36] For Cave, too many believers landed squarely on the unimaginative side of the religious spectrum, which he finds quite unappealing. "How can anyone be elevated spiritually if they are loaded up with the chains of religious jurisprudence? How can the imagination be told how to behave?"[37] He sees his growing relationship with Christ through the lens of imagination. He views Christ as the victim of "humanity's lack of imagination"[38] and says that he was "hammered to the cross with the nails of creative vapidity."[39]

Cave's theology starts with the recovery of imagination. He sees humanity locked in the mundanity of life. But Christ comes to set us free from the mundanity of life *and* religion by liberating our minds. His view anticipates creativity's increasing importance within postmodern theology. The faith community used to be the foremost patron of the arts and imagination. Yet in many realms of pop culture, religion inhibits and opposes art. Christians must get in step with the colorful and creative mission of Christ. As Cave says, "Christ came as liberator. Christ understood that we as humans were forever held to the ground by the pull of gravity—our ordinariness, our mediocrity—and it was through His example that He gave our imaginations the freedom to rise and to fly. In short, to be Christ-like."[40]

What Words Cannot Say: Music as Landscape

An ambience is defined as an atmosphere, or a surrounding influence: a tint. My intention is to produce original pieces ostensibly (but not exclusively) for particular times and situations with a view to building up a small but versatile catalog of environmental music suited to a wide variety of moods and atmospheres.

Brian Eno, *A Year with Swollen Appendices*

Brian Eno invented "ambient music" in 1977.[41] The idea came to him while he waited for a plane in Cologne, Germany. He envisioned a new genre of music designed to express moods and create atmospheres. Ambient music would serve as a backdrop to enhance particular environments. Eno wanted to "use music in a different way—as part of the ambience of our lives."[42] Technical advances in recording and instrumentation allowed him to realize his dream. His ambient music floated into the atmosphere, creating sonic spaces and being stored in our subconscious.

Yet the roots of Eno's innovations can be found in composers such as Gustav Mahler and Claude Debussy. Their compositions veered from more classic forms of music. Mahler, in particular, changed not only the rules of composition but the role of music itself. His Symphony no. 5 had five movements instead of the usual four and did not feature voices.[43] Mahler created a new shape for this musical piece. It evoked Eastern European folk melodies and created a "memory" for its listeners, allowing them to interpret and imagine worlds gone by and worlds yet to come. Symphony no. 5 epitomized the beginnings of ambient music.[44]

The film *Death in Venice* used Mahler's Symphony no. 5 to great effect. The longings and inner turmoil of the main character (Dirk Bogarde playing a fictitious Gustav Mahler) play out against Mahler's music. Mahler understood the emotive side of music, paving the way for its use as "background," the soundtrack for films.[45]

Music as atmosphere or a "soundtrack for living" has produced some of the most innovative and challenging tunes of the last twenty years. Four artists in particular contribute to this genre, and their music not only challenges assumptions about the form of pop music but also underscores the argument that the meaning of music resides in far more than simply the words. Music is not a discursive medium. It does not present linear, rational-based information; it is presentational. In other words, meaning is found as much in the emotions created by the music as in the words used.

SUGAR CUBES AND HIDDEN PLACES: ICELAND'S POP LANDSCAPE

Iceland? How did this remote place become a crucible for music innovation? Two artists entered the public spotlight from this small spot on the planet, female singer Björk and rock band Sigur Rós. Each of them pushes the boundaries of pop music. Björk travels in the world of drum and bass and hip-hop and challenges her listeners with each recording she releases. On her contemplative album *Vespertine* (from the Christian prayer cycle of Vespers),[46] Björk evoked the imagery of familiarity, of home, and of being wrapped in a safe cocoon. To accomplish this, she employed the services of New York recording artists Matmos, renowned for their eclectic uses of the sampling process. They used technology to record a vast number of familiar household sounds such as wind chimes, a hand rubbing fabric, and spaghetti falling from a pan on to a plate! They took these sounds, manipulated them with available technology, and created drum loops and sound samples, which provided the instrumental basis for Björk's lyrics. The effect is stunning, comforting, and amazingly contemplative. Sounds and words blend together to create the feeling of safety and comfort. Never has spaghetti on a plate sounded so warm, rich, and rhythmic! The lyrics are song cycles about love received and love lost mixed with mythic Icelandic folktales and neopagan imagery. But it is the feel of the music that really matters—the words are complimentary but not essential. Just as words have taken on new meanings within culture because of semiotics, structuralism, and postmodernism, so pop music lyrics have increasingly become symbolic, echoing feelings rather than definitions.

The primary proponents of words as feelings are Björk's fellow Icelanders, Sigur Rós. This four-piece band from Reykjavík has adopted novel approaches both lyrically and sonically. They play conventional rock band instruments—guitars, drums, and keyboards—but with a twist. Guitars are played with a violin bow, and effects pedals create more of a string synthesizer sound than traditional guitar noises. But Sigur Rós's lyrics demonstrate the most invention. On their debut release, *Agaetis Byrjun*,[47] they employed a self-invented language that they called Hopelandic. The band attempted to make statements about their own isolation from much of the world (because of location and language difference) by using an indecipherable language! According to the band, their music evokes meaning by creating a new language through which they convey their ideas about life (the "hope" in Hopelandic). Without learning a new tongue, listeners get involved in the moods created by the music. Interpretations begin from feeling, not thinking. This approach makes the recipient the sole interpreter of the material, and each listener brings a different interpretation to each song.

What then do we do with issues such as truth? How do we convey larger ideas through the medium of music? We need to see music and particularly language in music as largely symbolic and move away from using music as a platform for the transmission of ideology. At best, music, and pop music in particular, allows roughly four minutes to get a point across. A theology out of popular culture acknowledges both the limitations and the opportunities of the medium. Given just four minutes, pop songs still manage to communicate plenty about the wonder of love. Given the same four minutes, far too many theologians would just be finishing their introduction. In a post-rational, post-literal world, the communication of thoughts and ideas through "atmosphere" might prove to be a more effective means of communicating the gospel. St. Francis told his followers, "Preach the gospel wherever you can, and when all else fails, use words." For today's people, St. Francis may say, "Sing the gospel wherever you can, and when all else fails, use words."

RADIOHEAD

An electric piano opens the song in a minor key. After a few bars, a barely discernible computer-manipulated voice begins to swirl in and out of the chord. Each element continues to rise in volume. Suddenly, the words can be heard: "Everything in its right place." Over and over this phrase repeats like a mantra. This is how Radiohead's album *Kid A* opens, an album that was attacked as a commercial disaster by many within and outside the recording industry.

Radiohead, a band from Oxford, England, rose to prominence by creating fabulous, melancholic pop melodies full of angry, biting, irony-drenched lyrics. If U2 was the eternal optimist, then Radiohead was a pessimist veering toward nihilism. But Radiohead is celebrated for two things: its sound, driven by guitarist-keyboardist Johnny Greenwood; and Thom Yorke's angst-ridden falsetto.

Kid A abandoned both those strengths. For a five-member band renowned for creative and experimental guitar work, the absence of guitars troubled many of its fans. Thom Yorke's unwillingness to sing, in the proper rock sense, seemed to verge on madness. Yet they dared to confound critics and alienate fans. They played with their strengths and reconfigured the purpose and focus of their music. Radiohead is on some levels a protest band. It rails against the numbing qualities of living in a technological age while at the same time using all the creative advantages technology offers. It attacks globalization and free trade, economic injustices and environmental issues, but it does so through its album artwork.

The band's approach offers some challenges as we think through a theology out of popular culture. Three statements by various band members demand particular reflection. Ed O'Brien, bass player, said, "We can't do anything exactly right. But that's what makes our sound."[48] One of the banes of contemporary Christianity is its intense focus on orthodoxy. The problem is not orthodoxy but the fact that far too many people are running around making *their* particular theological posture the standard orthodox test. We all have glimpses of the truth, but, to echo Paul, this side of the grave we all "see through a glass darkly." The desire to appear orthodox has led to a dearth of creativity in virtually every realm of the contemporary Christian experience, particularly the realms of theology and music. This streak of perfectionism, which runs deep in the American religious mind-set, creates atmospheres of fear and trepidation, especially in regard to new ideas. Experimentation is a key ingredient of a contemporary theological construct.

A second point comes from vocalist Thom Yorke: "Aiming and missing is the whole premise."[49] This does not mean that to be wrong is right, but it affirms the need for room to fail and also the need to challenge right constructs by being wrong. The pop song demands on some level a degree of conformity. For the last forty years, the basic structure of the pop song has revolved around the verse-chorus-verse-chorus-bridge-chorus method.[50] Along with this approach to the structure of songs has come a similar conformity in the formulation of vocabulary and sentiments. In this environment, originality is at a premium, as most artists tend to fall back on the mundane and the mediocre. That is why rhyming is a key element of pop songwriting—words have to fit and sound right. Rhyming helps this process. Unfortunately, originality can get lost in the pursuit of the perfect rhyming word.

Radiohead bent and broke these rules both musically and lyrically. They allowed the authority of the lyrics to be controlled by technology. Taking a cue from David Bowie, they fed their lyrics into a computer software program that randomly reconfigures the words. They abandoned standard pop song structure and format in search of new musical horizons. They re-created the rules and boundaries of what a pop song is and what it can accomplish. Theology also needs to fiddle with its rules, not in random ways but with a sense of experiment, excitement, and creativity.

A final ingredient comes again from Ed O'Brien: "There's nothing more like the kiss of death vis-à-vis a musician than if he can do everything by age sixteen. . . . It's very, very dangerous, unless you approach it the way, that say, Picasso did as a painter . . . enough, I'm putting down my tools, I'm going to approach it in an entirely different way . . . forget all that, start anew."[51] Is starting from theological scratch something we should all consider every so often? Tradition can quickly become traditionalism when we stop thinking and assume we have arrived at our theological destinations. Many of the more traditional Christian faith expressions, particularly Orthodox and Catholic, offer positive contributions to aid an engagement with an image-driven, body-conscious, mystery-celebrating culture. These "slow-moving," sacramental churches affirm the arts and creativity. But their hierarchy, rules, and traditions have been challenged by the waters of contemporary culture, which demand a more responsive, "liquid church."[52]

MOBY: CHRISTIAN PLAGIARIST

A final artist who has used all available technology with great success is Moby. A writer for the *New York Times Magazine* said, "Moby is not a band, or a singer-songwriter exactly, or a producer, exclusively, or an 'electronic-artist,' strictly speaking. . . . One way or another he is present on every song he has ever made, since he does everything himself."[53] Using available technology, Moby creates songs that are eerily familiar and yet completely new. His album *Play* has sold in excess of nine million copies worldwide and has been one of the most discussed and critically acclaimed albums of the last decade. He recorded the entire work alone in his home studio in New York. Each of the eighteen songs on *Play* has been licensed to a television show, movie, or advertiser.

What makes Moby interesting is not just his use of technology but what he accomplishes *with* the technology. By raiding popular music, from early twentieth-century field recordings to samples from recent pop hits, Moby recycles the past but also reshapes it.[54] He may employ snippets of two hundred recordings to create a "new" song. This artistic process mirrors culture, looking forward but often seeking meaning in the comfort and history of the recent past. Continuing Eno's commitment to music as soundscape, Moby says, "Every song I write, I imagine this specific kind of person listening to it . . . a woman who's just come home from a hard day's work . . . a student on a train in Germany."[55]

This approach to music causes us to rethink what constitutes a musician. One can now create music and write songs without being proficient on any musical instrument. Many of today's most popular recording artists are DJs— people who make a living playing other people's music. "The realm of the dead is as big as a culture's capacity for storage and communication," wrote Friedrich Kittler.[56] In DJs' hands, "the realm of the dead" and "the realm of those still alive but not necessarily recording anymore" become a huge reservoir for what Ira Matathia and Marian Salzman call "pick 'n' mix nostalgia."[57]

Until the Renaissance, the artist's role was wrapped up in the life of society through religious services and functions. The artist was like a prophet or a seer and was in a sense a "marketer of ideology." Art generally served to undergird the values of the society. Only after artists such as Michelangelo and Leonardo da Vinci came along did artists begin to see their work first and foremost as a means of expressing themselves. The dawn of the modern artist, committed to self-expression, whose work often flew in the face of cultural norms or the status quo, followed.[58]

But now a new awareness of the "invisible artist" is emerging. The artist has disappeared but has not vanished.[59] The artist is, like the resources he plunders, multidimensional. Drawing from any number of sources and offering no authority to any of them, the DJ combines texts (in this case, musical sources) in new configurations and makes the old new again. "Now, in the late nineties, we have to start with a musical hybridity, of global cultural crossover and the profound interpenetrations of style, coupled with the reliance on often quite basic machines. . . . In short, music, has become artificially intelligent."[60] As Moby says, "What I'm not doing is spending my life playing just guitar accompanying my voice. On my records, I'm the composer and the musician and the engineer, but also the plagiarist and thief."[61]

Plagiarism and thievery are troubling self-definitions, but they are the hallmark of a post-ethical reality. Speaking of oneself as a plagiarist and a thief is, in this sense, a badge of honor. This stealing is done out in the open for all to see. Matathia and Salzman call it "pick 'n' mix nostalgia"; McRobbie, Beaudoin, and others might use the terms *collage* or *bricolage*. All of them acknowledge that contemporary life involves weaving together seemingly disparate pieces of information and reimagining them into something new.

This blended approach to creativity impacts postmodern spirituality. "Plagiarism" abounds in the religious environs, particularly among young people who cut and paste to form their spirituality: a little piece of the Buddha, mixed with a dash of Zen, covered with a splash of yoga, and topped by a dollop of Jesus. Many fret about such disrespect for religious tradition in the post-institutional world. When *all* religions and ideologies and opinions are afforded the same respect, the Christian faith faces a great challenge. Jesus' followers must figure out how to maintain a singular faith in a pluralistic age.

Moby regards himself as musician, plagiarist, thief, and Christian. He blends sources, crosses genres, embraces technology. He shapes his life after Christ and verbalizes this commitment in concert and on his album cover notes. Yet he also finds support for his vegan practices in the words of Mohammed and the Dalai Lama. His blended Christian faith troubles some, encourages others. He moves forward as techno's first superstar and one of Jesus' highest-profile followers.

The Urbanization of Pop

It's all about the beauty of hip hop. There are no constraints with this art form.

Grandmaster Flash, quoted in *The Hip Hop Years*

A rather tongue-in-cheek history of pop music goes something like this: It was invented by blacks (Little Richard) and stolen by whites (Elvis Presley).

African-Americans invented rap; white people stole it. And so on. Obviously, the history of popular music cannot be written simply based on race. However, there has been rivalry for supremacy among different genres of pop music since its inception. And the center of influence shifts every so often.

In the 1940s, Charlie Parker and others invented bebop as a means of rebelling against the more formal style of swing music. It was deemed vulgar by critics. Now it is appreciated the world over and viewed as a revolutionary form of music that changed the face of popular music. Rap music followed a similar trajectory.

Rap music, hip-hop, nu-soul, and other musical genres of the African-American urban experience are the biggest selling form of popular music today, and they are growing daily. "Rap music brings together a tangle of some of the most complex social, cultural, and political issues in contemporary American society," writes Tricia Rose.[62] She calls rap music "a black cultural expression that prioritizes black voices from the margins of urban America."[63] Though its origins and expressions are largely black, rap music comes in all colors. The main purchasers of rap music are predominantly white, suburban youth. Cypress Hill finds its largest following in the Hispanic community. The most significant rapper of recent history is a white, working-class kid from Detroit who goes by the moniker Eminem.

Rap music may have been formed out of the collective experience of urban black America, but the issues raised in the music strike chords with young people around the globe. Rap and hip-hop music can be found in virtually every culture. These artists are united by their urban experience rather than by race. Makale is a Turkish rap group based in Zurich, Switzerland. Their music blends traditional Turkish folk music with rap and hip-hop beats and lyrics sung in Turkish. As the swing toward city life swept the globe, rap and the urban experience went international. Urban life is often multicultural. Consequently, new musical forms tend to be multiethnic, cross-cultural, and interracial.

Urban music began with artists such as Curtis Mayfield and Stevie Wonder, who vocalized the plight of a predominantly black urban population. But performers such as Bruce Springsteen and Bob Seger voiced similar themes of alienation, unemployment, and despair found in the white working-class urban experience. Rock music that used to come from America's heartland now comes from the cities. The sound of the city infuses pop music with new rhythms and new intensities. Music born out of an urban context tends to be gritty, busy, and often angry. The anger in heavy metal music arose from its origins in economically depressed, high unemployment cities around the world. Before Kid Rock and Eminem, Detroit produced Grand Funk, Bob Seger, and Ted Nugent. Birmingham, England, unleashed Judas Priest, while Sheffield, England, gave us Def Leppard. White urban youth verbalize their frustration regarding the conditions in which they find themselves: "The North American heavy metal audience, by the early 1980s, consisted to a significant extent of suburban males who did not acquire a postsecondary education and who increasingly found that their socioeconomic prospects were not as great as those of their parents."[64]

Rap and hip-hop emerged in similar situations, in the projects of crowded American cities. Hip-hop's roots can be traced to the Bronx and a 1970s context of economic recession. "Afrika Bambaataa and his Zulu nation used their knowledge as consumers to become skilled producers of hip-hop. . . . Hemmed in by urban renewal, crime, and police surveillance, and silenced by neglect from the culture industry, the school system, and city government, they found a way to declare themselves through music."[65]

Rap, in particular, has a narrative form of vocal delivery spoken in rhythmic style over homemade rhythms called breakbeats. Breakbeats are created by DJs who piece together fragments of different songs to create an entirely new one. The narrative style of much urban music today points to a need to shift from a linear reading of Scripture to a more organic and narrative approach, telling stories rather than just providing information. Jesus often presented his theological constructs in the form of a story, whether it was a perspective on the character of God (the prodigal son) or the nature of the kingdom (the mustard seed). Telling a story allows listeners to have an active role; they use their imaginations to understand the story and draw their own conclusions. Urban music is also a communal and collaborative affair and, particularly in its early days, a spontaneous event. Again, theology can learn from this, offering a foundation (creating the breakbeat, if you will) on which the community can develop its own contextual and organic form of faith expression.

The Globalization of Pop

> I believe that spirituality is more important than politics and material things. When you create a work, you must do it not for yourself but for every human being.
>
> Baaba Maal, Senegalese singer-songwriter

When I was touring with AC/DC, we were supported by a vast array of bands, some good, some really bad. None matched the French band who opened for AC/DC's first big concert in Paris. We didn't expect much at the time. After all, the best bands came from Britain and America—who did the *French* have? Johnny Hallyday?[66] Exactly. Time was when pop music was strictly an export from either Britain or North America. English has been the lingua franca of pop music since its inception. Until very recently, if a song was sung in any other tongue, it was destined for local success and global ignorance—but not anymore. In our globalized world, the exchange of goods goes both ways. This is vividly seen in the burgeoning realm of "world music."

World music was coined by music marketers in Great Britain[67] who were trying to categorize new music from non-Western cultures. It is urbanized pop music from around the globe—Africa, Asia, and all points in between—that blends traditional music and postwar technology. It reveals a trend in pop music, namely, that the rest of the world has gotten on the pop music bandwagon and has married indigenous sounds with available technologies and Western influences. World music charts the amalgamation and adaptation of various music forces.

Although the United States still accounts for more than a quarter of worldwide music sales, its days of domination seem numbered.[68] Cross-cultural pollination is taking place all over the globe and produces compelling new sounds. DJ Rekha, a Punjabi-American, describes the current music environment: "For my generation, music is a cultural mix. We grew up hearing it all—the rural folk music of my parents' heritage in the Punjab, Bollywood soundtracks, the urban sounds of hip-hop, dance, reggae. At the Basement Bhangra party downtown at S.O.B.'s, I mix it all together. In the course of a single night, I weave all these different influences in and out. I put it all through my speakers."[69] Multicultural, multi-influenced, and genre-defying contemporary pop music is a cultural mix. Mono-cultural is out, and a global celebration of diversity and collaboration is in.

From Latin-based singers such as Jennifer Lopez or Shakira to the more exotic sounds of Algerian Rai singer Cheb Mami (whose vocals fueled the hit Sting song "Desert Rose"), global music reigns supreme. Damon Albarn of the English rock band Blur has a new side project, Mali. They mix English pop with traditional Maalian music and musicians. Asian music, with roots in India particularly, spins in clubs all over Europe and America. From Ry Cooder in Cuba giving us "The Buena Vista Social Club" to Paul Simon promoting the Sounds of Soweto on "Graceland," the results of musical blending have been utterly sublime. Globalization gives musicians all over the world new ways of making hybrid sounds and selves.[70] This is not just old-school, cultural exchange. While Western pop rock sound influences it, world music cannot be viewed simply as foreign regurgitations. Collaboration and appropriation are key ingredients in contemporary world music.[71]

A stellar example of the new era in world music can be found in a project called 1 Giant Leap. Two British artists, Jamie Catto and Duncan Bridgeman, traveled to twenty-five countries armed with a laptop computer and a digital camera. On the laptop were the sketches for some songs the two had already composed. They took these embryonic pieces to various musicians they met on their travels and invited them to contribute. The digital camera captured the recording sessions and the cultural contexts. The finished work, 1 Giant Leap, is more than just music. It is an album and a documentary. Musicians involved in the project added their thoughts about life and commented on the questions that every culture seeks to answer. Ultimate concerns about God, money, sex, and power are interwoven with geographic footage and music making. The project represents much of the contemporary global context. It combines technology and tradition. Laptop computers and state-of-the-art music programming meet traditional non-Western instrumentation such as the kora and djembe drums. *1 Giant Leap* blends art forms as music and film complement each other. The results are global and local—glocal.

Global pop resists imperialism. Other cultures' musical roots are not being eradicated and replaced. "New popular musics are being made, old ones altered or maintained, sometimes museumized and sometimes lost altogether."[72] More and more musicians around the globe wish to explore and collaborate, creating new musical horizons. This marriage of styles and forms is unprecedented in pop music history. How rare these days to hear a "pure" music form. Some may bemoan this loss, but others recognize that it reflects the world in which we live. It holds more promise than doom.

This production of new music relates to the idea of "new selves." World music indicates the growing understanding of peoples everywhere that we are in a new time. In this new time, we need new definitions of ourselves.[73] These musical developments point to the seismic changes taking place around the globe. They give us new ideas about where we live—culturally. They challenge the notion that we have a single cultural center. Much previous talk about culture assumed that a line could be drawn through culture and that the particular value of a certain thing could be judged by proximity to that line. The question, Is it art? arises from this assumption, the idea being that a standard exists by which all things can be measured.[74] World music presents us with a new alternative—that there is not a line but a network of connections inviting us to interesting and surprising places. New meanings, new stories, and new destinations are created through these collaborations.

What does this all mean? Pluralism has arrived. The days of cultural homogeneity are gone, in spite of the railings of fundamentalists from all faiths. Contemporary culture, connected by borderless media and computer technology, is more diverse, more open, and more collaborative than ever before. The unavoidable theological result? Diversity. The center of the Christian faith has shifted from the West to Africa and Asia. As with world music, voices from the outside, from non-Western nations, are seeking to be heard.

The Chinese revolutionaries used to greet one another with the question, "Are you living in the New World?"[75] We must continually ask ourselves that question as we seek a theology out of popular culture. The embrace of world music must carry over to the Christian community. What formulations of the gospel story might appear as we approach theology in such a collaborative way?

The Democratization of Pop

> Music fills and structures space within us and around us, inside and outside. Hence, much like our concept of place, music can appear to envelop us, but it can also appear to express our innermost feelings/beings.
>
> Sara Cohen, *Rock Culture in Liverpool*

Sitting in an auditorium, dressed in a suit, and coughing politely in the spaces between movements is a vastly different musical experience than standing on a chair, singing along with a band at full voice, in an arena full of screaming, die-hard fans. These differences arise from the social activities music addresses—what music is for. Until recently, music matched the space in which it was performed. This included the social space. Before recording equipment, before synthesizers and computers, to hear symphonic music one had to go to the theater and dress accordingly. Once the concert was over, only the memory of it remained. But technological developments have changed the process for musicians and listeners.

Recording shifted the relationship between performer and audience. With sound recordings, the social space necessary for listening to music changed forever. Music was liberated from both the performance and the performers. Recordings meant that music could be collected and listened to again and again, wherever and whenever one chose. Now one can listen to the Boston Symphony while in the bath, in the car, on the porch—anywhere. A guitar can be played in a small recording studio, but with reverb added in the mixing process, it can sound as though it were played in a spacious cathedral. The act of making music has become the art of creating new sonic locations. These and other developments created the democratization of music.

The advent of the digital age revolutionized every aspect of the musical experience—from creation to marketing to listening. In the sixteenth century, Vincenzio Galileo, father of the more famous astronomer, released a book entitled *Dialog of Ancient and Modern Music*. Vincenzio loved and played the lute, which was falling out of vogue, being replaced by the guitar. He was also a student of the physics of sound. The tuning techniques for the lute were based on Pythagorean mathematical formulas that required strict obedience to numerical properties and ratios. Applying the results of his own studies to the lute, Vincenzio developed a new approach to tuning that required fractionally shortening the distances between frets. Some of his findings went into his book, which challenged the existing concepts and rules about music and advocated a new form of tuning that favored the sweetness of the instrument's sound over adherence to strict relationships between notes. This trend toward feeling, sound, and atmosphere continues to this day. Musical rules continue to be stretched and challenged.

In the 1970s, inventions were already being introduced that would change the relationship between musician and music. When the Beatles recorded their landmark album *Sgt. Pepper's Lonely Hearts Club Band,* they had to record with four-track recording machines. They had bigger things in mind, so their producer, Sir George Martin, linked several four-track machines together. The Beatles recorded some parts, then "bounced" those recorded tracks on to a single track, recorded some more, bounced those and the other single track on to another track, and so on. Today, one can record up to ninety-six tracks on a digital machine without breaking a sweat! When the Beatles wanted strings on their recordings, they had to bring in trained musicians. Whether employing a string quartet or an orchestra, the costs were prohibitive. Today, a single keyboard contains hundreds of sounds—strings, orchestras, organic folk instruments—literally anything a musician needs. Technology begat musical democracy.

These technological developments forced the definition of a musician to change. Computer programs provide the various sounds a "musician" assembles to create a song. Electronic keyboards allow basic pianists to compose orchestral pieces. Recording decks outsell guitars at a rate of roughly four to one in the U.K. When young people dream of being a rock star, most of them aspire to be DJs. DJs, or disc jockeys, used to be people who played other people's music for people who wanted to dance. Now they are considered musicians in their own right. A flyer for a London club advertised the DJ equivalent of an open-mike night. Anyone who considered himself a DJ could bring his own records to the club and spin some tunes for the public. The crude and inexpensive flyer had a slogan that read, "Anyone can be a f— DJ." It reflected both the optimism (anyone can be a DJ) and the resignation (anyone can be a DJ) of the postmodern world. Technology allows anyone to create music.

The profusion of music technology forces a reassessment of the meaning of music. New technology allows for the sampling of sounds and ideas. When you hear a song on the radio, the music leaps between genres and styles. The songs snatch words, beats, and sounds from all over the pop landscape. Disparate things are placed side by side and on top of one another. Songwriting credits on recent CDs reveal long lists of writers from different ages and different record labels, all converging on a single song. Technology encourages countless remixes, a means of teasing audiences with the threat, or the promise, that they will never hear the same version again. We used to make sense of music by placing it in certain genres: punk, metal, rap, rock. Now, those categories seem obsolete and inappropriate. We have to start with an assumption of musical hybridity, of global cultural crossover, of interpenetrations of style.

DJ culture, born of the marriage of technology and art, displays a strong spiritual bent among its nihilistic tendencies. Club venues are rife with biblical names and terminology: Grace, Bliss, Heaven, Salvation, Sanctuary, and God's Kitchen. Simon Reynolds writes in the introduction to his book *Generation Ecstasy,* "Rave is more than music plus drugs; it's a matrix of lifestyle, ritualized behavior, and beliefs. To the participants, it feels like a religion; to the mainstream observer, it looks more like a sinister cult."[76] It is interesting that DJ music contains ideas of ritual, religious experience, and spiritual longing. But like rock and rap before it, dance music is perceived as yet another example of youthful nihilism and rebellion. Followers of Jesus must embrace those who are searching and seeking. We must honor their search, misguided though it may be at times, and join them as co-pilgrims, walking and dancing beside them.

Musical Conclusions

The present time of believers is no longer determined by the past. It takes its definition from the future.

Jurgen Moltmann

Artists such as Nick Cave, Bruce Cockburn, Creed, Moby, and U2 speak about spirituality from a distinctly Christian bias but have little or nothing to do with organized religion. Many consider it a hindrance to their own spiritual journey. This painful sentiment has been expressed by some of our kindest, gentlest, most faithful Christian students—even those so passionately committed to Christ that they enrolled in seminary! We must discover the difference between being organized and being institutionalized.

If those already on a journey with Christ seem unable to "get with the church," how will those who have yet to embrace Jesus be able to connect? Western Christianity faces a population raised on pop culture, interested in spirituality, who feel unwelcomed at Christ's table. What should we do? Pop music offers at least three glimpses into elements of the nature of the Christian faith that we may have forgotten: the creative nature of God and faith, the role of pain and suffering in life and faith, and the integration of body and soul in contrast to the dualistic approach of modernity.

ART FOR GOD'S SAKE

Christians must rediscover creativity. Pastors and missionaries have used rational and linear means to communicate scriptural truths with great success. But the world that responded to such methods has nearly vanished. Nick Cave suggests that Christ came to liberate humans from their "earthboundedness" and free them to use their creativity and imagination.[77] Using our imaginations in the propagation of the gospel does not mean merely co-opting the creativity expressed in popular culture (something that contemporary Christian music has been doing for years). That is only part of the equation. We must discover our own creativity and take it *into* pop culture. This includes the need to rediscover myth and story.[78]

Old Testament theologian Walter Brueggemann speaks of the "prophetic imagination." He makes a case for equating the Old Testament prophets with the Greek poets. Like the Greek poets, the prophets are "voices that shatter settled reality and evoke new possibility in the listening assembly."[79] We must recover the prophetic imagination, the creative use of language that has the power to stir and stimulate the imagination. Our means of dialogue and expression must change in order to keep the interest of the culture around us.[80] U2 may not care to see itself as a Christian band, but they may have done more to generate dialogue about Christian faith than all traditional evangelistic efforts put together. Fans can even go online and enter into more than one global conversation about their theological statements.

Art and artistry allow deep and sometimes difficult issues to be addressed without an authoritarian, preachy tone. In *Virtual Faith,* Tom Beaudoin quotes Thomas Groome, who suggests that "revelation comes first to meet us in our imaginations." Beaudoin then adds, "Imagination allows us to make and receive infinite interpretations of how symbols represent God's presence in the world."[81] In other words, there is more than one way to see things. Our imaginations offer countless interpretations of a given set of information. We need a "poetic-theology," a sort of bare-bones belief stripped of unnecessary baggage. We need a theological construct that does not use reason at the expense of the creative use of language and the arts nor sacrifices theological truth for purely artistic license. Such theology will require a new theological voice. God's people must embrace Nick Cave's example, rereading the biblical text in the reality of the lived world rather than in the safety of old assumptions.

PAIN AND SUFFERING

St. John of the Cross chronicled his deep and often anguish-ridden struggle with God, his dark night of the soul. As Christians we must incorporate our darkest emotions into the current theological mix. We have left the era of "be happy attitudes!"

Jesus was known as the Man of Sorrows, a metaphor that doesn't fit with triumphalist theological constructs. But the image of a suffering Man of Sorrows resonates with a post-traumatic culture. Nick Cave says, "Mark's Gospel is a clatter of bones, so raw, nervy and lean on information that the narrative aches with the melancholy of absence."[82] He captures in that statement an important element of the gospel story—namely, Christ's own loneliness and isolation—that can speak to the alienated, isolated, disenfranchised postmodern seeker.

U2 created a "postmodern psalmody" rooted in the Bible's greatest songs. The Psalms cover the entire gamut of human emotions. People groan, wail, moan, and scream their way through the songs, seeking answers and comfort from God to ease their pain. Contemporary music also covers all emotions. Jesus' followers must realize that "emotional-censorship" threatens artists and the faith. May we learn to sing all kinds of songs—songs of praise and songs of pain.

Body and Soul: A Holistic Approach

The modern era compartmentalized human life. We knew the difference between the sacred and the profane, heaven and hell. But a division of the physical and the spiritual, body and soul, now seems misguided and forced. Christians must adopt a holistic approach to humanity.

An overemphasis on statements of faith reduces Christians to "theology in a body bag." We're much more than our beliefs! Cave wrote that the eerie figure of Jesus who moves through the Gospels has "an essential humanness which provides us with a blueprint for our own lives."[83] Essential humanness unites body and soul. People are searching for a "lived theology," a practical faith that encompasses all aspects of what it means to be a person created by God.

Christians have viewed the imagination and the physical body as the devil's playground for too long. Imagination must be rediscovered as a seat for holy creativity. The body must be affirmed as the home for sacred sensuality and the worship of God. These are dangerous topics, fraught with tensions and challenges. But this is where people live. If we do not address these topics, what can we possibly hope to contribute to the contemporary spiritual search? Spiritual life cannot be lived in a vacuum. People want to experience God through their emotions and senses.[84] Why not take things a little farther and see what transpires? An embodied faith will spark worship we've never imagined, music we've longed to hear.

"YOU TALKIN' TO ME?"
- TRAVIS 3:16

movies

Look Closer

Perhaps the single most intense pleasure of movie-going is . . . escaping from the responsibilities of having the proper responses required of us in our official (school) culture. . . . It's the feeling of freedom from respectability we have always enjoyed at the movies. . . . They are stripped of cultural values.

Pauline Kael, quoted in *Life the Movie*[1]

I made it as a prayer, an act of worship. I wanted to be a priest. My whole life has been movies and religion. That's it. Nothing else.

Martin Scorsese on *The Last Temptation of Christ*,
quoted in *Martin Scorsese: A Journey*

The preeminent American movie critic, Pauline Kael, titled her first collection of reviews, published in 1965, *I Lost It at the Movies*. With her playful title, Kael acknowledged films' long association with sexuality and illicit images. Movies have always exposed the hidden, unseen, unacknowledged parts of the human experience. They allow us to be voyeurs, sitting in the dark, peeking into someone else's life. For many religious leaders, movies were an evil to be avoided, the last temptation of Christians.

Yet for many other people, they didn't lose it at the movies; they found it. Movies teach us (almost) everything about our world that we need to know. Film noir such as *The Maltese Falcon* reveal the evil hidden in every human heart. Romances such as *Say Anything* suggest that love is worth waiting for. Science fiction such as the original *Planet of the Apes* teaches tolerance. Fantasies such as *The Lord of the Rings* dream of a better world, challenging us to environmental preservation. The Marx Brothers promote laughter in the face of absurdity. Humphrey Bogart offers a code of honor and ethics. Katharine Hepburn demonstrates brains and bravura. Sean Connery models wit, grace, and style. Clint Eastwood communicates the power of silence.

But how spiritual can a film be? Can a relationship with God be as thrilling as *Star Wars*? Can the Holy Spirit move us with the ferocity of *Run Lola Run*? Can Jesus Christ be as revolutionary, tough, and inspiring as Rocky? When *Raging Bull* ends with a quotation from the Gospel of John, "Once I was blind, but now I can see," for many it can be an epiphany. Today, it isn't always a choice of movies *or* religion. Audiences can find God in movies *and* religion. This chapter dares to suggest that if God can speak to us through the pummeling effects of *Raging Bull,* then *Fight Club, Magnolia,* and *Dogma* might be God's latest, greatest sermons—but only if we follow the advice of the provocative poster and trailer for *American Beauty*: "Look closer."

Estranged Bedfellas?

> We are in the business to provide entertainment, but in doing so, we do not dodge the issue if we can also provide enlightenment.
>
> Darryl F. Zanuck

> Give me any two pages of the Bible and I'll give you a picture.
>
> Cecil B. DeMille[2]

Massive, meticulous histories have been written about the tortured relationship between people of faith and people of film.[3] Why do preachers rail about the evils of Hollywood? Why does Hollywood get nervous every time conservative Christian lawmakers decide to clean up sex and violence in the media? Have the church and Hollywood, two primal culture makers, always hated each other? Are the film studios' violent, effects-driven blockbusters a sign of *Apocalypse Now*? Or has a new generation of filmmakers gone to very dark places in order to proclaim, *"It's a Wonderful Life"*? Hollywood's avalanche of jarring images demands that discerning filmgoers "look closer" than ever before.

A century ago, many people of faith recognized the power and promise of motion pictures. Terry Lindvall documented the pro-film views of churchgoers in his important book *The Silents of God*. Writing in 1911, Herbert A. Jump asked questions that resonate today. "Why do not men, especially the common people, want to go to church more than they do? Is it not in part because they feel that the preaching of today, at many points, fails to fit their natures and meet their needs?"[4] What did Jump propose as a solution? He declared, "The growing possibility of the motion picture . . . is its usefulness to the preacher as he proclaims moral truth. It will provide the element of illustration for his discourse far better than it can be provided by the spoken word. It will make his gospel vivid, pictorial, dramatic, and above all, interesting."[5] Also writing in 1911, K. S. Hover announced, "Satan has a new enemy. They are fighting the evil one with the flickering films that were formerly used only to amuse. . . . The motion picture has actually become a part of the equipment of the up-to-date church. It is almost as necessary as a janitor, an organ, or the heavy and depressing looking pews of oak."[6] Unfortunately, Lindvall's book also reveals that churchgoers eventually decided to oppose moving pictures, seeing them as below their refined Victorian tastes.

While Hollywood turned Jewish immigrants into millionaires and prim debutantes into film fans, people of faith rose up in protest, labeling movies "the devil's incubator."[7] Movie studios, stung by scandals and threatened by faith-based boycotts, banded together to hire a teetotaling, God-fearing Protestant to clean up their industry. Will Hays acted as the studios' "front man," overseeing and enforcing the Production Code, a guide to acceptable on-screen behavior written by Catholic layman Daniel Lord in 1930. Classic films such as *Casablanca, Mr. Smith Goes to Washington,* and *The Wizard of Oz* followed. The Christian community can rightfully claim that their diligent activity as moral watchdog spawned the Golden Age of Hollywood. But should people of faith approach art and culture only as something to be monitored, a corrupting influence to be kept in check? Only recently has the "hidden history" of faith-based (mostly Catholic, immigrant) filmmakers been uncovered.

In *Afterimage,* priest and film scholar Richard Blake studies six of the most celebrated directors in film history: John Ford, Frank Capra, Alfred Hitchcock, Francis Coppola, Martin Scorsese, and Brian De Palma. One can imagine any number of comparative themes emerging from their work: the male psyche, the American Dream, redemptive violence, longing and loss. Blake traces those recurring motifs back to a unique, unifying concept: All six directors are Catholic. Blake draws heavily from Andrew Greeley's *Catholic Imagination* to find several Catholic "loves" that influence these auteurs' collective oeuvre. Catholics embrace the ordinary, physical world. They love the sacraments, the saints, and devotional activities. Their primarily masculine characters struggle with conscience, need spiritual mentors, and ultimately experience moral growth.[8]

Blake argues that a movie screen can take ordinary, mundane people and objects and add value; it can make the common and everyday "sacred." Why do Catholic filmmakers understand the movie camera's mysterious and sacred power? Because they watch ordinary wine become the blood of Christ every Sunday. Tasteless wafers are transformed into the broken body of Christ at every mass. While the Protestant Church concentrated on words and music (and produced many great writers and musicians), the Catholic Church preserved the image, the symbol. Catholics make better filmmakers because they understand the mystery and the power of images. So Michael Corleone takes a solemn oath to resist the power of Satan while his goons knock off his enemies at the conclusion of Francis Coppola's *Godfather.* And Harvey Keitel puts his hand over a candle, an open flame, hoping to be purged of his demons in Martin Scorsese's *Mean Streets.* Here are classic cinematic images forged in a religion of sacred images.

So what happened? If the church had such a strong start in Hollywood, when did the great divorce occur? Why can the Republicans in Hollywood be counted on a single hand? The injustices of the McCarthy era drove a permanent wedge between the church and Hollywood.

Consider Gary Ross's creative 1999 directorial debut, *Pleasantville.* After considerable success writing *Big* and *Dave,* Ross chose to chronicle the ugly underside of the 1950s in *Pleasantville.* What drove his most personal film? Vivid recollections of his father's blacklisting during the communist witch hunts fanned Ross's creative flames. A person of faith might view *Pleasantville* as a celebration of sex and infidelity. Yet artists in Hollywood celebrate *Pleasantville*'s defense of the five freedoms, from free speech to the right to assemble. Ross obviously remembers the upheaval and loss occasioned by well-intentioned, flag-waving defenders of the faith. He portrays dull, black-and-white conformity as the anti-American enemy of colorful artists everywhere. The passions surrounding artistic freedom and government intervention and the industry's betrayal remain real and palpable. When Jesus' followers align themselves with conservative congressmen seeking to censor Hollywood, they awaken old and justifiable fears. Faith-based film-makers are caught in this historical cross fire.

Do you align yourself with liberal Hollywood, understanding the long, strange path of persecution from the 1950s? Or do you associate with a church known for protests, boycotts, and pickets of the "secular media"? Rather than construct an elaborate, biblical defense of R-rated movies, I ask people of faith to consider what rating the Bible might generate if filmed verse by verse.[9] Since the Bible would be lucky to earn anything less than an NC-17, I will move past issues of content to the central question of movies and their greater meanings.

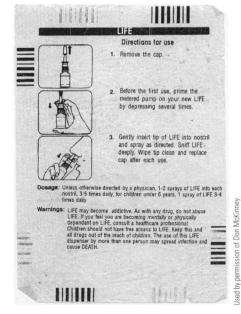

Used by permission of Don McKinney.

Mere Entertainment?

Making films solely for entertainment is like making soup with only one ingredient.

David Puttnam, producer of *Chariots of Fire*

Are moving images destined to create mere idols? Can the graven images dominating the big screen be redeemed? Can God speak through something as mundane as movies? Is it possible to encounter the holy himself in a movie theater? Before writing *Taxi Driver* and *Raging Bull,* before directing *American Gigolo* and *Affliction,* fledgling filmmaker Paul Schrader brought such lofty questions to his graduate work at UCLA. Schrader's rigorous Christian Reformed Church upbringing and undergraduate education at Calvin College schooled him in the power of logic, creeds, and words to describe a transcendent, wholly other God. Schrader sought to fuse his Calvinist training in thinking, writing, and apologetics with the power of moving images. He explored the spiritual possibilities of film in his master's thesis, "Transcendental Style in Film."[10]

For Schrader, "Transcendental style seeks to maximize the mystery of existence; it eschews all conventional interpretations of reality: realism, naturalism, psychologism, romanticism, impressionism, and finally rationalism."[11] In a fallen world, "the enemy of transcendence is immanence," the common stuff of everyday life. Borrowing heavily from Catholic theologian Jacques Maritain, Schrader identified two "temporal means" available to artists and theologians. Abundant means are practical, emotional, physical, and sensual. Sparse means are abstract, rigid, stylized, and stripped to the essentials, "the proper means of the spirit." Maritain considers the sparse means higher than the abundant means, "closer to the Holy."[12] For artists hoping to capture the divine on film, the less human, psychological, or realistic the filmmaking the better.

Schrader cites the failure of overtly religious films to inspire faith as proof of Maritain's theories. He suggests that whenever movies manipulate viewers' emotions via character identification, rational plot lines, and special effects, the end results undercut faith. Watching Charlton Heston part the Red Sea in *The Ten Commandments* doesn't make that miracle more "real" to viewers. When films such as *The Omega Code* or *Left Behind* combine special effects and Scripture to explain the future, God becomes cheesy, the wholly Other boiled down to a hidden code. Schrader summarizes: "The abundant means are indeed tempting to a film-maker, especially if he is bent on proselytizing. With comparative ease he can make an ardent atheist sympathize with the trials and agonies of Christ. But he has not lifted the viewer to Christ's level, he has brought Christ down to the viewers."[13] In Schrader's theology, God is not here. The transcendent can be found only out there, beyond human sin and failings.

Schrader found three models of "transcendent cinema" in directors Carl Theodor Dreyer, Yasujiro Ozu, and Robert Bresson. They created critically acclaimed classics such as *The Passion of Joan of Arc, Floating Weeds,* and *Diary of a Country Priest.* Languid camera movements, austere acting, and spiritual subject matter unite the three directors' films. How they tell their stories—via long takes, poetic compositions, and restrained performances—communicates what their films are about. Bresson used only "amateur" actors, believing paradoxically that non-actors better convey human reality. "We are not simple. We are extremely complex. And it is this complexity you will find with a non actor." Bresson summarized this rigorous aesthetic: "Your film is not made for a stroll with the eyes, but for going right into, for being totally absorbed in."[14] Unfortunately, Schrader's hallowed trio of directors is also united by their complete box office failure, consistently demanding too much of audiences looking for sheer entertainment. Even *New Yorker* critic Anthony Lane readily admits that he is afraid of Bresson and his films. "As I shuffle into the theatre I feel like a pupil approaching the principal's door, wondering what crimes I may have committed and how I must answer them."[15] What is it about their sparse style that makes audiences so nervous?

In an interview in *Cahiers du Cinema,* Bresson called his 1966 movie *Au Hasard Balthazar* "the freest film that I have made, the one in which I have put the most of myself."[16] Bresson's most difficult and acclaimed film offers a brutal, depressing, two-hour snapshot of a donkey's hard-knock life—not an animated donkey, not a talking donkey, but a plain old beat down dirty mule. "We see him taken from his mother by spirited children seeking a playmate. They baptize him—complete with a ritual of water and the sign of the cross—and name him after one of the three wise men. From there, Balthazar's life becomes one of drudgery and mindless abuse at the hands of grown-ups who know no better."[17] Bresson forces the audience to muster all the empathy possible for a lowly ass. After enduring countless beatings and abuse, Balthazar is shot in a careless accident. He wanders into the hills to die, the ass lying down with the lambs. Audiences wept at this transcendent moment, moved by the portrayal of suffering and the beauty of lying down after a lifetime of affliction. Famed critic Andrew Sarris claimed, "No film I have ever seen has come so close to convulsing my entire being. . . . In such moments, Bresson's Christian spirituality finds its most earthy, layered and life-giving expression. . . . 'Grace,' a mute thanks offered by the very act of living and accepting hardship as part of the gift of life, has never been dramatized more lucidly, or more movingly, than it is here, by Bresson or anybody."[18] Yet how many people of faith have ever watched or even heard of Bresson or *Balthazar?* What makes these transcendent films so difficult to watch? They are rigorously, doggedly sparse art created in an era of abundance.

The Trouble with Schrader

> I don't think it's very useful to open wide the door for young artists;
> the ones who break down the door are much more interesting.
>
> Paul Schrader

Having completed his research, Schrader welcomed the chance to test his theories, bringing sparse means to the physical, tangible, abundant medium of movies. Schrader noted that throughout history most art forms shifted from a religious purpose to a capitalistic enterprise, from the sacred to the profane. Motion pictures, born from a fusion of technology and the bottom line, offer the opposite, a chance to move from the profane to the sacred. Schrader's sparse, dry style pushed Maritain's theories to their logical extreme. But Schrader's screenplays for *The Yakuza, Rolling Thunder,* and *The Mosquito Coast* and his direction of *Blue Collar, Hardcore,* and *Mishima* received the same reaction as did his idols'—critical kudos and audience indifference. Only Schrader's slick reimagining of Bresson's *Pickpocket, American Gigolo,* broke through as a rare profitable venture.

The artistic success and financial frustrations of Paul Schrader's career provide some interesting parallels to his cinematic heroes. What kept audiences away? The first stumbling block involves content. Schrader goes everywhere and shows everything. He explores the truth within our ugly nooks, making R-rated films for the R-rated world he inhabits. Perhaps his strict religious upbringing ensured a lifetime fascination with and revulsion toward sin. His most blatantly "Calvinist" film, *Hardcore,* drags a father, Jake Van Dorn, from the Dutch "Reformation" Church in Grand Rapids to Los Angeles in search of his prodigal daughter. Van Dorn's search leads to the sleazy porn industry, where he poses as a producer to try to locate his lost child. Over time, the "heroic" father is revealed as a cold, brittle man whose emphasis on beliefs over practices drove his loved ones away. Schrader reveals the emptiness of law versus love, yet many missed this sermon because of its seamy subject matter.

Schrader also tackles plenty of uncomfortable "nonreligious" topics bathed in ambiguity. Who else would try to make sense of Patty Hearst? Would anyone want to see a film about her kidnapping, brainwashing, and transformation from millionairess to revolutionary? Schrader dared to reexamine the tangled legacies of the sixties during the height of the Reagan/Bush era, 1988. In 2002's *Auto Focus,* Schrader explores the secret sex addiction of *Hogan's Heroes'* star Bob Crane. You will not see a finer sermon on the power of temptation and the ability of sin to undermine a person's life and family. Yet the hardcore subject matter made it unsavory for most filmgoers. Schrader made the sparsest film possible about the most abundant of subjects, the lure of pornography.

Schrader's sparse art reached a critical and commercial peak only when he collaborated with Martin Scorsese. Schrader's Protestant, word-based upbringing met its perfect complement in Scorsese's violent, colorful, Roman Catholic imagery. Their 1976 Cannes Film Festival award winner, *Taxi Driver,* became a pop cultural landmark. Calvin College professor Roy Anker observed, "American movie audiences hadn't ever seen anything like *Taxi Driver,* an urban gothic version of Dostoevsky's underground man, a creature full of the malaise of utter disconnect—hungry, furious and nowhere to bring it."[19] Schrader and Scorsese mined the same veins in acclaimed films such as *Raging Bull, The Last Temptation of Christ,* and *Bringing Out the Dead.* Critics praise Schrader's tough, uncompromising, soul-searching protagonists who are riddled with doubt and searching for one moment of light. They celebrate Scorsese's haunting images and redemptive themes.

Yet large numbers of Jesus' followers chose to ignore or protest these violent but transcendent pictures. "Many church people, it's reasonable to assume, have never seen even a single one of his films, even though his insistent preoccupation is with how we understand personal evil and the possibility and shape of grace."[20] Schrader's recent films have reached a profound level of artistic achievement accompanied by a near total abandonment of audiences. *Mishima, Light Sleeper, Affliction,* and *Auto Focus* are tough, hard, honest explorations of human pain and a search for meaning. Ian Birney, the executive director of the Los Angeles County Museum of Art's film program singles out Schrader: "I can't think of any other filmmaker who survived the '70s with his vision intact. There's a level of stylistic consistency in his films that is rare in American movies."[21] He stands out as the most accomplished Protestant filmmaker, equal to the Catholic cinematic "saints."

So why don't audiences, particularly those who share his Protestant/Calvinist roots, patronize his films? Schrader reflects, "Both critics and viewers are pack animals and if my film doesn't fit into the pack mentality that given month, it takes a while for them to sort it out."[22] He observes that in the nineties "existentialism was replaced by irony."[23] He had all the wrong issues for his era—just like his heroes Dreyer, Bresson, and Ozu. In 1998, he lamented, "We're in a particularly fallow period. Audiences regard the arts as essentially trivial and decorative. When audiences don't demand much from artists, that doesn't mean they quit working. It means they start talking to themselves."[24]

The New Rules

A film is the world in an hour and a half.

Jean-Luc Godard

In March 1995, director Lars von Trier got together with a fellow Danish filmmaker, Thomas Vinterberg, and drew up the "Dogme 95 Vow of Chastity."[25]

It served as his artistic canon, a rigid religion to sharpen his creative life. Von Trier had already demonstrated a profound technical virtuosity. In his early films, such as *The Element of Crime* and *Zentropa,* von Trier employed every trick available since the birth of cinema: special effects, back-screen projections, colorization, dissolves, and fades. The results were impressive and off-putting, admirable but empty. But then von Trier experienced a psychic crisis when his mother revealed that the man who had raised him wasn't his biological father. Von Trier rejected his free-form, hippie-atheist upbringing and converted to Catholicism. He resolved to destroy the stylish artifice that had dominated his early work. "The idea for the Dogme film aesthetic emerged from a desire to submit to the authority and rules he did not have as a child."[26] Vinterberg recalls, "The very strict and serious manifesto was actually written in only 25 minutes and under continuous bursts of merry laughter."[27] "It was easy. We asked ourselves what we most hated about film today, and then we drew up a list banning it all."[28] They swore to obey ten rules: only location shooting, no props, only natural sounds, only handheld cameras, no special lighting, no optical work or filters, no superficial action (such as murders), only current time and space, no genre movies, and no credit to the director. Von Trier and Vinterberg added, "Furthermore, I swear as a director to refrain from personal taste! I am no longer an artist."[29] They considered their back-to-basics movement a rescue operation to counter certain tendencies in film.

"Dogme 95" opposes the auteur concept, makeup, illusions, and dramaturgical predictability. "Dogme 95" desires to purge film so that once again "the inner lives of the characters justify the plot."[30] Von Trier and Vinterberg even offered a scene-by-scene "confession" to use when they fail to obey their commandments. After outlining his "transgressions" in his 1998 film *The Celebration,* Vinterberg signed his confession with the words "pleading for absolution." Are von Trier and Vinterberg poking fun at religion, creating a smart publicity stunt to promote their own art, or are they rediscovering something significant about cinema's strengths? Their manifesto launched an artistic shock wave similar in scope to the reformation Martin Luther unknowingly unleashed when he posted his Ninety-five Theses on the door of the Wittenberg Castle Church.

Von Trier's 1995 *Breaking the Waves* served as the proto-Dogme film. It's about Bess, a simple, innocent woman who suffers through the paralyzing work injury of her beloved husband, Jan. In marrying "an outsider," Bess faces expulsion from the strict religious community she grew up in. Her childlike prayers include the deep, foreboding voice of God under which she was raised. Yet she challenges the church authorities with statements such as, "You can't love a work, but you can love another person." She wonders why religious people would banish bells from their house of worship. She debases herself in twisted acts of obedience and self-sacrifice designed to save her ailing husband—prostitution as penance. The taunts that come from her religious community echo the behavior of the Pharisees and the Romans and the mob that killed Jesus.

Bess's choices can be seen as crazy or Christlike. Yet the rampant nudity, cruelty, and persecution populating the film give viewers striving for moral perfection plenty to avoid. Surely Jesus' sacrificial love was never so sexual. The questions of her sanity demonstrate that Bess walks more in the footsteps of Joan of Arc than of Jesus. She is a woman who dares to speak in church, to challenge the prevailing masculine wisdom. For that, she is shunned, persecuted, "put on trial." Yet von Trier makes his verdict of Bess's sainthood and sanity abundantly clear. He breaks his own rules to use a special effect in his final shot, concluding the film with an absurd affirmation of faith that dares viewers to believe in heavenly bells and a God who loves his foolish followers.

At the movie's Cannes Film Festival premiere, von Trier wore an old tuxedo, previously owned by his idol, famed Danish director Carl Theodor Dreyer. Von Trier's film celebrates and updates the suffering sainthood Dreyer depicted in 1928's silent classic *The Passion of Joan of Arc*. The "new" Dogme consciously adopts the austere, transcendental style that Dreyer perfected (and Schrader identified) years earlier. Von Trier recalls, "I wanted to do a film with a religious motif, a film about miracles. At the same time, I wanted to do a completely naturalistic film."[31] Von Trier's intense close-ups of Bess force the viewer to enter into her mind and spirit. For those who endured the shaky cinematography and "suffered with" Bess, the results were sublime. *Breaking the Waves* won the Cannes Film Festival's highest prize, Europe's most prestigious cinematic honor. Catholic priest Andrew Greeley called it "a fable, a parable of grace superabundant, of a loving God who stands by us always, just as he promised Bess He [*sic*] would do."[32] Von Trier observed a strict Dogme in an effort to remember what drew him to filmmaking, to rediscover his own humanity and feeling.

He also created a slew of "disciples." Subsequent, officially sanctioned Dogme films include *Mifune, The King Is Alive, Lovers, Julien Donkey-Boy,* and *Italian for Beginners.*[33] As with most transcendental films, not a single box office champ resulted. But the seeds of experimentation and freedom emanating from such an affordable means of expression are only starting to grow. Notable films influenced by Dogme include Mike Figgis's *Time Code,* Wim Wenders's *Buena Vista Social Club,* and Richard Linklater's *Waking Life.* Acclaimed directors such as Allison Anders, Gus Van Zant, and Miguel Arteta welcomed the speed and economy of digital video. Director Steven Soderbergh adapted the handheld immediacy of the Dogme style to add dramatic realism to his Academy Award–winning study of the worldwide drug trade, *Traffic.*

Von Trier put the capstone on his accidental revolution with 2000's *Dancer in the Dark.* Once again, the subject is sainthood and suffering. Von Trier contrasts the simplest, most mundane melodramatic plot with the most joyous, cinematic musical sequences in forty years. The sparseness of the main character's everyday existence finds relief only in her abundant imagination. Von Trier breaks his own rules, employing hundreds of cameras in carefully choreographed, creative dance numbers. Yet the final a cappella song moves audiences the most.

Dancer in the Dark is a miracle, the rare film that gives viewers every reason not to care yet still manages to evoke a profoundly humane catharsis. Jaded, cynical filmgoers are forewarned: Von Trier will make you weep.

An Unexplainable Phenomenon

> The greatest achievement is that you come out of the theatre, not dull and depressed the way you feel after movies that insult your intelligence, but elated—restored to that youthful ardor where all hopes are raised at once.
>
> Pauline Kael[34]

Dogme's simplicity and ideals inspired a group of film students at the University of Central Florida. They created the most unlikely, unanticipated, unexplainable phenomena of 1999: *The Blair Witch Project*. Bloody, self-referential, overabundant horror films such as *Scream* had reached their apotheosis. What could truly scare jaded audiences overwhelmed by too many sensations? *The Blair Witch Project* used sparse means to rediscover very human fears. No special effects were needed to create suspense. The no-budget filmmakers used common experiences of isolation, the woods, spooky sounds, and the frightening power of viewers' imaginations. The video documentary shattered all previous records for profits versus costs, generating over one hundred million dollars on a thirty-five-thousand-dollar investment. Surely, such absurd numbers would generate a rash of imitations.

So why didn't Hollywood crank out a series of knockoffs? Screenwriter William Goldman coined a term that explains the studios' take on *Blair Witch*: "nonrecurring phenomena." "What this means, of course, is this: It was a freak, a fluke, a once-in-a-lifetime occurrence. The deeper and more important meaning is this: I don't have to think about it."[35] The box office failure of *Blair Witch 2: Book of Shadows* put executives at ease; crisis over. But why would a cheap, amateur video shot by three actors in the woods without a director on set threaten Hollywood? It undercuts the studios' monopoly on production, distribution, and audiences. If anybody with a camera, three actors, and free time can make a film, why do we need Hollywood?

Perhaps *The Blair Witch Project*'s Sundance Film Festival pedigree means truly independent film has finally arrived. Longtime indie guru John Pierson says, "It's not an independent film phenomenon. What you really have is a convergence of old and new media."[36] Many experts eventually linked the success of *Blair Witch* to a clever web site containing creepy misinformation. But the new media that actually built *Blair Witch* is much more obvious and elemental. It represents the blooming of digital video, the triumph of no-budget filmmaking. To the next generation of filmmakers, *Blair Witch* was much more than a gold rush. It was a manifesto, Hollywood's worst fear, the beginning of a visual tidal wave.

Moviemaking has never been easier, cheaper, or more democratic. The co-chairman of Jersey Films, Stacey Sher, declares, "Directors are the rock stars of the end of this century. You can see the burst of new energy everywhere. Kids now think they can pick up a camera and express themselves in the same way they used to pick up a guitar and start a band."[37] Digital cameras and video mean that the prohibitive cost of Kodak film has vanished. The post-production revolution introduced by Avid technology and Apple's Final Cut Pro software allows anyone with a computer to edit at home. The rise of the Internet created direct distribution channels completely outside the Hollywood system. In an age in which anyone can afford to make a movie, the sheer volume of moving images may become overwhelming. Tomorrow's technology will change the way we watch movies. By shooting *Star Wars: Episode II* exclusively with digital cameras, George Lucas slowly forced theaters to accept digital projection. But will new technology change the kinds of movies we watch?

The Year That Changed Movies

Art is born and takes hold wherever there is a timeless and insatiable longing for the spiritual, for the ideal: that longing which draws people to art.

Andrei Tarkovsky, *Sculpting in Time*[38]

Despite all the press releases touting record box office receipts and technological breakthroughs, Hollywood studios have been struggling. Strong sales of DVDs featuring previously released movies long since paid for have created an unexpected financial buffer for the film business. But a dearth of ideas caused executives to raid their own vaults in search of a hit. Marginal, forgotten television shows such as *Car 54, Where Are You?*; *Sergeant Bilko*; and *The Mod Squad* became embarrassing feature films. Occasional hits such as *The Brady Bunch Movie* and *Charlie's Angels* convinced studio chiefs to resurrect *The Beverly Hillbillies* and *Scooby Doo*. Measuring box office success in dollars rather than tickets sold allows studios to announce record-breaking feats almost weekly. Yet an adjusted comparison of audience size for *Gone with the Wind* and *Titanic* would show how significantly moviegoing has declined.

During Hollywood's golden era of the 1930s and 1940s, eighty to ninety million Americans went to the movies *every week*. Now, Hollywood celebrates one hundred million dollars in total receipts on a given weekend. At almost ten dollars per ticket, that's just ten million weekend viewers. The rise of television, the Internet, and sports has cut into movie theatre attendance. But mostly, a steady diet of loud, moronic, fairly predictable fare has kept all but the youngest moviegoers away. Behind the hype, movie studios are running scared.

Yet *Entertainment Weekly* called 1999 "The Year That Changed Movies." In a splashy cover story, *EW* announced, "You can stop waiting for the future of movies. It's already here. Someday, 1999 will be etched on a microchip as the first real year of 21st-century filmmaking. The year when the old, boring rules about cinema started to crumble."[39] The *Los Angeles Times* agreed, calling directors Paul Thomas Anderson, Spike Jonze, M. Night Shyamalan, and Andy and Larry Wachowski "The New New Wave." In the same article, the president of Artisan Films, Bill Block, noted, "These young directors have a fascinating, new kind of browser mentality. They've grown up immersed in MTV and Nintendo and PlayStation, and it's the software that's influencing the sensibility. Most of these films have bypassed the old studio-executive character arc rules."[40] Films from 1999 presented as exciting evidence of the future of film included *The Matrix, Fight Club, The Blair Witch Project, Being John Malkovich, The Limey, Go, Run Lola Run, American Beauty, The Sixth Sense, Dogma,* and *Magnolia.*

Jeff Gordiner discusses what makes these films and their maverick directors so unique and fearless. "Time doesn't move in a straight line. . . . There's no such thing as death, . . . and why get hung up on logic?"[41] That's a virtual definition of our post-rational, post-literal society. A sixteen-year-old high school student wrote:

> *Fight Club* marks a reinvention of cinema as we know it: What will surely be seen as one of history's most insensitively violent pictures is, in fact, violent for the sake of reinventing an entire storytelling medium. By breaking conventions, by trampling "the norm," the film not only grabs the audience's attention but also forces it to observe what will soon be the future of movies: work that is nonlinear, multi-layered, shockingly visual and moving at the speed of thought.[42]

For all its prescience, *Entertainment Weekly* missed one obvious common bond linking these films: their edgy exploration of ultimate questions. Each of these movies reveals a belief in the transcendent, in unexplainable phenomena, in the random, the unknown, the wholly Other. "1999: The Year That Changed Movies" was the most spiritually charged era in Hollywood history.

Some may attribute the phenomenon to turn-of-the-millennium fever. Thrillers such as *End of Days* and *The Omega Code* exploited Y2K worries. But that doesn't explain other films from 1999 drenched in unprecedented theological questioning: *The Third Miracle; Stigmata; The Green Mile; Jesus' Son; The Straight Story; The Big Kahuna; Keeping the Faith; The End of the Affair; Dracula 2000; Bringing Out the Dead; South Park: Bigger, Longer, and Uncut; Stir of Echoes;* and the extraordinarily sublime Japanese film *After Life.* The philosophical questions have continued since then, from wrestling with evil in *Lost Souls,*

Bedazzled, Little Nicky, Harry Potter, Frailty, and *The Body* to exploring faith in *O Brother, Where Art Thou? A Walk to Remember, Moulin Rouge, Waking Life, Changing Lanes, We Were Soldiers, Signs, Levity, The Count of Monte Cristo,* and *The Lord of the Rings.* Why do we now have so many spiritually themed films? Perhaps the breakdown of old rules, whether in society or in Hollywood, causes profound discomfort. When the system no longer works, artists step into the gap as critics, as questioners, and as theologians. Let's examine the spiritual undercurrents of six key films from 1999: *The Matrix, American Beauty, Fight Club, Magnolia, Dogma,* and *Run Lola Run.*

A Matrix of Meanings

> To shoot a film is to organize an entire universe.
>
> Ingmar Bergman

Seeing is no longer believing. It's just one of five senses available to the postmodern consumer in a virtual universe. *The Matrix* represents Generation X's first blockbuster franchise, an answer to Spielberg and Lucas, *Indiana Jones* and *Star Wars.* Two films directed by Australians anticipated the themes and issues of *The Matrix.* Alex Proyas's *Dark City* and Peter Weir's *Truman Show* questioned our limited perception of reality yet inspired far less enthusiasm and obsession from young audiences. That's because *how The Matrix* communicates says more than *what* it communicates. Twenty-something filmmakers Larry and Andy Wachowski fused the most stylish elements of global pop culture, particularly Japanese anime, Hong Kong chop-socky films, and cyberpunk comic books, into one potent, postmodern package.[43] The kung fu sequences, the computer-created effects, the dark visuals, and the spooky metallic music all contribute to the central question, What is real?

The first part of a trilogy, *The Matrix* was submitted to intense theological scrutiny. While some may have dismissed the characters' lofty names—Morpheus, Cypher, and Neo—as comic book posturing, filmgoers decoded them as much more. In *Entertainment Weekly's* article "Matrix Mania," Lori L. Tharps broke down the religious symbolism packed into the film.[44] She linked Keanu Reeves's character, Neo, to an anagram for one, as in "the One." Tharps pointed out the similarities between Christ the Messiah, who delivers humanity from sin, and Neo the One, who leads humankind out of bondage to computers. *The Matrix* and the Bible are both driven by the search for a savior, the fulfillment of prophecy. Jesus had John the Baptist; Neo has the Oracle. Tharps also connected Zion from the Book of Revelation to *The Matrix's* Zion, the city where humans gather following the destruction of the earth. The association between Morpheus's ship, *Nebuchadnezzar,* and the Babylonian king obsessed with his dreams seems apt. Tharps connected Judas's act of selling out Jesus for thirty pieces of silver to Cypher's (perhaps Lu-cipher's) betrayal of Morpheus for a steak dinner. And do not overlook Neo's love for Trinity, comparable to Christ's relationship with the Holy Spirit.[45]

Several critics connected the style of *The Matrix* with the killings at Columbine High School. The similar fashion choices of Columbine's trench coat mafia and *The Matrix's* Neo and Trinity stand out as a spooky coincidence. While most social critics ultimately identified Leonardo DiCaprio's fantasy school shooting in *The Basketball Diaries* as the closest role model for the shooters at Columbine, *The Matrix* clearly glamorizes violence and the use of guns to resolve most problems. One could argue that Neo must learn a new way of seeing to defeat the machines, but he also employs a well-stocked arsenal to implement his vision. The use of guns to solve problems has a hallowed place in Hollywood cinematic history.

Yet the Christian faith was also born via violence. The blood associated with Jesus' death serves as a symbol of hope in the Christian community. The cool, stylized violence in *The Matrix* connects with classic Christian notions about blood being spilled en route to redemption. But Jesus didn't commit violence; he suffered and died under it. Jesus wrestled with forces as shifty as Agent Smith, but he didn't use guns or karate kicks to save humankind. He saved his most powerful moves for Easter morning, resurrection day.

Are parallels between Christian theology and *The Matrix's* mythology overstated? While Christians may see the choice between the red pill and the blue as self-deception versus abundant life in Christ, can't others claim *The Matrix* as their story as well? Wouldn't acolytes of Joseph Campbell find archetypes that tie all humanity together? Gnostics could affirm their distrust and disdain for the physical—only the spiritualized is real. The Wachowski brothers suggest that connections between Buddhism and mathematics make up the bulk of *The Matrix's* philosophy. In an online interview, the reclusive Wachowskis revealed, "*The Matrix* was an idea that I believe philosophy and religion and mathematics all try to answer. Which is, a reconciling between a natural world and another world that is perceived by our intellect."[46] In a post-rational, post-literal, post-human culture, *The Matrix* offers a new mythology, a spiritual shaping story that gives life meaning. Irrespective of one's theology, the lessons to be drawn from *The Matrix* reside in substance *and* style. It is critique of computers created on computers. It uses virtual technologies to tell us that what we see is not always true. *The Matrix* asks viewers to look beyond the surface, to distrust what they've been bought and sold, taught and told. *The Matrix* dares viewers to adopt Neo's enlightened perception. To ensure our future survival, we all must learn to "look closer."

Ugly Beauty

The more opinions you have, the less you see.

Wim Wenders

How appropriate that the poster for *American Beauty* invited audiences to "look closer." In a classic sexual tease, the naked, nubile stomach on the poster appeals first to the voyeur, searching for something illicit. The film pulls Baby Boomer fathers, raised on sexual liberation, back to their carefree, halcyon days of free love. Lester Burnham masturbates in the shower, turned on by his daughter's friend, a high school cheerleader. The rose petals fluttering about the story always come back to the innocence and purity of that cheerleader, the "American beauty" of the title. Oscar-winning screenwriter Alan Ball purposely provoked audiences, saying, "A Puritan would look at his visions of Angela and go, 'Oh, that's disgusting, a middle-aged man lusting after a young girl like that.' I look at that and I go, 'You know, here's a man who hasn't felt anything for years, and all of a sudden he's feeling something. That's not disgusting.' His choice not to follow through with it redeems him, because she's not really the goal, she's the knock on the door. And I didn't even know that myself when I wrote the first draft of the script."[47]

"Look closer" also suggests peering behind the "perfect" families populating suburban America. The white picket fence surrounding the Burnham household disguises the dissatisfaction rumbling between husband and wife, parents and child. Certainly, next-door neighbor Ricky Fitts suffers in silence like his mute mother, the threat of violence from his military father, Colonel Frank Fitts, creating an air of dread. Ball recalls, "I grew up in a household with a somewhat troubled father figure and somewhat shut-down mother figure, so Ricky's household certainly resembles mine in ways."[48]

But what ultimately lifts *American Beauty* beyond the familiar suburban critique is Ricky Fitts's ability to "look closer." While walking home from school, Ricky and Jane are passed by a funeral procession. Ricky says, "When you see something like that, it's like God is looking right at you, and if you're real careful, you can look right back." Jane asks, "What do you see?" Ricky responds simply, "Beauty." For practical, financial reasons, the producers wanted to cut the scene. Ball insisted that it's one of the most important scenes in the movie. "If one line . . . is the heart and soul of this movie, that is the line."[49]

Ricky celebrates the fragile beauty in the world, a beauty that makes him cry at the poignancy around him. His videotaping habit has enabled him to develop eyes to see beyond the horror of his family life. He shows Jane the most beautiful thing he has ever captured on tape. The random freedom found in a plastic bag blown by the wind serves as reason enough to carry on. If one looks closer, one will see past the horror of Lester Burnham's murder. When Ricky bends over the kitchen murder scene and smiles, it is not the perverse smile of a video opportunist. This isn't exploitation. No, legendary cinematographer Conrad Hall lights the scene so that Lester's blood is practically luminescent. The filmmakers create a beautiful shot of a dead man to challenge viewers to "look closer," to adopt Ricky's worldview. In a post-traumatic culture, he can find beauty amid an abusive father, closeted homosexuality, and a brutal murder.

American Beauty did not win best picture because it was a sharp satire. In fact, director Sam Mendes actually trimmed the satirical bite of Ball's original screenplay. Mendes made *American Beauty* a meditation on truth, beauty, and transcendence. Despite the self-destructive events of Waco and Oklahoma City, a new generation dares to find "beauty" amid such American tragedy.

Piercing Truths

It's not hard to make decisions when you know what your values are.

Roy Disney

Fight Club also dares to comment on the self-immolation fueling American males. Following the killings at Columbine, people kept asking why two affluent suburban kids would attempt to blow up their school. What created such anger among (primarily) white, male outsiders? In typically vexing postmodern fashion, *Fight Club* wrapped the most potent answers in the most volatile, violent package possible. Far too many critics failed to "look closer." *Fight Club* dared to take on the near impossible task of being a broad, mass-marketed, movie star driven critique of commercial culture. How do you tell a commodified, sedated, therapeutic culture that the things you own end up owning you? Evidently, in something other than a dark, dank, violent, stylish, in-your-face, misunderstood movie.

Who directed this impossibly smart, savage rant against all things commercial? David Fincher created the most abundant groundbreaking music videos and advertising spots of the past decade. In *Fight Club,* he tries to destroy the world he created. He admits, "I'm extremely cynical about commercials and about selling things and about the narcissistic ideals of what we're supposed to be. I guess in my heart I was hoping people are too smart to fall for that stuff."[50] For a cynic, Fincher exhibits lots of faith.

The producers, studio, and critics who supported *Fight Club* never wavered in their devotion to the film, which was perhaps the most important movie in Hollywood's most spiritual year. Critic Gavin Smith calls it "the first film of the next century. . . . An anti-New Age satire of both the dehumanizing effects of corporate/consumer culture and the absurd excesses of the men's movement."[51] How ironic that a movie that dares to identify the causes of Columbine gets critiqued and picketed as an example of the exploitative, violent films that caused Columbine. What appropriate irony for a film drenched in postmodern irony. *Fight Club* is the emerging generation's most trenchant critique of the false bill of goods and empty bromides handed down by their forebears. One of the sharpest observers of consumer culture, Bret Easton Ellis, declared that "*Fight Club* rages against the hypocrisy of a society that continually promises us the impossible: fame, beauty, wealth, immortality, life without pain."[52]

The film follows the misadventures of Jack, an upwardly mobile executive with a classy, furnished-by-Ikea lifestyle. After work, Jack wanders through a variety of twelve step groups, hoping that a hug a day will keep his aching inner child at bay—until he meets Tyler Durden, a dark and mysterious stranger oozing an unchecked masculine id. Tyler calls Jack's self-improvement efforts "masturbation" and obliterates a series of Jack's sacred truths: "You are not your job, you are not your khakis, you are not what you have in your bank account." When shopping serves as the new hunting and gathering, what's a testosterone-riddled man-child to do? Punch, prod, and pierce oneself in an act of defiance. "I bleed, therefore I am" serves as *Fight Club*'s rallying cry. And the legions of students with earrings, tattoos, and body modifications confirm author Chuck Palahniuk's vision. Screenwriter Jim Uhls says that the novel is "about numbness and alienation and finding self-empowerment through drastic means."[53] There isn't a better summation of the motivations behind the Columbine killings.

Unfortunately, most culture critics missed the film's desperate cry for meaning. The acid Tyler pours on Jack's hand in *Fight Club* speaks volumes about young people's hidden pain. Tyler challenges Jack to move past therapy, to be in the moment, to truly live. Jack's chemical burn accompanies the realization that "our fathers were our models for God. If our fathers bailed, what does that tell you about God? . . . In all probability, he hates you. We're God's unwanted children, so be it."[54] What a bald, defiant appeal for love, for meaning, for divine intervention. Yet the *Los Angeles Times* thought the movie was full of "whiny, infantile philosophizing and bone-crunching violence."[55] The *Wall Street Journal* called it "an appalling excursion into social satire . . . a theater of cruelty."[56] Roger Ebert saw "some of the most brutal, unremitting, nonstop violence ever filmed."[57]

Kids got it confused too. The Utah governor's son was arrested for staging a fight club in a Mormon Church gym. Many failed to recognize the film's critique of a community bound together by rage and anarchy. Yet to attack the film with a shoot-the-messenger mentality only reinforces the frustration. The fact that Dylan Klebold and Eric Harris blamed their marginalization on Christian America only underscores the need to understand *Fight Club* within the church. High school student David Green called *Fight Club* "the voice of a new generation: It is a subversive, cerebral rush, and it must be viewed with open eyes."[58]

So upon closer inspection, what does *Fight Club* reveal? The reasons behind an earring, a tattoo, or a pierced tongue are often more than a rebellious pose or an act of defiance. To those tired of being anesthetized by shopping, piercing can serve as a wake-up call. Suffering, even for a short time, becomes a means of feeling, an occasion for caring. In his book *Virtual Faith,* Tom Beaudoin finds spiritual significance behind body modification. It serves as a rite of passage, a sacred ritual, a visual reminder, and a signpost along the journey.[59] In Genesis 28, Jacob dreams of a stairway to heaven. The next morning, to commemorate the vision, Jacob erects a pillar, pours oil over it, and renames the place Bethel. In Genesis 32, Jacob wrestles with God in the form of an angel. He receives a new name and a wrenched hip, a permanent reminder of his divine wrestling match. When people mark their bodies, pierce their skin, they may be trying to commemorate God's movement. In the movie *Memento,* tattoos are the primary means of remembering. Piercing can establish spiritual signposts, constant reminders of where we've been, what we've endured, and God's presence through it all.

Fight Club is probably the most violent, sadistic, negative, pro-life movie ever. In an early cut of the film, Jack's desperate girlfriend, Marla, proclaims her love by announcing, "I want to have your abortion." This sounds like the height of nihilism. Yet for a generation forged in the suicide of its primary poet, Kurt Cobain, affirmations of faith start in the pit of hopelessness. Only after self-annihilation gets a hearing can Jack make a conscious choice to live. His double-mindedness ends when he lets the promise of love slip in. Jack and Marla look for beauty amid the collapse of fallen financial centers. We've gone to that dark space as a society, forced to ask "Why?" after 9/11. Viewers must look closer at the desperate acts of desperate men as a desperate cry for help, a plea for life, for meaning, for community, for significance within a culture that has stripped them of God-given humanity. Tyler Durden delivers a speech that echoes the angry words of Ezekiel, Jeremiah, and Isaiah, prophets in exile.

> I see in Fight Club the strongest and smartest men who've ever lived. I see all this potential. And I see squandering. . . . An entire generation is pumping gas, waiting tables, slaves with white collars. Advertising has us chasing cars and clothes, working jobs we hate so we can buy . . . [stuff] we don't need. We're the middle children of history, men. No purpose or place. We have no Great War, no Great Depression. Our Great War's a spiritual war. Our Great Depression is our lives. We've all been raised on television to believe that one day we'd all be millionaires and movie gods and rock stars. But we won't. We're slowly learning that fact. And we're very, very pissed off.[60]

That's a shocking sermon kids are desperate to hear. In a society created by, for, and about "selling soap," *Fight Club* offers a bracing cry for something much more spiritual.

Turning Over a New (Magnolia) Leaf

The creative spirit and negative capability of William Shakespeare stirs in the sprawling, ambitious work of young Paul Thomas Anderson. He demonstrates Shakespeare's ability to create characters of all ages and both genders, drawing on wisdom far beyond his years. In *Magnolia,* the complex, interlocking leaves of a magnolia blossom serve as an apt metaphor for a film that attempts to juggle and reconcile twelve major characters. Anderson builds on the earlier cinematic quilts created by director Robert Altman. Altman's satirical 1975 film, *Nashville,* managed to weave twenty-four characters into one probing portrait of America. As Altman dissected the capital of country music, Anderson chronicles life in the capital of entertainment, Los Angeles. But Anderson delves into life on the other side of the Hollywood scene, in the San Fernando Valley, specifically along Magnolia Boulevard. Instead of the high-profile movie moguls populating Malibu, Anderson tracks an anonymous game show mogul dying in Sherman Oaks. He chronicles the fringes of the entertainment business, the stories that continue after the cameras stop rolling. Drawing on his own childhood, being raised by a divorced and frustrated actor, Anderson creates remarkably profound character studies.

What happens to the instant celebrities who rise and fall on quiz shows? In *Magnolia,* game show host Jimmy Gator deals with a shattered offscreen life. While he battles cancer, his daughter, Claudia, struggles with addiction. Former quiz kid Donnie Smith, who fails to forge a "second act," to follow his early genius with something substantive, serves as a foreboding precursor to another budding quiz kid, Stanley. Stanley pees in his pants under the show's lights, crippled by pressure from his father to succeed. Behind the scenes, the producer of the show, Earl Partridge, lies dying. His trophy wife, Linda, seeks emotional relief at a nearby drugstore. Earl's estranged son has reinvented himself as a cocky motivational speaker, Frank T. J. Mackey. Tom Cruise shines as this slick media manipulator, hiding behind his new persona. Only those outside show business provide any sense of grounding and health. Earl's live-in nurse, Phil Parma, pursues Mackey, hoping to create a deathbed, father-son reconciliation. And a decent, hard-working, Christian police officer, Jim Kurring, tries to talk some sense into Claudia, the addict, and Donnie Smith, the crushed child star.

The sins of the father discussed in Exodus 20 find ample expression in the characters' cycles of suffering. The wages of sin appear to be profanity, pill popping, misogyny, robbery, and suicide. Critics admired Anderson's attention to psychological realism: "About an hour and a half in, the movie achieves a veritable ecstasy of cross cutting. . . . *Magnolia* becomes a swirling, barely controlled fantasia of juxtaposed emotional predicaments."[61] The fatalism contained in the notion "We might be through with the past, but the past isn't through with us" suggests that things will get even darker.

So what makes (some) viewers stumble during the second half? Anderson's anything-goes worldview. When his characters reach their bleakest moments, they don't act "normal"—they break into song. Aimee Mann's poignant single "Wise Up" ends with the potentially stark conclusion, "Just give up." In the face of endless suffering under familial sin, why go on living? Anderson pushes his characters (and the audience) to the brink of emotional collapse before offering a seemingly random ending. He explores the Old Testament theme of sins handed down from fathers to sons with an Old Testament–style plague. But first he drops plenty of visual hints that something big and biblical is coming. The numbers eight and two pop up on billboards, on a hanged man's chest, in a weather forecast (82 percent humidity), in apartment and mug shot numbers, in a posted meeting time (8:20 P.M.), in cards dealt in a blackjack hand, and even in the shape of a long electrical cord.[62] Anderson completes his repeated planting of Exodus 8:2 with an actual, biblical-scale rain of frogs. Viewers expecting a logical ending to a finely nuanced, psychological film are blasted by a deus ex machina. Anderson gives rationalists a twist so big, so unexpected, and so unexplainable that they are forced to "lose their mind."

Yet for postmodern filmgoers, a plague of frogs is perfectly apropos, a welcome relief, the last refuge. They're willing to endure three hours in hell for three minutes of grace. "Just give up" doesn't mean despair; it means letting go, renouncing self-control, surrendering to the possibility of divine intervention. For modernists, such a supernatural phenomenon is unconscionable. Anderson explains:

> I don't want to get too personal, but maybe there are certain moments in your life when things are so confused that someone can say to you, "It's raining frogs" and that makes sense. That somehow makes sense as a warning, that somehow makes sense as a sign. I started to understand why people turn to religion in times of trouble, and maybe my form of finding religion was reading about rains of frogs and realizing that makes sense to me somehow. And then of course to discover it in the Bible and the reference that it makes there just sort of verifies it, like, "Hey, I guess I'm on the right track."[63]

Magnolia is about finding the right track, connecting the dots between seemingly unconnected events. Anderson introduces his central thesis with a random prologue. In a dark drama, such random comedy appears inappropriate. Yet a postmodern mind-set easily reconciles the tragic and the comic as complementary sides of the same coin. Anderson admits, "I want to always go to the place where I'm going to write the saddest happy ending I possibly can. That's just the way that feels good to me."[64] So a missing gun falls from the sky. Stanley offers the painfully simple request, "Dad, you have to be nicer to me." A cop with Christian convictions sloshes across the squishy frogs to deliver a simple smile and a message of grace, of second chances, of new life. Certainly for Anderson, the chance of forgiveness for conniving criminals, for washed-up stars, for estranged families is as far-fetched as a rain of frogs—and just as possible.

Raging Angels

Bad taste is simply saying the truth before it should be said.

Mel Brooks

The most overtly spiritual film of 1999 is Kevin Smith's *Dogma*. It is a theological comic book stuffed with every random thought and ultimate question Smith could muster. It deals with race, abortion, gender, and evil in absurd ways. *Dogma* throws fallen angels into a theological stew, complete with gender bending, profanity, and a monster formed from excrement. Critics called it "extravagantly foulmouthed and excessively pious simultaneously."[65] Can such seeming incongruities be reconciled? Smith calls *Dogma* "the cumulative effect of religion, faith and spirituality, filtered through the pop cultural maze."[66]

The film's central questions arise in a parking garage as two fallen angels rage against God. "Why did God have to disturb paradise and upset the perfect harmony between angels and him? Why did God complicate everything with humans, particularly by giving them free will, a choice? Why would he give people another chance? Why not wipe humanity from the face of the earth? Why not start over?" As the angels take out their frustration and vengeance on God's behalf, the blood, the bodies, and for many, the laughs, pile up rapidly. The angels make a particularly violent stop at a Disney-like corporation that promotes Mooby, a cuddly singing character similar to the dreaded purple dinosaur Barney. After their killing spree, the angel Loki turns to alcohol for consolation. Bartleby lets his rage flow, taking out random victims. Where is God amid the carnage? In the hospital, on life support, listed as John Doe.

Smith stops the carnage when God appears (portrayed by pop star Alanis Morissette). Smith envisions a playful God wearing boxer shorts, stopping to smell the flowers, falling on her face from failed handstands. Bartleby faces divine judgment. God's expression hardens. Metatron, the literal voice of God, recommends that the crowd cover their ears. Bartleby nods in understanding, manages a half smile, and says, "Thank you." In a moment of power and beauty, Alanis opens her mouth and emits an overpowering sound that Smith's script describes as "a mixture of trumpets, whale-songs, fog-horns, and a sonic-boom." Bartleby's head explodes. God closes her mouth and walks away. This scene offers Smith's most complex portrait of God.

Some viewers interpret Bartleby's demise as judgment, a death sentence to eternal damnation. At the Academy of Motion Picture Arts and Sciences annual screenwriting lecture, Smith was asked to deconstruct the scene. "What happened to Bartleby?" Smith declined to answer, preferring to let the viewers' answers reflect their theological assumptions.[67] Why would Bartleby smile and say "Thank you" to eternal damnation? After kicking and screaming at God's grace throughout *Dogma,* Bartleby finally understands. He finally receives the forgiveness that humans so frivolously dismiss. He says "Thank you" to a God who offers a severe mercy—an end to his psychic suffering, a chance to return home, a fallen angel welcomed back into the fold. *Dogma* broke ground as an R-rated Christian tract. It also broke ground as a radical depiction of the fathomless limits of God's love.

Smith hoped the film would "raise questions, spark discussion and allow young people to speak about religion without being bedeviled by images of holy wars and pedophile priests."[68] Asked to describe the underlying theme of the movie, Smith quipped, "Church good, God better."[69] He considered *Dogma* "nothing more than a kick-back, two-hour commercial for Catholic belief. . . . This is a pro-faith movie. If one person walks out of the movie and goes back to the church, I'll have done my job—though that would make the person the most expensive convert ever."[70] When eight hundred fans crammed the Academy's theater to hear Smith talk about screenwriting, he called *Dogma* "a big . . . valentine to God, a way to pay back. I've always been a big fan of the Lord. What better way to honor God than to make a movie?"[71] He pointed to his unlikely success, reaching the Sundance Film Festival with his nearly no-budget, suburban New Jersey, black-and-white feature debut, *Clerks,* as a miracle. "What happened with *Clerks* and my career—there is no better proof that there's a God."[72]

So how was his irreverent attempt to move beyond a packaged "Buddy Christ" received by a church desperate to remain hip? It nearly incited a holy war. The Catholic League for Religious and Civil Rights denounced the film as offensive months before it was released. Catholic League spokesman Patrick Scully said, "The entire plot is one situation after another of making fun of the Catholic faith." He concluded this without seeing the film.[73] If he had caught the disclaimer that opens the film, "Remember even God has a sense of humor," perhaps the whole, ugly controversy could have been avoided. The original distributor, Disney-owned Miramax, grew nervous about a Christian protest similar to that waged against Universal Studios over Martin Scorsese's equally sincere *Last Temptation of Christ* in 1988. Miramax president, Harvey Weinstein, normally a courtier of controversy, sold *Dogma* to smaller, low-profile, Canadian distributor Lion's Gate.

Smith sought to understand the position of the average protestor. He actually joined protestors outside a theater in Eatontown, New Jersey. Smith declared, "I just wanted to find out what was on everyone's minds. These were people like my grandmother, who out of true feeling were there defending their faith."[74] By the end of the entire exhausting experience, Smith was discouraged to find that Christian brethren wrote "thousands of pieces of hate mail." He lamented, "I wouldn't want to go through it again. It will be another 24 years before I make another picture about religion."[75] His loyal fans wait with eager expectation.

The Power of Love

> If there's a way of saying "I love you" without saying it—that's film.
>
> Buster Keaton

Berlin seems like an unlikely setting for a meditation on the importance of prayer and the healing power of love. Yet the pulsating German film *Run Lola Run* demonstrates the spiritual possibilities arising in postmodernity. *Lola* is an ultra-abundant film cut at a breathless pace that traffics in ancient virtues. Although loaded with artifice, *Run Lola Run* was inspired by the gritty, back-to-basics style of Lars von Trier. Filmmaker Tom Tykwer calls *Lola* "my dogma film."[76] He juxtaposes the profound and the silly, placing quotations from poet T. S. Eliot alongside those of a famous German soccer coach. After asking life's most essential but unanswerable questions, Tykwer kicks things off with the most basic rules of soccer: "The ball is round; the game lasts ninety minutes." Yet *Lola* demonstrates that anything is possible within those parameters.

The plot seems straightforward. Lola's boyfriend, Mani, needs one hundred thousand marks in the next twenty minutes or he will face the wrath of gangsters. Lola races against the clock, running to get the money. She appeals to her banker father for assistance, but he's distracted by an affair at work. So Lola resorts to drastic means to save Mani. Her persistence demonstrates the lengths she will go to for love.

Viewers follow Lola through the same scenario three times, but the slightest variations in timing create radically different consequences. The bumps in Lola's path, from a rabid dog to a line of nuns, determine what information she gathers and what traps she avoids. As Dinah Washington sings on the soundtrack, "What a difference a day [or even a moment] makes." The changes in Lola's run have huge repercussions for Mani. In the first scenario, he resorts to armed robbery with horrific results. Like Lola, he's given a chance to start over, to learn from experience. The movie illustrates how connected we are, even in the most impersonal of urban settings.

The style of *Run Lola Run* is also the substance. Writer-director-composer Tykwer employs multiple formats to present his multifaceted story. He splices together video, animation, still photographs, and conventional 35mm film to advance his sneaky narrative. *Run Lola Run* pulses to a techno soundtrack, and the flow of the story mirrors the rising and falling energy of a rave. *Lola* also resembles a video game, with the reset button snapping the story back to the beginning just when it appears to be "game over." Spiral imagery recurs throughout, in a grocery store sign, winding stairs, a woman's hair bun, and a roulette wheel. The passionate color red beams from Lola's hair to the "chill out" scenes in which she and Mani ask life's most basic questions: "Do you love me? Will you remember me after I'm gone?" *Run Lola Run* "feels" random, but its style reveals incredibly intelligent design.

The film deals with the consequences of crime but suggests that death is not the end. Tykwer says, "You can beat time only in movies. In reality, we all know we're victims of time—it's going on, we can't stop it. Every second we come closer to our own death. But in the movies there's a miracle quality, the feeling that there is control of time. It's one of the basic elements why cinema for us is so magic. We beat time."[77] In the first two (failed) scenarios, Lola thinks of Mani as she runs, urging him to wait for her arrival, not to do anything rash. In her third attempt, a breathless Lola prays to an unnamed force, "Please . . . please . . . I'm waiting . . . I'm waiting" while she runs. She finds God's answer in a casino. Short on money, she depends on the kindness of a stranger to fund her high-stakes bet. The stuffy, upper-crust atmosphere of the casino echoes the formality of a high church, where Lola's dyed hair and tank top draw disapproving stares. Lola's bet is blessed by "chance," but her love for Mani manifests itself in a scream of sheer willpower. Lola's happy ending comes from a combination of running, praying, gambling, and screaming—the recipe for almost any enduring relationship.

Mani's breakthrough arises when he discovers that the blind can see. He learns to accept charity, to receive blessings he doesn't deserve. Yet he demonstrates how much he's learned to trust when he offers his gun to the homeless man who found the missing bag of money: The gift of love comes to us when we're ready to receive it. An encounter with grace should inspire us to extend grace (even in the odd form of a firearm!).

Lola's ultimate reward comes not from gambling but from connecting with a long-lost father. Disappointed throughout the film by her parents' indifference, Lola finds a moment of healing in the back of an ambulance. She extends a healing hand of love to a father she's never truly known. Love has the power to resurrect a faltering heart, to reconcile the most estranged families.

The movie's what-if possibilities are almost endless. Tykwer's mere entertainment withstands many close and conflicting readings. Those who consider postmodernity random and chaotic may fail to appreciate the film's deliberate structure. Tykwer tells one story three different ways. The ending cannot start at the beginning. It has logic, order, a progression rooted in experience. The movie is about what Lola learns along the journey while moving forward at dizzying speeds. It offers profound insight into how future audiences will enter into and appreciate the Bible.

Readers hoping to find a clear plot flowing through Scripture may be frustrated by the disconnected events and odd characters popping up every few chapters. But the Gospel of Matthew connects the disparate dots of the Old Testament, suggesting that the stories of Abraham, Ruth, and David culminate in the arrival of Jesus, the Messiah. *Run Lola Run* demonstrates how seemingly unrelated characters spread across Berlin are all united and touched by the sacrificial love of one heroine. The lessons Lola learns along the journey, about prayer, sacrifice, and seeing, prove almost as important as the destination. The Bible also offers an assortment of life lessons en route to God's overriding goal, the saving actions of Jesus Christ. Like the Bible, *Run Lola Run* stands as one story composed of many seemingly random stories or encounters. But these side trips, loaded with flawed but interesting characters, ultimately reveal how connected we are by the healing power of love.

The New Temptations

> The future of cinema no longer lies in its past.
>
> Wim Wenders

> The moving picture machine has become a preacher, and its sermons are most effective because they are addressed to the eye rather than to the ear.
>
> K. S. Hover, 1911, quoted in *The Silents of God*

Paul Schrader's vision of a transcendent cinema pushing viewers to a direct encounter with the divine has manifested itself in surprising ways. Digital technology allowed filmmaking to get louder, faster, and even more manipulative—punching viewers straight in the gut. Lars von Trier, troubled by his own technically accomplished but unfeeling films, vowed to strip his future projects down to their barest, sparsest essentials. "Dogme 95" injected much-needed humanity and spirit back into the filmmaking process. Yet the simplified digital videos of Dogme filmmakers met the same fate as Schrader's original "transcendent trio": critical kudos and public indifference.

In director Martin Scorsese, Schrader found the most abundant collaborator possible, a Roman Catholic steeped in the experiential, the material, and the bloody. Enduring films such as *Taxi Driver, Raging Bull, The Last Temptation of Christ,* and *Bringing Out the Dead* resulted. Schrader's sparse means needed an abundant interpreter, a visual stylist par excellence to bring transcendence to the silver screen.

The next generation of filmmakers worship at the church of Scorsese. They are ultra-abundant filmmakers, employing new tools and techniques with a dizzying force. Yet their finest films reinforce Schrader's hope that movies may progress from the profane to the sacred. Wes Anderson, Paul Thomas Anderson, the Wachowski Brothers, Tom Tykwer, and David Fincher definitely serve as filmgoers' high priests. Without trying to proselytize, they've inspired audiences to expect the unexpected. They've proven that dense, overly abundant films can touch the transcendent. Loud, fast, and manipulative can also be profoundly, surprisingly spiritual. And the ultimate questions keep coming. M. Night Shyamalan offers *Signs,* in which everything fits together for a reason. *Minority Report* raises troubling issues about free will and human choice. *Bruce Almighty* finds God giving Jim Carrey an overwhelming dose of divine responsibility. Mel Gibson cashes in his star power to do a study on Jesus' last hours in *The Passion.* Filmgoers are being offered an unprecedented array of ambitious, transcendent cinema.

Yet the audience indifference that dogged Bresson, Ozu, and Dreyer could also undo the current spiritual renaissance. The original, sparse, transcendental style put viewers to sleep, demanding too much emotional and spiritual investment. The current abundant style may overwhelm viewers who fail to look beyond the initial provocation to the ultimate questions being raised. Both the sparse and the abundant transcendental styles may expect viewers to look closer than they want to on an average Friday night. It is more likely that the next generation of filmgoers will be forced to educate the previous generation of filmgoers on how to watch a film.

The widely diverging responses to Darren Aronofsky's shocking second film, *Requiem for a Dream,* illustrates this visual generation gap. Based on a Hubert Selby Jr. novel, *Requiem* deals unflinchingly with the downward spiral of drug addiction. Pretty people, portrayed by Jared Leto and Jennifer Connolly, become ugly shells of their former selves. Ellen Burstyn gives a frightening and brave performance as a housewife descending into diet pill addiction. A normally comedic actor, Marlon Wayans, goes to dramatic places he never even suggested in previous films. Harry Knowles of "Ain't It Cool News" (the Roger Ebert of the Internet generation) raves about *Requiem,* insisting, "This film should be REQUIRED VIEWING by every . . . High School kid in the country. It should be unleashed upon them. Will it disturb them? Will it shake their fragile little minds? Will it possibly make a lifestyle change for them? Oh God YES. YES YES YES."[78] *Requiem* offers two gut-wrenching hours of "just say no," telling all sides of the drug story. Aronofsky shows the lure, the pull, and the "beauty" of drugs alongside the life-draining, crime-inducing, jail-resulting debasement of addiction.

Yet teens comprised the one group not allowed to see the film. The Motion Picture Association of America (MPAA) rated the film NC-17. An outraged Aronofsky wondered what the MPAA objected to? Did particular scenes need to be edited or adjusted? Repeated conversations and appeals led to the same conclusion: The film's rating wasn't rooted in content but in *style*. Aronofsky's rapid-fire, split-screen, frame-shaking editing brutalized the ratings board. A "normal" Hollywood film has six to seven hundred edits. *Requiem* crams in two thousand separate splices.[79] The sheer volume of images beat up the ratings board, made them cry uncle. They objected to what they thought they saw while missing the overall positive impact the film could have on its intended audience.

Perhaps the culture clash that inspired America's initial movie rating system in 1968 will result in a new standard for what tomorrow's teens can handle. Large, sociopolitical (and epistemological) shifts lead to large generation gaps. The gap in *Requiem for a Dream* is visual. The next generation has already evolved into a much more discerning, sophisticated, visual culture. Aronofsky lays out the challenge: "It's about figuring out ways to entertain people who have been bombarded by billions upon billions of images."[80]

Film viewers and filmmakers face new temptations that may potentially derail this spiritual renaissance before it reaches full fruition. What types of pledges or dogmas may be necessary? "Dogma, like many a religious movement, is less avant-garde than revivalist. Its rules respond to a changed situation, to marvelous new temptations."[81] Will the digital revolution take moviegoers to more inviting and inspiring places than ever imagined? Or will reliance on new technology replace storytelling with pure sensation?

If 1999 was "the year that changed movies," the time since has been "the years that need changed." The promises of a transcendent cinema have not been realized. Instead, Hollywood has trotted out an array of mindless action films and sequels that have hauled in major coin: *Mission Impossible II, The Mummy Returns, Rush Hour 2.* Perhaps Michael Bay, the director who brought us visceral sensations such as *The Rock, Armageddon,* and *Pearl Harbor,* represents the cultural zeitgeist of overabundance. Or perhaps movies will get more varied, more creative, and more personal, like Lars von Trier's tragic and celebratory musical *Dancer in the Dark.* Dogme films put cinematic illusions to death, constantly reminding us with their grainy handheld images that a human operator is filming a living, breathing, "acting" human. Why do we go to the movies? To escape? Or to transcend our everyday lives? What's the difference?

Audiences will ultimately decide what they want their movies to offer. To the degree that moviegoers patronize senseless sequels, Hollywood will produce more thrilling but forgettable on-screen roller-coaster rides. Yet when smart, articulate, probing films such as *Erin Brockovich* and *Traffic* pass the one-hundred-million-dollar mark, audiences prove what kinds of varied films they also will support. The dean of the next generation of directors, Steven Soderbergh, declared independent film dead when Christopher Nolan's brilliant film *Memento* failed to find a distributor. But when audiences made the smart postmodern mystery a surprise hit, all independent-minded filmmakers and filmgoers should have been encouraged. How does a small, sharp film that forces viewers to confront their own self-deception cut through the clutter of *Lara Croft: Tomb Raider* and *Coyote Ugly*? By offering viewers a visual puzzle, a mental exercise. Audiences don't mind being manipulated by all the new technology if it serves a greater purpose, linking us to the deepest parts of our humanity.

Soderbergh also issues a healthy warning: "For a young filmmaker, the enemy isn't the studio or the critics, it's self-importance. It takes a great amount of effort to stay hungry, but it's far preferable than self-importance, which is what has brought down every great filmmaker."[82] Thank goodness for vows such as "Dogme 95" that push filmmakers past dehumanizing technological perfection to what made movies matter: characters, stories, redemption. Twenty-first-century filmmakers will be tempted to blast us with visions of *Apocalypse Now*. But enduring works of art will dare to remind us that *It's a Wonderful Life*. Filmmakers may prove humble enough to hear the creative whispers of their Creator, but it's up to audiences to learn to "look closer," to discover and support films that offer truly moving images, that nudge us closer to one another and closer to the divine.

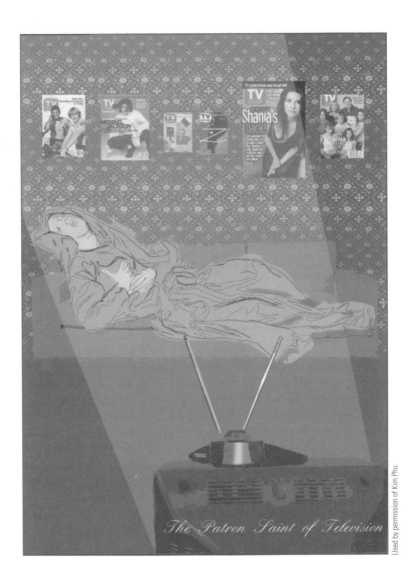

The Patron Saint of Television

television

Our Constant Companion

> Nothing is as ruinous to the character as sitting away one's time at a show, for it is then, through the medium of entertainment that vices creep into one with more than usual ease.
>
> Seneca, Roman stoic philosopher,
> writing two thousand years ago

How strange to see a *Newsweek* magazine cover story announce, "Why TV Is Good for Kids." Television has so few defenders. It's been called the idiot box, the boob tube, and the plug-in drug. Renowned architect Frank Lloyd Wright called it "chewing gum for the eyes." It is blamed for social ills ranging from weight gain to murder. Some of us approach television with indifference: "I don't really pay much attention to it." Others, when pressed, will admit to the occasional guilty pleasure: "I checked out *The Osbournes* once" or "I only watch *The West Wing*." Those who don't own a television use it as an opportunity to claim certain superiority: "I have better things to do" or "I'd rather read a book."

Most of our reticence comes from television's content. It promotes false values. It harms girls' self-image. It makes boys more aggressive. It underrepresents minorities. This may all be true, but as a democratic art form, committed almost exclusively to audience interest, it tells us much about our God and ourselves. Television is a mirror, an extension of our hopes and dreams, desires and depravities. Perhaps that's why we feel so ambivalent. Not only do we hate to admit we watch TV, but we also hate ourselves while we watch it.

Yet God wants to extend love to us, and he wants us to extend love to our neighbors. How can this take place while we're engaging in an isolating and distorting activity? We devote so many more hours a week to television than to church or community life. What should we think about television? While debates rage about its harmful effects, television continues its expansion, offering more choices on more channels every day. If we're worried about television's five-hundred-channel impact today, how will we respond to tomorrow's five-thousand-channel universe? Should we fear or embrace our almost constant companion?

Overlooked in the debate about television's content is its subtle but significant effect as a technology. It is first and foremost an appliance. It is a value-neutral invention that performs multiple functions simultaneously. It offers us endless choices to suit our moods—news, sports, drama, and comedy. It delivers us from boredom. But what matters more is *how* it delivers us. Television alters how we think, how we relate to others, and how we behave by constantly adapting to what we want it to be. We can blame television for manipulating us, or we can accept our role and responsibility as the ultimate arbiters of what television offers.

This chapter traces television's evolution from a technology to a salesman to a teacher to a parent. This brief historical overview will inform our subsequent theological reflection. Television has shifted from a town square to a tribe to our own private universe. This impacts our understanding and practice as a community. Television serves as a comfort, a companion, a sedative, and an adventure. It can awaken our senses or lull us to sleep. To those closest to it, television executives, it remains a mystery. Television offers a mirror that provokes pride, envy, and disgust. Yet it increasingly functions as both an art and a religion. We can criticize it for appealing to our worst tendencies or embrace the sometimes painful wisdom and truth it imparts.

By studying television's adaptability, we will inadvertently consider the promises and temptations of another delivery system with huge potential, the Internet. Radio, television, and the Internet were each created by scientists, overtaken by advertisers, and turned into entertainment. None of these technologies has wiped out previous systems. Each has simply upped the ante of information and electronic inputs. As former *NBC News* president Lawrence Grossman explains, "Printing made us all readers. Xeroxing made us all publishers. Television made us all viewers. Digitization makes us all broadcasters."[1]

Many find the information age overwhelming. We've been accused of "amusing ourselves to death." And yet the channels and choices continue to proliferate. We're living through "the rise of the image, the fall of the word."[2] For people of faith committed to the Word of God, this can be a frightening statement. Yet the evolution of television offers reasons to hope. Hopefully, our tour of television history will reveal enduring truths about the human condition and the nature of God.

A Technology

TV is a free public hanging.

anonymous confession
of a television producer

TV was invented by a twenty-one-year-old. What began as a bright idea turned into a real-life soap opera full of lies, lawsuits, depression, and death.[3] Mormon teenager Philo T. Farnsworth was tilling a potato field in Utah when "he turned at this little high spot to see if his rows were straight and it just hit him like a thunderbolt—'I can scan a picture that way, by taking the dots, the electrons, back and forth as you would read a page.'"[4] He realized light could scan images the same way he was plowing the field: line by line. On September 7, 1927, Farnsworth introduced the world's first television show, a vertical black line swinging back and forth like a pendulum.[5] One of his investors asked, "When are we going to see some dollars in this thing, Farnsworth?" And immediately a dollar sign appeared on the screen.[6]

Farnsworth's ingenuity was rewarded when the powerful Radio Corp. of America (RCA) offered him one hundred thousand dollars for his services and patents. He rejected RCA's overtures, insisting royalties be included in their offer. RCA harassed Farnsworth with a series of lawsuits that tied up his patents through endless appeals. Despite incessant, contrary legal claims by RCA, the courts consistently affirmed Farnsworth's patents, eventually ordering RCA to pay him one million dollars in damages. But before Farnsworth collected all his money, his patents expired in 1947. With Farnsworth's technology now freely available to all corporations, television production and sales soon exploded. In 1957, suffering from ulcers and depression, Farnsworth appeared on *I've Got a Secret* as "Dr. X," inventor of "a machine." To the first question he was asked, "Is this a machine that might be painful when used?" Farnsworth replied, "Yes. Sometimes it's most painful."[7]

An Appliance

Television is not a luxury, it's a necessity.

Arthur C. Clarke, author of *2001: A Space Odyssey,*
quoted in *Television*

The TV revolution started slowly. In 1946, there were only 10,000 television sets in use in America. In 1948, the year after Farnsworth lost control of the medium, the number of televisions rose to 1.5 million. By January 1953, 50 million people watched Lucy Ricardo give birth to little Ricky on *I Love Lucy.*[8]

Farnsworth died in 1971, before television entered every room in the house and personal digital satellites made one thousand entertainment options just a click away. Three networks, CBS, NBC, and ABC, ruled television from 1945 to 1975.[9] When cable television arrived, network proliferation soon followed. ESPN debuted in 1979, CNN in 1980, MTV in 1981, and the Home Shopping Network in 1982. The comparatively small and unobtrusive DirecTV digital satellites replaced the dishes that used to occupy an entire backyard. Beyond the United States, the global acceptance and prevalence of television are equally incalculable. Farnsworth certainly hoped his invention would educate viewers around the world about how others live. What he could not have anticipated is how much this household appliance would *shape* how we live.

People crowded into shantytowns around the globe struggle for food, shelter, and basic health care. Yet even the smallest houses usually feature a rooftop antenna and a television. Reporting from Iran in 1997, Thomas Friedman found "that some of those in South Teheran who had television were setting up a few chairs and selling tickets when the most popular American television show [*Baywatch*] came on each week."[10] The government banned satellite dishes, but the Iranians simply hid them under laundry lines or plants on their balconies.

Television has become the most essential, ubiquitous household appliance. This simple appliance serves as the ultimate dream machine—what we turn to for advice, from what to wear to how to behave. That is entirely appropriate considering the financial fuel that keeps most television programming afloat. From the beginning, American television has been fueled by advertising dollars.

A Salesman

Television may be the Trojan horse of Western civilization.

Quentin J. Schultze, *Redeeming Television*

In the 1930s, advertising agencies realized they could build a massive radio audience through soap operas. By tuning their radios to the same station at the same time each day, housewives could follow the lives, loves, and losses of people like themselves, characters who served as trusted role models, dear old friends. Why did advertisers target housewives? Because housewives were the decision makers who determined what brands and products their families used. Television took soap operas to a new level by adding showing to telling. TV demonstrated how new products "fit" within a "successful" American home.[11] From the beginning, television programs served as filler between the real business of wooing consumers and selling products.

In the early days of television, a single advertiser funded each particular program. Such arrangements ranged from Milton Berle on *The Texaco Star Theater* to Chevrolet presents *The Dinah Shore Show.* The shows' hosts paused in the middle of the program to tell viewers about the virtues of a cleaning product or to sing about a smooth, refreshing cigarette. Eventually, the star as salesman was replaced by commercials, thirty- or sixty-second mini-movies that could be repeated on multiple networks and competing programs. The singular show sponsor gave way to multiple sponsors, with advertisers paying premium dollars for airtime on the most popular television programs. Television ratings compiled by Nielsen Media Research using viewer diaries and a device called an audimeter determined advertising rates.[12] Higher ratings generated higher advertising rates.

The economics behind top-rated television series are staggering. How can NBC and Warner Brothers afford to pay $25 million to each of the six cast members of *Friends*? They make the money back from advertisers many times over. NBC made news when it offered the producers of its top-rated series, *ER,* $850 million in a three-year contract.[13] Yet in the 1998–99 television season, *ER* generated $355.7 million in ad revenue. NBC charged advertisers nearly $1 million per minute during *ER.* NBC can pay *ER*'s producers $13 million per hour because they can make $13 million per hour. Networks have complained that the price of original sitcoms and dramas has gotten out of hand. ABC scheduled the comparatively cheap game show *Who Wants to Be a Millionaire?* four nights a week. Yet host Regis Philbin earned $20 million per year as host of the show, and $62 million in prize money was awarded in the first two years.[14] Where is the network's profit? In the $271,000 they charged for each thirty-second ad, twenty times per show. While movie stars make headlines, television stars make much bigger bucks. In fact, the television industry accounts for roughly 70 percent of production in Los Angeles, resulting in a $7-billion business.[15]

Such a significant economic engine must reveal hidden secrets about our wants and desires. Do we hate television for selling so incessantly? Or do we hate ourselves for wanting so much? Either response fails to appreciate the evolving nature of television. It has moved far beyond sales into a voracious, self-promoting, 24/7, one-stop shop.

A Store

I hate television. I hate it as much as peanuts. But I can't stop eating peanuts.

Orson Welles[16]

When *Entertainment Tonight* touts an upcoming episode of *Everybody Loves Raymond,* most viewers don't connect the dots between the production company (David Letterman's World Wide Pants), the CBS network, and *Entertain-*

ment Tonight. Yet Viacom ultimately owns each of these entities. The same "coincidence" occurs when *Access Hollywood* offers exclusive behind-the-scenes footage from the set of *ER*. Few viewers realize that the exclusive coverage is rooted in Warner Brothers' mutual monetary interest in both *ER* and *Access Hollywood*. While *Entertainment Tonight* may deny a journalistic conflict of interest, does it offer equal coverage of its rivals? When *Access Hollywood* does more in-depth reporting than *ET* on whether *Survivor* was rigged, could it be because Viacom owns CBS, *Survivor,* and *Entertainment Tonight*?[17]

When ABC telecast college football's 2001 Rose Bowl game, the halftime commentators were reporting live from Disney's California Adventure. It seems a random location, until we realize that ABC's parent, Disney, wants to attract visitors to their underperforming attraction. Even networks proudly devoted to "independent visions," such as the Sundance Channel, reside under corporate umbrellas. Sundance is a subsidiary of the Showtime Networks, which are a subsidiary of Viacom. Where do the nesting Russian dolls stop?

Two networks founded in the early eighties perfected the art of "advertainment." MTV broadcasts hours of music videos, funded and provided by record companies as "original" programming. Between the videos plugging a band's new album, MTV offers more commercials, essentially operating as all advertising, all the time. Yet viewers flocked to the station, following the network's urging to tell their cable company, "I want my MTV."

Long before he created faith-friendly PAX TV, Lowell (Bud) Paxson started selling merchandise over the radio on WWQT in Clearwater, Florida. He soon realized that television offered an even better medium to showcase his products. In 1985, Paxson's Home Shopping Network brought consumers and products together through the magic of television, a 1-800 number, and a major credit card. HSN grossed over one hundred million dollars by its second year. By 1992, the Home Shopping Network was selling one billion dollars in merchandise annually.[18] HSN's telephone capacity expanded to field up to twenty thousand calls *per minute*. Home Shopping eliminated a residual gap between television and advertising. TV no longer simply advertises products found in a local store. It has become the store.

Does it matter? Should we be scared? In efforts to engage students in a discussion of the ethics of television and advertising, professors are met with utter indifference. Observations of European critics such as Theodor Adorno that accuse television of producing "the very smugness, intellectual passivity, and gullibility that seem to fit in with totalitarian creeds" fall on deaf ears.[19] Kids know television is selling a false (or at least constant) bill of goods, but they're willing to enter into that social contract. James Twitchell takes on Adorno and the founders of cultural studies by dismissing their Marxist interpretation of a vast entertainment/advertising conspiracy as presumptuous. In labeling consumers blind sheep duped by networks and advertisers, Adorno and the Frankfurt theorists set themselves up as the one true source of enlightenment. They feared that TV could be used for ugly political purposes, as the ultimate propaganda machine.

Yet a half century of televised political debates has made viewers only more skeptical of their leaders.[20] Television's ability to brainwash has been seriously over-calculated by the Frankfurt school, except when it comes to promoting democracy and capitalism. James Twitchell embraces popular culture and capitalism as expressions of the "people's" general will.[21] Television has simply connected and perfected people's innate drive to shop, to acquire goods. A thoughtful theological response to television must treat viewers with dignity. Let's consider why we watch certain shows.

A Comfort

> We're in the boredom killing business. Nothing sinks a program faster than an audience response of "Boring!"
>
> Howard Beale, crazed newscaster-prophet in *Network*[22]

Why do we watch television? What keeps us coming back to certain programs? What makes us "love Lucy"? Why do we consider Phoebe, Rachel, Ross, Chandler, Monica, and Joey our "friends"? Like any appliance, television is judged by its ability to perform a desired function. When we turn on the television, we rarely want to be challenged. We want to relax, unwind, be entertained. Television's placement inside our homes has turned it into the most conservative and comfortable form of pop culture.

Television's intimate relationship with advertisers has none-too-subtly shaped the type of programming offered. While movie studios welcome the "free advertising" that controversial films can create, television networks shy away from divisive programming. As far back as 1963, *TV Guide* described television as "a Timid Giant." "Despite official freedom from censorship, a self-imposed silence renders network documentaries almost mute on many great issues of the day." Newscaster Howard K. Smith found that "the networks are delighted if you go into a controversy in a country 14,000 miles away. They don't want real controversy, real dissent, at home."[23] Shows that depress, anger, or upset audiences are anathema to television. Networks avoid tragic or controversial themes because advertisers want shows that put viewers in the buying mood. Whether implicitly or explicitly, the spirit of consumerism drives almost every television programming decision.[24] In the late sixties, *The Smothers Brothers Show* lured viewers to CBS with an edgy combination of sketch comedy and topical humor. The show's political content caused CBS to cancel the series despite stellar ratings. It took producer Norman Lear three years of lobbying to convince CBS execs to take a chance on Archie Bunker. *All in the Family* became the top-rated television series of the seventies. Lear recalls, "Their worst fears were not realized, and I think we all learned together . . . that America was more grown up than they had thought."[25]

Politicians and critics have accused television of having a liberal bias, but most network executives view their business in anything but ideological terms. Robert Niles, the vice president of marketing for NBC, said, "We're in the business of selling audiences to advertisers. They [the sponsors] come to us asking for women 18 to 49 and adults 25 to 54 and we try to deliver."[26] Roger King, an executive for *Wheel of Fortune* and *Jeopardy*, declares, "The people are the boss. We listen to the audience, see what they want, and try to accommodate them."[27] CBS's vice president for research, Arnold Becker, explains, "I'm not interested in culture. I'm not interested in pro-social values. I have only one interest. That's whether people watch the program. That's my definition of good, that's my definition of bad."[28]

Television's most enduring contribution to culture is the twenty-two-minute solution. The twenty-two minutes between a sitcom's introduction of a problem and the tidy solution often do not correspond to lived experiences of detox, the D.M.V., or divorce court. Some argue that television's timely resolutions create pent-up frustration, increasing expectations of timely results. Television heightens our impatience with how long things take to get fixed in the "real" world. Yet the sitcom remains one of America's primary exports, a distinct cultural commodity.

Susan Borowitz, a TV comedy writer, believes that "the sitcom has taken the place of the church in religious training. Sitcoms work better if they're little sermons or parables."[29] Why have viewers consistently invited the Beaver, Fonzie, and Alf into their homes? Viewers turn to television because of its familiarity, its comfort, its predictability. Critics deride the formulas that sitcoms follow. Yet after a hard day's work, viewers apparently like to come home to familiar friends who behave in predictable patterns. It gives the illusion of feeling connected, of being with old friends at the same hour each week.

Weekly religious services perform similar functions. We check in with the same people at the same time and follow the same formula each week. Yet young people often describe worship services as boring, particularly in comparison to the pace of television. In an effort to respond to the media culture, many of the fastest growing churches have made Sunday mornings more entertaining. Such sincere contextualization may have overlooked the formulaic and liturgical rites of TV. Comfort comes from familiarity, from repetition, from ritual. Television's twenty-two-minute liturgy manages to comfort and entertain. No wonder we tune in so regularly.

A Teacher

I find television very educating. Every time somebody turns on the set I go into the other room and read a book.

Groucho Marx

A thirteen-year-old Connecticut boy goes to the hospital with second- and third-degree burns after imitating a Johnny Knoxville stunt on MTV's *Jackass*.[30] Another thirteen-year-old, charged with murdering a family friend, claims a professional wrestling show made him do it.[31] How did television become the most convenient scapegoat for all of society's ills? Why has an appliance inspired TV-turn-off week? How have electronic images become the battleground for the blame game? Parents blame television for corrupting America's youth and promoting violence. Legislators blame television for angering their constituents, and television networks promise to clean up their act via a self-instituted ratings system. Yet parents and legislators continue to ignore the root causes of violence such as poverty, alcohol abuse, and the quality of public education. Television producers are equally disingenuous when they claim to be reflecting rather than influencing culture. If they honestly believe that television doesn't influence behavior, then why do they charge advertisers millions of dollars for thirty seconds of airtime? Does television mold social behavior, or does it merely reflect our values like a constant, flickering mirror?

Most of the debate swirling around television involves its influence on children. Does TV rot kids' brains, drive down test scores, and make kids fatter? In *Glued to the Set,* author Steven D. Stark traces the passionate debate about kids and TV back to the beginning of broadcasting, 1947's *Howdy Doody*. Five days a week, Buffalo "Bob" Smith would ask his youthful audience, "What time is it?" The answer became television's first theme song to sweep the culture: "It's Howdy Doody time!" Fifty years before *Teletubbies, Howdy Doody* was praised as an ideal electronic baby-sitter. *Variety* raved, "In the middle-class home, there is perhaps nothing as welcome to the mother as something that will keep the small fry intently absorbed and out of possible mischief."[32] *Parents Magazine* predicted, "Television is going to be a real asset in every home where there are children."[33] Howdy also introduced the vast possibilities of product tie-ins, selling toys to kids. By the early 1950s, critics questioned Howdy's profound pull on impressionable eyeballs, wondering, "Is Television Good or Bad for My Children?" and "Should You Tear 'Em Away from TV?"[34]

The U.S. Congress commissioned numerous studies on the effects of television violence on children's impressionable minds. These congressional reports came out in 1954, 1961, 1964, and 1970.[35] The surgeon general's 1972 *Report on Television and Social Behavior* devoted four of its five volumes to studies of the effects of violent television programs.[36] The National

Television Violence Study looked at ten thousand hours of television over a three-year period. The study estimated that a preschool child, watching two hours of cartoons per day, would be exposed to ten thousand on-screen acts of violence per year. By age eleven, viewers will have witnessed eight thousand murders and one hundred thousand other examples of TV violence.[37] Should we be appalled by the sheer volume of violence we, the audience, tolerate? Or should we be encouraged that despite such a constant barrage of jarring images, teen crime statistics are declining? Countless scientific studies of television violence have failed to find evidence establishing a direct connection.

The gap between public posturing (*The Simpsons* undermines the family) and private practices (Homer cracks me up) can be found in conflicting statements made by government officials on the same day in 1961. Newton Minow, the chairman of the Federal Communications Commission (FCC), called television "a vast wasteland . . . of blood and thunder, mayhem, violence, sadism, and murder." Vice President Hubert Humphrey called TV "the greatest single achievement in communication that anybody has ever known."[38] Politicians and parents continue to offer mixed messages, *using* television to make statements *condemning* television.[39]

In 1996, network executives haggled with legislators and children's advocacy groups over TV ratings and the V-Chip. Then-president of NBC, Warren Littlefield, admitted, "In my 20 years of broadcasting, I have never been more afraid than I have been of the ratings issue."[40] In 1997, the networks "voluntarily" adopted ratings of TV-G, TV-PG, TV-14, and MA. Five years after these parental guidelines were introduced, the Annenberg Public Policy Center found that only 50 percent of parents were aware of their existence. The Kaiser Family Foundation reports that just 17 percent of parents who own a V-Chip television (mandatory in all sets since January 2000) use it to block programming. A television exec laments, "The reality is, this was never an issue that parents cared about. This was something that only 10 people in America cared about—members of Congress and children's advocacy groups."[41] Another anonymous network chieftain called TV ratings "a false solution to a false problem. The V-Chip should truly be in the parents' brain."[42]

A Baby-Sitter

I let my child watch TV only when: A) There's an education show on public television, B) I have time to narrate the action for him, C) I want to take a shower.

Parents Magazine survey[43]

Television has been called an electronic baby-sitter. Parents worry about too much sex and violence being transmitted to kids. Yet a half century of rhetoric about television's harmful influence hasn't changed the simple fact that most viewers don't care. They don't consider television a classroom dedicated to the moral development of youth. While legislators grabbed headlines carping about kids and content, they chose to ignore a far more important development. In *Lead Us into Temptation*, James Twitchell chronicles television's shift from "infotainment" to "advertainment." He traces the shift to the early 1980s, when President Reagan's administration enacted massive deregulation. The chair of the FCC, Marc Fowler, defined television as "just another appliance—a toaster with pictures."[44] The rules limiting the time stations could devote to commercials were relaxed. Infomercials for the Pocket Fisherman, the Smokeless Ashtray, and the Ronco Clean Air Machine resulted.[45]

While adults spent one billion dollars on the Showtime Rotisserie and BBQ, children paid the highest price. *He-Man and the Masters of the Universe* became the first program designed specifically to sell toys. *Thundercats* followed shortly thereafter. The producers of *Thundercats,* Lorimar Telepictures, actually gave kickbacks to the stations based on toy sales in their local markets. The more toys kids bought, the fatter the stations' bottom lines. Independent stations got rich by essentially selling airtime directly to toy companies. Children's programming has never been the same. Saban Entertainment's *Mighty Morphin Power Rangers* brought this "art form" to a new level in the nineties.

Congress passed the corrective Children's Television Act in 1990. Six years later, President Clinton was still brokering a deal between the National Association of Broadcasters and the FCC to enforce the act. The NAB and FCC agreed that broadcasters must offer three hours of educational programming for children per week. But the FCC agreed to "ordinarily rely on the good faith judgment of broadcasters."[46] Just five years later, NBC sold its three-hour block of Saturday morning programming to the Discovery Communications Corporation for eight million dollars. Discovery Channel stores springing up in suburban malls will benefit from this as well. Fox recently auctioned off its four-hour Saturday morning programming block to competing bidders DIC Entertainment and 4 Kids Entertainment. DIC produced toy-driven hits such as *Inspector Gadget* and *Super Mario Bros.* 4 Kids represents Nintendo and Pokemon.[47]

While we've been arguing about sex and violence, television has quietly been teaching our kids that their central purpose in life is to shop. With all due respect to the sincere folks at organizations such as the Parents Television Council, we do not need more statements about sex and violence. Instead, kids desperately need a theology of consumption. Our children need to understand the power and pull of toys—why they like to shop. Perhaps shopping reflects a God-given desire for beauty. Maybe our constant interest in newer, improved products suggests something deep about our hunger for new life. Kids need to learn about the real magic of advertising, our ability to impart value on seemingly inanimate objects. The bread and wine of the Eucharist may reacquire its magic when we've helped the next generation get in touch with the mystical experience that occurs every time they think the latest version of Sony's PlayStation will transform their lives. As James Twitchell says, "If we craved objects *and* knew what they meant, there would be no signifying systems like advertising, packaging, fashion and branding to get in the way. We would gather, use, toss out, or hoard based on some *inner* sense of value. It is that inner sense of value we don't have."[48]

From a Town Square to a Tribe

> No survey is needed, of course, to establish that television has brought the family together in one room.
>
> Jack Gould, TV critic, 1949[49]

In 1987, three networks attracted two-thirds of all viewers.[50] Now, the up-start Fox Network seems like a grand old man compared to the fledgling UPN and WB. Stations didn't always need to constantly superimpose their network logos to identify themselves. Viewers knew their VHF channel choices were limited from 2 to 13. Yet ABC, NBC, and CBS grew comfortable with their mo-nopoly. Reporter Ken Auletta traced the networks' decline from 1986 to 1991, calling them the "three blind mice."[51]

While American TV viewership has reached an unprecedented one hundred million households nightly, that audience is divided into smaller and smaller pieces. Television used to be a national gathering place; now it has evolved into a hundred separate, narrowcast networks. If the big three networks offered a cultural rallying point, "our common church," the proliferation of networks corresponds to a new tribalism.

How did a medium designed to bring people together gradually segregate audiences? The Fox Network built an audience base by catering to underserved, niche markets. African-American sitcoms such as *Living Single* and *Martin* at-tracted black viewers shut out from programming on CBS, NBC, and ABC. In fact, *Living Single* pioneered the concept of twenty-somethings hanging out to-gether in New York City a full year before *Friends* hit NBC. A 1994 survey found that 48 percent of black homes tuned into *Living Single*, while only 3 percent watched *Friends*.[52] Top 20 Nielsen hits such as *Frasier, Seinfeld,* and *Mad about You* ranked 87th, 109th, and 110th in programming among black households. In the 1995–96 TV season, the advertising firm BBDO found that the top five programs in black homes were *New York Undercover, Living Single, The Crew, In the House,* and *Fresh Prince of Bel Air.*[53] While schools taught tolerance, television divided audiences quite clearly along racial lines.

When Fox replaced black dramas such as *New York Undercover* with *Ally McBeal,* upstart network UPN went after the African-American market. *Moesha, Malcolm and Eddie,* and *The Secret Diary of Desmond Pfeiffer* resulted. The WB built its network by targeting advertising's most valued consumer, those still forming brand loyalties: teens. Shows such as *Dawson's Creek* and *Buffy the Vampire Slayer* enabled the WB to distinguish itself as "teen friendly." Programming such as *Murder She Wrote* and *Diagnosis Murder* made CBS the "gray" network. In the 1998–99 season, the median age of CBS viewers was 52.5 years old. The WB was heralded as the only network to actually increase its viewership, with a median age of just 26.6.[54] Plans are underway to create a "gay" network, with homosexually sensitive programming. Niche programming continues to subdivide American viewers by age, class, race, gender, and orientation.

LA CUCARACHA © Lalo Alcaraz. Dist. by UNIVERSAL PRESS SYNDICATE. Reprinted with permission. All rights reserved.

As the networks have expanded, so have the number of television sets residing in U.S. homes. In 1970, only 6 percent of sixth graders had a TV set in their rooms. By 1999, 77 percent of sixth graders had their own television.[55] A survey of kids ages eight to nineteen found that less than 5 percent of their TV watching occurs with their parents.[56] Marriages fare no better, as husbands and wives spend three or four times as much time watching television as they spend in conversation with each other. More than half of our television viewing is done alone.

To some degree, the fragmentation has only just begun. If five hundred channels have subdivided us, what will five thousand channels of tomorrow do? Digital television, video games, and the Internet will all be united through one ever widening broadband entry point into the home. A "smart TV" will combine a digital video recorder, an interactive game system, and a personal computer. Even the new and pricey HDTV and plasma screens seem destined to become antiquated next to these future TVs. Smart TV will offer access to entire libraries of programming. We'll finally be able to watch what we want, when we want. Hollywood is just discovering the most profitable, completely underutilized revenue stream: personal programming.

A Constant Companion

Ironically, the important, undiscussed truth behind the *fragmentation* of audiences is the rapid *consolidation* within the television industry. There appear to be hundreds of competing channels, visions, and choices. But actually, comparatively few corporations control those "competing" channels. The FCC's Telecommunications Act of 1996 removed barriers guarding against information monopolies. Deregulation allows Disney to own Lifetime, ESPN, the Disney Channel, A&E, ABC, and the Family Channel. Fox can capture viewers on FX, Fox News, or Fox Sports Net. NBC owns pieces of MSNBC, CNBC, and PAX. AOL Time Warner's holdings include the WB, CNN, HBO, TNT, TBS, and the Cartoon Network.

AOL's grip on the airwaves pales in comparison to Viacom Entertainment, the behemoth behind MTV, VH1, BET, TNN, Country Music Television, Nickelodeon, Paramount Pictures, and Blockbuster Video.[57] The FCC overturned a fifty-five-year-old prohibition (basically, the entire history of television) when it allowed Viacom, the owner of CBS, to purchase UPN.[58] Viacom offered an early example of the cross-promotional possibilities during television's biggest annual event, the 2001 Super Bowl. Carson Daly hosted "CBS Sports Presents: MTV's TRL at the Super Bowl," luring MTV's younger viewers to a CBS network plagued by an older demographic. MTV brought Aerosmith, Mary J. Blige, Britney Spears, and *NSYNC to the normally stodgy halftime show.[59]

Such consolidation has also led to instant reruns, referred to in the television industry as "repurposing" or "multiplexing." New episodes of *Law and Order: Special Victims Unit* play on USA after they're on NBC, ABC's morning talk show *The View* appears on A&E that evening, and the WB's *Charmed* repeats on TNT.[60] Giants such as Viacom don't have to worry whether viewers are watching MTV or CMT, CBS or UPN. They can now deliver eyeballs to advertisers across networks.[61]

Consolidation has turned broadcasters into "narrow casters," programming for smaller, clearly identified audiences grouped by age and interests. This subdivision carries over to kids' programs. *Sesame Street* was originally designed for kids ages three to five. When viewers under two started watching, the network introduced *Elmo's World.*[62] Ph.D.s raised on *Sesame Street* have now become consultants for Nickelodeon and Disney. The *Teletubbies* was created with only the youngest viewers in mind. *Dora the Explorer* introduces English-speaking three-year-olds to Spanish. *Bear in the Big Blue House* covers potty training.

Some rail against television's broken promise to create a "global village." Television has devolved into a place where people of all backgrounds gather with people who share only their own backgrounds and interests.[63] Yet the lived theology of growing churches has adapted to this fragmentation. The future of Christian community also appears to be "narrow casting," dividing congregations into like-minded focus groups—junior high, young married, seniors, single again, and so on. As we gather around particular television shows aimed at us, we also gather around sermons, worship styles, and groups made for us. This challenges the understanding of fellowship—*koinonia*. Should the faith community provide a rare opportunity for families and individuals to unite in one room for one shared experience? As television divides us, can't God unite us? Certainly, but our understanding of God appears headed toward even more diversity.

Custom TV has led us toward a custom God. Theology will be forced to find an ever smaller central core to accommodate the multitude of faith expressions sure to flow from smaller and smaller audiences. We must unite around *the fact* that we break bread to celebrate Jesus' salvific actions rather than argue about the particulars of *how* it should be done. The explosion of television channels forces Christians to focus on the sacraments that unite us rather than the dogma that divides us. Perhaps God embraces television as the means to create a global village after all.

A Window on the World

> Mankind might be better off if television was never invented.
>
> Reuven Frank, former *NBC News* chief, quoted in *Television*

In the short history of television, cataclysmic events caused viewers to tune in for around-the-clock, televised updates. In November 1963, America grieved the death of President John F. Kennedy over three and a half arduous days, from the initial shock in Dallas to the lighting of the eternal flame in Arlington Cemetery. In the seventies, the Iran hostage crisis spawned nightly updates hosted by Ted Koppel called "America Held Hostage." By the time the crisis ended 444 days later, *Nightline* had become a permanent 11:30 P.M. fixture on ABC. Many can recall watching the space shuttle *Challenger* explode in 1986. The twenty-first century received an early, defining, television tragedy when the World Trade Center's towers collapsed on September 11, 2001. During trying times, network newscasters become true "anchors," a comforting and authoritative presence.

Tom Brokaw, Dan Rather, and Peter Jennings have continued the tradition established by respected, pioneering television journalists such as Edward R. Murrow, Walter Cronkite, and David Brinkley. News coverage of the Vietnam War, the NASA space program, and the Watergate scandal cemented television's reputation as a credible source of important information. Only thirty years later, exhaustive, twenty-four-hour coverage of press conferences featuring lawyers, managers, uncles, and neighbors all chiming in on utter minutia have turned the news into a steady stream of what Daniel Boorstin calls "pseudo-events."[64]

A Harvard study of network news discovered that in 1968 the average sound bite from presidential candidates lasted 42.3 seconds. By 1988, candidates' quips had been reduced to an average of 9.8 seconds.[65] For the 1996 Clinton-Dole election coverage, the sound bite had shrunk to 8.2 seconds.[66] Politicians' efforts to discuss substantive issues on television are doomed to fail. Dan Rather followed his coverage of President George W. Bush's stem cell research speech by saying, "If you're really interested in this, you'll want to read it in detail in one of the better newspapers tomorrow."[67] In a speech to news directors, Rather accepted blame: "We should all be ashamed of what we have and have not done."[68] How did network newscasters become mere talking heads? When did "serious" journalism get co-opted by entertainment? Does it matter that television serves as the primary news outlet for the majority of Americans? And that younger viewers pay almost no attention to television news?

Ted Turner gambled that the public would support a twenty-four-hour TV news service when he launched the Cable News Network in 1980. Turner undercut the network news anchors by insisting that at CNN "news is the star."[69] Investing in technology rather than personalities, CNN beat the networks to coverage of the *Challenger* disaster, China's Tienamen Square, and the Gulf War.[70] With successful spin-offs such as *Headline News* and *CNN/Sports Illustrated,* Turner's tiny Atlanta operation has gone international with access to one billion viewers through fourteen outlets, including CNN en Español, N-TV in Germany, and even CNN Turk.[71] CNN's only consistent challenge has been finding enough quality news to occupy twenty-four hours of programming.

An unlikely source of news debuted as a syndicated show in September 1981. *Entertainment Tonight* treated celebrities, premieres, and award shows as legitimate news. Mary Hart and John Tesh served as the anchors, with correspondents reporting from the field. They took the graphics and inserts of network newscasts to another level, introducing animation, charts, and spin frames. Soon the network newscasts were imitating them. Bill Moyers recalls, "In meeting after meeting [at CBS], *Entertainment Tonight* was touted as the model—breezy, entertaining, undemanding."[72] *ET*'s success spawned a rash of imitators such as *A Current Affair* in 1987, *Inside Edition* in 1988, and *Hard Copy* in 1989. They took *ET*'s obsession with celebrity much farther by focusing on the scandalous side of fame, no matter how salacious. Gossip grew into a new form of news, "tabloid TV." CNN now covers scandals because it needs to fill airtime and because such stories generate strong Nielsen ratings. Al Primo, the creator of the local "Eyewitness News" format, admits, "Our whole industry has become a part of show business . . . using the same tools they use to make a movie or a comedy show: lights, cameras, an actor and a script."[73]

Used by permission of Don McKinney.

The New News

> There are lots of reasons fewer people are watching network news,
> and one of them, I'm convinced more than ever, is that our viewers
> simply don't trust us. And for good reason.
>
> Bernard Goldberg, CBS news reporter, *Bias*

Yet the emphasis broadcast news has placed on personalities and sex appeal has still failed to woo younger viewers. The audience for nightly network news plummeted from 60 percent of adults in 1993 to 38 percent just five years later. In a 1997 study, NBC found that the average age of viewers of all its news programs was forty-two. For nightly newscasts, the average leapt to fifty-seven.[74] For viewers under thirty years of age, network news anchors are simply old people reporting on things other old people did. They have little connection to what teens care about or consider news.

To attract a new generation, CNN and Fox News have altered their on-screen appearance, borrowing heavily from the Internet to create a denser format. Older viewers complain about on-screen "clutter," too much information entering the picture in too many ways. But the stock ticker of Bloomburg TV is only the beginning. CNN's revamped *Headline News* has crammed the anchor into the upper right-hand corner to make room for more updates and scrolling text. *ESPNews* has followed suit with a steady stream of sports scores and transcripts of online chats. The general manager of *Headline News* declares, "Younger people involved in the computer today are so used to seeing lots of information on a screen. They want information in fast doses."[75] Walter Isaacson, CNN's News Group chairman, adds, "In this day and age, you need information at the speed of your life, and you need to absorb (only) some of it."[76] For better or worse, focusing on one thing well has become a dated, twentieth-century notion.

For many younger viewers, the primary news outlets are *Oprah, Leno, Letterman,* and MTV. Talk shows reign as agenda setters and public opinion shapers. In a recent poll of news media preferences, 22 percent of Americans said they get their news every day from talk radio hosts such as Rush

Limbaugh. Rosie O'Donnell's advocacy for the Million Mom March did more to hurt the NRA than any anti-gun legislation before Congress. Oprah can create a best-seller in a single hour. Jay Leno and David Letterman provide a running political commentary, joking about vice president Dan Quayle's spelling of "potatoe," Bill Clinton's ogling of Monica Lewinsky's thong, and George W. Bush passing out from eating too many pretzels.

Even "serious" talk shows such as *Larry King Live, The O'Reilly Factor,* and *Charlie Rose* offer mostly promo spots for celebrities pimping their newest products. *Politically Incorrect* with Bill Maher allegedly offered a forum to discuss "the issues." It mostly provided a forum for Maher's particular predilections. Jon Stewart's *Daily Show* on Comedy Central and *Saturday Night Live's Weekend Update* offer younger viewers a faster, funnier, alternative *Headline News.* For better or worse, news is now being communicated in a light, bright, entertaining format that leaves little room for serious, "hard" news.

Teachers, pastors, and activists must learn how to enlighten and entertain simultaneously. While many may question his conclusions, documentarian Michael Moore has exhibited a profound understanding of how to communicate a serious message in a manner that engages today's audiences. *Bowling for Columbine* made audiences laugh and cry, sparking outrage and activism. The Evangelical Environmental Network demonstrated media savvy rare among policy-driven organizations when it found an entertaining way to raise serious questions about the gas-guzzling S.U.V.s racing through our suburban streets. Their "What Would Jesus Drive?" campaign crossed over into the major news outlets.

With hard news no longer our window on the world, conscientious Christians must develop a theology out of pop culture if they hope to promote a theology of social justice. It will not be enough to report on genocide in Rwanda or Kosovo via journals, magazines, and Bible studies. Moving images will be the means to move us. If activists want congressional phones to ring, then television must be respected and understood as the first wave of any international act of relief. The question "Who is my neighbor?" must be answered via captivating stories and compelling images. We must rediscover what Jesus meant when he declared, "The eye is the lamp of the body" (Matt. 6:22). Instead of focusing on keeping our eyes pure by filtering out what not to watch, we need to focus on the positive potential of Jesus' teaching: "If your eyes are good, your whole body will be full of light" (Matt. 6:22). We are called to develop good eyes, not blind eyes. We must train the next generation to see the world through God's compassionate eyes for the poor, the widow, the orphan. We desperately need to create entertainment that moves beyond escape to engagement. Only then will our bodies be full of light.

A Sedative or an Adventure?

> There are two kinds of people in the world—those who walk into a room and turn the TV on, and those who walk into a room and turn the TV off.
>
> Frank Sinatra, *The Manchurian Candidate*

After a hard day's work, many people look forward to turning on the television to unwind. Television allows people to leave the pressures of work or school behind. Yet research suggests that the term "veg out" all too accurately describes what happens when we watch TV.

In *Bowling Alone,* Robert Putnam connects increased television viewing to the collapse of community. He cites Sue Bowden and Avner Offer's report on "Household Appliances and the Use of Time." These British researchers found that "television is the cheapest and least demanding way of averting boredom. Studies of television find that of all household activities, television requires the lowest level of concentration, alertness, challenge, and skill."[77] What a perfect way to slow down or shut off your brain. Yet overexposure or addiction to television can have the opposite effect. Other research revealed that people who complained of headaches, indigestion, or sleeplessness were dependent on television. While physical health, financial insecurity, and a lack of education also contributed to a general malaise, the amount of time spent watching TV had a direct correlation.[78] In other words, when we feel bad, watching television, "being entertained," only makes matters worse.

Putnam suggests that television has turned us into an isolated, disengaged culture. We no longer participate in civic activities such as volunteering at charities because our leisure time is invested in television viewing. The implications for an organization such as the local church are huge. The more TV people watch, the less likely they are to attend church—making television one of religion's most formidable challenges. How does television serve as a substitute religion if most of our viewing is passive and uninvolved? In other words, if we don't care about what we watch, how does television compete with something as devotion-driven as faith?

The Roper polling organization asked Americans, "When you turn the television set on, do you usually turn it on first and then look for something you want to watch, or do you usually turn it on only if you know there's a certain program you want to see? Do you find you frequently will just have the set on even though you're not really watching it?"[79] The Roper organization discovered that Americans have become less selective in their viewing habits and are more likely to turn the TV on and leave it on in the background. We're also watching more television than our parents watched, roughly four hours per day.[80] More of us are watching "whatever's on" for longer than ever before. Only television has managed to change kids from irresistible forces into immovable objects.[81]

The remote control has changed the way we watch television. A 1996 survey by the *Yankelovich Monitor* found that younger generations are more likely to channel surf through a wide array of programs.[82] Men use their remote controls like a flashlight in a forest, constantly hunting for bigger game behind the next bush, lurking on the next channel. The Discovery and Learning Channels offer instant trips to exotic destinations with programs featuring Top 10 lists of places to go. Television has become an adventure, with the remote control replacing the rocket ship. TV connects with our restless search for new lands to conquer.

Teachers must educate students accustomed to switching subjects at the moment boredom arises. Ministers preach to congregations steeped in steady visual stimulation. What are the implications of constant channel changing? Has the ability to zap from one corner of the television planet to another in a flash made our world seem smaller or expanded our intellectual and spiritual horizons? Kids are bored in church and school because they want more—more info, more exposure, and more life.

Yet kids raised on remote controls have no problem imagining a God communicating to every corner of the globe. God can hear and sort out all our prayers just as the converting box can receive and distribute multiple signals from the DirecTV satellite. Media analyst Tony Schwartz calls modern media a "'second God'—invisible but everywhere, all knowing, and working in mysterious ways."[83] Critic Stephen Stark finds eerie connections to St. Augustine's definition of God as "a Being whose center is everywhere and whose borders are nowhere." But is television a rival god, like the Old Testament's Baal, or merely a God-friendly metaphor? Research suggests that passive TV watching inspires complacency. But what about active engagement with stories and characters? Why do people get addicted to soap operas? Or obsessed with certain shows? Perhaps we can gather important theological truth by looking closer at shows that inspire the most rabid devotion.

A Mystery Religion

> The experience of watching television has become the social and intellectual glue that holds us together, our "core curriculum," our church.
>
> James Twitchell, *Lead Us into Temptation*

> Commercial television is ruthlessly secular. Its emphasis is on the immediate, the here-and-now, the accumulation of goods, and the denial that there is any higher experience than consuming and watching TV. . . . Ultimately, conventional religion is heretical to television's very notion of itself.
>
> Stephen Stark, *Glued to the Set*

Despite the best data marketing and demographics can offer, the "science" of TV programming remains a crapshoot. The number of new programs that become mainstream hits, renewed for successive seasons, remains low, and network executives fail regularly. For *Inside Prime Time,* media scholar Todd Gitlin interviewed television programmers. He found that the element that most consistently drives the industry is not politics or morals but sheer uncertainty. "No one in the industry knows exactly which shows will be popular and which will flop in the audience ratings. Moreover, there seems to be no sure way to predict success; the business is mired in its own chaos."[84] To broadcasters, television remains a mystery. Yet once viewers fall in love with a show, television becomes a religion.

Few programs are lucky enough to reach the magic number of one hundred episodes. What makes the number one hundred magic? Television's form of heaven, syndication, guarantees "eternal life" in reruns. Pioneering sitcoms such as *I Love Lucy, Leave It to Beaver,* and *My Three Sons* developed a corpus large enough to occupy a daily time slot. With one hundred episodes to choose from, local stations can air a sitcom such as *Seinfeld* Monday through Friday without the repeats wearing out their welcome. In syndication, the creators of these shows receive nearly eternal rewards called "residuals." Thirty years from now, *M*A*S*H, Friends,* and *Mad about You* will still be playing in TV land, their one hundred plus episodes in permanent rotation.

Shows that inspire passion, that fuel hours of online chatter, that attract a dedicated cult following are quite rare. But when viewers find their show, they tape it, anticipate it, and refer back to it. Conventions, costumes, and communal celebrations follow.

The original *Star Trek* was canceled before the *Starship Enterprise* completed its five-year mission. In just seventy-nine episodes that aired from 1966 to 1969, Gene Roddenberry created a universe that has been broadcast in forty countries, translated into fifty languages, and continues to be shown two hundred times a day.[85] *Star Trek: The Next Generation* doubled the output of the original, lasting for 178 syndicated episodes from 1987 to 1994. The sequels and spin-offs continue, from *Deep Space Nine* and *Star Trek: Voyager* to the prequel, *Enterprise*. As the most successful "failure" in television history, *Star Trek* defined the formula for creating a cult following. There may not be enough hard-core science fiction fans to create a network television hit, but those fifteen million Trekkies can jump-start a new program, guarantee a movie's opening weekend box office, and ensure eternal syndication.

The X-Files has come closest to duplicating *Star Trek*'s sci-fi success. Special agents Mulder (David Duchovny) and Scully (Gillian Anderson) complement each other as believer and skeptic, respectively. Their conviction that "the truth is out there" in the form of extraterrestrial life buoyed the fledgling Fox Network from 1993 to 2002. Creator Chris Carter says, "I think faith informs almost every episode. I'm a skeptic who desperately wants some reason to believe."[86] In an episode in which a satanic hit man stalks a boy with genuine stigmata, Mulder and Scully respond in surprising ways. The alien-affirming Mulder doubts the divine explanation of the stigmata, while the normally skeptical Scully finds herself drawn in.[87] A quick glance at a bookstore's television section reveals scores of books, manuals, and compendiums exploring *The X-Files'* "universe." The series concluded in May 2002 with a two-hour finale that featured super soldiers, mind readers, the nefarious cigarette-smoking man, and scads of government cover-ups.[88] Scully looked longingly at Mulder and concluded, "You want to believe. But believe in what?" After nine years of searching for the truth, Mulder longed to know that "the dead are not lost to us. . . . We're part of something greater than this [and greater than aliens]." He tenderly grasped the cross around Scully's neck and whispered, "Maybe there's hope."

Cult TV goes beyond sci-fi. The relaxed southern charm of *The Andy Griffith Show* continues to unite fan clubs around the world. *Buffy the Vampire Slayer* inspired countless web pages and chat rooms. By charging subscribers just twelve dollars per month, HBO acquired enough fans to make original series such as *The Sopranos* and *Sex and the City* instant cult classics.

Cult TV provides a detailed, self-contained, alternative universe. *Star Trek* devotees can buy the blueprints for the *Starship Enterprise*. *The Simpsons* has a massive gallery of recurring characters. Dedicated viewers eventually get complete back-stories for peripheral characters such as Principal Skinner, Groundskeeper Willie, and Christian neighbor Ned Flanders. Fanatical devotion leads to a deeper understanding of the interconnectedness of the program's universe. The creators' worldview comes into focus, allowing dedicated followers to analyze the creative choices for hours. That's why many new programs start with a "show Bible," a complete overview of the world the fictional characters will inhabit. Some fans go into obsessive detail creating time lines, architectural renderings, and family trees usually reserved for serious academic study.[89]

Cult TV shows bring perspective, offering pointed commentary on today's culture often wrapped in either nostalgia or science fiction. *Andy Griffith* takes viewers to a world that no longer exists. *Star Trek* takes viewers to a world they hope will exist. Some might call that an escape. But it can also be seen as a mythology. Such shows present a self-contained universe with values that make sense. External forces may threaten Mayberry or the *Enterprise,* but in the end, order is restored, peace is maintained. *Andy Griffith* and *Star Trek* offer a chance to discuss and process our world by viewing theirs. Cult TV shows give us the bigger perspective, maybe even a God's-eye view.

Finally, cult TV provides a sense of community. Fan clubs and conventions provide a gathering point for discussing a shared mythology, a common bond. Once the canon of a show is fixed, the characters' traits can be celebrated, the finer points of controversy reviewed by episode, chapter, and verse. It sounds exactly like a church gathering, right down to battles over the Bible. The former dean of the Annenberg School described television as the "new state religion" of the modern era, the primary dispenser of our allegories, gospels, and parables.[90] It may offer the best advice when read like the Bible's wisdom literature.

A Sage

> The answers to life's problems aren't at the bottom of a bottle. They're on TV!
>
> Homer Simpson

If television serves as a substitute church, what kind of theology does it communicate? The WB's *7th Heaven* focuses more on the Rev. Eric Camden's family than his preaching. Ministers such as the BBC's *Father Ted* and *The Vicar of Dibley* show the human and humorous side of Christianity. Viewers looking for the gospel message will likely be disappointed. But television still communicates plenty of truth. It serves as our collective wisdom literature. Like the Book of Esther, television doesn't have to mention God to be God-haunted. Like the Book of Ecclesiastes, television makes viewers look between the lines for answers. God is found in relationships, in ethical decisions, in the mundane. In an issue of *TV Guide* devoted to "God and Television," Jack Miles, the Pulitzer Prize–winning author of *God: A Biography,* found that "God on prime-time television is like God in American culture: submerged most of the time, emerging only as a guest star whose appearance is rarely announced."[91] Yet those guest appearances seem to be occurring more frequently, from the halls of *ER* to the legal chambers of *Judging Amy.*

Moral dilemmas arise naturally in dramas such as *NYPD Blue* and *Picket Fences.* Bill D'Elia, the executive producer of *Chicago Hope,* admits, "It's difficult to run a medical show and not deal with issues of God and religion. Each and every week, you're dealing with healers who believe they can prolong life and make it better. The very nature of the profession touches on issues of God."[92] When his cocky disregard for his supervisor's instructions endangers the life of a ten-month-old baby, ER's Dr. Benton ends an episode murmuring, "The Lord is my shepherd." The entire premise of CBS's *Early Edition* involves divine intervention. How does Gary Hobson receive a newspaper twenty-four hours before the rest of the world? What type of force wants him to prevent calamities? Executive producer Bob Brush says, "There is no question that some kind of force clearly steers events, but we specifically stay away from identifying what the nature of the spirituality is."[93]

On *The West Wing*, President Jeb Bartlet sends for his childhood priest when struggling with the death penalty. Actor Martin Sheen kneels on the presidential seal in the Oval Office while making his confession. For *West Wing's* 2001 season finale, President Bartlet raged against God behind the closed doors of National Cathedral with a passion comparable to that of Job.[94] On *The Sopranos,* another powerful leader brings his rage into therapy. Tony Soprano has wealth, power, and frustration comparable to the Bible's King Solomon. Tony and his wife, Carmen, have achieved all their goals and still feel, like the writer of Ecclesiastes, that "everything is meaningless."[95] On *Ally McBeal,* an eight-year-old leukemia patient hires Ally to sue God. Ally recalls her own anger following the death of her five-year-old sister. Yet she also remembers her mother saying, "God had man make the blimp to remind people that he's up there watching." After the boy succumbs to cancer, Ally ends the episode walking alone. She looks up and spots a blimp flashing the message, "Just Looking."[96] Serious questions about this disengaged God can be found in Old Testament writings from Job to the Psalms.

Sitcoms have also made room for God, most often in an African-American context. In the late eighties, Sherman Hemsley played an egotistical deacon on *Amen.* His comedic foil was a young reverend portrayed by real-life minister Clifton Davis. In an episode of *Living Single,* Khadijah goes back to church after a two-year absence. Executive producer Yvette Lee Bowser confessed, "I hope that episode encouraged some people to get back to the church. After all, it doesn't matter how often you go, but that you keep God at the center of your life."[97] On the clever Claymation series *The PJs,* Thurgood Stubbs sees a vision of a black Jesus and decides to become a daredevil for God. The episode concludes with Thurgood learning to "be still and know that I am God." Comedians Steve Harvey and Robert Townsend regularly incorporated faith as a "normal" part of their programs. Bernie Mac turns to the Bible to settle arguments with his television family.

The creators of *Home Improvement* chose a God metaphor so subtle that most viewers missed it. Tool man Tim Taylor repeatedly found advice behind a fence, in the hidden face of his all-knowing next-door neighbor Wilson.

The conversations between Tim and Wilson can be viewed as confessions, prayers, and advice. *King of the Hill*'s Texas setting demands plenty of references to football, riding mowers, and church. In an episode titled "Revenge of the Lutefish," the installation of a new woman minister prompts a protest from the misogynistic Grandpa Cotton Hill. When Bobby Hill accidentally burns down the church, Cotton is accused of committing a hate crime. The episode concludes with Cotton's apology and Bobby's confession. Peggy Hill gets the final word: "I forgive you." The short-lived NBC series *Kristin* made the title character's Christian faith the center of dramatic and comedic tension. Series star Kristin Chenoweth's real-life Baptist beliefs mirrored her fictional character's convictions.

The most consistently religion-obsessed sitcom is *The Simpsons.* In Mark Pinsky's excellent and detailed *The Gospel according to the Simpsons,* Ned Flanders is celebrated as "television's most effective exponent of a Christian life well-lived."[98] In the book's preface, famed evangelical Tony Campolo confesses, "*The Simpsons* provides me with a mirror that reflects my own religious life." Satirical Christian magazine *The Door* declares with all seriousness, "There is more spiritual wisdom in one episode of *The Simpsons* than there is in an entire season of *Touched by an Angel.*"[99] If that's true, then why have Christian viewers embraced *Touched by an Angel* but shunned *The Simpsons*? Many prefer witness to wisdom. A revealed message requires less reflection than a veiled theology.

After almost being canceled during its first two seasons, *Touched by an Angel* took off when scheduled for Sundays at 8 P.M. Five years after its shaky debut, *Angel* was CBS's top-rated drama and the second most-watched drama on television. The pilot episode featured drug jokes, angels who threatened people, a smoking and cussing Della Reese, and God as a dismissive joke. When CBS asked Martha Williamson to fix the pilot, she said, "This is a show without rules, and every successful series has to have rules that an audience can buy into and remember from week to week."[100] (Remember television's sense of liturgy.) When the CBS brass asked about her "rules," she suggested, "Angels have to believe in and respect and love their boss and that God doesn't screw up." Williamson recalls, "It was professional suicide in 1994 to walk into a network president's office and tell them they needed to apply biblical principles to a television show."[101] Yet Williamson got a chance to establish her rules.

In each episode, angel in training Monica gets a divine assignment from Tess, usually involving an unsuspecting person heading toward a personal crisis. Most shows end as the angels reveal themselves to the troubled guest star and offer comfort, guidance, and inspiration. Characters meet God in a blinding light and are changed forever. Andy Hill, then-president of CBS Entertainment Productions, recalls, "It's fair to say there has never been a show in the history of network television to go on with lower expectations than 'Touched by an Angel.'"[102] Yet the show has consistently communicated inspiring, faith-affirming messages while highlighting the plight of overlooked peoples in China and the Sudan. *Angel* ended in 2003, but over two hundred episodes will continue to spread faith, hope, and love in televised perpetuity.

ABC countered the success of *Angel* with their religious drama *Nothing Sacred*. Critics praised Kevin Anderson's earthy portrayal of an inner-city priest wrestling with doubt. *Nothing Sacred's* stories came from a writing staff of practicing Catholics that included a priest using a pseudonym. Episodes tackled gritty issues of poverty, homelessness, and unwanted pregnancies. *Nothing Sacred* addressed complex, troubling issues encountered by the priest and his parish. Yet religious groups such as Opus Dei and the Catholic League protested vocally and voraciously. *Nothing Sacred* didn't survive a season.

Nothing Sacred and *Touched by an Angel* tackled similar problems of infidelity, addiction, and anger. Yet one inspired religious protest, while the other generated Christian praise. What made *Touched by an Angel* connect with viewers while *Nothing Sacred* languished? Williamson cites two reasons:

> I think one is that we did not treat people of faith as jokes, as they had been treated everywhere else for years; and two, CBS gave the show enough time for the right viewers, the viewers we needed, to discover the show. The ones we needed, the ones who already believed in angels, were the ones avoiding the show like the plague—why watch when they know they are going to be made fun of? That changed with our show.[103]

Nothing Sacred treated its entire parish of characters with profound humanity and respect but generated rafts of protest letters. What separated the two shows were their final five minutes. *Sacred* ended with questions (and answers) rooted in wisdom literature, while *Angel* offered a consistent witness of hope. In fact, *Angel* got consistent complaints from Christians that it didn't offer enough witness: "Where was the magic 'J word'—Jesus?" A majority of Christians in America prefer a message to a meditation. They want prime-time religion to offer hope, not despair, to tie up problems rather than raise theological questions. Like network executives, television viewers shun controversy. *Touched by an Angel* provides a valuable service, offering a weekly dose of hope to hurting audiences. Maybe television didn't invent the twenty-two-minute solution; viewers demanded it.

But what happens to hurting audiences after the show ends, when a harsh "reality" returns? Ministers must offer a message of hope while slipping in the odd and troubling assurance that we don't always get the answers we want to hear. Television has heightened our desire for easy answers but works best when it demonstrates the wisdom of a sage.

An Art

As a relatively young art form, television has just begun to study itself. A&E introduced "TV-ography," a historical overview of classic series such as *The Mary Tyler Moore Show.* ESPN dug into ABC's sports archive to create *ESPN Classic.* The early days of MTV replay on *Classic VH1.* What are the implications of defining "classic moments"?

A potentially dangerous by-product of television is national amnesia. With TV as our primary source for education and information, events that happened B.T. (before television) will rarely be rehearsed. Music history starts with Elvis on *The Ed Sullivan Show;* presidential history begins with the 1960 Kennedy-Nixon debates. In *The Age of Missing Information,* Bill McKibben points out that television remembers and reports only what television has already reported.[104] So today's students have strong associations with the fifties and sixties, rooted in the endless recycling of Martin Luther King Jr.'s "I Have a Dream" speech, Neil Armstrong's one small step on the moon, and hippies frolicking at Woodstock. But Teapot Dome, Hoovervilles, and the Black Sox register blank stares equal to blank screens. "The history—social, cultural, musical, economic, political—of the last forty years appears every day a thousand times on our screens, more and more frequently all the time."[105] McKibben worries that we're "happily trapped in a familiar museum," stuck with the styles and attitudes of one limited time zone—the era of television. When attacks forged in ancient grudges and historical hatreds strike, we're often left dumbfounded, unable to reach back beyond TV land. Does the creation of a television museum suggest that the best has already been broadcast?

Then why have many critics celebrated recent sitcoms and dramas as the golden age of television? The brightest Ivy League graduates continue to gravitate toward the television business. A generation raised on moving images seems deeply committed to advancing this still-emerging art. Executive producers such as David E. Kelley (*Picket Fences, Ally McBeal, The Practice*), Aaron Sorkin (*Sports Night, The West Wing*), and David Milch (*NYPD Blue*) have merged ancient wisdom with a new medium.

The creative content of most television shows begins with these "showrunners." These executive producers craft the scripts, manage the productions, and steer a show through arduous twenty-two-episode seasons. Showrunners often start as staff writers, cranking out a steady stream of scripts to feed TV's insatiable appetite for original programming. Bruce Helford, the creator and showrunner of *The Drew Carey Show,* laments, "Television is a *really* bad art.

It's like someone going into a museum and saying, 'You know we have a lot of blank walls, let's make some paintings to fill them up.' *That's* what TV is—space trying to be filled."[106]

The producer of *The Beverly Hillbillies* liked actor Ed Wynn's description of TV as "the glass furnace," "because it burns up scripts; it burns up talent. It's just a fierce thing."[107] Showrunners work incredibly long hours under intense deadlines to produce new programming every week. Showrunner of *Mad about You,* Larry Charles, recalls, "It really did require eighteen-hour days, often seven days a week for weeks on end. Coming home I would be just a silhouette climbing into bed as my wife and kids were getting up. We really did not see each other for two years, which was damaging, no doubt about it."[108] After a while, Charles decided to simplify his life by wearing only pajamas to the office.[109]

Yet these overworked showrunners receive huge financial compensation for their efforts. *Forbes'* 1998 list of the highest paid entertainers is loaded with television producers, with Bruce Helford's $38 million yearly salary topping poor Leonardo DiCaprio's lowly $37 million. But no salary could compare to the dollars lavished on the creative team behind the top-rated sitcom *Seinfeld.* Showrunner Larry David raked in $200 million, and the star-producer-namesake Jerry Seinfeld topped him at $225 million—for one year![110]

The economics of television will continue to attract the sharpest and wittiest minds on the planet. Disney and Warner Brothers offer competitive fellowships to attract and train the most promising college grads. Fox's *24* has changed the shape and pace of television drama. *Malcolm in the Middle* and *The Bernie Mac Show* have expanded the art of the sitcom by using a single camera and creating a filmic quality. Yet the quality of television programs will likely go up and down at the same time.

The proliferation of channels will spread the talent pool too thin. Yet programs that emerge from the five-hundred-channel clutter will likely be more accomplished than ever before. As always, the pressure will be on viewers to discover what they like within a very crowded marketplace. Some suggest that the greatest threat to the emerging art of television is economics. The networks' hunger for affordable programming led to the ever expanding trend known as "reality TV."

A Mirror

> We are threatened by a new and peculiarly American menace. It is
> not the menace of class war, of ideology, of poverty, of disease, of
> illiteracy, of demagoguery, or of tyranny, though these plague most
> of the world. It is the menace of unreality.
>
> Daniel Boorstin, 1961, *The Image*

> I don't want realism; I want magic.
>
> Blanche Dubois, *A Streetcar Named Desire*

Court TV debuted on July 1, 1991, banking on the far-fetched notion that viewers would appreciate a sneak peek into courtroom trials. Cofounder Steven Brill recalls, "When I thought of Court TV, I had been in lots of courtrooms and had always been struck by the gap between what the public thought the process was all about, and what those of us who watched it up close knew it was all about. People thought trials were like Clint Eastwood or Perry Mason movies. I think we did open the legal system."[111] Columnist Joe Bob Briggs became an early advocate: "They show the same gol' dang trials over and over again, all day long, like MTV for lawyers. This stuff is great. I can't believe these trials won't bump soap operas off the air inside of three years. And if you think these trials are bloody, wait till they start doing divorce trials."[112] When O. J. Simpson was arrested for Nicole Brown Simpson's murder, the real world of Court TV suddenly became the hottest drama on television. By June 2001, Nielsen rated Court TV the fastest-growing cable network in the country, with subscribers up 40 percent from one year earlier.[113] Previous arcane legalese such as "sidebars" has become a permanent part of most Americans' vocabulary.

MTV's *Real World* followed in 1992 without much fanfare or expectation. It has become MTV's longest running series, with 191 episodes spread across ten houses and ten years. The cocreator of the series, Mary-Ellis Bunum, recalls, "We started with the two of us [Jonathan Murray and Bunum] working around the clock. Now we have a company of 160 people."[114] Why have reality series proliferated? They deliver all the favorable elements in television's bottom line—audiences, advertisers, and economics. Producers love reality series because they're cheap to produce. One location, a handful of nonprofessional "actors," and a bare-bones video crew put producers in business. Compared to the arduous costs of producing an hour of prime-time drama (estimated at $1.5 million in 1998),[115] *The Real World* looks like a bargain. And it attracts audiences, particularly younger, more impressionable viewers—the kind advertisers love. While critics carp, *Real World* fans continue to vote with their eyeballs, basically saying, "Let me be a fly on that wall." Naturally, equally low-budget programming such as *Cops, America's Most Wanted,* and *Road Rules* followed.

One can question the predictable cross section of America crammed into another house on *The Real World.* One can debate the ethics of crafty producers who manipulate the outcome of who gets voted off the island on *Survivor.* One can also bemoan the rash of copycats following in the wake of their fiscal success. But the television business has always preferred to duplicate a current success than to program another risky proposition. So CBS's *Survivor* spawned *Big Brother,* ABC's *The Mole,* Fox's *Boot Camp* and *Temptation Island,* and UPN's *Chains of Love.* The economics make sense. NBC president Jeff Zucker took heat for degrading his "must-see TV" network with *Fear Factor.* He rationalizes, "We still stand for quality. But c'mon—we're broadcasters. If we're going to survive, we have to attract a younger audience. The success of *Fear Factor* demonstrates a generational shift in television. People under the age of 35 grew up with O. J. as entertainment."[116]

What attracts viewers to reality TV? Some critics find the fake torment of *Fear Factor* an inadvertent tribute to our overprivileged lives. For those struggling in the third world, such obvious excess only fuels outrage at Western opulence. Syndicated columnist Norah Vincent suggests that inane reality shows might be a residual cause of September 11. By broadcasting our staged sufferings, Americans communicate just how wealthy and insensitive we've become. Vincent questions how MTV can stage a game show called *Kidnapped* after *Wall Street Journal* reporter Daniel Pearl was abducted in Pakistan. Is it emblematic of how far we've strayed from the volatile, genuine reality in the other two-thirds of the world?[117]

In a post-human era, reality TV should actually be seen as an encouraging sign. Younger viewers don't want acting; they want to follow real people, warts and all. They want models shaped like them caught up in stories with unpredictable endings. Reality TV suggests that audiences are tired of being passive—they want more participation, to judge their own "American idols." The manufactured contests of *Survivor* and *The Amazing Race* take cues from extreme sports. They offer experiences beyond the routine and take place in the most beautiful and exotic places. Rather than celebrating overabundance, reality TV critiques consumption, pointing to a search for significance outside life as we know it. Reality programming also offers television's clearest, most unvarnished mirror of who we are as people. Perhaps that's why it frightens so many critics. Reality TV presents human depravity.

A savage cinematic satire of reality TV, *Series 7,* was produced prior to *Survivor's* success. Filmmaker Daniel Minahan worked as a producer of Fox's *Cops* series, and his film, *Series 7,* captures the look, feel, and arch-importance of reality TV. Minahan's faux "real" show is called *The Contenders.* Contestants are drafted at random, given guns, and assigned a cameraman. Their objective is simple—to kill their fellow contestants before they're killed. Minahan considers producers who push people into these terrible situations the true villains. He comments, "There's a tendency in *The Real World* toward humiliation, toward ostracizing the person you don't like. *Survivor* and *Big Brother* are completely mean-spirited, all about singling out the person the group hates [or envies]. To me, that's completely anti-social and it's because the producers want it that way." He sums up the genre by saying, "It's interesting that these shows have chosen to be about mistrust and hatred. They could easily be the other way around. They could all be about people trying to work together."[118]

Perhaps producer Mark Burnett heard such objections after the victory of unapologetically self-interested Richard Hatch in the first *Survivor.* If Burnett does indeed manipulate the voting (as a contestant's lawsuit alleges), then allowing an all-American southern nurse and mother like Tina "Sunshine" Wesson to win *Survivor: The Australian Outback* over the more controversial and colorful Jerri Manthey was a stroke of public relations genius. With the victory of Ethan Zohn, another "good guy," on *Survivor: Africa,* the show almost became immune to accusations of promoting back-stabbing, self-interest, and the almighty dollar. *Survivor: Marquesas* winner Vecepia Towery referred to the Book of Habakkuk and celebrated the chance "to see God's hand at work." Have the producers "voted out" duplicitous "look out for No. 1" champions like Richard?[119] When *Survivor: The Australian Outback* supplanted *Friends* as television's top show, did audiences exhibit a preference for fair, team-minded role models?

Time will tell whether a steady diet of "lord of the flies" style entertainment increases sensitivity or heightens jadedness. But in the meantime, people of faith should embrace reality TV. It offers viewers an unvarnished portrait of our capacity to lie, cheat, and steal. The dark side of human sin gets revealed every hour. Perhaps the reality that evil sometimes triumphs over good scares us. We hate to think that Darwinian "survival of the wiliest" rules. Yet the Bible describes countless examples of injustice and indifference, the rich and strong trampling the weak and the poor. Reality TV offers a chance to discuss kingdom values, to question a winner-takes-all philosophy.

We can hate the portrait in the mirror or welcome it as a starting point for ethical engagement with the real world. The emerging generation has decided where to turn to understand how the system works. Teens caught in the high-stakes game of college admissions already know how intense competition can be. They're deciding what corners they might cut to outlast and outwit others. People of faith must understand that video voyeurism can inspire critical self-examination. The implicit question driving reality TV's manufactured conflicts remains, "What would you do?" Disgust viewers feel for duplicitous contestants might inspire a lifetime of integrity. The ethical and theological dimensions of reality TV launch discussions on school buses, in lunchrooms, around water coolers. Christians need to get into the grittiness and grayness of *Survivor* before they're voted off the island for irrelevance.

Former rap star MC Hammer demonstrated how people of faith can make a difference on even the most questionable of reality shows. The WB series *The Surreal Life* placed seven "C-list" celebrities in a house together for ten days. The cast included actors from *Baywatch, Webster,* and *Beverly Hills 90210.* To ensure a certain volatility, the producers of *The Surreal Life* added Vince Neil, the lead singer for notorious heavy metal band Motley Crue, and Jerri Manthey, the most contentious *Survivor* ever, to the home. Executive Producer Mark Cronin said, "We wanted worlds in collision."[120] On the first show, Hammer had his newfound faith as a minister tested. He refused to participate in their dinner, "sushi in the raw," served on a naked woman's body. But as the series evolved, Hammer also found out about Vince Neil's anger with God over his loss of a child to leukemia. When Hammer was invited to preach at the First AME Zion Church in Los Angeles, the entire house went along. As Rev. Hammer started his sermon, he called on Neil, inviting him to bring his anger forward, and church ministers surrounded him with prayers of comfort. Neil and all the other house members wept at this moment of confession, prayer, and purgation. By the conclusion of the series, Hammer presided over the wedding ceremony of former teen idol Corey Feldman. A situation designed as disposable entertainment turned into a genuine ministry opportunity for a faithful former celeb willing to get into the mix. MC Hammer concluded, "It has turned out to be a life-changing experience for everyone in this house."[121]

A Confessional

> More theology is conveyed in, and retained from, one hour of popular television than from all the sermons that are also delivered on any given weekend in America's synagogues, churches and mosques.
>
> Phyllis Tickle, *God-Talk in America*

Reality TV allows viewers to be much more than voyeurs. We're invited to sit in as electronic priests. The cast of *The Real World* and *Big Brother* give up their secrets on camera. The cocreator of *The Real World,* Jonathan Murray, acknowledges the source: "Too bad you can't put a copyright on a confessional, but I guess the Catholic Church has that."[122] Not for long.

For many, talk shows have become the confessional of choice. Almost every talk show begins with a guest who has a secret to reveal. They bring their mother, brother, or ex-lover to Jenny or Jerry or Sally Jesse, spotting an ideal time to reveal some painful, hidden truth. Dirty laundry gets aired in public with the cameras rolling.

Some viewers get a kick out of such shows. The tangled relationships revealed on *Ricki Lake* allow audiences to feel superior. Our problems look mild compared to the perversities explored on *Jerry Springer.* Desperate guests longing to know somebody cares end up mocked by studio audiences *and* home viewers. Those hoping for validation from television end up ridiculed and reviled. The television confessional that should restore relationships has destroyed the participants, even leading to murder after a *Jenny Jones* show. Viewers who stand in for priests regress from sympathy to superiority.

Like many sharp, intelligent people, *Newsweek* columnist Anna Quindlen attempted to understand why "garbage" such as *Judge Judy* and *Ricki Lake* continues to attract viewers. She inverts the conventional wisdom that TV is the first choice of those with nothing better to do. Perhaps the boom in vicarious "shock" TV corresponds to having too much to do. She suggests, "An entire nation living at warp speed has no time for tedium."[123] Television has become the audiovisual equivalent to a Starbucks fix—a direct electric jolt to our already overextended system. With no time to finish our to-do list, we certainly can't be expected to manage a personal emotional life. Click on the tube, and *Jerry Springer* provides all the emotional range we'd possibly need, from shock to rage to tearful confessions. The proliferation of talk shows demonstrates our hunger for feelings, a need for personal resurrection.

Christian Century explored the power of talk shows in a cover story on Oprah. Writer Marcia Nelson noted how Oprah incorporates roles traditionally reserved for the church. She encourages confession on her talk show because for her, "Talk is crucial, even salvific."[124] When she interviews pop star Brandy about an abusive relationship in her teenage years, Oprah insists, "You're gonna save a lot of girls today." With the help of Dr. Phil, Oprah has spread therapeutic language so broadly that psychologists have almost become irrelevant. People engage in self-analysis while following along at home. Kids raised on talk shows can decide whether to give guidance counselors and therapists what they want to hear. Oprah promotes the power of public confession because she can testify from her own life. She offers stories about being abused as a child that liberate her and her audience. She deals with her diet and weight in public and empowers thousands of viewers struggling in private. She offers community, a voice that says, "You are not alone."

Dating games offer two religious rites—a confessional and premarital counseling. *Blind Date, Change of Heart, Rendez-View, Meet My Folks, Fifth Wheel,* and *Elimidate* expose the machinations behind our mating rituals. Viewers hear contestants' immediate reactions and previously private thoughts. Awkward first dates and painful breakups are equal opportunities for on-camera confessions. The snappy thought balloons on *Blind Date* mock the contestants. Yet the proliferation of these contests suggests how complex and confusing the post-sexual world can be.

ABC's *The Bachelor* combines dishy voyeurism with Cinderella fantasy. As Alex Michel, the bachelor, sorted through twenty-five candidates, searching for Mrs. Right, viewers could feel superior to the aspiring wives, pick up romantic pointers, and have their dreams fulfilled when Prince Charming chose one lucky lady.[125] No wonder the ratings were huge among women eighteen to thirty-four, advertisers' most desirable demographic. When feminist critics carped, producers reversed the roles on *The Bachelorette.* The jilted runner-up from *The Bachelor* assumed the position of power and wept every time she had to break another aspiring husband's heart. As in real life, such dating games are painful, high-stakes, and humbling.

Television has responded to the widening gap between the arrival of puberty and the sacrament of marriage with comedic relief. Dating games offer a welcome reminder of how painful mating rituals can be, especially for viewers who'd rather view dates than go on them.[126] They also suggest how close viewers are to despair. Every time the ratings rise for *Joe Millionaire,* churches should offer another seminar on sexuality. Talk shows and game shows exploit the elusive nature of love. The ridiculous lengths people will adopt to find a mate underlines our intense longing for love. Contestants take risks, look foolish, and expose themselves to heartbreak and public humiliation in search of love. Perhaps the rise of dating games corresponds to renewed spiritual interest. We can castigate those who look for love in all the wrong places or affirm the long and restless search that fuels the dating game. Every new talk show or dating game underscores how much more love and compassion the postmodern church must offer.

A Reflection of God

> I believe that television is going to be the test of the modern world and that in this new opportunity to see beyond our range of vision we shall discover either a new and unbearable disturbance of the general peace or a saving radiance from the sky. We shall stand or fall by television, of that I am quite sure.
>
> E. B. White, 1938, quoted in *Disconnected America*

When Marshall McLuhan declared, "The medium is the message,"[127] he pointed out that *what* we watch is far less important than *how* we watch. McLuhan anticipated both our shorter attention spans and our increasingly sophisticated visual vocabulary. "Before TV, there had been much concern about why Johnny couldn't read. After TV, Johnny has acquired an entirely new set of perceptions."[128]

Unfortunately, many of McLuhan's disciples failed to embrace these new perceptions. Neil Postman condemned the rise of television in his best-selling polemic, *Amusing Ourselves to Death*. Postman considered Johnny's reading problem an early warning, the death of discourse, the end of all logic. He boldly announced, "I believe the epistemology created by television not only is inferior to a print-based epistemology but is dangerous and absurdist."[129] Postman traced his disdain for moving images all the way back to the Bible, to the second commandment against the creation of idols, "graven images." As a college professor, Postman saw his students' growing expectation that education be entertaining as problematic. He blamed *Sesame Street* for confusing kids, blurring the lines between learning and laughing.

Nevertheless, the way forward is not a return to the printed word. Television technology is still in its infancy, and we literally ain't seen nothing yet. With HDTV on the way, the need for discernment is just starting. We will get only more visual stimulation. In this evolutionary struggle, adaptation is inevitable. People of faith need not fear the triumph of images. The Word of God spread far and wide in a pre-literate society. God will thrive even in a post-literal world. We have plenty of experience talking about the message. What we need is a theology rooted in the medium.

Mitchell Stephens's *Rise of the Image, the Fall of the Word* celebrates a future filled with moving images. He looks forward to exploring the possibilities of image-based storytelling:

Our eyes were selected over millions of years of primate evolution for their ability to notice, search, compare, connect, and evaluate. Increasingly, in the five thousand years since the development of writing, they have been reduced to staring at letters of identical size and color, arranged in lines of identical length, on pages of identical size and color. Readers, in a sense, are no longer asked to see; they are simply asked to interpret the code.[130]

Stephens responds to altered perceptions by optimistically quoting Nietzsche: "The more eyes, different eyes, we can use to observe, the more complete our vision will be."[131] We must abandon the notion that "surfaces" are inherently superficial. Stephens suggests that looking out may offer a healthy alternative to looking in. In fact, looking for signs and images may inspire us to look up in a search for transcendence.

The expansion of television can inspire a much bigger view of God. An early preview is offered in the documentary *The Face of Jesus in Art.* It offers a tour of the colorful history of Christian art, from stained glass windows to Rembrandt's canvases. Viewers float through the great churches and museums of Europe, discovering surprisingly diverse portraits of Jesus. The program concludes with a blending of ancient images and digital technology. The face of Jesus morphs from one painting to another, from lily white to dark brown. Jesus is portrayed as European, African, Asian, and American Indian in a space of seconds. These images communicate more than any sermon about Jesus' universal appeal. History is compressed, barriers are broken down, by pictures of Jesus spliced together at the postmodern pace of MTV.

We've only just begun to see a God who looks like all of us. Television can provide a window into the world, to the many faces of Jesus. In fact, the changing functions of television reveal forgotten aspects of God. A theology of television must borrow from icons, from the non-Protestant Church. In Orthodox and Catholic traditions, icons provide a two-way street. We may stare at the face of Jesus, but Jesus also looks at us, entering our space. Looking at television can slowly put us to sleep. But realizing that television stares back can wake us up to a world of possibilities.

What started as a technology, an appliance, evolved into a comforter of choice. It began as a salesman but became a store. The town square divided us into tribes and sent us toward separate rooms. Custom TV will follow us all the days of our lives, serving as a constant companion. Yet when we hate TV, we hate ourselves, revolted by the reality it presents. Efforts to control it end only in frustration. It remains a mystery, even for those who've devoted their lives to studying it. We want it to offer a tidy message, but it's best when offering the wisdom of a sage. It is a burgeoning art form that reflects our highest aspirations and most devious behavior. Television reveals human sin and our longing for love. The message may confuse us, but the medium reflects the changing perceptions of our eternal, immutable God.

fashion

Dressing Up the Soul

Clothing gives human beings their anthropological, social and religious identity, in a word—their being.

M. Perniola

Fashion is the sartorial expression of a given group of people at a precise moment in their history.

Bruno du Roselle

Of all the subjects tackled in this book, theology and fashion present some of the biggest challenges. What on earth does clothing have to do with theology? Or perhaps more importantly, how does one construct a theological position based on contemporary fashion trends? Jesus said in Matthew's Gospel, "Do not worry about . . . what you will eat or drink; or about your body, what you will wear. Is not life more important than food, and the body more important than clothes?" (6:25). This statement alone would seem to discourage efforts to construct something of lasting value from the way in which we clothe ourselves. But what if we turn things around and attempt to "decode" fashion to see if it leads to theological conclusions about the state of contemporary culture?

The term *decode* points to the fact that fashion is a series of signs that unlock at least part of the pop culture psyche. Goods contain value in their immaterial aspects. The immaterial aspect of fashion, for instance, is found in the cultural references that clothing expresses and the signs and information it incorporates. For example, a pair of "bondage trousers" (the official name of punk pants) are not that different from a pair of suit trousers, except that they not only create an appearance but also modify the identity of the wearer. This may seem to be nothing more than a matter of appearance, but in terms of appearance, it is quite significant.

We live in an age in which what we wear and how we present ourselves are important issues. "Fashion is always the product of the culture that spawns it, embodying the concerns of the wider society in its myriad styles."[1] The ability to express oneself in clothing and style was once the domain of the wealthy. Appearance meant little to the vast majority of people on the planet. But the industrial era changed that dynamic by lowering costs and allowing access to more and more materials. Gradually, fashion has become everyone's opportunity, and it has created a topsy-turvy world.

I (Barry) grew up in a working-class British family with little discretionary income. Hand-me-down clothes, or secondhand items, stigmatized our class. I love the newness of things and have little patience for scouring vintage clothing stores for someone else's castoffs. Yet those with the resources to buy anything and everything new buy clothing that looks used, even when it isn't. Worn and broken-in clothing carries an entirely different cultural meaning for them. In our post-technological world, full of new things and new experiences, we hunger for things that have weathered time, that signify lasting value, that offer a lived-in feel. What we wear expresses the spirit of the times in which we live. Someone walking around the high-priced stores of Rodeo Drive in Beverly Hills wearing an Elizabethan doublet with tight leggings and pointed shoes would be viewed as either a little nutty or on his way to a costume party. We attach sign value to clothing.

At conferences I've attended, a definite look identifies those in postmodern ministry. It may involve tattoos or piercings, facial hair (soul patches, not beards!), and casual dress (no three-piece preacher suits here). These are the signs of the Gen-X minister. What is worn on the outside often reflects what is going on inside.

In his book *Virtual Faith,* author Tom Beaudoin sees fashion as a "way for the body, or even the self, to communicate itself to society."[2] He goes on to say that to "begin any fashion-oriented interpretation of popular culture, one must choose which fashion 'events'—that is, which particular costumes and bodily adornments—to take into consideration."[3] In other words, any number of issues can be examined in this realm. As with the other aspects of popular culture, fashion remains highly personal and subjective.

Jesus may tell us not to worry about what we wear, but we do. Our culture places a high priority on outward appearance. Appearance often signifies how we feel inside, and it can reveal what's happening in contemporary society as we search for identity, meaning, and shape for our lives. We also do a lot of judging by outward appearance (something for which at least one of the prophets was chastised by God). We are shocked by body piercings and bare navels, by scantily clad teens and goths, punks, rockers, and all the other fashion subcultures we encounter. But ever changing fashion scenes offer ways to "read" culture. Beaudoin argues that the way people "adorn their temples" provides a way to interpret their "lived theology."

The ways we look and dress make huge statements about where we are going and who we are. The transitory and changeable nature of fashion matches the changing sense of self that permeates our post-human culture. Photos, newsreels, and movies up until about the mid-fifties reveal that men usually wore suits, ties, and hats—think of Humphrey Bogart, Clark Gable, Cary Grant. Men both young and old dressed basically the same. Suits were worn for a lifetime. The message communicated was that the body remained unchanged. Now, fashion changes every season, even for men. What's the new message? The body, like everything else in contemporary culture, is in a constant state of flux.

In fact, fashion itself has been transformed. It involves style[4] more than fashion. The fashion industry generates ever changing signs that we, to varying degrees, consume. The old rules no longer suffice. We have been freed from traditional and religious constraints about dress, as we have in other arenas of human life. A far more complex and nuanced set of ideas about the construction of identity has arisen in their place. This is what fashion means and what this chapter explores. Religion wishes to speak to us about how we construct our identities. Indeed, it offers us explanations for our identities—telling us that God has a say in this regard. Therefore, if another medium speaks to this territory of the soul, it must be explored as well. Let's see what fashion has to say.

Fashion's Roots

The fashion of this world passeth away.

1 Corinthians 7:31 KJV

A store called Oki-Ni opened recently on Savile Row, London's famous street for bespoke tailoring. The store itself is very modern, a stripped-down open space made out of recycled timber, steel, and felt. It resembles a gallery more than a store and aims to turn the act of shopping into a thing of beauty. Customers are invited to view and try on limited edition designer merchandise made exclusively for the store by designer labels such as Adidas, Evisu, and Fake of London. The only problem is that you can't take any of the goods with you. The store carries little stock, just a few sizes of each piece to try on, and offers a three-day turnaround for purchases. Following the Savile Row tradition, the store focuses on personal service and attention to detail. In an age of immediate gratification, Oki-Ni serves as an experiment in shopping, getting rid of the end (buying something immediately) so both customers and staff can concentrate on the means (enjoying the clothes and the store itself). As a final deterrent to immediate gratification, there is no cash register in the store.

Oki-Ni's experiment in both retail and fashion demonstrates the changing world of consumerism. The store uses novelty to generate notoriety and create a loyal customer base founded on exclusivity. But it also points to the broader cultural effort to find a sense of individuality in our consumer society. We laud individuality, while producers ply their wares in mass-marketing ways. As a result, our streets are full of "individuals" who express their individuality by wearing the same Banana Republic khakis, Gap T-shirts, and Timberland boots as everyone else. But before we critique the present, let's consider the fashion past.

Dating the birth of fashion is difficult because people have been wearing clothes since the Garden of Eden! Just as the Bible has a story about the fall and the subsequent application of the fig leaf, so many cultures possess creation stories that discuss personal adornment. But fashion as an idea—a way of looking at and thinking about clothing—began around the fourteenth century.[5] Clothing helped to denote rank, status, and gender. The first dictionary reference to fashion appeared at the turn of the seventeenth century, but the use of decorative features in clothing had already begun. Silk and velvet grew in popularity in the sixteenth century, and black was introduced into men's wardrobes around the same time. The invention of looms large enough for mass production took place at the end of the eighteenth century, and fashion as an industry exploded in the nineteenth century.

In 1830, Barthelemy Thimmonnier invented the sewing machine, which provided the final ingredient necessary for the mass production of clothing. Dress designers also began to appear at this time, and their role was not only to design dresses but to sell them as well.[6] This role initiated a new industry and provided work for thousands of people. Interestingly, this new industry did not loose a wave of individuality in dress. To keep costs low, clothing was kept very simple. Straight pants, loose jackets, and shirts with detachable collars were appropriate for men. Women wore long gathered skirts and simple white blouses. It would take another development, the department store, to encourage the creation of newer, more attractive outfits. These stores initiated the transition from clothing as a means of protecting and covering the body, shielding it from the elements, to clothing as fashion.

France became the center of fashion for the Western world, whether through the influence of kings such as Louis XVI or the haute couture designers of Paris's Left Bank. It remains the center today, although it is a center held together by global conglomerates, with designers from Japan, America, and Great Britain. Clothing has become a major part of the global economic culture. Three and a half million tons of nylon are made every year, and seven billion pairs of jeans were sold in 1995.[7] Companies such as Levi, Gap, Gucci, and Chanel are brand names with global recognition.

This incomplete history demonstrates the basic shift that took place in fashion in the last couple hundred years. Clothing changed from being merely functional to a means by which self-revelation or self-identity can be demonstrated. Fashion provides a space for image makers and consumers to experiment with culturally held views about the body and the person. Fashion affirms these views through traditional folk costumes, uniforms, and dress codes and challenges them through street wear, "political clothing" (as in T-shirts with slogans), and clothing that reveals more of the body such as miniskirts and halter tops. Fashion constructs and reflects ideas about the physical body. In every country, social, cultural, and political changes are manifested in the ways people dress. In Europe, this was demonstrated in loose empire-cut dresses worn by French women after the Revolution and in the flapper clothing styles that swept Great Britain after World War I. The miniskirts that came along in the 1960s crystallized women's liberation and a new sexual revolution. Fashion also plays a part in the development of ethics and morality. London designer Katherine Hamnett has often used her political agenda as a foil for her fashion designs. She recently released a series of pieces reflecting her antiwar views in the wake of September 11, 2001.

As the modern world experienced a collapse of its central political, economic, and religious values, new means of constructing morality came into play. As Richard Stivers says in his book *The Culture of Cynicism,* "In the past, public opinion formed around Christian morality and was subservient to it. Today, public opinion is largely but not exclusively wedded to the growth of technology and its promise. This form of morality is an expression of the instinctual power of desire."[8] Fashion shows that postmodern morality is a fluid, developing idea, not a fixed set of absolutes. These shifting ideas about ethics and morality can be challenged and affirmed as different social groups use fashion to undergird their views. Various groups—rockers, bikers, hippies, yuppies, punks, goths, skaters—use clothing to communicate both their alienation from mainstream society and their particular take on morality.

Fashion involves more than how we dress. Issues of body image and perception as well as gender and sexuality form an intrinsic part of the dynamics of fashion. They will be considered here.

Luxury and Power

a wolf in sheep's clothing: someone dangerous disguised as
   someone harmless
to give someone the boot: to dismiss a person from his or her work
in one's birthday suit: to be naked

In the U.K. edition of *Esquire,* a monthly column takes readers "from the catwalk to the sidewalk" and shows them how to re-create expensive clothing "looks" on differing budgets. The column covers four price levels: catwalk, splash, spend, and save. The economic disparity between catwalk luxury and low-budget save is quite amazing, but it is possible to "get the look" even if you can't afford the real thing.

Modernity brought a level of comfort and opportunity to the lives of working-class people that was unheard of before. The emergence of a middle class reflected the new opportunities available to people willing to work hard and better themselves. Fashion enabled working-class people to achieve the look of the wealthy. In our culture, appearance plays a large part in how we relate to one another. We all tend to make judgments about people based on their appearances. Developments in fashion allowed people to create the appearance of having and being more than they actually had and were.

"If you want to understand material culture at the beginning of the twenty-first century, you must understand the overwhelming importance of unnecessary material."[9] So begins the latest book from culture watcher James Twitchell. Not only do we pursue the unnecessary, but we want luxury as well. Luxury is the new thing we all want, even if we have to pretend we have it! Fake designer clothes, watches, and bags reflect the power labels have on the cultural psyche. A shift took place as we changed from a producing society to a consumer one. Individuality has been subsumed to fitting in.[10] We have to consume the right brands in order to compete and interact with others.

U.K. artists Gilbert and George have taken a rather eccentric posture within British culture. The pair has collaborated, lived, and worked together since art school, and their lives are one huge interactive performance piece. They eat at the same restaurant every day, wear the same kinds of clothes, and ignore film, television, and all the other elements of our entertainment culture. Their reason for doing so is based on an observation that we live in a time characterized by "fascism of taste." "Nobody has a capacity to look and decide what they feel about it [fashion] anymore. Nobody's allowed to have an opinion about it."[11] Their reaction may seem a little extreme, but their point remains well made. We live in a time in which conformity drives cultural affiliation. Going to the right films and the right clubs, listening to the right music—and wearing the right labels—have become cultural must-dos. "In a world informed by marketing," writes Twitchell, "the shame of consuming too much has been reconfigured into the shame of not consuming the proper stuff."[12] This is not a purely Western phenomenon but a global trend. "For millions of people around the world the cake of luxury is becoming the wafer of presumed salvation."[13]

The late Italian designer Moschino sent a model down the runway for his 1991 spring/summer collection in an outfit that seemed to exhibit over-the-top power dressing. But the gold embroidery on the jacket carried a message that read: "Waist of Money."[14] Ever the satirist, Moschino combined our desire for the power of fashion clothing with the idea that we've been taken for a ride. Nevertheless, we succumb to the lure of expensive clothing because we understand that identity in our culture often starts with appearance. While many adopt a careless attitude toward dress as a statement about the values and opinions of others, most of us dress in ways that will ensure our acceptance, if not in the culture at large, then at least within a particular subculture. "Consumerism is far more than just economic activity; it is also about dreams and consolation, communication and confrontation, image and identity."[15]

Clothes denote status and create desire. When Jesus was crucified, lots were cast for his clothing. A seamless garment was apparently something to be desired. Rappers and hip-hop artists have made dressing an art form. Not only do many singers have their own clothing lines (P. Diddy has Sean Jean, Jay-Z has Rock-a-Fella, Jennifer Lopez has J-Glow), but they also frequent designer stores and shows and take great delight in demonstrating their social and economic power through their clothing. "A frisson of envy and desire is added to the clothing worn by those within a particular circle."[16]

I have a magnet on my fridge that reads, "Good clothes open all doors." Clothing, cosmetics, and perfumes have long been offered as a route for social advancement in our culture, and this truth has not been lost on those raised on popular culture. A desire for consumer goods stems from more than possessing certain items. It is connected to the search for new experiences, new relationships, and even a new sense of "me." We have come to believe that we can find those things by transforming ourselves via fashion.

Anti-Fashion

mad as a hatter: crazy
talking through one's hat: talking nonsense
if the shoe fits, wear it: you decide whether a particular description
   fits you

A single phrase summarizes an entire decade's commitment to excess: Greed is good. The movie *Wall Street* was released at the height of 1980s Reaganomics and reflected an unrivaled global pursuit of economic success. Developer Donald Trump reveled in his newfound wealth and celebrity by buying huge, garish homes and living an extravagant lifestyle. Power suits demonstrated determination and a will to succeed. But that particular economic wave crested, and a new group of people tried their hand at economic success. The "greed is good" generation gave way to the "dot.com" generation. Computers and Internet technology initiated a whole new way of dressing.

Remember how everyone in business used to wear some sort of suit? Now, most banks and other businesses have casual Fridays—when the person handling your finances can be seen wearing an "I Love Marge Simpson" T-shirt! Dress has become more and more relaxed. A friend of mine who works for a major investment firm told me that his company no longer requires brokers to wear suits. Banks are no longer the economic power brokers they once were. Technology wizards, who generally shunned suits in favor of far more relaxed clothing, attracted much of the new capital. Forced to compete with the new economy, banks now try to appear cool. Fashions in the financial world acknowledged the shift in the economic power base. "New wealth" customers now form the core of the financial viability of many banks and investment firms, and these customers have a different set of values and goals than did their predecessors.

Casual dress challenges the ideas and values that fueled the modern age. If power suits reflected the final gasps of old-school economics, then today's dressed-down look reflects disdain for those values. This process began in the late 1950s with the biker look, gained momentum with the hippie movement, and continues today with goth, punk, and vintage clothing. These styles reflect distance from the values and ideals of another age.

The Streets

> The first spiritual want of a barbarous person is decoration.
>
> Thomas Carlyle, quoted in *Virtual Faith*

As fashion goes global and the world connects through new technologies, the streets of the world's major cities resemble one another more and more. Contemporary street fashion reveals three recurring fashion statements: a fascination with things military, a growing movement toward tattooing and body modification, and a cult-like approach to vintage or retro-fashion.

When U2 opened the 2001 Grammy show with their song "Beautiful Day," Bono was wearing a military style jacket. Its drab green color resembled the fatigues of combat soldiers everywhere. Yet Bono's jacket was covered with embroidered roses designed by Italian fashion maverick Roberto Cavalli. His 2001 fall collection relied heavily on military style clothing, but much of it was covered with flowers—war and peace combined. The utilitarian and functional nature of military clothing was blended with the pastoral and the beautiful. Incongruous? Of course. Culturally relevant? Absolutely.

Pop culture has often appropriated military clothing in nonmilitary settings. Army surplus stores do a brisk business selling military clothing in urban settings. How strange that we wear military clothing while resisting armed conflict. But urban life can feel like war at times. Military clothing sends strong signals about how we feel about our lives. Tom Beaudoin interprets this fashion choice as a statement about our battle for meaning in our lives.[17] We reflect what is going on inside us and the values by which we live in the clothes we wear. Military clothing matches our rough and rugged times.

During the 1960s, civilians wore military dress uniforms. Gold buttons, brocade, and bright colors fit well with the sense of liberation from social norms that marked the era. Wearing a military uniform made an antiestablishment statement. Coupling a uniform with long, unkempt hair and sandals sent the message that ties to the prior generation had been severed. The pride of war veterans became a fashion accessory for the new generation.

Post-traumatic people prefer the combat and camouflage gear of real warfare. Gangsta rappers wear bulletproof vests onstage, and hip-hop performers wear camouflage uniforms made of leather. The streets are filled with young people dressed for urban guerrilla living. They've stripped down to the basics, equipping themselves for mobile lives full of countless threats. Life in the postmodern world involves risk. What better way to symbolize that risk than through combat gear.

Camouflage clothing makes a great equalizer. It is difficult to tell who is who when people dress in camouflage. Rank and position get blurred. This reflects the equalizing attitude of a post-institutional culture in which rank and authority are suspect. Authenticity, not entitlement, carves the path to acceptance and influence. Camouflage also provides a defense by "canceling out" the person wearing it. Soldiers can avoid being seen by the enemy. In a highly individuated society, sometimes we need to be invisible to get around unnoticed and undisturbed. Camouflage suggests, "Leave me alone!"

Fashion houses have incorporated the military look into their designs. Dolce and Gabbana created postmodern military uniforms for their 2001 winter collection, complete with combat boots (covered with paint and slogans). In fact, heavy-duty work boots have become a staple of urban living. Beaudoin states that "military boots, which are made for lengthy, heavy-duty marches, implied a prolonged trek toward wholeness and out of suffering."[18] Many feel embattled. In *Fight Club,* Tyler Durden identifies the front lines as our lives. A uniform helps prepare us for that war.

A couple of other street styles fall into similar categories of interpretation. Punk clothing started in 1970s Great Britain, a time of great social and political upheaval when the working class reacted to the government's stripping away of nationalized industries and social systems. It found inspiration in the Situationist movement of 1960s France, which was characterized by the "politics of boredom."[19] The Situationist Internationale was formed by a group of European intellectuals and avant-garde artists in 1957 and was dedicated to the subversion and critique of modern society. Members railed against the role that capitalism and technology played in creating a culture that rendered true individuals powerless by making them dependent on entertainment and consumerism. They used art to practice their subversion, often taking what was considered low art—comic books, newspapers, and romance novels—and reconfiguring it into political and antiestablishment statements. The "politics of boredom" was a slogan created by fashion designer and Sex Pistols' creator Malcolm McLaren. It was a reworking of the Situationist slogan "Boredom is always counterrevolutionary."[20] The Situationists believed that boredom was a product of modernity and was a form of social control created by those who controlled the flow of capital and the power of technology and media. Punk was an attempt through music and fashion to challenge the establishment's perceived control over individuals' freedom.

Punk's torn and ripped clothing stopped traffic when it first appeared. McLaren and his then-wife, fashion designer Vivienne Westwood, introduced political and social sloganeering: bondage trousers and "bovva boots" (heavy, steel-toed, rubber-soled work boots). Their strange antiestablishment, anti-monarchical, nationalist bent resulted in colored and spiked hair. Punks wore safety pins in their clothing and in body parts as anti-jewelry. Such decoration was decidedly tongue-in-cheek because there was nothing "safe" about punks—their entire demeanor was threatening. Punk clothing articulated the massive unrest sweeping through British youth culture as the '70s unfolded in layoffs, unemployment, fuel shortages, and declining social services. Punk clothing was a reaction against the perceived emptiness and shallow promises of the previous generation.

Today, punk clothing functions in much the same way as military clothing. It sends a message of disconnectedness with the values of mainstream society and a desire for an aggressive push into new modes of meaning.

Gothic clothing is easy to spot. It's black—all black except for an occasional crucifix. The style is also characterized by heavily dyed hair, black lipstick, and white kabuki-style face makeup. Goths look as though they could use a few days in the sun to put some color back into their cheeks. Goths send a message of suffering-induced apathy and isolation. They also embrace androgyny. In goth circles, males and females wear similar clothing and makeup. Such people seem lost and unable to connect with culture. They want something but are not sure what. They resort to nihilistic and self-destructive attitudes and actions out of desperation. Like punks, they bear the weight of culture's sense of disappointment and loss. Beaudoin notes a sense of humor, gallows humor perhaps, within goths. Their slightly clownish portrayal of their internal feelings—the over-the-top use of white makeup and black lipstick—demonstrates their ability to commodify their suffering.[21]

Goth clothing and music developed as a subgenre of heavy metal rock music and is characterized by a fascination with death; hence, the proclivity toward black clothing and white makeup. There is also copious use of predominantly Christian symbolism surrounding death: crucifixes, skulls, sacred hearts. Goth appearance points to disaffection with the present world, with all its discontents, and acknowledges the world beyond—a world in their view filled with the absence of God. The embrace of religious imagery is not so much a statement of belief as it is of unbelief, of the ineffectual nature of faith to provide hope in the face of the onslaught of society's disintegration. The goth style is embodied pain and suffering—fashion and music for the brokenhearted and hopeless.

Four logos of the apocalypse

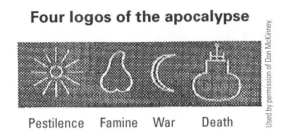

Pestilence Famine War Death

Used by permission of Don McKinney.

A Retrolution

> Fashion is what one wears oneself. What is unfashionable is what other people wear.
>
> Jean Cocteau

Fashion used to look forward. Designers focused on innovation, forgetting the past in order to introduce new ideas. Breakthroughs included the miniskirt, the maxi-skirt, the bikini. When punks first began to appear on the Kings Road in Chelsea, the new still had the ability to shock. Now, we live in a post-traumatic age beyond shock. Tabloid TV, political scandals, horror films, and graphic sex and death have left us immune to shock, particularly when it comes to fashion. Today, not the now or the new but the old generates buzz and holds power.

The past dominates current pop culture. The Volkswagen Beetle rolled back into car dealerships. Austin Powers celebrates all things from the sixties. Adam Sandler praises '80s music in *The Wedding Singer*. The Eagles were the best-selling band in 2000. This trend is reflected in parts of the church, with the embrace of Celtic Christianity and various forms of Orthodoxy. These ancient forms of faith offer a pre-Reformation spirituality.

When it comes to fashion, ancient actually means the '60s, '70s, and '80s. L.A.-based clothing designer Henry Duarte built a following among rock stars by drawing on a U.K.-based design trio called Granny Takes A Trip. This 1960s-style palette forms the backbone and the appeal of Duarte's designs.[22] Julia Roberts wore a vintage designer dress at the 2001 Academy Awards—not a one-hundred-year-old dress but a twenty-year-old one. "Retro" is the term, and in fashion it is the rule. If Jean-François Lyotard could declare the "end of ideology,"[23] fashion designers have heralded the end of new ideas. Everything seems to be recycled from a recent decade.

If you can't afford new clothes designed to look old, try rummaging through a vintage clothing store. Aardvark's stands out as the most popular vintage clothing store on L.A.'s trendy Melrose Avenue. Aardvark's may offer vintage, but you won't find much that was around before the 1950s. Vintage means "recent past." This mining of the recent past is more about superficially embracing a look and style and using it today than about fully appreciating the context in which the clothes were first worn. "Fashion, in this sense seems to be more about creating costumes than it does just clothing," writes journalist Josh Sims. "Retro filters out all the downsides of the past and only selects the attractive. . . . Retro is history without context. It is the past consumed not for the bigger picture but as a commodity."[24] We return again to the cut-and-paste nature of current pop culture—take whatever you want from wherever you choose and remake it into something new that smacks of old. As Moby combined early field recordings by Alan Lomax with computer-generated dance beats to create his smash album, *Play,* street fashion fuses tie-dye, peasant, and polyester fashions to create the new cool.

Having grown up in the 1970s with its clash of punk and glam clothing, I never imagined the fashion styles of my youth would make such a comeback. I always thought we all looked ridiculous teetering around on our platform boots with our smoothed down shag haircuts—but I was wrong.

This fascination with retro suggests at least a couple of things.[25] Fashion in the twenty-first century is about the presentation of identity. It states who we are and how we feel about ourselves. The ripped, faded jeans and worn-out plaid shirts that characterized the Seattle-based grunge movement attempted to express the sentiment, "We are on our own."[26] But a second and more important issue springs from notions of safety and refuge. Modernity promised a bright future that let us down. The progressive Enlightenment project failed, leaving us feeling disoriented and disconnected. The Sex Pistols summed up the sentiment in their song "No Future." When the future holds dubious promise, retro gives us a refuge from the sadness and the disappointment of that realization.

Our culture, which has lost faith in the future, brings to mind a couple instances in the Bible: first, the cynical people who, in response to the life of Jesus, said, "Can anything good come out of Nazareth?" and second, the disciples, who, when told of the resurrection of Jesus in Luke's account, "doubted for joy." They were frightened to believe. The disappointment if it were not true would simply be too much to bear. So they adopted a more resigned posture as if to say, "Well, we knew him once, back in the good ol' days. We will live with the memories of our recent past rather than look into the future and be disappointed again." There is a sense that for many the future and ideas of the new and revolutionary are not worth the disappointment. So they take comfort in an idealized, romanticized, already-worn recent past.

The plethora of ideas and creativity that bombards us moment by moment has left us with a jadedness toward it all. In an environment such as this, uniqueness is a potent commodity—and unfortunately, there is so little of it. "Retro-activity encourages derivation rather than inspiration. Looking back is easy. It is already there, in the textbooks, in the archives, endlessly repeated on

TV. Looking forward to produce truly original work, to embrace the unknown of the future, is much harder."[27]

We live in an age that is the product of too much rebellion and too little revolution. Things that have stood the test of time are appreciated. This is a hopeful sign when considering the relationship between church and culture—a faith that has stood the test of time is a viable commodity in a rootless world. Buddhism and other ancient faiths presently in vogue also benefit from this retro fascination. The otherworldliness, the rootedness of those practices in another time and place, and the mystery of those spiritual disciplines carry weight. Yet faith communities must also be willing to practice revolution. Jesus' followers must not settle for recent history.

Four logos of the apocalypse

Truth   Beauty Goodness Unity

Used by permission of Don McKinney.

Body Modification

A pin named *safety*—an artifact meant to avoid harming babies— becomes a social statement about harm, danger, and social effrontery.

Tom Beaudoin, *Virtual Faith*

Fashion encompasses anything we do to our bodies. The rise in the rituals of tattooing and body piercing demand careful reflection.

A friend of mine held a conference at his church for a national organization committed to exploring postmodern ministry. The sanctuary of his church featured local artists, a couple of film ministries, and a Christian tattooist! In spite of some hard sayings in the Old Testament related to marking the body and a certain amount of controversy over the practice, more and more young Christians are electing to mark themselves with permanent tattoos and various kinds of body piercings. Another friend of mine incurred the wrath of his church elders when he had himself tattooed during a service while talking to youth about servanthood and sacrifice.

Not too many years ago, tattoos were the domain of drunken sailors and convicts, the rebellious, the outsider, the outcast. But not anymore. Today, tattoos and body piercing are more than de rigueur. They are pervasive. Teen idols Britney Spears and Christina Aguilera both exhibit belly button rings. The permanence of these practices separates them from other fashion trends. Clothing is exchangeable and transitory; tattoos are for life. While piercings can be removed, not every trace vanishes. This permanence deserves theological attention.

A research project for my doctoral work involved surveying people getting tattoos and body piercings at local parlors in my area. Why do people mark themselves, and what might it mean for them in terms of how they view themselves and others in relation to questions about life's meaning and purpose? I took a low-key approach to my study and had no set questions. I began conversations by asking a person why he or she was getting a tattoo or piercing. Everyone I interviewed said virtually the same thing: The tattoo or piercing marked a significant moment in life's journey or served as a highly personal act of remembrance.

One girl I spoke with had designed intricate combinations of initials, which she had tattooed down her spine. Each set highlighted a particular moment of transition and importance to her. The initials of her college stood for the day she graduated, representing her final transition from childhood to responsible adulthood. The initials of her first dog marked the first significant loss in her life. Her mother's initials at the base of her spine honored the passing of the one who had given her the gift of life. As I talked with people, I realized these were not frivolous, spur-of-the-moment decisions but well-thought-through actions that were intended to make personal statements about their individual lives. The tattoos were highly individualized and personalized rites of passage.

Body piercing is a newer cultural phenomenon and is done at most tattoo parlors. There is definitely a correlation between the two. By piercings I do not mean simply ear piercings but navel, lip, tongue, eyebrow, nipple, and genital piercings. Tom Beaudoin suggests that these markings signify "immediate, bodily, and constant attention to the intimacy of experience. To pierce one's body is to leave a permanent mark of intense physical experience, whether pleasurable or painful . . . as proof that something marked me, something happened."[28] Most of the people I interviewed echoed that sentiment and felt the experience had a spiritual dimension. One said, "I had my first ear piercing after the death of a close friend. It was an attempt at marking my own life given the loss of his. He had worn an earring, and I decided to get one in his honor." The willingness, perhaps the need, to feel something—even pain—drives the marking experience.

In a post-human society, body modification identifies flesh as the last "permanent" possession. With the demise of traditional forms of life, from marriage to community to neighborhood, the physical body has become the only safe place where we can leave a sign. Marking the body has been associated with religious rites of passage in numerous cultures over the course of human history. But in contemporary society, it is detached from a broad social rite of passage. It is not something we all undergo as a culture, like baptism or some other rite. Instead, it has become a symbol of the alienation common to our culture. Disengaged from broader religious experiences, many attempt to fashion their own rites of passage.

This aspect of fashion can help to shape and form theology. Where are Christian rites of passage? How can we help people acknowledge meaningful events in their lives? And what about the pain and suffering we experience in our lives? From the rage and anger in punk fashion to the nihilism and resignation expressed in goth, fashion reflects our uncertain times. Pain and suffering expressed in body modification echoes the pervasive sense that we have inherited the burden of the previous ages' failings. We have lost faith in science, technology, and institutions. The subsequent sense of alienation and loss dominates much of today's fashion.

Pain and suffering, however, are recurring aspects of the gospel story. Jesus was known as the Man of Sorrows. This Jesus may be the catalyst for another generation to reconnect with the community of faith. A bloody theology marked by pain and suffering rather than one that focuses on success may prove effective in ministering to a post-therapeutic culture. The alienation reflected in many aspects of popular culture needs to be acknowledged, even dignified, by the church. We need to help those in pain root their suffering in Jesus and find wholeness in God.

The Sexualizing of Fashion

> I have always had more faith in fashion than in God. . . . I believed that the right clothes could make me perfect. I still do.
>
> Monah Li, designer[29]

Perhaps it's all Madonna's fault. She can usually be blamed for upsetting the status quo. From the moment she appeared on MTV, writhing and grinding provocatively while singing "Like a Virgin," she has been a flash point for controversy. Yet despite her penchant for underwear as outerwear, leather corsets, and dominatrix outfits, Madonna can't be the sole reason for the explosion of sexually charged fashion.

A loss of faith in the future has placed immense importance on the here and now. Regard for the body, for physicality, has soared. People want to be seen as sexy; they aspire to being desired and wanted. Sex in advertising appeals to our cultural obsession with the body, and it seems to achieve the desired results for the companies whose products are advertised. People look at the sexually charged ads and choose to be identified with such products. Consider recent ad campaigns for major clothing designers. For Marc Jacobs, a model lies on her back and pushes her legs back over her head. Her dress does not follow, revealing the top of her hips to her feet. In an ad for Ungaro, a model rolls around on a carpet, her dress riding up, her crotch provocatively facing the camera. A Chanel ad features a model so happy with her new designer boots that she wears nothing else. An ad for a scent called Opium features a naked woman lying on her back with her legs raised and open. It was banned in Great Britain from billboards and other public spaces because of the traffic jams caused by drivers slowing down to ogle it.[30]

As photographers and ad designers push the boundaries of convention, controversy and contention swirl. The philosopher Michel Foucault imagined a world in which people would become more and more obsessed with sex until it became the primary mode of discourse. The Hays Code of 1930 stated that in Hollywood films "undressing scenes should be avoided and never used save where essential to the plot. Indecent or undue exposure is forbidden. Dancing costumes intended to permit undue exposure or indecent movements are to be regarded as obscene."[31] How tame that seems these days. We've seen and heard too much since then. In 1958, film audiences in Great Britain reacted in shock to the first direct screen reference to sexual intercourse—"Oh, wasn't it super?"[32] Yesterday's vulgarity generates blithe and casual nonchalance in today's pop culture.

Teen idols such as Britney Spears and Christina Aguilera offer an overtly sexualized vision of young womanhood. Taut and youthful abs hold diamond-pierced belly buttons. Clothing covers less and less. Angela McRobbie calls it "in yer face—the new politics of femininity." These new forms of self-expression "break decisively with the conventions of feminine behavior by representing girls as crudely lustful young women."[33] Popular culture seems to feed and reinforce an endless cycle of chicken and egg—creating fashion, reflecting fashion. Magazines have played a definitive role,[34] but so have films and television. Sex sells, but that statement does little to help us understand the new social views of sexuality itself.

Female empowerment, an outgrowth of the feminist movement, contributed plenty to the changing sexual mores of society. In an era of AIDS and STDs, sexuality faced a new set of obstacles and challenges. The movie musical *Moulin Rouge* contrasts Christian, a writer who believes in the power of love, with Satine, a courtesan who resigns herself to a cold and clinical "love" at any price. But what are the roots of that mind shift?[35]

Sex and sexuality offer a major challenge to Jesus' followers. We desperately need a renewed theology of sexuality. Perhaps the Song of Songs can offer a sexual ethic that goes beyond the morality or immorality of specific acts to a more expansive construct that explores and understands the meaning of sexuality itself. Christine Gudorf argues for a new sexual ethic because "the Christian sexual tradition uses Scripture and theological tradition as supports for a code of behavior which developed out of mistaken, pre-scientific understandings of human anatomy, physiology, and reproduction. . . . We are still teaching a sexual code based in fear of the body and of sexuality."[36] The complex world of postmodern sexuality desperately needs some help unraveling the webs we have woven. It's too little too late to focus on the acts at the expense of a biblical perspective on sex and sexuality that takes tradition into account but also faces the challenges and opportunities that contemporary understandings about what it means to be human bring to the conversation.

Boys to Men

> The fashion wears out more apparel than the man.
>
> William Shakespeare, *Much Ado about Nothing*

Women are not the only ones affected by new trends in fashion and sexuality. Men's fashion has reached unprecedented heights in the past few decades.

One of my favorite films, *Beau Brummel,* stars British actor Stewart Granger playing Beau Brummel, the eighteenth-century English dandy. It is not a particularly great film, but its upper-class Britishness makes it enjoyable to watch. It follows the ultimate downfall of a man consumed with finery, gentlemen's manners, and trendsetting. In some ways, Brummel fits with today's man. Men have fallen into a beauty trap previously set for women. Since the 1970s, men have changed their attitudes about how they present themselves. The *New York Times* Sunday magazine called women the "real story" of the twentieth century,[37] and in the wake of women's movements, men have struggled to redefine themselves. With male identity eroded, some turned to cosmetic surgery (to the tune of five hundred million dollars in 1996) and hair transplants (eight hundred million dollars in 1997).[38] Face cream made promises to eradicate wrinkles from around the eyes so a man can look younger. How times have changed!

In her insightful book *Looking Good: Male Body Image in America,* author Lynne Luciano cites significant events that transformed the way in which men view themselves: a changed view of the male body resulting from feminism, shared economic power, changing sexual mores, and a shift from a culture of character to one of personality.[39] The concept of personality holds great import in a post-sexual world, and it requires external forces to back it up. A certain look gives credence, whatever persona is being constructed. And, of course, we must not forget our cultural fascination with all things youthful. Craig and I live and work in Los Angeles, where people can be too old before they are even out of their twenties!

Men used to follow unwritten rules of fashion, but expectations of masculinity have crumbled. The deconstruction of codes of behavior and comportment have created a crisis (and an opportunity) for the contemporary male. The British newspaper the *Independent* reported on the new phenomenon of men who actually enjoy shopping![40] Men have reached new pinnacles of consumerism as they have taken a personal interest in how they look. They now take responsibility for their own appearances rather than leaving the shopping to spouses or partners.

Lines previously etched in concrete with regard to gender and gender roles have been challenged and redefined. In fashion magazines, male models often look feminine. Some female models are so gaunt and thin that they look like prepubescent boys. This gender confusion is a by-product of a culture rethinking the boundaries of sexuality and gender. The move toward sexual equality (at least on paper!) has ignited a growing debate about the very nature of gender roles. Elaine Showalter writes, "In periods of cultural insecurity, when there are fears of regression and degeneration, the longing for strict border controls around the definition of gender, as well as race, class, and nationality, becomes especially intense."[41] Pop culture has contributed to the blurring of those lines. From the androgynous rock stars of the 1970s, such as David Bowie and Marc Bolan, to 1980s artists such as Duran Duran and Prince, music blurred lines, changing gender definitions and sexual roles. The fashion of male musicians, with its earrings and tight pants, scarves and leggings, set the stage for gender confusion.

Rebecca Arnold suggests, "Androgyny indicates uncertainty."[42] But does it? Perhaps it also serves as a reminder that roles are changing. The patriarchy that characterized much of our history needs to be replaced. What the future will look like may not yet be clear, but the desire for new definitions certainly remains. Androgyny signifies the tension of living with a constant and continual loss of boundaries.[43] "In highlighting difference, incongruity becomes another way of suggesting that things are not as they seem. Cross-dressing disguises one's sexual identity and presents an outer appearance that does not match the inner reality of one's sexual self," writes Sybil Del Gaudio.[44] There are at least two ways to view this challenging issue. It can be seen as destructive and harmful—a generation blurring and destroying boundaries for the sake of it, eager to offend cultural propriety. Or as Beaudoin does, we can view androgyny in a "prophetic" light,[45] as indicative of a cultural uncertainty that is not limited to sexuality, and see conversation with this uncertainty as a means to more effective mission in the postmodern world.

Androgyny offers a tough theological challenge. It seems to launch us into the choppy seas of questionable orthodoxy, heresy even. If gender definitions are deeply embedded in culture, even deeper are the roots of religions' definitions. But the old categories do not suffice. They are too static and are rooted in a world different from the one in which we find ourselves. Can we find traces of God in this arena of popular culture? When lines of gender and sexual identity are blurred almost beyond recognition, can we still engage in effective ministry without getting bogged down in a clash of categories and categorizations?

Return of the Cross

> Fashion is that by which the fantastic becomes for a moment universal.
>
> Oscar Wilde

A recent edition of *Los Angeles Magazine* declared that we live in an age of "buddhist-chic."[46] The magazine commented on the popularity of Buddhism from interior design to spiritual choice. Yet while Buddhism may be the "cool" religion of choice, the cross remains fashion's religious symbol of choice.

I was recently asked to contribute to a New Testament class being taught at Fuller Theological Seminary. Professor Marianne Maye Thompson invited me to discuss conversations I had had about faith and the meaning of the cross with people outside religious settings. She suspected that for many people outside the institutional church, the cross really didn't mean that much. Rather than the scandal, the foolishness, or the stumbling block St. Paul claimed it to be, the cross seems to generate little if any response. Yet the cross still has a place in contemporary culture—just a slightly different position than what followers of Jesus might hope for.

We live in a time in which religious imagery and rituals have been turned into lifestyle choices. The current vogue of using candles and incense and creating "sacred spaces"[47] reflects this. I showed the class some magazines that featured crosses, mainly in the Catholic folk art style, as this season's home design choice.[48] This is not a new thing. The cross as a design element has been noted in many ancient cultures: Aztec, Phoenician, Hindu, Buddhist, Persian, Assyrian, and Native American.[49] While the cross and the religious meaning attached to it have been wrested away from the mediation of the faithful, its potency as a religious symbol has not diminished.

I focused on the appropriation of the cross as jewelry. This may disturb followers of Christ who view the cross with reverence and believe it has more significance than merely serving as a means of adornment. (In fact, on the Third Street Promenade in Santa Monica, I heard a couple street preachers screaming at passersby to "rip those crosses off your necks—you are not worthy to wear them!") Yet one must wonder why a large number of people in our society adopt the cross as a fashion statement. Madonna and a number of hip-hop artists are seldom seen without some form of a cross. Rappers seem to delight in sporting large platinum and diamond jewelry, and crosses and dollar signs are their symbols of choice. Italian fashion designers Dolce and Gabbana sell a line of solid gold rosaries alongside their designer clothing. A friend of mine makes expensive gothic jewelry that is carried in designer stores around the globe. One of her most popular pieces is a classic signet ring with a raised cross on the top. Countless celebrities, actors, and musicians wear this ring.

Jeweler Theo Fennel attributes this interest in crosses to the 1960s,[50] when the cross was appropriated by hippies along with symbols of peace and love. *Harpers & Queens* magazine's jewelry editor, Vivienne Becker, says, "It is the prerogative of youth to subvert symbols of the establishment."[51] Becker's point has merit. The appropriation of religious symbolism matches the attempts by members of our society to grapple and wrestle with religion and spirituality outside the confines and influences of the establishment.

Fordham University's chairwoman of modern languages, Catherine Randall, sees this phenomenon in largely negative terms. "I don't like the way religious symbolism is being appropriated and commodified. . . . The culture of the 21st century is all about display and ornamentation."[52] She's right. The reduction of a symbol into a mere fashion accessory reveals the harsh consumerist attitude that prevails. This attitude has little respect for what has been sacred to prior generations. Yet religious symbols have long been used in talismanic ways. People throughout the centuries have worn images in order to draw on the supposed protective power of the particular deity invoked by the image.

People I converse with don't doubt the power and potency of the person of Jesus or the cross. Only the institutionalized religion surrounding Christ and his cross has been rejected. The postmodern person has, for the most part, rejected institutional forms of religious expression but wholeheartedly embraced more premodern folk religious expressions in which symbolism and the use of religious artifacts feature prominently. Becker adds, "The biggest trend we're seeing in jewelry today is increasing spirituality. There is an age-old need to ward off evil spirits, and jewels have always fulfilled that role. The cross symbol inevitably makes celebrities feel safe and protected."[53] Not only celebrities feel the need for protection these days. We live in vulnerable times, and winds of change are gusting. In such times, spiritual searches are more common. All the crosses dangling from necks reflect this trend.

An Oddly Godly Mood: Fashion's Religious Turn

> Every generation laughs at the old fashions but follows religiously the new.
>
> Henry David Thoreau

U.K. fashion magazine *Harpers & Queens* featured an article entitled "Holy Muses."[54] In it, fashion journalist Clare Coulson notes the post 9/11 trend of purity and the liberal use of religious imagery on the fashion runways. "It's about love, we felt a real need for goodness,"[55] declared designers Viktor Horsing and Rolf Snoeren. Coulson roots this trend for all things religious in post-traumatic desires for goodness and even godliness. Arkadius, a Polish-born clothing designer, used the inspiration of Roman Catholic imagery in his collection to show how influential a society's religious values can be. Through his clothing, Arkadius attempted to highlight how religion can divide instead of unite.[56] *Harpers* also noted the ample use of white as a symbol of purity by designers famous for their use of black. "White is the new black" declared the March 2002 edition of *Arena* magazine. Fashion, which often loves to shock, has instead decided to soothe. Tom Ford, designer for Gucci, says, "People want to be soothed, and when words fail, I think beauty can fill the void. Anything with edge feels wrong right now."[57]

Singer-songwriter Elvis Costello has written about love and the loss of innocence in a song called "All This Useless Beauty."[58] The song recounts the story of a woman walking around in an art gallery being confronted with the mythic images of beauty immortalized in paint. They serve as painful reminders of the loss of her own innocence and beauty. Age and the troubles of life had assaulted her emotionally and physically. Much of popular culture has adopted a similar slant right now, offering ideals, images of the way things ought to be, in the harrowing face of what they recently have become. Fashion seeks to serve as a reminder that love and purity are far better expressions of true religious faith than violence, terrorism, and forms of fundamentalism.[59]

There seems to be some sort of sacramental element contained in contemporary fashion. In a culture of isolation, experiencing, as it has, the disintegration of many supporting structures, the body has become a sort of "last stand" against the world. We inscribe it with meaning with tattoos, piercings, hair cuts, and clothing. We literally "wear our politics on our sleeves" in the postmodern world. Fashion is a barometer by which we can read the cultural psyche, from the dismay and pain of the goths to the flamboyant "coming out" of those rethinking their sexuality. "We piece together our own meaning—our own religiosity—through popular culture. We cobble together a lived theology in a realm over which we have creative influence."[60] For theology, this means we have a visual clue with which to engage culture. A theology of fashion that reads the signs worn around us is a theology that will speak to the times.

The Patron Saint
of Sports

8

sports

Board Generation

Q: Is sports a religion in America?
A: Yes.
Q: Is it an organized religion?
A: No. It does not *appear* to be organized—but if it were, we would all be members
   of a very powerful church.

Hunter S. Thompson, "Enough to Make a Man Believe,"
in *The Gospel according to ESPN*

For many of us, friendships forged and lessons learned on athletic fields
still mean plenty. Trophies from Little League or youth soccer still gather
dust on a shelf. We saved the program and ticket stub from the first sporting
event we witnessed in person. We cherish the baseball cards and athletes'
autographs collected over the years. Before I (Craig) was a filmmaker,
before I was a divinity student, before I got married, had kids, and wrote
this book, I was first and foremost a jock—not in any kind of three-sport-
star, college scholarship, make-millions-as-a-pro sort of a way, but in the
"healthy" manner that many kids, male and female, work out their evolving hormones.

Like many institutions, sports have been challenged by a shift in public
tastes and perceptions. Once sacred traditions must compete with relative
upstarts that defy gravity (and reason). While team owners have been trying
to find new ways to squeeze water from a rock, the emerging generation has

moved on, creating new sports that reflect its desperate need for risk taking, solitude, and group identity. Bored by established sports and old rules, this board generation has taken its activity to the streets, to the mountains, to the waves, to anywhere but well-defined, clearly lined fields. Kids no longer join teams and wear uniforms. They simply grab a board and start grinding. The changing nature of sports parallels our evolving relationship with God. Worship is no longer a spectator sport but an active, engaging practice.[1] People consider themselves spiritual yet often have little or no connection to organized religion. With fears rising during these uncertain times, we still must enter the game of life, responding to risks with expressive tricks that mirror the most extreme sports. At this critical crossroads for Western Christianity, perhaps America's big four sports of football, baseball, basketball, and hockey can provide a lesson in what *not* to do.

Higher Purposes?

Heavenly Father, Divine Goalie . . . Help us stay within the blue line of Your commandments and the red line of Your grace. Protect us from being injured by the puck of pride. May we be ever delivered from the high stick of dishonesty. . . . May You always be the Divine Center of our team and when our summons comes for eternal retirement to the heavenly grandstand, may we find You ready to give us the everlasting bonus of a permanent seat in Your coliseum. Finally, grant us the courage to skate without tripping, to run without icing, and to score the goal that really counts—the one that makes each of us a winner, a champion, an All-Star in the hectic Hockey Game of Life. Amen.

invocation of Father Edward Rupp before the 1976 World Hockey Association All-Star game[2]

In the charming 1999 film *The Cup,* young Buddhist monks in training sneak out of their monastery to watch soccer's World Cup. The boys are willing to risk expulsion from their religious order because they've found a more compelling object of devotion in Ronaldo and the Brazilian soccer team. *The Cup* treats the tension between sports and religion as lighthearted, comedic, and reconcilable. Contrast this with *Bull Durham,* in which the narrator, Annie Savoy, declares at the start of the film, "I've tried 'em all, I really have. And the only church that truly feeds my soul day in and day out is the church of baseball."[3] Are sports a substitute for religion, or are they a separate religion with its own set of rules and beliefs?

Sociologist Harry Edwards draws striking parallels between sports and religion. Millions of worshipers congregate each week to bear witness to the manifestations of their faith at churches and stadiums across the land. Each sport has its own shrine—a national hall of fame complete with trophy rooms. In departed legends such as Babe Ruth, Lou Gehrig, and Knute Rockne, sports canonize their saints. Coaches and commissioners form the ruling patriarchs, and the mightiest athletes, like Michael Jordan, rise like gods above all challengers.[4]

Scholars call the national pride and local heroes that emerge from athletic contests a form of civic or folk religion.[5] Brazil worships Pele. Ethiopians laud barefooted Olympic marathoner Abebe Bikila. Romanians revel in gymnast Nadia Comanici's unprecedented perfect tens. Note the religious language associated with the most memorable victories. Argentineans still celebrate Diego Maradona's "hand of God" goal in the 1986 World Cup. Americans call the Olympic hockey team's 1980 gold medal "the miracle on ice." Pittsburgh Steeler football fans replay Franco Harris's "immaculate reception." Nashville remembers "the Music City miracle," when a controversial last-second lateral sent the Tennessee Titans to the Super Bowl.[6] High schools, Little Leagues, and neighborhoods all have their particular hometown heroes. Communities segregated by race, class, and religion rally around their team and their sports stars.

But what happens when teams lose? When the Buffalo Bills become a study in Super Bowl futility? When Chicago Cubs or Boston Red Sox fans talk about curses keeping their teams from winning the World Series? What causes British soccer fans to engage in hooliganism and riots after a loss? As far back as 1608, a Manchester, England, ordinance prohibited soccer, complaining of "a company of lewd and disordered persons using that unlawfulle exercise of playing with fotebale in ye streets."[7]

The word *fan* derives from the word *fanaticus,* meaning "inspired by a deity, frenzied." *Fanaticus,* in turn, comes from the Latin word for temple, *fanum.*[8] Michael Novak's own fandom inspired him to write *The Joy of Sports.* What made him cheer for the Dodgers? Why did he care whether they won or lost? He equated sports with a "natural religion" that re-creates "symbols of cosmic struggle, in which human survival and moral courage are not assured. . . . To this extent, they are not mere games, diversions, pastimes. Their power to exhilarate or depress is far greater than that." Novak says, "A game is a symbol. . . . To lose symbolizes death and it certainly feels like dying; but it is not death." Novak finds the same effect in religious rituals such as baptism and communion in which "the communicants experience death, symbolically, and are reborn, symbolically."[9] Cubs and Red Sox fans are still waiting for rebirth in baseball's World Series.

A Muscular Faith

> Praise the name of baseball. The word will set captives free. The
> word will open the eyes of the blind. The word will raise the dead.
> Have you the word of baseball living inside you? Has the word of
> baseball become part of you? Do you live it, play it, digest it, forever?
> Let an old man tell you to make the word of baseball your life.
>
> W P Kinsella, *Field of Dreams*

While scholars debate the similarities or differences between sports and religion, most ministers look to stadiums crammed with thousands of paying spectators on Sundays and see serious competition. Many decide to accommodate rather than oppose sports' intrusion on religion.

With the 2002 World Cup staged in Asia, England's first match kicked off at 10:30 A.M. on a Sunday morning. "The Church of England, realizing that soccer is a religion unto itself, sent an e-mail to dioceses throughout the country, advising they arrange to televise the game for parishioners and also approved changing the time of services." St. James Church in London cut short its customary Sunday services to make way for *futbol* star "Saint" Michael Owen. St. James not only screened the game but also allowed parishioners to bring their own beer. Vicar Andrew Baughen said, "It is part of our way to show Christians are not complete weirdos who sit in a monastery and never have any fun."[10] It also demonstrates which "church" has the most influence in Europe.

As a new pastor at a Presbyterian church in Kansas City, Brian Ellison learned a hard lesson on a fall Sunday. A colleague offered some pointed advice: "Don't ever, *ever* again schedule anything at the same time as a Chiefs game." Upon closer inspection, Ellison found the tailgate parties in the parking lot before a Chiefs game to be a model of *koinonia*, the New Testament Greek term for fellowship or community. "Speaking and listening together. Breaking bread and offering the cup. Part of a group that is diverse and inclusive. United with a shared sense of purpose. All in all, it's not a bad way to spend a Sunday," Ellison said. "What have we [the church] been doing—and not doing—that leaves people looking to football for fellowship, service opportunities, pastoral care and identity formation?"[11]

Rather than confront the larger theological questions that sports presented to religion, many in evangelical Christian circles simply handed athletes a microphone. Randall Cunningham credited God for his comeback as quarterback with the Minnesota Vikings. Basketball player A. C. Green was lauded for his abstinence. All-pro wide receiver Cris Carter praised the Lord after every touchdown reception from Cunningham. Chicago Bear linebacker Mike Singletary made his commitment to Jesus a hallmark of his induction into the Pro Football Hall of Fame. New York Jet lineman Dennis Byrd's remarkable recovery from a paralyzing on-field injury was turned into the Gospel Films production *Rise and Walk*. Pastor-sacker Reggie White defined "muscular Christianity" while leading the Green Bay Packers to the Super Bowl.[12]

Kurt Warner's sudden rise from the Arena Football League to quarterback of the Los Angeles Rams offered ample opportunity for him to praise his surprising God. Broadcasters loved to hear and tell his dramatic story. After the 2000 Super Bowl victory, to television's largest audience, Warner declared, "With the Lord, all things are possible. I believe in him. I believe in myself. With the two of us together, there's nothing I feel we can't accomplish."[13]

The most surprising testimony has come via "Neon" Deion Sanders. On Fox Sports' *Beyond the Glory,* Sanders admitted, "My thing was fornication. My thing was to have sex with as many women as possible. I didn't discriminate." He hit rock bottom with a 1997 suicide attempt. Sanders recalls, "I got in that car and drove off that cliff and got to the bottom of that fallout and I was still alive. I was like, 'Lord, you saved me.'" Sanders found religion and now encourages others. "You can't escape the call. The phone is going to keep ringing and ringing and ringing until you answer it. And it's a collect call. If I were you, I would accept the charges."[14] Deion "Prime-Time" Sanders turned everything over to God's time.

These faith-filled athletes modify the either/or stance exhibited by Scottish sprinter Eric Liddell of *Chariots of Fire* fame. Liddell celebrates the transcendent nature of sport: "When I run, I feel his glory." Yet in the Oscar-winning film, Liddell refuses to run on the Sabbath. He misses a qualifying round and forgoes a potential gold medal. Today's Christian athletes believe in a more practical both/and faith. At the conclusion of every NFL game, players from both teams unite to form a prayer circle. They now play *and* pray on Sunday.

As sports' influence exploded over the past century, the Christian community adapted. Pastors rarely preached against the competition. While other pop cultural expressions were derided, sports were embraced. Like Paul, we pressed on, toward the goal, to win the prize. We longed to fight a good fight, to finish the race, and to keep the faith. We started Fellowship of Christian Athletes and Athletes in Action. Promise Keepers brought men to stadiums for recommitment and reconciliation. We encouraged athletes such as boxer Evander Holyfield to share their testimonies after every victory. These efforts were sincere, savvy, and successful.

But our embrace of a muscular faith neglected some of the significant theological underpinnings that keep us coming back to sports. Sports became a means to deliver a message rather than a God-given gift, an essential physical and spiritual practice. We were created to play. Fans flock to stadiums for a touch of the divine. Sports unite communities, inspire prayers, and offer transcendence.

But now, the traditional American sports of baseball, football, basketball, and hockey face their own challenges. The board generation has moved on, creating new ways to play. A faith wedded with games that no longer work is in trouble. The big four sports and the institutional church both suffered from their success as they drifted toward complacency together.

An analysis of what went wrong with American sports may offer potent warnings to Western Christianity. What was intended as a break from business became a big business. Something born out of joy turned into an institution that put personal profits before broader community interest. Yet fans' rising frustration may actually reveal sports' original sacred purpose and offer theology a recipe for either marginalization or recovery. The test will come not on the fields but in the streets.

Bye-Bye Big Four

> Baseball is something more than a game to an American boy. It is his training field for life work. Destroy his faith in its squareness and honesty, and you have destroyed something more—you have planted suspicion of all things in his heart.
>
> Judge Kenesaw Mountain Landis,
> quoted in *The Faith of Fifty Million*

> Take me out to the corporate-sponsored megaplex.
>
> David Letterman, *The Late Show with David Letterman*, April 10, 2003

America's love affair with football, baseball, basketball, and hockey dates back only one hundred years. From humble beginnings of bus rides, civic auditoriums, and radio broadcasts, the big four spectator sports have enjoyed unparalleled, unpredicted prosperity. Franchises purchased for thousands of dollars are now worth millions, such as the Yankees in major league baseball, the Lakers in the National Basketball Association, and "America's team," the Cowboys, in the National Football League.[15] What enabled certain sports to expand so rapidly and so significantly? Television. Soccer has languished on American shores because its continuous action does not conform to television advertisers' need for time-outs.[16] The stop/start structure of baseball, basketball, hockey, and football has offered the perfect merger of sports and commerce. Fox Sports recently offered professional baseball $2.5 billion for six years of broadcasting rights. The NFL signed an even more lucrative $17.6 billion, eight-year television deal with a combination of networks.[17]

So why are so many articles chronicling the demise of pro sports? Why is the commissioner of major league baseball testifying before Congress, asking for government aid? How can Montreal's storied Canadiennes hockey team be sold to American buyers? Since 1997, postseason Nielsen television ratings for the NFL dropped 10 percent, for major league baseball 28 percent, and for the NBA a frightening 29 percent.[18]

What's wrong with the big four team sports? Certainly, fan loyalty and community support have waned. The big four spectator sports were originally supported by their local box office. Legendary New York Yankee lineups of Ruth and Gehrig were funded without television revenue. With community support in the stands, owners could make a profit. Father-son trips to the game became a rite of passage, an essential part of growing up.

Rising ticket prices have gradually forced families out of the ballparks and stadiums. In the last decade, the average price for NFL and NBA tickets has doubled, to above $50. And that's before parking and hot dogs. According to Team Marketing Report, a family of four spends an average of $145 to $300 to attend a game. Tim Leiweke, the president of Los Angeles's Staples Center, laments, "We can't just cater to the 5% that happens to have a high discretionary income. Our ticket prices are getting to the point where we're limiting our audience."[19] Yet owners continue to concentrate on luxury skyboxes rather than affordable seats. While other industries pursue customers by offering more for the dollar, the sports industry treats spectators as incidental, as the "background" for sports' real revenue source—television broadcasts. "Television did not make sports possible. . . . Sports made television commercially successful."[20] In fact, sports drive television sales. Big-screen television sales rise before each Super Bowl. Michael Novak links sports' problems to a Chaucerian proverb: *Radix malorum cupiditas*—"The root of all evils is greed."[21]

Baseball's decline may be traced to the Dodgers move from Brooklyn to Los Angeles. Teams were no longer tied to civic identity. They moved wherever the grass (and the cash) was greener. For sports fans living in the west or the Sun Belt, that meant good news. But for die-hard supporters of baseball's New York Giants or football's Baltimore Colts, it meant a long commute to see their former hometown team. Even stadiums, a symbol of civic pride named after native sons, are up for sale. The Oakland Coliseum became Network Associates Coliseum. In four years, the Philadelphia Spectrum became CoreStates Center and then First Union Center. Denver rose in protest when fabled Mile High Stadium was renamed Invesco Field.[22]

Collegiate athletics benefit from the capricious nature of these pro franchises. Alumni are assured that their universities will play in the same cities under the same school colors. Yet professionalism has invaded even amateur athletics. In college football, Miami now hosts the Federal Express Orange Bowl, and New Orleans hosts the Nokia Sugar Bowl. The Heisman Trophy is presented by Suzuki.[23]

How can new stadiums, hundreds of millions of corporate dollars, and increased television revenue hurt sports? They have slowly taken athletics away from their original purpose. A gift from God meant for play has become a business. A business intended to bring people together has priced out many fans.

Fans wanting a break from the corporate grind have rejected what has evolved into just another corporation. Athletes energized by a love of the game have gotten fat, greedy, and complacent. Instead of lifting us above this mortal coil, sports have become a prime example of institutional and ethical decay.

America's Past Time?

> Professional baseball is on the wane. Salaries must come down or the interest of the public must be increased in some way. If one or the other does not happen, bankruptcy stares every team in the face.
>
> Albert Spalding, Chicago White Stocking owner, 1881[24]

Baseball entered the nineties as America's national pastime. In a world of tumult, baseball seemed pure, with meticulous rules and a measured pace worth preserving. But when a labor dispute between players and owners cut into spring training in 1990, baseball's bad news was only beginning. The 1994 strike lasted 232 long days, bringing the season to a premature conclusion and canceling the hallowed World Series.[25] For many fans, baseball's time had passed.

Many maintained that baseball had rebounded from adversity before and would again. The Black Sox scandal threatened baseball's reputation back in 1919. So when Mark McGuire and Sammy Sosa engaged in 1999's thrilling home run derby, the media declared, "Baseball is back," despite flat attendance and television ratings. The 2000 World Series between the marquee Yankee franchise and subway rivals the Mets failed to increase viewership. The 2001 World Series was an instant classic, a seven-game, nail-biting battle with last-inning heroics between the Yankees and the Arizona Diamondbacks. But the post-series euphoria proved short-lived when team owners threatened to eliminate two teams before the 2002 season. Teams and cities slotted for elimination had to use injunctions to ensure another season.[26] Why is the national pastime threatening franchises and alienating fans? Why is Commissioner Bud Selig begging Congress to allow baseball to continue its seventy-nine-year-old antitrust exemption? Selig says, "Baseball has $4 billion of debt, the bankers are nervous and the losses are very real. . . . I would say six to eight [teams] can't exist another year, another year and a half."[27]

What's killing America's pastime? First, baseball choked on its own success. The rise of television revenue created survival of the fattest. A small market team such as the Pittsburgh Pirates could not compete in the 1990s. Rare talents like Barry Bonds left small towns like Pittsburgh for greener pastures in San Francisco. Wealthy owners decided revenue sharing was good for baseball's long-term health, so smaller markets such as Minneapolis and Pittsburgh now share equally in baseball's network TV pie. Still, the rights to broadcast games in local markets remain a separate and unequal system. At the start of the 2003 season, the Tampa Bay Devil Rays' entire on-field payroll of $15 million was just 10 percent of the New York Yankee payroll and less than the salary of shortstop Derek Jeter.[28]

Second, the talent has gotten more and more expensive. In the late seventies, Curt Flood challenged baseball owners' control. Being a trailblazing free agent may have killed Flood's career, but it guaranteed unparalleled riches to the next generation of ball players. The escalation in salary can be chronicled from Andy Messersmith to Alex Rodriguez. It took thirty years for Joe DiMaggio's 1950 salary of $100,000 to rise to Nolan Ryan's $1 million with the Houston Astros. By 1997, Ryan's $1 million mushroomed to $11 million for Albert Belle, thanks to the generosity of the Cleveland Indians.[29] Just three years later, Belle's salary looked paltry compared to Rodriguez's ten-year, $252-million contract with the Texas Rangers. Rodriguez's contract exceeds the total estimated value of eighteen major league *teams*. The color of greed doesn't inspire many fans.

Third, baseball's heroes lost their luster. Where are today's charismatic heroes on the level of Babe Ruth or Mickey Mantle? Cal Ripken Jr. broke Lou Gehrig's endurance record of consecutive games, yet baseball's all-time hit leader, Pete Rose, is banned from the Hall of Fame for gambling. Barry Bonds broke home run records but refused to talk to the media. In a previous era, who wouldn't have recognized the Yankees' highest paid all-star who won four World Series? Yet how many people could identify Derek Jeter if he were to sit next to them at a restaurant?

What is the way forward for our nearly past time? The New York Mets and the Chicago Cubs opened the 2000 baseball season *in Japan*.[30] The next generation of baseball stars are coming from the Dominican Republic, from Panama, from Korea, from anywhere but America. The 2002 World Series was televised in 224 countries and in 14 languages.[31] In a post-national era, baseball has learned to go global.

The color line broken by Jackie Robinson now extends to all races. Sammy Sosa and Pedro Martinez make Latin Americans proud. Livan Hernandez led an exodus out of Castro's Cuba. Japanese press and fans flocked to Dodger Stadium for each of Hideo Nomo's starts during his spectacular rookie season. After Nomo was traded, Korean baseball fans gathered every time Chan Ho Park took the mound. The Seattle Mariners acquired the runaway 2001 rookie of the year, Japanese veteran Ichiro Suzuki. The Yankees wooed Japan's "national treasure," Hideki "Godzilla" Matsui, away from the fabled Yomiuri Giants. In the 2002 all-star game, twenty-three of the sixty players honored were born *outside* the United States. With the rise of globalization, the World Series is finally starting to live up to its name.

Yet while other nations have adopted baseball, the next generation of Americans has moved on. American teams won seventeen of the first twenty Little League World Series from 1947 to 1967. Since then, a United States team has won only eight times, while Taipei teams have claimed seventeen championships.[32] The number of Americans age six or older playing baseball has declined 25 percent since 1987. In the last five years, the Little League organization has lost 8 percent of its baseball and softball participants.[33] Kids who don't play baseball today are less likely to grow up to become baseball fans later on. To the average American teen, MLB is DOA.

Is the sport too slow for active kids? Or will the deliberate pace of baseball eventually offer a strange, nostalgic appeal to a frantic culture? Baseball is built on drama, on waiting and watching for something to happen amid all the balls and strikes and foul tips. Fans learn to cherish the rituals that occur in the on-deck circle and the bullpen. Batters practice their swings, and pitchers search for signs before each encounter. In the field, players shuffle the dirt. In the stands, spectators crack open peanuts. Everyone prepares for that rare opportunity when a ball flies toward them at lightning speed. But most of the time, nothing much happens. Patience is no longer a virtue, and baseball is no longer America's national pastime. But perhaps both will recover their place when we can no longer find peace of mind in any other pastime. Churches tempted to speed up services, to make them snappier and jazzier, would be advised to watch baseball. If the slowest team sport recovers, then perhaps there is also hope for the quietest, most reflective church liturgy. We must teach kids how to enjoy and cherish all that boring, "dead" space in between the home runs. Can we learn to wait and watch for that rare moment when God shows up in a flash of insight and blinding intensity? Can we practice our swings and look for the signs that only rarely result in exhilaration? Most of the time, nothing much happens. But when something does, nothing can beat it for surprise, delight, and transcendence.

Gridiron Gains and Losses

It's not whether you win or lose, but how you play the game.

legendary sportswriter Grantland Rice[34]

Winning isn't everything; it's the only thing.

legendary football coach Vince Lombardi

Football once appeared poised to become America's new national sport. Visionary commissioner Pete Rozelle oversaw the merger of the NFL and the upstart AFL, created the interleague Super Bowl, and expanded television revenues from $300,000 in 1960 to more than $2 billion annually today.[35] Team owners learned to share the wealth in order to avoid baseball's pitfalls. To close the gap between major and minor market teams, football now splits television money equally among franchises irrespective of the size of their cities. Schedules are adjusted to ensure that the strongest teams face the toughest schedules. Salary caps have made it difficult for winning teams to retain high-priced talent. The NFL proudly boasts that on any given Sunday any team can win. In the past seven seasons, only Cincinnati and San Diego have failed to make a play-off appearance. Worst-to-first Cinderella stories have become commonplace. The 1999 St. Louis Rams, 2000 Baltimore Ravens, and 2001 New England Patriots rose from losing seasons and relative obscurity to win the Super Bowl. Yet many fans consider such parity another word for mediocrity.[36]

With no dynasties in place, is football becoming so unpredictable and random that fans have stopped caring? When anyone can win, does nobody win? Nevertheless, football has managed to avoid the labor strikes that crippled baseball, basketball, and hockey. New franchise purchase fees rose from $140 million for Carolina and Jacksonville in 1995 to $700 million for Houston in 2002.[37] Fox, ESPN, ABC, and CBS combined to pay the NFL a staggering $17.6 billion to broadcast games from 1999 to 2007.[38] *Monday Night Football* remains a cash cow for ABC, generating $350 million in advertising dollars from beer and car companies desperate to reach elusive male viewers.[39] Super Bowl ratings continue to dwarf every other sports championship. Super Bowl Sunday has become "a national day of gluttony for Americans to unabashedly embrace the joys of advertising, consumerism and greasy foods."[40]

So why have football's ratings been in decline for the past decade? Santana Moss, the Jets' top draft pick of 2001, received a $200,000 reporting bonus as part of his $7.119 million deal.[41] The next day he injured his knee and missed the entire preseason. After signing a $75 million contract, the Vikings' Randy Moss had the gall to admit, "Do I play up to my top performance, my ability every time? Maybe not. . . . I play when I want to play, case closed."[42]

Whether it's Michael Irvin at a strip club, Mark Chmura in a hot tub with his baby-sitter, or Ray Lewis at the scene of a murder outside the Super Bowl, football players' reputations have taken their share of hits. As with baseball, repeated reports of pampered athletes have cut into fan interest.

Hollywood couldn't have scripted a more compelling story than the New England Patriots' upset of the St. Louis Rams in Super Bowl XXXVI. With American soldiers fighting the war on terrorism in Afghanistan, the Patriots overcame their underdog status behind unlikely second-year quarterback Tom Brady. It was the rare Super Bowl in which viewer interest rose during the game, right up to Adam Vinatieri's last-second, forty-eight-yard field goal. Yet the 2002 game's overall Nielsen ratings remained flat, hovering just above the record-low ratings of the 1999 and 1992 Super Bowls.[43] So where have the viewers gone?

Perhaps parity has undercut football's appeal. The NFL owners graciously shared the wealth and created balanced schedules. But in the parity process, they drifted from one of sports' most seminal themes: rooting for the underdog. The mythic power of sport resides in overcoming the odds and accomplishing the impossible. We want (and need) to see David defeat Goliath. If they had entered the battle with the same height, same weight, and same experience, we wouldn't remember the outcome. No drama equals no story. But we can all cheer for the little guy, armed with a single rock, taking on a fearsome giant. With no giants left to kill, the NFL has replaced the mythic with mush. Sports can teach morality and fair play. There is certainly a place for Grantland Rice's interest in how we play the game, but Vince Lombardi's "winning is the only thing" permeates every sector of our society. Theology may have gotten trapped in the muddy middle, answering questions of morality and fair play. Theology must recover the mythological, the epic struggles of the under-equipped and overwhelmed. We're interested in little guys beating the odds, knocking down giants, not parity.

Football taps into our most violent, survival instincts. It repeatedly draws a line in the dirt and dares opponents to cross it. While it offers rules of engagement, often the meanest and nastiest prevail. We may wish that football weren't so appealing. We may train our kids to turn the other cheek. But the realities of the playground, of people taking sides and encroaching on our property, continue to haunt us. Every weekend, football underlines what the bloody twentieth century of "progress" taught us: We love to wage war.

The Bible offers a wealth of bloody scenes to rival any of the NFL's greatest hits. While Jesus introduced a radically different kingdom, the Old Testament still stands as a violent, epic chronicle of God's messy wars. We may prefer that Scripture passages such as 1 Samuel 15:18 were cut out. What does it mean that God sent his people on a mission saying, "Go and completely destroy those wicked people, the Amalekites; make war on them until you have wiped them out." Reading about the battle of Jericho raises troubling questions. In Joshua 6:21, after the trumpets sounded and the walls collapsed, "They devoted the city to the LORD and destroyed with the sword every living thing in it—men and women, young and old, cattle, sheep, and donkeys." The world is a bloody, ugly mess irrespective of which god people serve.

Football reminds us of who we are and how we got here, what battles had to be fought, what bodies had to be sacrificed to forge a nation. Does football affirm such violence or purge the aggression that continues to plague us? In a world without football, we would still find plenty to fight about. Having played football and experienced the grime, the grit, and the gore of the field, I would rather see my son head to the gridiron than the battlefield on any given Sunday. Despite Jesus' blessing of the peacemakers, football, violence, and war are still very much with us.

Prophets and Saviors

> Without sports, there'd be no reason to get up on Sundays.
>
> ESPN billboard

Bill Russell and Wilt Chamberlain took the classic duels between the Celtics and the Lakers to new heights. After Larry Bird's Indiana State team lost to Magic Johnson's Michigan State Spartans in the 1979 NCAA college basketball championship and the two players brought their college rivalry to the NBA, a new basketball era emerged. Both were 6'9". Both practiced the vanishing art of passing, promoting team play. Of the ten championships available in the 1980s, Magic and the Lakers took five, Bird and the Celtics won three. Magic's unprecedented $25 million, twenty-five-year salary became the benchmark for player appreciation. Before Bird arrived, the NBA was perceived as "too black" by the media. *Sports Illustrated*'s Frank Deford said, "Bird's race was crucial at the time. I don't think it's crucial anymore. He made it so that you'll never need another white guy to be important."[44] They ushered in a post-racial NBA. *The Gospel according to ESPN* calls Magic and Bird "saviors." Yet they were more like prophets, paving the way for sports' true messiah, Michael Jordan.

Choose your moment. The NBA all-star dunk. The Bulls' first championship. His "three-peat repeat" for a total of six championship rings. Whatever accomplishment you cherish, Michael Jordan elevated the NBA to unprecedented global attention. In 1990, NBA games reached 200 million homes in 77 countries. By the time of Jordan's second retirement in 1998, the NBA's reach had extended to 600 million households in 190 countries.[45] When reporter Thomas Friedman visited Moscow to cover the 1996 presidential election, the hottest-selling Matrushka dolls did not feature politicians. He found "Dennis Rodman inside Scott Pippen inside Toni Kukoc inside Luc Longley inside Steve Kerr inside Michael Jordan"—da Bulls.[46] *Fortune* magazine estimated that Jordan's impact on the American economy since entering the NBA in 1984 was *$10 billion.*[47] Divinity measured in dollars.

Vancouver and Toronto moved NBA teams beyond American borders. European stars such as Arvydas Sabonis, Toni Kukoc, and Drazen Petrovic joined Nigerian Hakeem Olajuwon and the Congo's Dikembe Mutombo to initiate the first wave of immigration. China's Yao Ming was the first of seventeen foreign-born players drafted in 2002. French-born Tony Parker led the San Antonio Spurs to the 2003 NBA championship. The NBA now features sixty-six players from thirty-five countries.[48] Michael Jordan inspired disciples who went into all the world.

Yet just six years after Vancouver entered the NBA, the Grizzly franchise moved to Memphis. For all of basketball's global gains, Jordan's retirement in 1998 coincided with an unparalleled slide in basketball's popularity. Pat Williams, senior vice president of the Orlando Magic, concluded, "Now we know, it was Michael Jordan who was selling tickets all over the league. He was the one who produced the high television ratings, sold all the jerseys, and took the game around the world."[49] Commissioner David Stern blames the erosion of basketball's market share on the plethora of television channels. But the fact remains that fewer fans are watching fewer games on more and more channels.

So the race to proclaim a new savior heats up every year. Harold Miner was called "Baby Jordan" as a prolific scorer from the University of Southern California. He's no longer in the NBA. Vince Carter's explosive exploits in the 1999 all-star dunk contest thrust him to the foreground, but his failure to advance his Toronto Raptors through the NBA play-offs damaged his "new Jordan" status. Allen Iverson has skills and charisma, but his thug persona will never match Jordan's class act, especially in the eyes of the NBA brass.[50]

With panic setting in, NBA scouts have started their search earlier and earlier. Kobe Bryant jumped from Lower Merion High School to his role as "heir Jordan." The NBA hyped Kobe's first all-star appearance opposite Jordan, suggesting a passing of the torch. The Lakers even brought in Jordan's "Zen master," Coach Phil Jackson, to train their designated savior. Bryant broke single game records, making twelve three-point shots and nine in a row. In a convincing sign of things to come, Kobe has helped lead the Lakers to three consecutive NBA championships. The Jordan mantle may have found a new home.

Did Jordan sully his savior status with his long-awaited yet misguided comeback? Rumors of his second coming as a Washington Wizard had sportswriters buzzing for months. The Wizards' 2001 season opener against the New York Knicks drew huge press coverage and audience interest. Yet just a few weeks into his comeback, Air Jordan had become "chair Jordan," sent to the bench with a leg injury. At the time, he was shooting 40 percent, leading the NBA in shots taken *and* shots missed. The unthinkable happened in his first game of the 2002 season. The crowd laughed at Jordan when he muffed a breakaway dunk.[51] He admitted, "My body is sending me messages, and I need to listen."[52] He accomplished one final feat, becoming the first forty-year-old to score forty points in an NBA game. But his retirement felt like a mercy, a relief, a sign of how mortal our old god had become.

The NBA desperately needs a savior. Don't we all? As a high school junior, LeBron James appeared on the cover of *Sports Illustrated* accompanied by the caption "The Chosen One." ESPN broadcast his high school's game from UCLA's Pauley Pavilion. That's as close as LeBron ever got to a college campus on his way to becoming the NBA's top draft pick of 2003. Many have critiqued the media's hype as premature, even unethical. Yet the NBA's longing for new heights matches our own.

Critics should not assail pro basketball for seeking a messiah. Michael Jordan gave us a foretaste of the divine, a peek into infinite possibilities. We want more. A glimpse of greatness *should* make us long for more, whether in sports or religion. An improvised 360-degree cradle dunk deserves to be celebrated. It should be replayed, studied, and duplicated. Basketball at its best combines the creativity of jazz, the beauty of flight, and the majesty of physics. Surely, God must be a hoops fanatic.

The search for a basketball savior parallels the culture's hunger for transcendence. May people of faith affirm the Jordans of the world, touched by the divine, to offer a sneak preview of the Almighty's high-flying power. The feats of Michael Jordan, etched on to highlight reels for centuries to come, can help us reexperience the awe and wonder that Jesus inspired. The Gospel writers captured his shocking improvisations, his daring riffs, his devastating teaching. Ralph Wiley describes the shouts that accompany our athletic saviors' accomplishments: "He can't do that. . . . Hey! *Nobody* else can do that! Nobody would have even *thought* of doing that! . . . Only *he* coulda done that! Yes! That's how the game can be played!"[53] Jesus took his game and our life to another level. He performed feats that would make even the mightiest NBA god weep. Jesus created a thrilling, enduring highlight reel we need to rediscover.

Ice Age

Without sports, how would we know what season it is?

ESPN billboard

Wayne Gretzky is to hockey what Michael Jordan is to basketball. The Great One shattered all NHL scoring records. He led the Edmonton Oilers to four Stanley Cups. He brought celebrity status to the long-beleaguered Los Angeles Kings. His marriage to actress Janet Jones was a Hollywood script for Americans and a royal wedding for Canadians. As the ultimate sign of respect, the NHL retired Gretzky's jersey. No player will ever wear number 99 again.

The Great One's retirement left a gaping hole. The Pittsburgh Penguins' Mario Lemieux wore the messiah mantle until Hodgkin's disease caused his early exit. Like Jordan's return from his baseball experiment, Lemieux's triumphant comeback as owner-player for the Penguins gave hockey fans momentary pause and excitement. A *Sports Illustrated* cover declared Mario's return "The Second Coming."[54] Different sport, same story: Everybody needs a savior.

Ultimately, hockey's relative rise in popularity has not come from charismatic players but from a visionary commissioner. The thuggish behavior of the Philadelphia Flyers, 1970's championship team, gave hockey a reputation as boxing on ice. Hoping to change its image, the National Hockey League hired its first commissioner, Gary Bettman. He guided the league through its first work stoppage, a 102-day lockout in 1994–95. Human-interest stories such as that of all-star defenseman Ray Bourque's twenty-two-year quest for the Stanley Cup made the Colorado Avalanche's 2001 NHL championship front-page news. Astounding slapshot stoppers such as Patrick Roy and Dominik Hasek took the art of goaltending to a new level. In 2001, for the first time since the late 1980s, hockey attendance exceeded that of pro basketball.[55]

Bettman has embraced globalization, encouraging NHL athletes to participate in the Olympics. During the winter Olympics, the NHL schedules a break, allowing hockey players to join their nations' teams. Bettman recalls, "I saw a piece of research that said something like 80% of what I'd call our strong fans think going to the Olympics is a good thing to do."[56] Through a series of strategic moves, ice hockey has become hot.

But bankruptcy still threatens several NHL franchises. The Ottawa Senators suffered from insolvency while leading their division. The Buffalo Sabres were dragged down by the collapse of their owner's Adelphia Cable empire. With the NHL labor agreement expiring in 2004, Commissioner Bettman faces a chilling future.

What can we learn from ice hockey? Globalization works. Sports must offer more than brawls. Faster is better for today's audience. With the constant substitution of players, hopping on and off the ice, hockey comes closest among the team sports to providing constant action. Players enter in waves, keeping fresh skates on the ice at all times. Opposition arrives from unexpected angles, just as in real life. While nothing will replace the fearsome glory of a Bobby or Brent Hull slap shot, games often are decided by a flick of the wrist or an unintended deflection. Momentary breaks in concentration can undo hours of diligence. Final scores may not reflect what happened on the ice. Wisdom literature such as Ecclesiastes teaches us that life is not always fair. But rather than lament our surroundings, we need to eat our food with gladness and drink our wine with a joyful heart, for it is now that God favors what we do. "Enjoy life with your wife, whom you love, all the days of this meaningless life that God has given you under the sun" (or on the ice!) (Eccles. 9:9).

Hockey proves that humans were born to play. The coldest winter conditions could not keep us from sports. Lakes froze, and we adapted. People strapped on skates, took up sticks, chased a puck. Nature does not need to cooperate. Games continue in rain, sleet, and snow. Our hunger for competition, for pushing ourselves, cannot be abated. Our bodies demand exercise, cry out for an embodied faith. If necessary, we will employ new technologies (skates) in an effort to practice ancient rituals (playing games).

If faith is a muscle, then people will always find ways to exercise. If our current Sunday services seem stifling, we will adapt. We may not strap on skates, but we will add turntables, video projectors, and PowerPoint. We will exercise our faith on the job or in community service. If we grew up in a hot religious environment of charismatic expressiveness, we may head toward a cooler, understated service. If we have felt trapped among God's frozen chosen, then we will probably gravitate toward more vocal and ecstatic forms of worship. But we will find a place to grow, stretch, and play. An ice age may have killed the mastodon, but ever resourceful, ever adaptable humans have learned to thrive in even the most foreboding environments.

On the Sidelines

Anyone who will tear down sports will tear down America. Sports and religion have made America what it is today.

Woody Hayes, Ohio State football coach, 1976,
quoted in Hunter S. Thompson, "Enough to Make a Man Believe," in *The Gospel according to ESPN*

Sports' most brutal hit occurred in the most obvious and overlooked place. Today's fan base is shrinking because the major sports have failed to attract tomorrow's players. Boys and girls don't watch baseball, football, basketball, and hockey in the same numbers because they don't play baseball, football, basketball, and hockey. Soccer stands out as the only team sport to experience growth, an 11 percent increase in the 1990s.[57] But soccer's growth doesn't account for all the big four's losses. Can we really blame the big four's ills on soccer moms?

Robert D. Putnam's ambitious and comprehensive book *Bowling Alone* chronicles the declining participation in youth sports.[58] Putnam found that the fitness boom that sparked a proliferation in health clubs did not extend to younger generations. Organized youth sports may show an increase in the number of participants (due primarily to the offspring of the massive baby boom), but the rates of participation have consistently declined. The number of youth soccer players increased significantly during the 1980s, but growth has remained stagnant for the past decade. In 2001 in California, the land of year-round sunshine, 77 percent of students in grades 5 through 12 failed a basic fitness test involving running, push-ups, and pull-ups.[59] Twenty-five percent of U.S. schoolchildren do not attend a physical education class.[60] An American government study found that the number of young people (ages six to nineteen) rated obese tripled between 1980 and 2000. Nine million youths are seriously overweight.[61] According to the surgeon general, the long-term health costs of such a slovenly populace spell national crisis.

Putnam's concerns extend far beyond weight gain. He is disturbed by the decline of social capital, the network of relationships that results from people helping people, whether formally or informally, through civic clubs, volunteerism, and other community-based activities. The decline in team sports, in bowling leagues, sounds a larger warning bell for Putnam. He argues that less sports activity corresponds to smaller amounts of civic activity. In other words, we've become a society of isolated watchers content to stand on the sidelines, letting professionals play the game of life. "We spend less time in conversation over meals, we exchange visits less often, we engage less often in leisure activities that encourage casual social interaction, we spend more time watching (admittedly, some of it in the presence of others) and less time doing."[62] Is this a problem? How did we get into this mess? Can something as "silly" as sports somehow rescue us from becoming a passive culture?

Christopher Lasch finds a direct correlation between spectatorship and passivity. "Commercialization has turned play into work, subordinated the athlete's pleasure to the spectator's, and reduced the spectator to a state of vegetative passivity—the very antithesis of the health and vigor sports ideally promotes."[63] The instrumental and utilitarian impulses of Western culture have separated us from the restorative power of play. College students seem more driven, stressed-out, and overscheduled each year. Yet adults and educators have increased workloads to boost test scores, robbing today's students of precious downtime. After a draining workday, we're too tired to play anything but video games. Our exercise involves watching the Rock wrestle on the TV. We desperately need to recover a theology of play.

In *The Christian at Play*, Robert K. Johnston celebrates play as a God-given end unto itself, independent of any material interest or ulterior motive. Sports allow us to enter a new time and a new space, with boundaries and rules beyond the concerns of everyday life. We can find joy and release from the workaday world whether we win or lose.[64] Most would agree that if God chose to take a break from his creative act in Genesis ("and on the seventh day, he rested"), surely we are created to work *and* play as well. But Johnston builds a persuasive biblical argument that play should be viewed as more than a reward that follows work. Israel was commanded to celebrate the Sabbath as an act of restoration and worship, a chance to luxuriate in the graciousness of God. Festivals, feasting, and dancing were encouraged throughout Hebrew history, even during trying times of exile (Neh. 8:9–12). Such holidays (holy days) demonstrate that "holiness is better associated with joy rather than solemnity, with happiness rather than gloom."[65] Jesus followed the same plan, earning a reputation as "a glutton and a drunkard, a friend of tax collectors and 'sinners'" (Luke 7:34). Jesus also reserved a special place for the most playful of people, children. Yet the drivenness that characterizes so many of us causes us to miss out on the banquets, celebrations, and feasting that Christ frequented. We were born to play.

So what's really happening on the sidelines and in the stands? Why do we attend sporting events? What's God's intention for fans? From the introduction of the wave in 1981 to extravagant face painting and flag waving, sports fans seem more rabid than ever. Barbara Ehrenreich sees such flamboyant fanaticism as a rebellion *against spectatorship,* a chance for audiences to say, "We want to play, too."[66] Increasing fan fervor could be a sublimated cry for more community and less passivity. The longing for experiences, for an embodied faith, a lived theology, will only grow alongside spectatorship. How ironic that sports intended to hone and stimulate the body created a nation of ever expanding couch potatoes. Why have parents been unable to motivate their kids to play more? Probably because sports' original purposes have been both drained and maimed.

Many exercise because it's good for the body. But what about the soul? Athletes no longer perform for the love of the game but for the love of the green. The joyous discovery of what a body can do has been replaced by bottom lines. The big four sports turned a game into a commodity—with coaches calling the plays, decisions being dictated by statistics, and nobody remembering why they once started playing. An embodied faith can renew our fallen pastimes. Will we demonstrate a commitment to a holistic faith that integrates body and soul?

While corporations allot additional resources to keep their executives in shape, schools are experimenting with cutting recess entirely.[67] Blame us— the taxpayers who demanded tighter bottom lines for school systems across America. Texas phased out elementary physical education in 1995, deciding to put more emphasis on academics.[68] Their failed experiment was reversed in 2002. When Harold W. Dodge, the superintendent of the Mobile County, Alabama, school system faced state-imposed budget cuts, he decided to save $1.3 million by cutting supplemental salaries paid to coaches and band directors. To balance the budget, Dodge proposed eliminating all extracurricular activities, including football. In the home of legendary football coach Bear

Bryant and the Alabama Crimson Tide, parents were outraged. The manager of the local stadium declared, "Football in this part of the country is more than a sport. It's a first cousin to a religion." A local math teacher considered Friday nights without football "like Catholicism without the pope." While the religious metaphors abounded, questions of Dodge's sanity flew. Yet he was merely dealing with the "will of the people," which had rejected a raise in school taxes by a 3 to 1 ratio in the last election.[69] The big four sports are dying because today's voters aren't interested in investing in tomorrow's athletes.

Yet the explosion of women's sports demonstrates what a little government and community support can do. The passage of Title IX, which banned sex discrimination in school sports, initiated a tidal wave of new opportunities for those previously on the sidelines. The next generation of women can participate in a variety of athletic options, from soccer to field hockey, from golf to water polo. The number of high school girls playing sports exploded from 300,000 in 1972 to 2.5 million in 2002.[70] Books such as *In These Girls, Hope Is a Muscle* celebrate the grit, determination, camaraderie, and ability emerging from high school athletes. The University of Connecticut's women's basketball team made headlines during an undefeated season en route to an NCAA championship. The Los Angeles Sparks, led by Lisa Leslie, dominate the fledgling WNBA. When 90,000 fans packed the Rose Bowl to watch the United States defeat China in 1999's Women's World Cup, cultural commentators finally took notice. Talk of Brandi Chastain's overtime goal was exceeded only by her shirt-ripping, bra-baring celebration. While golfers on the LPGA tour bristled at encouragement to dress in a more provocative manner, Annika Sorenstam made headlines by competing against men at the PGA's Colonial tournament. Venus and Serena Williams took the focus of women's tennis off Anna Kournikova's endorsements and brought it back to the court. The rise of female sports stars such as Mia Hamm, Marion Jones, and Se Ri Pak suggests that strong, aggressive, and athletic women will redefine "feminine" for generations to come. As a new father, I am excited to see what games my daughter will play.

Board Generation

> The true skater surveys all that is offered, takes all that is given, goes after the rest and leaves nothing to chance. In a society on hold and a planet on self-destruct, the only safe recourse is an insane approach.
>
> John Smythe[71]

When the big four sports became bloated, when communities failed to invest in kids' futures, many teens found new, more extreme ways to play.

Between 1996 and 2001, American boys between the ages of seven and seventeen voted—with their feet. Participation in football rose 2 percent, baseball activity remained flat, and basketball playing dropped 9 percent. Yet participation in the expensive sport of snowboarding rose 46 percent. Skateboarding skyrocketed 123 percent.[72]

Extreme sports are killing the big four—not instantaneously but slowly. They are replacing batting practice, tackling dummies, and free throws. Such shifts worry old-school sports moguls such as Tim Leiweke, president of hockey's Los Angeles Kings. He does the math: "If they're not playing traditional sports, that means they're not watching traditional sports."[73] The commissioner of the made-for-TV Arena Football League, David Baker, would like to take his teenage sons to a baseball game, but "they think it's too slow and too long. They come from a video-game culture where everything has to be slam-bang-hit-boom." His nineteen-year-old son, Benjamin, confirms, "If something doesn't happen in the first five minutes, I'm gone."[74]

One phrase sums up the action sports revolution: Life is not a spectator sport. The board generation believes in active participation—on a bike, or board, or blades. They want to be mobile, embracing new forms of transportation. In 1999, inline skating had twenty-seven million participants, followed by skateboarding and mountain biking with eight million each. Extreme sports enthusiasts have no time for rules. They require no field, no referee, and no teammates. They defy reason, logic, and gravity. They long to get away, to scale the most distant mountain, to merge with the most powerful wave. They are alternative, or at least they used to be.

Action sports are rooted in advanced technology. The original board sport, surfing, expanded only with the introduction of fiberglass. Skateboarding exploded in the seventies with Frank Nasworthy's discovery of the polyurethane wheel.[75] When Jake Burton started snowboarding, rubber straps held his boots on custom wooden boards. Thirty years later, Burton Snowboards dominate the industry. In 1980, two brothers in Minneapolis, Scott and Brennan Olson, fused an ancient Dutch design with the latest technology to introduce the rollerblade. Mountain biking also began by borrowing from the past. Pioneers such as Gary Fisher, Charlie Kelly, and Joe Breeze merged the solid chassis of old bikes from the 1940s with modified brakes and gears to race down San Francisco's Mt. Tamalpais. BMX (bicycle motocross) began as an effort to duplicate dirt track motorcycle racing. In each extreme sport, lighter, faster, and stronger equipment led to ever more expressive "freestyle" efforts.[76]

Each action sport has established an icon. Tow-in surfers marvel at the exploits of big-wave rider Laird Hamilton. Jeremy McGrath put motocross on the map, winning seventy-four events and seven championships.[77] John Tomac has reigned as the Michael Jordan of mountain biking for a decade. Stylish surfer Kelly Slater makes his sponsor, Quiksilver, the leader in "active" apparel. Tony Hawk's place in skateboard history was secured with his "sick" 960-degree trick at the 1999 X Games. As far back as 1996, *Thrasher* magazine declared, "Never in the history of our sports has one personality dominated it more than Hawk."[78] And these seemingly "foolish" superstars are savvy businessmen, creating clothing, equipment, and entertainment empires. Check out the video games shelf. Tony Hawk's ProSkater series dominates the sales charts. The skateboards designed by Mark "the Gonz" Gonzalez have been exhibited in art galleries and generate millions of dollars annually. Leading BMXer Matt Hoffman also owns leading BMX supplier Hoffman Bicycles. Forget baseball cards. Stunt biker Dave Mirra has his own brand of bubblegum.[79]

If you still don't believe action sports rule, then I suggest you pay attention to those who pay the most attention: television and advertisers. In 1995, Ron Semiao's "alternative" Olympics, ESPN's X Games, debuted in Providence, Rhode Island. It featured skateboarding and BMX biking competitions. It's now a summer *and* winter event. In 1999, 270,000 people attended the summer games in San Francisco. Thirty-seven percent of all male teenagers watching television in the United States were tuned in.[80] In 2001, the X Games generated six hundred hours of programming for ESPN and ESPN2, including a four-hour weekend slot on their sister network, ABC.[81] NBC (and its advertisers) countered with the Gravity Games. Ratings remain minimal compared to the Super Bowl, but for advertisers, suburban kids between the ages of twelve and twenty-five constitute a "dream demographic."[82]

Will advertising undermine this alternative movement? Mountain Dew commercials manufactured extreme sports such as street luge and sky surfing. Hollywood tried to cash in with women surfers in *Blue Crush,* Vin Diesel in *XXX,* and *Stuart Little 2* on a skateboard. I am proud of the independent film I cowrote titled *Extreme Days.* But just a year later, the forced scenario of *Extreme Ops* made this emerging genre look ridiculous. Semiao reflects on the phenomenon he helped create: "It's interesting that in the soft advertising marketplace the ad guys are always talking about, this genre shows real resiliency."[83] Rachel Newsome, editor of the magazine *Dazed & Confused,* says, "The big question faced by the post-ism generation is how you communicate your ideas without selling out."[84] Can action sports stars rooted in rebellion take the money and keep their credibility? In the either/or world of the past century, absolutely not. In the both/and tension of the twenty-first century, why not? Newsome suggests, "This means using the system and all that goes with it—sponsorship money, media partnerships, strong brand image, marketing strategies—to set their own agenda. In other words, *Selling In*. Translation: getting away with it."[85]

The "other" Olympics serve as an interesting test case. Olympic viewership among eighteen- to twenty-four-year-old men dropped 55 percent between the 1992 games in Barcelona and the 2000 summer games in Sydney.

How did the International Olympic Committee attract the next generation of viewers? Freestyle skiing of aerials and moguls became official Olympic events in 1994's winter games in Norway. Mountain biking premiered as a medal event in Atlanta's 1996 summer games. The staid International Olympic Committee's ads for the 2002 winter games in Salt Lake City featured a rapid-fire montage of snowboarding and hot dog skiing backed by the high-energy techno sounds of Daft Punk. Esteemed advertising guru Lee Clow of TBWA/Worldwide admitted, "Younger generations tend to be more cynical about the [Olympic] Games. Sports like snowboarding and freestyle skiing seemed more appropriate for that audience."[86] Teen viewers want sports with "a liberal sprinkling of music, entertainment and fashion to create a tasty lifestyle stew."[87] The record ratings for the 2002 winter games affirmed the IOC's instincts. When America swept the men's snowboarding half pipe and eighteen-year-old Kelly Clark won the women's event, the Olympics finally landed on the Millennials' map.[88] When Simon and Garfunkel sang, "Where have you gone, Joe DiMaggio?" they never dreamed the answer would come from a snowboarder. Olympic bronze medallist Chris Klug replaced the baseball legend as spokesperson for "Mr. Coffee."[89]

What's the lesson for the church? Will labeling the Bible "extreme" make it suddenly hip to be godly? Christian publisher Thomas Nelson paid attention to cultural trends, establishing the Extreme for Jesus product line. "We were looking for something that resonated with teens," said Hayley Morgan. "We got in front of kids and asked, 'What's cool with you?'"[90] The company introduced the Extreme Teen Bible, which featured the phrase "No fear, no regrets, just a future with a promise." Thomas Nelson normally sells thirty to forty thousand Bibles to adolescents annually. In the first sixteen months of the Extreme Teen Bible's release, it sold four hundred thousand copies. Morgan explains their marketing breakthrough: "At his time, Jesus was a freak. He was going to parties, hanging out with prostitutes, hanging out with the dregs of humanity. He would definitely have been considered extreme."[91]

How long will the extreme marketing phenomenon last? With products such as Right Guard Xtreme Sport, Extreme Polo Sport, and Extreme Butter entering the market, extreme will soon mean passé. "True extreme sports are if you screw up, you die," said Kristen Ulmer, a professional ice climber, para-glider pilot, and mountaineer. "I get annoyed with the general public's perception of extreme where they look at a skateboard and a taco and go, 'That's extreme.' I just laugh at that."[92] The president of Extreme Coffee, Dan Parodi, reflects, "I think people don't like being lumped in with everybody else. We're all part of this group that wants to be an individual. Maybe that's an oxymoron."[93] Sociologist Armond Aserinsky suggests, "People are insulted by the ordinariness of life. Everything has to be grand; everything has to be great, nobody can be average. When that's the societal norm, it has to be feeling pretty empty inside."[94] How long will extreme for Jesus remain an effective marketing tool? Hayley Morgan surmises, "If I were marketing to parents, I'd say we have another five or six years. But I think for teens, I've got maybe one more year at most. Then, we're going to have to get another word to get their attention."[95] Will people of faith latch on to extreme sports just as the phenomenon fades? Should we ignore trends and stick to the King James Bible? Do we risk riding ever shifting cultural waves? Is it a matter of simply finding the next cool, ultimate, or extreme word?

DILBERT reprinted by permission of United Feature Syndicate, Inc.

A Risky Proposition

> The ocean for me is a totally spiritual thing. . . . It's my place. You can have all kinds of things going on in your life, all kinds of problems and worries, and the second I begin surfing I'm completely focused on that and the rest of the world goes on hold. It's almost like someone going to church. Without a doubt, the ocean is my church.
>
> Mike Parsons, surfer, quoted in *Being Extreme*

Extreme is much more than a word. It represents a major shift in orientation, in thinking, in how people live. To some, these trends present a threat. Skateboarding appears to be rebellious, disrespectful, and destructive. To others, action sports herald opportunities galore—a chance to explore exotic places with new technologies that rise to unparalleled heights. Like much of postmodernity, extreme sports present a paradox. They're individual and communal, alternative and co-opted, hopeless and hopeful. They respect nature and wreck property. They present theological challenges and conundrums. Some call them a pose or an attitude. Consider them a new way of being.

The board generation does not join bowling leagues. They go where they want, when they want, with a friend or two. But that doesn't mean they don't believe in community. Extreme sports *appear* to be all about the individual. Participants take turns catching big air. One competitor rides the half pipe while the others watch. Yet skateboarders practice their "faith" in community, surrounded by those who have gone before them, setting examples for those making their first cautious moves. A skate park may look like chaos, but with the exchange of very few words, kids manage to develop an order of "worship." The array of ramps and rails should prompt a lot more accidents and collisions. Action sports are a stirring tribute to freedom, creativity, and community.

Action sports also represent a refreshing approach to competition. Most athletes perfected their art out of love, not a will to win. In fact, many started practicing before televised competitions and prize money were a possibility. They approach their sport as a personal challenge. At the X Games, new tricks are attempted with an understanding that a fall may spell instant defeat. But riders don't care. The games aren't played against others but oneself. Participants push one another out of respect and are genuinely thrilled when fresh moves and unexpected styles emerge. In fact, style is the substance. As Grantland Rice said, "It's not whether you win or lose, but how you play the game."

Why are kids so drawn to extreme sports, to extreme behavior? Perhaps a cloistered upbringing begs for something more. Soccer moms kept their sons off the football field to prevent broken bones. What are emergency room doctors seeing? Boys and girls with broken bones connected to skateboarding and rollerblading. Why do teenagers resist parents' efforts to protect them? Is it just willful disobedience? Or does risk taking, gambling with the body itself, point to a larger psycho/social/religious need?

Teenagers push the limits because they're trying to find them. "How much abuse (physical and chemical) can my body take? What am I capable of? What have my parents told me that isn't true?" Behind every absurd skateboarding trick is a desperate desire to reach out, to accomplish more, to touch the sky, to find a transcendent high. A popular song finds "Heaven in a Half Pipe." Every time a rider crashes to the ground, he or she discovers what's real, what hurts, what determination costs. Bloody is beautiful.

Teenagers must be allowed and even encouraged to take risks.[96] Parents, teachers, youth leaders, and pastors who deny kids risk-taking sports arrest their children's development. Twenty-nine-year-old adolescents jump off mountains to attain an ever elusive, delayed adulthood. Extreme sports are a clear, defiant challenge: "Either let me take chances now—or pay for my future spent on your couch." Kids want to grow up—physically and spiritually. Coaching and team sports no longer seem sufficient to inculcate values. Instead, kids want to land frontside ollies. Will we help them put wheels on their faith? Or will we keep them sheltered (and hindered) in our overprotective arms? "Skate or die" may be a bumper sticker or a profound theological truth—the board generation's affirmation of a "sick" faith.

To Christians who consider themselves guardians of the truth, this will be threatening. In a time of competing philosophies, Jesus' followers may circle the wagons, opting for purification and clarification. Yet they will miss the fun God may have intended. Kids long for experience, for an embodied, lived faith. They may find that in a faith community or at a skate park. We must come alongside them, bringing our breadth of biblical wisdom and thoughtful theology. But we must also be willing to listen, to allow our blind spots to be identified, our weaknesses exposed.

James Naismith founded basketball "as a means to evangelize people about morality and Christian values."[97] He felt his new game could meet both social and spiritual needs. The YMCA movement offered athletics as a means of promoting physical and spiritual health. With extreme sports on the rise, will we see pro skateboarders and BMX riders as convenient Christian witnesses? Or representatives of the post-rational, post-institutional future? Perhaps the church will invent new games for a board generation desperate for something to do with all that unfocused and unfettered testosterone. Will the next James Naismith please stand up?

If the YMCA gym united a previous era, the skate park serves as the new Mecca. The polished wood floors and chipper coaches of the Young Men's Christian Association have been replaced by concrete and peer relationships. What should the postmodern Y include? All the concrete kids can eat. Can you imagine a place where teens are actually allowed to skateboard? Where they're encouraged to congregate? Most church parking lots have plenty of concrete available, Monday to Saturday. A half pipe, some ramps, and you're suddenly relating to kids.

Some have already started a skateboarding ministry. A Baptist youth pastor in Florida said, "We wanted to reach out to a group of kids that weren't really being reached. They were getting kicked out everywhere else. . . . We wanted to model to them that God would accept them."[98] A Salvation Army captain thought, "The skating is just the worm on the end of the hook."[99] Yet many who skate every day outside the church don't come for the message on Sundays, and the skate park suffered so much vandalism that the church considered shutting it down.

Many sincere ministries will fail because those involved see sports as a means rather than an end. We must alter such outmoded assumptions. God did not create extreme sports to proclaim a message. Kids created extreme sports as a subversive form of worship. It is a radically new theology, not a convenient evangelistic opportunity. Don't make skaters conform to your youth program. They defy formulas. They resist carefully laid marketing plans. Each person with a uniquely decorated board and individualized tricks demands a personalized, relational gospel—just like the one Jesus presented.

Extreme sports cut through theological hegemony. They destroy the notion of one message for all. We must recover Jesus' highly personalized theology. Some are told to sell all they own; others are given a cloak to cover their shame. Jesus created better fishermen but ruined the careers of tax collectors. He overturned tables, attacked the self-righteous, and broke the law. What a cool, alternative dude. The board generation can help us rediscover this Jesus only if we learn to see them as the messenger—and look long enough and close enough to discern their message to us. A healthy balance of mind and body, work and play, religion and sports awaits.

St. Andy --- Popus Maximus

art

Sharks, Pills, and Ashtrays

Il s'agit de saisir ce qui ne passe pas dans ce qui passe. ("What matters is to grasp what does not pass away in what passes away.")

in a letter from Vincent van Gogh to his brother Theo

It's about very, very simple things that can be really hard. People do get really lonely, people do get really frightened, people do fall in love, people do die. . . . These things happen and everyone knows it but not much of it is expressed. Everything's covered with some kind of politeness, continually, and especially in art because art is often meant for a privileged class.

Tracy Emin, on her artwork, quoted in *High Art Lite*

To speak of art in the twenty-first century is to enter a huge, swirling, circular debate that has gone on for much of the past one hundred years. Since the dawn of the modern age of advancements and inventions, questions have raged about the role of art in society. All went well until the invention of the camera. Before then, artists' renderings of all aspects of life were embraced and understood by everyone. Art served as the only means of creating a visual record. Artists made faithful reproductions of geography, family, sexuality, religion, war, architecture. The human form was captured in oils or bronze or marble, as were other aspects of life on planet earth. Whether sketches in charcoal, etchings in brass, crude daubing on the walls of caves, or the tight and fine brush strokes of the Old Masters, art played a vital role in documenting human life in all of its guts and glory.

But the inventions of the nineteenth and twentieth centuries changed all that. Suddenly, a camera could fulfill the work of an artist. The hours spent faithfully capturing a likeness on canvas were challenged by the relatively quick (in the early days of photography, lengthy poses were still required, but nothing like the time needed to sit for a painting) and easy process of photography. And these inventions, like many other modern advances, did much to democratize the arts, which were the domain of the wealthy and privileged. A camera could capture aspects of life not given too much credence by artists: street life, the plight of the working classes, the immediacy of the modern age's horrific wars. And where did this leave the arts? It opened a door of creativity, new horizons of possibility, and a world of debate.

Freed from the need to be realistic, artists explored new forms: abstract, impressionist, cubist, modernist. Artists opened a Pandora's box of ever increasing opportunities for creativity. For viewers and critics, a new question arose: What is art? Like many rhetorical questions, it will probably never be answered, and the debate will continue.

Before looking at recent art and exploring the meanings and theology contained in it, a quick word will prove helpful about three key artists whose contributions created a basic framework that influences artists at work today. We can call them the trinity, if you like. I (Barry) picked them primarily because they remain influential and widely embraced[1] and are still referenced by artists and critics today.[2] They also hold some fascination in the larger public eye. In fact, most people in the Western world know who these figures are.[3] All three have even been portrayed by other famous persons in recent films: *Surviving Picasso* (which starred Anthony Hopkins), *I Shot Andy Warhol* (starring Jared Harris), and *Pollock* (starring acclaimed actor Ed Harris).

Each of these artists offered at least one significant contribution to the current art scene, an overarching idea that still carries weight and influence in the art world. They form a rather uneven and sometimes difficult to trace chain through the trajectory of modern art. Picasso was followed by Pollock, and he was in turn followed by Warhol. Each not only built on the contribution of others but also rejected others. No one creates in a vacuum. Picasso's contributions to art did not come out of thin air; they were born out of rejection and embrace. He rejected the more traditional approaches[4] to art that had characterized his predecessors and in turn explored new horizons. The same is true for the other two. But each of them offered something important to the artistic community.

The first is Pablo Picasso, one of the twentieth century's larger-than-life figures. He introduced new movements and new ideas with one flick of his paintbrush or turn of his pottery wheel. He transcended the art world and became a cultural icon for people who knew nothing of art. He was prolific, creating art in a wide range of styles and mediums. Oils, sculpture, pottery, drawing—there was not a medium he did not at least attempt to use. Picasso became a key figure in the development of a significant number of periods in modern art.

Picasso's 1907 painting *Les Demoiselles D'Avignon* is often called the first modern painting. It is a portrait of five women presented in cubist form. It is a very flat, on-the-surface painting with no real background, just different colors serving as a backdrop for the figures. It is also quite ugly. That is, perhaps, the great contribution Picasso made to modern art. Picasso replaced beauty with ugliness[5] and in the process opened up a new world of what modern art could be, the ramifications of which we are still experiencing today.

Jackson Pollock embodies the artist as an immensely troubled and self-destructive soul. Riddled with insecurity, grappling with genius, struggling to break free of the artistic constraints of his day, Pollock found new mediums and avenues of expression. He was a classic American figure, an almost mythic cowboy. He was rugged, hard-living, heavy-drinking, and promiscuous. As with all myths, truth and fiction blend together to create a whole new persona—Pollock was exactly that. In the movie *Pollock,* actor Ed Harris portrayed him as a tormented genius, destroyed by his hard living and drunkenness. Yet Pollock's paintings reveal his sensitivity. His art pours out of his brokenness, from his wounds.

Pollock's place in art history stems from his birthplace. To be more precise, he was an American, *not* a European. That is not to diminish his achievement, but because he was an American, Pollock broke down the authority and domination of European artists. Consequently, artists from all corners of the globe can find their way into the art world today. Pollock also represents the quest for authenticity, which makes his art so compelling. His commitment to paint on canvas seems belied by the apparent randomness of his dripping approach to the medium. But Pollock's commitment was nevertheless intense, a commitment to a form of art free of all phoniness.

Andy Warhol represents the opposite end of the spectrum from Pollock. If Pollock stands for authenticity and follows in the tradition of the artist as a tortured soul (a path well trodden by such artistic forbears as Goya and van Gogh), Warhol stands for the rejection of torment and the embrace of both commercialism and irony. In fact, Warhol's public persona was quite bland, almost a blank slate. Did he plan it that way? Much of Warhol's life—his lifelong Catholic faith for instance—was not held up to public scrutiny.[6] Warhol attended mass every day and often worked in his congregation's soup kitchen and shelter, a fact seemingly at odds with his outrageous celebrity-ridden existence.

Warhol began as a commercial artist but eventually turned "high art" into commerce. Warhol embraced art as a means to another end, not art for art's sake but art for fame, celebrity, and, of course, money. Those who dismiss Warhol as shallow and devoid of substance only underscore Warhol's genius at creating and hiding behind fake personae. He was famous, yet people didn't really know him, an intention on Warhol's part to generate continual fascination in a culture fascinated by celebrity and gossip. His adoption of wild, platinum wigs and an outsider posture was an attempt to remove personality and emotion from his art. His paintings are flat, but not like Picasso's, which seem to want to burst out of the canvas. They are flat in an almost two-dimensional manner (this approach has been picked up by Japanese artists such as initiators of the "superflat" medium). With Warhol everything is placed on the same level. Elizabeth Taylor and Jackie Onassis are placed alongside electric chairs and household items. None is given special pride of place; they coexist in contradiction and ease at the same time. In this way Warhol was the first postmodern artist: ironic, iconic, iconoclastic, plastic, navigating a fame-hunting world of emptiness and contradiction.

These brief outlines merely lay a groundwork for exploring the roots of some postmodern artists and understanding the shoulders they stood on and the things they both embraced and rejected. These three artists are also significant in understanding the rise of modern art.

Shock Art

> I'm classically trained, though I've since broken all that down. But the training was important, otherwise you don't really know why you are doing something and it's just gratuitous. (Who does he think he is, Picasso?)
>
> interview with Guido, hairdresser, *Independent on Sunday*

At the end of the twentieth century, a new kind of art emerged, an art form beyond the prerogative of the art elite. It was populist and incredibly successful. It utilized the new opportunities presented by a mediatized culture hungry for celebrity and willing to embrace virtually anything thrown at it. As with other forms of popular culture, this new art is fully ensconced in consumer culture. It is art for a prime-time society—a society fueled by radio shock jocks and Jerry Springer, by celebrity news programs and reality shows. Museum shows such as "Sensation" and "Apocalypse" characterized this prime-time art, which placed heavy emphasis on art that shocks and repels.

Shock value seems to be one of the major prerequisites of contemporary art. The content and nature of some of these works generate much uproar and concern from the more conservative elements within society. For example, New York Mayor Rudolph Giuliani vocalized outrage over the Brooklyn Museum's 1999 art show featuring a painting of the virgin Mary by Nigerian-born painter Chris Ofili. The work included the use of cow dung (a tribal artifact) and clippings from pornographic magazines. As with many protests, few protestors actually took the time to see the work. In fact, the uproar started with rumors *about* the show. Some investigation and conversation about the pieces in the show would perhaps have revealed the artist's deep interest in Catholicism and his honest attempts to characterize faith in a way that reflects his cultural heritage as well as his present social contexts.

Many contemporary art works shock those from older generations, reflecting changing social values and perceptions. Few postmoderns actually find this kind of art shocking. Artists follow the rock 'n' roll tradition in which the ability to shock stands as a must-have credential. From Elvis shaking his hips on *Ed Sullivan* to the Sex Pistols, Marilyn Manson, and Eminem, important artists incite protests and riots. Consider also the cultural fascination with violent and graphic horror movies and video games. Art has assumed this mantle of shock, and today's young painters and sculptors are often viewed like rock stars and accorded the same column space in the celebrity press.

Dissected cows, sharks, and sheep floating in formaldehyde-filled Perspex containers are the stock-in-trade of British artist Damien Hirst, one of the leading examples of the artist as shock maker and a direct descendant of the art-as-ugliness school of Picasso. Hirst has generated much debate with his shock tactics. Is it art? is a question commonly asked of Hirst's work. He does paint, but his primary medium is a modified form of sculpture. This is perhaps the reason the age-old question of artistic validity is continually asked in regard to his work.

Such new artists bypass the usual cultural capital needed in order to get artistic validity. Their art is, instead, a product of a prime-time society. It is immediate, and in that sense it is divorced from history and the need to embody lasting values. It is also populist, drawing on the present state of the cultural psyche. Some critics claim that this art has been downgraded and is therefore less important. But those comments draw from a modern rather than a postmodern view of life and history.

Unlike other painters who portray images, Hirst simply stages shock tactics. At least that is how he is often viewed. This leads some to dismiss the artistic value and content of his work. One must scratch below the surface, beyond the shock, to get to the issues at hand. There is genuine emotion at work. The pieces are designed to vent, to express and portray key themes at work in the postmodern psyche.[7]

Tracy Emin, another leader of the shock school, became famous by presenting her bed and all the detritus around it—empty alcohol bottles, cigarettes, ashtrays, underwear, used condoms—as a work of art. She said, "I would give up the art tomorrow—I would instantly give it up—if I could get rid of these feelings."[8] She verbalizes elements of the artistic-tortured soul along with the celebration of ugly. But she also highlights the continuing role that art plays in aiding humans to express the wide and full range of the emotional experience.

One of the most shocking art experiences of my own life occurred during a visit to the Royal Academy's 2000 show, "Apocalypse." The juxtaposition of highly creative and modern art pieces with the Baroque surroundings of the Academy's galleries only heightened the dissonance. One room was devoted to a single piece created by brothers Dinos and Jake Chapman, famous for works that deal with death, sexuality, bestiality, dismemberment, and pain. One particular piece entitled *Hell* consists of plastic toy soldiers, each one painstakingly made and painted by a team of workers over a three-year period. It reflects the horrors of war, the depths to which humanity can sink. There are torture chambers, dismembered bodies, and buildings reminiscent of Nazi concentration camps. Of course, *Hell* intends to shock. But once the novelty, or the shock value, wears off, a profound meditation on man's inhumanity to man remains. Viewers must ponder the horrific things that one human being can inflict on another. This work critiques the Enlightenment's progressive view of life, especially in light of September 11, 2001.

This particular genre of art declares that "we"—the public—cannot be shocked by what confronts us because "we"—our societies—produced it. Our culture's willingness to embrace these art forms points to the veracity of this observation. It seems that our collective consciousness is ready for this stuff.

Beauty

I don't think about art when I'm working. I try to think about life.

Jean-Michel Basquiat, *Basquiat*

When I was younger and still living in England, I used to make regular pilgrimages to what was then called the Tate Gallery in London. Now completely reconstructed and reopened, the Tate Britain displays the works of British painters. I found myself drawn to painters such as Joseph Turner and John Constable. I loved the way they evoked the pastoral nature of much of Britain, the colors of the countryside, the scenes of quiet lives from less driven times. And I particularly loved the light and beauty of their work.

Beauty has not been a major thrust of recent art. Picasso and others opened a door on the use of ugliness in art, and its effect is still in force. In many ways, ugliness served as a great metaphor for life in the modern world. A century filled with world wars, dictatorships, totalitarianism, global hunger, terrorism, and weapons of mass destruction is effectively captured with brutal brush strokes, distorted, disjointed figures, and the obtuse and abstract. But life is not all ugly. Beauty is still important and still celebrated.

I look for beauty in art, for soul, and I find it particularly in the works of two artists: Jean-Michel Basquiat and Patrick Heron. Basquiat died young, burned out in a blinding flash of celebrity, drug addiction, and pain. He was the Jimi Hendrix of the art world, and his life was portrayed on celluloid in 1998's beautiful film *Basquiat*.[9] Heron lived a more pastoral life as a holdover from another age. He visited the impressionist painter Henri Matisse toward the end of that great painter's life and was deeply influenced by his use of color and light.

Both offer contemporary perspectives on beauty, though Heron is a decidedly more modern painter rather than a postmodern one. The difference between them relates to self-expression. Heron's art, like that of Picasso and Matisse, is intensely personal and decidedly not ironic, demonstrating the contrast between modern and postmodern attitudes toward irony.

Basquiat offers several reasons why he should be studied. He stood out as a true pop cultural artist. He was multi-literate—a poet, DJ, and rapper, as well as a painter. He was also the first "black" painter to be given a retrospective by a major gallery. His work reflects his own pop cultural influences: Charlie Parker, Miles Davis, Muhammad Ali, and Andy Warhol (with whom he later collaborated on many paintings). His initial notoriety came through his graffiti. He peppered the walls and sidewalks of 1980s New York with pithy comments. His graffiti was an attempt to put an "end to mind wash religion, nowhere politics, and bogus philosophy."[10] His later paintings and drawings continued a graffiti tradition with their use of words and phrases. Yet his very primitive approach to painting went beyond folk art and had a calculated style. He said of his own work, "Picasso arrived at primitive art in order to give of its nobility to western art. And I arrived at Picasso to give his nobility to the art called 'primitive.'"[11] The childlike quality of his painting came from a calculated approach.

The second reason to study Basquiat stems from his postmodern understanding of beauty. Basquiat's paintings are not beautiful in the classic sense of the word. But conventional ideas of physical beauty have been turned on their heads in the twenty-first century. Look at the world of fashion models; multicultural beauty fuels the catwalks and runways of today's globalized fashion industry. But the post-racial future represents just one aspect of our evolving standards. Postmodern beauty goes beneath the surface, beyond skin-deep. It is sometimes simply the idea of beauty.

Basquiat yearns for beauty as lost innocence, no longer available in postmodern times. He fills his intensely personal work with the detachment so common today. He draws from complex source material, loading his work with references from jazz, his color (he was of Haitian and Puerto Rican descent), medical reference books, New York. You name it, and Basquiat incorporated it into his work. Basquiat's concept of beauty can be described as soul.[12] It can be felt in the fluidity of his paintings, in the clash of colors, and in the juxtaposition of words, primitive figures, and cultural symbols. Some cite Basquiat as a symbol of the 1980s, but beauty remains the distinctive of his work.

Third and perhaps most importantly, Basquiat represents the rule-breaking, redefining of the art world. If Andy Warhol merged commerce and fine art, Basquiat merged the culture of the streets and the world of high art. He offered a new idea of the possibility of what makes for art. "My subject matters are royalty, heroism and the streets," he said in 1985.[13] Interesting choices for an artist like Basquiat, especially when we consider a theology informed by art.

Basquiat did not design his art to shock. A naive innocence permeates his work, especially when placed against more recent art. Yet it still packed plenty of punch. He turned an already reeling art world on its ear by redefining painting and stripping away the cultural elite's last grasps on the art world. In contrast to Pollock, who had a tortured soul, Basquiat gleefully immersed himself in the thriving New York celebrity circuit.[14] He was a hip, fun-loving soul. His work proved more accessible than Warhol's because it had more emotion in it. He took objects—tires, refrigerators, whatever he saw—and covered them with his vibrant painting style. His great contribution to art was his ability to defy preexisting standards and redefine who was and who could be an artist. He was the first black painter of the twentieth century to be given a major museum show. While largely formally untrained, Basquiat demonstrated that he knew his stuff. Like many rock musicians today, he was self-taught through listening to others and learning on the run, and he used his art as a way of acquiring the things he desired in life. His style paid homage to his influences—Picasso, Cy Twombly, the streets of New York, his heritage, his love of jazz and hip-hop—but his style was unique, a bricolage of influences refashioned into something new and totally postmodern.

Whole Lot of Nothing

> Art is a collaboration between God and the artist, and the less the artist does the better.
>
> Andre Gide

A play called *Art* ran successfully in London before crossing the pond for a successful American run. It centers on three male friends and a piece of art one of them has purchased: a blank white canvas. The play focuses on the nature of relationships and differing views on the nature of art and questions the large number of blank canvases in today's art. How can nothingness really be considered art? Shouldn't art be about something, something you can get your teeth into, like a drawing or a portrait or at least a couple of lines?

Blankness, nothingness troubles many people. Its use as an art reference is even more difficult for some to grasp. Yet art about nothing abounds today. It descends from the minimalist movement of the 1960s and stretches back to the dawn of the twentieth century, when absence first appeared in art. As the century unraveled, artists adopted nothingness to express their feelings and ideas about contemporary life. Minimalists in the '60s used small things to make larger, radical statements that were often political in tone. Today's nothingness relates to the blankness of much of postmodern life and is an attempt to remonstrate against the soul-lessness of life today. We are the most entertained generation in the history of the world. America has become a virtual coast-to-coast amusement park. Yet we are bored. We go shopping to fill our souls, we eat to feel better, we drink to mask the pain and isolation we feel, and what do we feel? Nothing.

Consider Martin Creed's 1994 work titled *A Sheet of A4 Paper Crumpled into a Ball*. It is just that—a piece of A4-sized paper crumpled into a ball. Later, Creed amplified the sound of a doorbell through a guitar amp. The sound is heard every time someone rings the doorbell to get into the gallery. But if no one rings the bell, there is no sound, no show, nothing! Martin Creed became the surprise winner of the 2001 Turner Prize for Art, Britain's most prestigious and sought-after award for contemporary artists. The prestige of the award grew when England's newest, hip resident, Madonna, presented it. She did so in her typically shock-inducing way, using an expletive live on British television, much to the chagrin of the event organizers and the censors of the BBC. Creed's victory was the source of much debate in the press, for his "work of art" was an empty room in which the lights went off and then came back on every couple of minutes! It presented yet another opportunity to drag the old "is this art" debate out of the closet. Creed spoke at length, post-prize, about his indebtedness to Marchel Duchamp and the minimalist movement. Yet he also spoke about alienation, isolation, and loss.

What should we make of blank canvases, white lights, and white noise? Some dismiss it all as rubbish. But I find myself greatly troubled by such art. Were it the isolated work of one artist, it could perhaps be seen as simply the quirkiness of an individual. But the preponderance of blankness demands a thoughtful reflection. Does it point to postmodern nihilism? The emptiness of contemporary life? Loss of soul? Loss of meaning? All of these and more. Contemporary life seems too comfortable with the concept of nothingness. Surely we can find something to reflect on. Why choose nothing? In a post-rational culture in which entertainment has been made reality and vice versa, in which so much information is available and all of it is imbued with the same level of importance, whether war or plastic garden gnomes, the ease with which postmoderns relate to nothing presents the greatest challenge to the religious community. The biggest mistake to make of this "nothingness art" is to assume that it is about nothing.

"There is no such thing as a painting about nothing," said the minimalist painter and deeply spiritual man Mark Rothko.[15] Perhaps a series of blank, empty canvases, such as those in the Rothko Chapel in Houston, Texas, are as able as any creedal or doctrinal statement to capture and characterize the holy. The postmodern mind does not always need an explanation. Sometimes the silence and the emptiness are more than enough.

Art and Technology

> Contemporary artists have so many visual options and technologies to work with, but the medium is never the message, the message is the gesture.
>
> Jeff Koons

> Art consists in drawing the line somewhere.
>
> G. K. Chesterton

Technological advancements revolutionized the art world, democratizing it like movies and music. Computers enable people with little or no artistic aptitude to create things in the comfort of their own homes, which would have taken roomfuls of equipment only a couple decades ago. L.A.-based U.K. artist David Hockney published a controversial book called *Secret Knowledge*.[16] He proffers the thesis that the Old Masters used an array of technological developments that were available to them to advance their craft. The use of lenses and mirrors, according to Hockney, revolutionized art from the mid-fifteenth century on. To underscore his thesis, he built a "great wall" of art over five centuries and highlighted where technology and change met.

While Old Masters such as Rembrandt, Hans Holbein, or Leonardo da Vinci may have kept the use of technology in their work a secret, today's artists advertise the fact. Andy Warhol called his painting studio in New York the Factory and used photography, screen printing, and commercial art processes in his work. That trend continues chiefly in the art of New York artist Jeff Koons. Koons is a painter who doesn't paint. He designs his works through technology and then hires a team of assistants to execute the actual paintings in excruciating detail. His Easyfun-Ethereal paintings are amazing. This series of seven paintings are replications of artwork Koons first assembled on his computer. He combined a seemingly disconnected collection of images from fashion magazines, cereal boxes, and nature books. His collages were then manipulated by computer programs before his assistants duplicated them on large canvases as traditional oil paintings.

Koons follows in the Warholian pop tradition, celebrating elements of popular culture. Like many of Warhol's contemporaries and descendants, he moves easily in the world of fame and celebrity. Whereas Warhol turned household items such as detergent packages and soup cans into art, Koons uses more personal items, particularly from childhood: dogs sculpted from skinny balloons, children's plastic toys, chocolate chip cookies. And whereas Warhol applied a mass production technique to his artwork, creating numerous copies of each piece, the perfectionist Koons creates one-of-a-kind pieces too labor intensive to replicate. His works are huge and showy but also carry strong messages about the world in which we live. The Easyfun-Ethereal series deals with adult sexual desire and the childhood pursuit of simple pleasure and examines the world of the sensual, the touch, taste, smell, and sights of the human experience. At first glance, his work seems preposterously juvenile. His 1994 *Balloon Dog* is a ten-foot-high stainless steel sculpture of a child's balloon dog. But standing in a museum, all bright and shiny, *Balloon Dog* comments on the plastic, shallow nature of postmodernity. Koons's work, like much postmodern art, bypasses the artist's personality. It is meant to be conceptual, offering a common experience for all who view it.

Technology's influence extends beyond the creation of a piece. It replaces aspects of the artist's craft formerly done by hand, such as the repositioning of figures or the mixing of color. Koons adds layers of computer-generated color palettes together to "mix" the perfect color for a piece. This combination of creativity and technology allows for horizons to be explored that weren't even dreamed of in the past. Technology allows for the creation of virtually any idea one can imagine.

The Pain Gate

One eye sees, the other feels.

Paul Klee

The art of life is the art of avoiding pain.

Thomas Jefferson

Jackson Pollock was a tormented soul, haunted by depression, who turned to art to ease his pain. The tortured life and art of Vincent van Gogh inspires art lovers around the world. We all experience pain, but culturally we seem intent on eradicating it. We have a hard time seeing any redemptive value in pain. We appreciate pain's contribution to art, but most of us would gladly forego the creative muse to live free from pain. A tortured life is not what we are after!

Yet pain is a central fact of human existence. We have two kinds of nerve fibers, one for acute pain, the other for nagging pain. Pain and suffering can often degrade life, but sometimes they can ennoble it. Pain warns the physical body of damage, launching a stimulus to activity. Friedrich Nietzsche believed that pain was given as a goad to creativity. Consider the case of Mexican artist Frida Kahlo. She suffered terrible injuries and experienced lifelong pain after a terrible bus crash in 1925. She underwent numerous surgeries, was unable to bear children, and spent the rest of her life in continual pain. But she painted and most often painted her pain, infusing it with a spiritual element, using powerful physical and religious imagery to convey her awareness even as her physical body disintegrated.

The Spanish painter Francisco Goya was struck with deafness at age forty-seven.[17] He suffered from depression and personality changes, which may have come from lead poisoning. The heaviness and pessimism that fill his later work must be attributed to the isolation of deafness and the weight of pain in his life.

In 1992, New York artist David Wojnarowicz died at age thirty-seven after succumbing to the AIDS virus. The disease had decimated his community of friends and ultimately the artist himself. His work explores his struggles with sexual identity, both his own and that of contemporary society. He attempted to capture the struggle with maleness that has become a hallmark of postmodern men, hetero- as well as homosexual. He was both an artist and a writer. In the midst of his struggle with AIDS, he said, "I'm not so much interested in creating literature as I am in trying to convey the pressure of what I've witnessed or experienced."[18] His disinterest with making a "grand statement" with his art is another element in postmodern art and life and is linked to the search for authenticity and rootedness and a hunger for meaningful experiences rather than propositional ideas.

In *Virtual Faith,* Tom Beaudoin declares that pain is a key to unlocking ministry opportunities when dealing with Generation X.[19] He goes on to say that pain and suffering lay the groundwork for their religiousness: "Suffering is a sort of boundary experience that forces us to confront questions about our own human limits."[20] The art world presented this idea throughout the twentieth century. Examples include Picasso's *Guernica,* the work of Max Ernst and other German artists who experienced the Nazis, and Stanley Spencer's paintings of the First World War. Postmodern art continues to confront us with human limits, challenging them dismissively, ironically, emotionally.

The search for understanding and healing can be found on canvases or in pews. But a case can be made that the art world offers a more open environment for expressing pain and suffering than does the church. This may explain postmodern culture's embrace of the arts and rejection of organized religions. There is much talk of returning creativity to Christian experience, but such creativity must allow for the expression of pain, recognizing it as a catalyst for making spiritual connections.

The Symbolic Use of Words

> All the time and space of his [working man's] world becomes foreign to him with the accumulation of his alienated products.
>
> Karl Marx

> Humor is the last stage of existential awareness before faith.
>
> Søren Kierkegaard

I was in my local convenience store a couple months back when a man came in pushing his baby in a stroller. He was obviously quite fashion conscious, wearing the most amazing lime green colored pants. I felt I had to comment on them! It turned out that he was also British, so we talked a little more and reached the subject of occupations. He was a painter in town for his first U.S. opening at a small gallery. Once he told me his name, Bob Smith, I immediately knew who he was. He paints with his wife, Roberta, and they are quite well known in the British art world for their politically incorrect and often funny works of art. They engage in a sort of postmodern sloganeering, and their art is comprised primarily of words painted on brightly colored canvases. They use words as art, turning the written into visual, making words both iconic and symbolic. Art used to be about image, people, landscapes, animals, but increasingly, words have made their way into art, assuming a key role in the artist's armory.

Andy Warhol took brand labels and turned them into art. Robert Rauschenberg perfected the art of collage and silkscreen, liberally dotting his works with words and slogans. Basquiat used words to great effect in his art. And now we have reached a point where words have become art themselves. One of Gillian Wearing's best-known projects is a series of photographs titled "Signs that say what you want them to say and not Signs that say what someone else wants you to say." For the series, this photographer approached people on a London street and asked them to participate in her project by writing something on the blank card she offered them. When they finished, she photographed them. Many of the respondents were the more marginalized elements of London's streets, and their cards were both political and moving. The words were more than personal expressions of those who wrote them, becoming a part of the art in and of themselves.

"Words are flowing out like endless rain into a paper cup," wrote the Beatles. Popular culture suffers from an overabundance of words. In the information age, we can access almost anything we desire if we have a computer. Words wash over us everywhere we turn. This endless stream of words has a numbing effect at times, part of the statement made in Bob and Roberta Smith's work. But words and language have changed dramatically in the ways they are used and how they are understood.

Semiotics has unlocked new understandings about the nature of language. The foundation for the Western understanding of signs was influenced by the teachings of St. Augustine. Augustine developed the theory of signa data—conventional signs—and narrowed the focus of the study of signs to the relationship between mental words and the verbal.[21] But the twentieth century saw revolutions in the understanding of language and signs. The work of Ferdinand de Saussure changed the way we understand language and its role in society.[22] But the sheer abundance of words has precipitated the biggest changes. Words have largely become meaningless. We co-opt words, give them opposite meanings: Bad means really good, cool is hot, and so on. Different ethnic groups have invented their own versions of language, from the cockneys of Victorian London to the homies of the African-American inner-city hoods. The situationist and the fluxus movements both used words to political ends, using the arts to advance their particular views on contemporary society. No wonder religions tied to words both written and spoken have so little identification among the mediatized world.

Bob and Roberta Smith paint canvases covered with political slogans drawn from popular culture. They are ironic and lighthearted at the same time: "Farmers are the new miners," "Shop Locally," or "Queen Camilla." In an age of slogans and branding, are these merely more of the same or an ironic commentary on them? Humor comes in all forms: lighthearted, dark, political, and so on. This is true of performance comedy as well as artistic humor.

David Shrigley is another artist who uses irony in his work. He draws childlike, spindly figures and adds liberal doses of pithy commentary. A review in *Face* magazine of his latest work, *Do Not Bend,* written by author Will Self, says, "This artist takes on everything: memory and forgetting, love and hate, murder and preservation, god and godlessness."[23] Shrigley's humor can be sarcastic and caustic, but postmodern humor is rarely sanitized or polite. Richard Prince also makes art out of jokes.[24] His first foray into art was a piece on which he copied not a particularly funny joke and then sold it for ten dollars. He repeated that process again and again and now has become recognized for his work. He still paints jokes, but now his work is not about the actual joke but the joke's role as a part of his artistic process.

The Spiritual Side of Art

And so the Spirit sweeps through the universe with resounding, inspiring, and igniting power, evoking the response of renewed vitality until the last day. This is the purpose and action of God, who has no beginning and no end. He created humanity as the wonderful work of his hand, by equipping people with an impulse and inclination to higher things by enabling them to make their own responses. God did this because he loved people. After all, he is Love itself.

Hildegard of Bingen

The spiritual life to which art belongs and of which it is one of the mightiest agents, is a complex but definite movement above and beyond, which can be translated into simplicity.

Wassily Kandinsky

Much art has been created to serve religion. In fact, the church was the great patron of the arts for centuries. Religion fueled art, and art was filled with religious imagery and spiritual devotion. Artists of the twentieth century largely abandoned religious imagery. But Mark Rothko's and Wassily Kandinsky's gestures toward a vague transcendence have been supplanted by a fair amount of spirituality floating around today's art.

Religious imagery dominates popular culture, whether in Madonna's videos or the goth subculture's affectation for religious clothing and icons as jewelry. However, such imagery is usually removed from its original meaning and purposes, co-opted as a symbol for any number of personalized statements. Thus, religious belief, issues of doubt, and questions of faith are usually not part of the dialogue surrounding contemporary art. Still, there are a few exceptions. In fact, the cover story in the April 20, 2003, edition of London's *Sunday Times Culture Magazine* was about the resurgence of the Christ figure in contemporary art. "Twenty years ago, no artist was interested in Jesus. Now his image is everywhere,"[25] declares the author.

Two other examples are video artists Bill Viola and Mark Wallinger, who deal almost exclusively with issues of religion and faith. Viola's most recent installations were ethereal works that focused on such things as angels and heaven. Floating figures against dark backgrounds were highly charged emotional forays into the realm of the spirit. Wallinger adopts a different approach. In *Angel,* Wallinger portrays the artist as a blind man at the bottom of an escalator on the London Underground (the Angel station), walking toward the camera but getting nowhere as the escalator moves against him. While this continues, Wallinger recites in a garbled voice the opening of John's Gospel: "In the beginning was the Word." It sounds strange because Wallinger is actually saying the words phonetically and backward. The entire film plays backward so that everything is interrelated. Handel's *Messiah* kicks in when he stops walking, and the escalator finally scoops him up to the street and out of sight. The references are complex: moving but getting nowhere, mouthing words we don't really understand, going forward but actually moving backward. Perhaps Wallinger is critiquing post-Christian societies that pay lip service to the idea of religion, to Jesus.

Wallinger made a significant contribution to a revolving art project in London's Trafalgar Square. Artists were invited to submit a sculpture to be placed on a large marble plinth. Wallinger's contribution was a life-sized figure of a man with a crown of thorns on his head, his hands bound, wearing a loincloth. It was called *Ecce Homo*—"Behold the man!" The figure was beardless but eminently recognizable as Jesus. It was a strange sculpture, way too small for such a large plinth and too religious for its secular environment.

The sculpture was a representation of Jesus in the public realm, the marketplace, and the discrepancy of a life-sized statue set on a plinth designed for something much bigger pointed to the difficult place the presence of Jesus now creates in the postmodern world. To some extent, the Western world is still stuck with Jesus, and we don't really know what to do with him. He hangs around the edges of our culture and makes us a little uneasy. Many people have no issues with Jesus. They are often more than a little interested, but they don't really know what to do about him. Others cannot make the connection between Jesus and the church. While they can connect with Jesus on some levels, the shadow of the church pushes them away. The presence of Jesus on a public plinth may remind us of Christianity's power and influence, now gone. Or it may stand as a rebuke to a culture that seeks power. Either way, Wallinger's work pushes emotional buttons about the spiritual state of Western society.

At the other end of the spectrum of religious artists lies Howard Finster. A native of Georgia, Finster was a classic southern Bible-thumping revival preacher. He did not begin to paint until he was sixty-five years old and claims that a paint smudge on his finger spoke to him and urged him to "paint sacred art."[26] He heeded that call and became world famous for his folk art style. His work gained even more public interest when he was commissioned to make album covers for rock bands such as Talking Heads and R.E.M. Finster's apocalyptic-fueled theological perspectives filled his art. His death in 2001 translated Finster to one of his heavenly visions.

Art Goes Global

Jackson Pollock took the focus of art off Europe. Fifty years later, the art community has become multicultural and globalized. Galleries in Paris, London, and New York now feature works by Asian, African, and South American artists. Art from anywhere has a chance in ways that it didn't before.

While artist Chris Ofili lives in London, his Nigerian ancestry informs his artwork. His afro-centered take on the imagery of Western popular and religious culture borrows the style and effects of African folk art. Similarly, Manuel Ocampo, a Filipino artist now based in Spain, fuses issues of racism, colonialism, and the clash of folk and official religion in his works. London's Heyward Gallery presented an exhibition of contemporary Japanese art in the summer of 2002. Such art has generated interest among young people because of their fascination with cartoons and particularly the Japanese version called anime. Japan's superflat movement finds inspiration in anime.[27] Artists of this movement create two-dimensional art, believing that contemporary society is two-dimensional, or superflat. Their artwork blends pop art, high culture, technology, and animation to create a new genre. It also represents the influence of Western culture on traditional Japanese society and charts the results. Issues of globalization and cultural exchange fuel this work.

Such art forces us to take off our Western-focused glasses and to see the world as a multicultural, multiethnic, globally local community. We can no longer afford to assume a position of elevation, to see ourselves as the arbiters of how faith or theology should be constructed. As the art world learns from the approaches and influences of global artistry, theology could well do the same.

All the Colors of the Sun: An Artful Theology

Jesus is the supreme artist, more of an artist than all others, disdaining marble and clay and color, working in the living flesh.

Vincent van Gogh, quoted in *Eternity's Gate*

The greatest tragedy of theology in the past three centuries has been the divorce of the theologian from the poet, the dancer, the musician, the painter, the dramatist, the actress, the movie-maker.

M. D. Chenu, quoted in *Quantum Spirituality*

Art has always been about meaning, and contemporary art offers a complex matrix of meanings. Understanding modern art, particularly the work of the abstract impressionists and minimalists, required much reflection and a willingness to work through the initial puzzlement over what was being presented. Postmodern artists tend to avoid the "hidden" aspects of meaning in their work, choosing instead to put the meaning front and center, reflecting a broader cultural trend of putting things directly in front of people's faces. Such art reflects the post-racial, post-sexual, and post-ethical challenges. It also draws from the library of familiar pop cultural references to soften its blows.

Some claim that contemporary art can be easily understood because of its emphasis on surface appearances. The vacuous nature of today's art makes meanings obvious. But the matrix of meanings offered in contemporary art includes the role of media in society (the Big Brother factor, the nature of surveillance and media exposure), illness (AIDS particularly but not exclusively), the relationship between humanity and technology, physicality and sexuality, fragmentation, and repetition. Combined with these themes are the importance of seeking silence, the pursuit of meaningful experiences rather than grand statements, the changing role and meaning of words, globalization and its discontents, and a fascination with bricolage and the blurring of categories. All these elements are important to a theological conversation with culture.

During Sunday services, the faith community of which I am a part has spent a great deal of time reflecting on the arts and the role they can play in developing one's spiritual life. Like most religious communities, we use music in a variety of ways. But art unlocked the door of understanding for many people. We have explored the relationship between art and spirituality and religion, looked at various works and styles of art, and, more importantly, made art together. We have preached from the paintings of Vincent van Gogh. We have put large canvases in the parking lot and painted about issues of racism and community. We painted dream stones after discussing the story of Jacob's wrestling bout with the angel and then built an altar. We have had artists within our group paint during our gathering times, responding to words and prayers and music with paint. Such activities may sound too ethereal for some, but they have helped people in our community understand the nature of faith and enabled them to grasp ideas that words could not convey.

I am a bit of an artist myself, though not a particularly good one. I find something compelling about paint on canvas and the things it brings to the surface of my life. If my life is devoid of some form of creative outlet, I sense that something is lacking. I realize that art is not for everyone, yet it may speak to people who don't even realize it. Art has an amazing ability to help people find release; it can be immensely therapeutic. But my concern here is not to defend the role and function of art. It is to examine what a theology funded by art might look like, to consider what the arts can contribute to theological reflection.

Others have reflected on the way in which the arts can undergird current theological paradigms. The intention here is to think about how a theological perspective can be shaped out of the arts. There are a few points worthy of consideration. First, in spite of much talk about the disinterest of people today, particularly young people, with large ideas and questions of ultimate meaning, the arts contradict this view. It is not that people are no longer interested; their fields of interest have merely shifted. They approach these questions from different angles and find few answers in the old ways of doing things. The old hierarchies have been torn down, and the doors have been thrown open to anyone who cares to enter the fray. This connects with postmodernity's shift toward a more level playing field in life, with a healthy suspicion and distrust of authority and hierarchy.

If, as Tom Beaudoin asserts, institutions are suspect,[28] and postmodern culture seems to affirm that view, what then for theology? Much of theology is structured around the authority of the church to speak for God. If the church is no longer viewed as a legitimate authority, the future of its message is cause for concern. But that future is shaky only if we insist on linking theology to existing structures rather than perhaps exploring how theology might lead to the creation of new incarnations of faith in our culture. "The church will only live insofar as it is prepared continually to die in order to experience afresh the resurrection power of the Holy Spirit."[29] A change of form is a theological must based on the contemporary shift away from hierarchical and authoritarian-based systems and structures.

Second, words have made their way into art in a variety of creative ways during the past few decades. We discussed our culture's changing relationship with words and the new symbolism. We saw the importance of the shift from word to image in the discussion of TV. But one must not simply dismiss words. They continue to enjoy a prime place. We have merely added more communication options and in so doing have changed the role that words play in society. The Internet, for instance, is primarily about words. It is about the exchange and accessing of information. Words are still at work, but how we perceive them has changed. Words have become art in and of themselves. Jenny Holzer has made art out of words with her truisms, presented in neon, projected on to buildings, painted in galleries. She teaches us to be more careful with our words. In a culture saturated with information, words can quickly become background noise and the content can be ignored. With so many options available to us, it is easy to avoid things we don't like or no longer want to hear. Theologian Walter Brueggemann has argued for a theology of poetry instead of prose for many years. He calls for a changed relationship between faith, preachers, and words.[30] Contemporary art suggests the enduring power of words and our evolving cultural perceptions.

The shift in focus toward an ascendancy of image over words presents some challenges for the theological endeavor. We have built a faith based on words—Christianity is a religion of "the book" and is driven by preaching and teaching. But we have conducted a rather one-way dialogue with culture. The changing use of words, the embrace of the symbolic and metaphoric alongside more literal uses of language, provides lots of room for experimentation. Two-way conversations may well be the way forward—a sort of postmodern midrash approach in which dialogue and discussion fuel theology.

Finally, artists embrace risk, attempting to form new ways of looking at life. That's why they consistently challenge the definitions of art. "All those sheep submerged in formaldehyde, dissected cows, larger-than-life ashtrays, and unmade beds—anyone could do that. I could take my bed and install it in a gallery and call it art, couldn't I?" But perhaps that is exactly the point—anyone can! Such a democratic approach to art must inform our theological constructs and presentations. Let the people in and help them practice the important and colorful work of theologizing.

If art represents anything in my theological and spiritual journey, it calls me to risk new ideas of holiness. I was first drawn to this idea through my interest in Jean-Michel Basquiat. His entry into the art world tore down the final curtain between the streets and the establishment. He took the streets of his everyday life and put them on the walls of galleries and museums. His social circles were broad and diverse, and he opened up to those diverse circles the possibilities of art.

I associate Basquiat with a story Jesus told the Pharisees about holiness. They were disturbed by the actions of his disciples, who were picking heads of grain in the fields as they walked with Jesus on the Sabbath. The Pharisees were incensed by the obvious violations of the holiness code of their faith. They fully expected Jesus to rebuke his followers. Instead, Jesus turned to the Pharisees and told them a story about a time when David was on the run from Saul. David managed to find food for his men by convincing a priest that the consecrated bread in the tabernacle could be freely given away. David sanctified his own mission and made holy that which was not holy. He risked a new notion of holiness. Jesus referenced this act of risk a few centuries later to underscore his own mission. Jesus ended his dialogue with the Pharisees by announcing, "The Sabbath was made for man, not man for the Sabbath" (Mark 2:27).

Art continually risks new ideas about what is beauty, what is holy. Whether it is Picasso's crude, beautiful-ugly creations; Pollock's tender, anguished paint pouring; or Basquiat's art for the people, art continually explores new ways of expressing timeless facts about human existence. Theology often seems intent on simply maintaining the status quo, and that will not suffice in these times. It is surely time to take the consecrated bread out of the tabernacle and place it in the hands of ordinary people, offering them a new portrait of holiness. Popular culture continues to redefine the relationship between the sacred and the secular, the holy and the profane. People of faith should do the same.

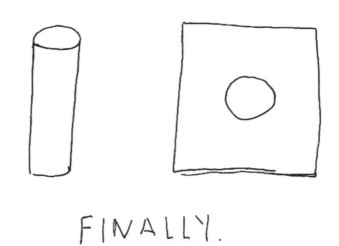

FINALLY.

conclusion

A Top 10 Theology

It is not the achievement of the past that a millennium appraises; it is the quality of
our aspirations for the future that are in question now.

Joan Chittister, *Seeing with Our Souls*

In the 1980s, the Coca-Cola Corporation responded to its declining market
share with a bold plan. They decided to alter the secret formula (and taste)
of Coke. On April 23, 1985, New Coke debuted to public outrage. People
snatched up all the original Coke remaining on the shelves. Groups such as
the Society for the Preservation of the Real Thing demanded a return to the
traditional formula. After two contentious months, Coca-Cola Classic returned
to the production lines, and New Coke was relegated to the sidelines.

Many find postmodernity as distasteful as New Coke. It appears to mess with
a sacred formula and to undermine "the real thing." Yet despite the New Coke
fiasco, the Coca-Cola Corporation continues to unveil new variations on their
old theme. Diet Coke, Cherry Coke, and now Vanilla Coke offer consumers
more choices than ever. While Coke worried about Pepsi, fruity new beverages
such as Snapple captured the public's interest. Coca-Cola responded to this shift
in tastes with Fruitopia, which comes in all kinds of colorful combinations and
attempts to offer a healthier alternative to soda.

There are at least three ways of dealing with changing cultural contexts. A
classic approach may resist change and preserve a prior way of life. Another
route fiddles with existing formulas, repackaging old truths in new cans. The
path we've chosen acknowledges the changes, embraces the culture, and re-
constructs life and practices accordingly.

Some may dismiss this book as a trip to Fruitopia. Our notions could be a colorful, frothy fad. During uncertain times, Coca-Cola Classic (and traditional Christianity) will undoubtedly inspire renewed, nostalgic devotion. Other churches will dare to alter their formulas, yet sincere efforts to create a hip taste could go the route of New Coke.

We've written this book to affirm the refreshing faith options beginning to emerge. Time will tell whether these emerging churches will endure. New Coke lasted less than a decade. It is a forgotten, failed experiment. We embrace Classic Coca-Cola (and its many permutations), salute (but snicker at) New Coke, and ask our readers to give Fruitopia a try. We're confident that the future church will offer drinks to suit every tribe (and tongue)!

We've highlighted the colorful spiritual quest driving pop culture. Unfortunately, religious practices and theological content rooted in the Protestant Reformation often fail to embrace the artistic and the colorful. An exhibit at the J. Paul Getty Museum offers a poignant example.

"Sacred Spaces" features the work of Dutch artist Pieter Saenredam created in the aftermath of the Reformation. His exquisite paintings focus on church architecture, documenting the sparse, sacred spaces in minute detail. What happened to the art that used to be displayed inside churches via icons, sculptures, and paintings? The Reformation severed the relationship between the arts, at least visual art, and religion, and churches were stripped of visual cues. Artists, therefore, shifted their attention to depicting the churches themselves. Art moved elsewhere, and the Reformed Church lost contact with the visual. As a result, Reformation theology as is cannot deal with the arts in a way that incorporates the visual and the material into the spiritual.[1]

We began this book by talking about creating a theology *out of* pop culture, rather than a theology *for* pop culture. Ultimately, theology is contextual and local: Where you stand determines what you see. Three major disciplines form the shape of our theology out of pop culture: cultural studies, sociology, and a practical contemporary theology.[2]

Cultural studies originated in England, with origins centered in the discipline of sociology.[3] Cultural studies examines popular cultural forms produced and generated through media and technology, all forms of mass communication on local, national, and international levels. Traditionally, cultural studies focused on the marginalized within the dominant culture. For Carla Freccero, what distinguishes cultural studies (and makes it pertinent to the intersections of culture and the gospel) is a "commitment to examining cultural practices from the point of view of their interaction with, and within, relations of power."[4] Cultural studies deals with politics and politicking—hence, the continual culture wars that rage over the arena. The study of popular culture deals with the relationship between cultural artifacts (movies, music, art, ads, fashion, etc.) and the way we use them to frame our societies.

We have argued that the cultural artifacts we create and use change the way we live, from the religious to the sexual, the sacred to the profane. Rather than passing judgment on certain elements of pop culture to determine if they are "good" or "bad," we've tried to analyze them and ask, "What are they doing? What do they represent? and What do they say about the world in which we live?" The latest pop stars may mean little to us, but they mean something significant to millions of teens around the globe. Determining what that meaning is might aid us in the future of Christian mission. John Fiske calls this approach a study of the culture of "everyday life."[5] In *The Practice of Everyday Life,* Michel de Certeau writes, "Everyday life is what holds us intimately, from the inside."[6] We've aimed to identify and understand this "holding from the inside."

While cultural studies focuses on the cultural artifacts we create, sociology focuses on the societies that create them. Sociologists study the institutions we build, our organizations, the way we structure our societies. Massive paradigm shifts during the last fifty years have put sociology in a state of flux. The organization of our lives around media and technology has created a heretofore-unseen crucible. George Ritzer's influential book *The McDonaldization of Society* explores the ramifications of a society that has adopted a "fast-food" approach to social construction.[7] Ritzer subtitled his book *An Investigation into the Changing Character of Contemporary Social Life.* This kind of sociology adds an important ingredient to the development of theological constructs and responses. Sociology looks to the back story, behind the scenes of issues. It suggests that nothing occurs in a vacuum. Forces gave rise to changes and continue to fuel them. Popular culture did not appear out of nowhere; social forces gave rise to it and continue to fan its flame.

Theology stands as the final ingredient. To develop a theology out of popular culture demands an a priori construct of some kind, not a particular denominational construct but a particular type of theology. Rather than a systematic or historical theology, we advocate a practical contemporary theology—practical, because theology needs to deal with lived life, not just propositions and abstract ideas, and contemporary, because theology needs to speak to today's world. Art historian Kenneth Clark noted that artists seeking to create a masterpiece "cannot escape using the language of the day, however degraded it may seem."[8] While theology must be faithful to tradition and rooted in Scripture, it also must speak to the times, not just vernacularly but in emphasis and focus. Every age presents new issues and challenges. Theology must move with the era and shift with the Spirit. "A paradigm shift in theology must include this very important claim—that there is a new way of reflection, a new procedure of interpretation, a new orientation of knowledge."[9] Our Top 10 theology is part of the new crop of theologies developed since the 1960s that includes theologies of liberation, play, and creation. This is a tract for the times, not a system for the ages (see fig. on page 296).

Theology: A Portrait of God

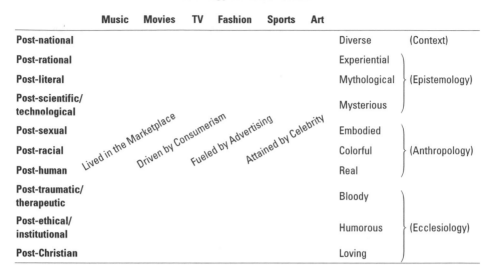

	Music	Movies	TV	Fashion	Sports	Art		
Post-national							Diverse	(Context)
Post-rational							Experiential	
Post-literal							Mythological	(Epistemology)
Post-scientific/ technological							Mysterious	
Post-sexual							Embodied	
Post-racial							Colorful	(Anthropology)
Post-human							Real	
Post-traumatic/ therapeutic							Bloody	
Post-ethical/ institutional							Humorous	(Ecclesiology)
Post-Christian							Loving	

(diagonal labels across the center: Lived in the Marketplace · Driven by Consumerism · Fueled by Advertising · Attained by Celebrity)

The gospel of Jesus Christ has always been a fluid, living entity. In the New Testament, a primarily Jewish Jerusalem church faced challenges in communicating Jesus' message to Greek cities. As theologian and friend John Drane says, "In order to stay the same, the gospel must be constantly changing." We must rethink, reform, reinvent, and reimagine the gospel for the times in which we live. What can we offer our culture to connect it with Jesus' profoundly good news? As mentioned in chapter 4, the Chinese revolutionaries led by Mao Tsetung had a greeting: "Are you living in the New World?"[10] The implications of that question and its revolutionary roots call out to us today. We conclude with some practical suggestions for tomorrow's Christian revolutionaries.

In the Marketplace

> In the rest of life practical thinking is the center of human thinking and . . . theoretical and technical thinking are abstractions from practical thinking.
>
> Don Browning, *A Fundamental Practical Theology*

Top 10 theology takes the charts seriously. It suggests that the popularity of a song, movie, or show corresponds with its ability to connect with viewers' core hopes, feelings, and desires, and it does not automatically dismiss those desires as base, sexual, or sinful. It believes that if God chose to speak through the warmongering Chaldeans in the Old Testament (Hab. 1:13), then the Almighty can certainly communicate through a debauched rock star or a giggling starlet. At Jesus' triumphal entry on Palm Sunday in Luke 19, the religious authorities told Christ to rebuke his disciples, to get his mob under control. Jesus fired back, "If they keep quiet, the stones will cry out" (v. 40). Unlike those who decry the decline of Western civilization, we believe a profound, profane, honest discussion of God, the devil, death, and the afterlife is sweeping pop culture. The stones are screaming, loud and proud, giving God all kinds of unorthodox and creative "props." We can curse culture, ignore it, and hope it goes away, or we can wake up and raise the questions to which people want answers. We begin by excavating the spiritual insight lurking behind most artistic endeavors, even when those endeavors make our hearts ache and our ears burn.

Ironically, Top 10 theology works from the bottom up. It looks to popular tastes, the masses, to discern and define core insights and experiences. Andrew Greeley points out that historically, church leaders were selected via popular election. Catholicism was so democratic that "several popes said it was a grave sin to choose a bishop by any method other than a free election of priests and people."[11] He suggests:

> If one believes that people are sacraments of God, that God discloses Himself/Herself to us through objects, events, and persons of life, then one must concede the possibility that in the sacramentality of ordinary folk, their hopes, their fears, their loves, their aspirations represent a legitimate experience of God, legitimate symbols of God, and legitimate stories of God.[12]

In the seventies and eighties, the implications of such "inclusive" thinking extended to the poorest sections of the Catholic Church. As small, local, "base" communities in Latin America studied the Bible, a theology of liberation was formed. Uneducated laypeople taught priests how to rediscover Jesus and the Gospels. Tom Beaudoin adopted this principle in *Virtual Faith:* "Basic to my proposal is that people [or forms of pop culture] who profess to know little or nothing about the religious, may indeed form, inform, or transform religious meaning for people of faith."[13] Of course, a close reading of Scripture should have prepared us for this dramatic reversal.

The prophetic books of the Bible show God using unlikely sources to sharpen and refine his chosen people, Israel. In Isaiah 10, God dispatches the king of Assyria (the rod of my anger) to judge Judah (a godless nation), even though this is not what the king of Assyria intended. Later, in Isaiah 45, God uses Cyrus, the king of Persia, to restore his exiled people. The wisdom gathered in the Book of Proverbs draws from sources outside Israel in the sayings of Agur and King Lemuel. Most Bible scholars also acknowledge that the Book of Proverbs adopted the format of thirty sayings of the wise from the Egyptian *Instruction to Amenemope* (Prov. 22:17–24:22). Furthermore, Jesus chose an unlikely collection of fishermen and tax collectors to carry out his ministry. Beaudoin writes,

"The kingdom of God is constantly revealed and enacted through the least likely person or circumstances. If the first are to be last and last first, then popular culture itself, as a quintessential instance of what counts as 'last' in importance for many cultural high priests, may be granted its moment of significance."[14]

In the post-Christian West, people of faith have expended much energy trying to interest people in the Bible. Instead of encouraging the reading of Scripture alone, we recommend engaging literate "nonreaders" with a thorough rereading of culture. A fresh take on the marketplace will help us rediscover a path to Jesus and the Gospels. As Fuller Seminary president Richard Mouw says, "Educated people are in no better position than the uneducated when it comes to knowing about God."[15]

Top 10 theologians may question the commercialization of politics, religion, and art, but they will not dismiss or condemn it. They deal with capitalism's triumph as a fact, not a plot. They accept the same terms that almost all artists eventually agree to—signing away copyrights in exchange for distribution, because getting the message out supersedes the highest of principles. Have such people compromised? Sure. Haven't we all? Idealized either/or-ness undercuts the messiness inherent in the Bible. Old Testament heroes such as Moses and David were plagued by sin, hounded by doubt, full of contradictions. Whether typing on an Apple iBook or using Microsoft Windows, we all end up paying AOL Time Warner (or their competition) for access to the Internet. You can "rage against the machine," but even the "purest" of bands eventually ends up as part of a conglomerate purveying pop culture. In *The Last Temptation of Christ,* Jesus flirts with getting off the cross. His last temptation is to get married, have kids, and live happily ever after. Such a comfortable reality is the assumed goal, the starting place of democratic postmodernity. America's founding fathers called it "life, liberty, and the pursuit of happiness." Jesus lived with the tension and so must we. The church may call us to something more, to a life of the Spirit beyond consumption, but this will not replace our listening to the radio, cruising the web, or watching television. Deplore popular culture, but also explore it. Top 10 theology won't go away as long as we have electricity or campfires—someplace to share our stories, sing our songs, paint our dreams. We desperately need a marketplace theology, a rediscovery that Jesus dealt with his world in the centers of commerce.

Entering the marketplace should come easily to people of faith. The highest profile preachers and largest megachurches have often been the most effective marketers. Rev. Pat Robertson turned modest donations to the *700 Club* into ABC's Family Channel. Bud Paxson went from a few radio stations in Central Florida to NBC's purchase of his PAX Network. Warner Brothers bought Christian music label Word Music. Small, Oregon-based publisher Multnomah Press saw *The Prayer of Jabez* become the best-selling nonfiction book of 2001. Faith-based production companies such as Big Idea sold twenty-five million *Veggie Tales* through the home video market. Christian writers, singers, and broadcasters have made millions offering "alternative entertainment" to the faithful.

But a discussion of God does not need to be limited to a subculture safely inside the temple. (In fact, Jesus didn't seem too fond of money changing hands within the temple.) The marketplace is wide open, ready to embrace ambitious, meaty trilogies such as *The Lord of the Rings* or *The Matrix*. It is eager to dance to Moby. It is desperate and willing to pay big bucks to "have church" in concert with U2. Bono made his intentions clear on U2's Elevation tour when he declared, "God is in the house." And the stadium. And the television station. And the fashion runway. Let us enter the marketplace to recover forgotten or hidden truths about ourselves and our God.

10. Post-national—Diverse

> The Malaysians go to Kentucky Fried and the Qataris go to Taco Bell for the same reason Americans go to Universal Studios—to see the source of their fantasies.
>
> Thomas Friedman, *The Lexus and the Olive Tree*

Does globalization threaten indigenous cultures? American television introduced blue jeans to native peoples in Peru. *Playboy* expanded into Russia as soon as the Soviet Union collapsed. Merchants in Oaxaca have tried to ban McDonald's from their marketplace.

Whatever blending occurs around the globe usually starts with American pop culture. The majority of pop cultural exports arises from the film, television, and music industries based in Los Angeles. Hollywood has spread the gospel of consumption via the church of pop culture. Celebrities are the new saints. Television, sports, concerts, and movie theaters are the places we gather to worship. Shopping has become our salvation. The reasons to condemn California and the pop culture industry are legion.

Yet we remain incredibly hopeful about the effects of globalization *because* we live in Los Angeles and create pop culture. It is an early testing ground for what our blended, urban future will look like. The bumper sticker "Think Globally, Act Locally" is not an empty phrase but a lived reality. The ethnic and religious diversity we encounter in California forces us to "get glocal" every day. Rather than dismissing California as "the land of fruit and nuts," we've chosen to consider it a sneak preview of the shape and color, problems and possibilities coming to your town.

California serves as a stellar example of how Hollywood's "Americanization" can still encourage "theodiversity." Rather than squelching faith, the clash of cultures in California has propelled religious expression. The Self Realization Fellowship in Pacific Palisades offers visitors a quiet walk past quotations from every major religious tradition. Malibu houses a Thai Buddhist temple. Saudi

Arabia paid for an ornate mosque in a nondescript strip of Culver City, California. The Bahai Temple in south central Los Angeles houses the progressive New Roads School, a trendy favorite for Hollywood parents who want to teach their kids tolerance. A trip down Hollywood Boulevard feels like a tribute to Scientology as stars such as John Travolta and Tom Cruise sing the praises of L. Ron Hubbard. Southern California welcomed America's first Buddhist college, Soka University. The freedom, rootlessness, and pluralism endemic to California makes it the perfect petri dish for new religious movements.

Amid such historic ethnic and religious diversity, California continually spawns major Christian movements. Our "sin city" was founded by Catholic missionaries, funded the tenets of fundamentalism, and served as the flash point for the Pentecostal revival. The Jesus People of the 1970s began with California hippies getting baptized in the Pacific Ocean. Surfer churches such as Calvary Chapel eventually became nationwide phenomena. California's Vineyard Movement led the rediscovery of worship and praise songs.

Many of the largest, most dynamic churches in Los Angeles are Asian, African, and Latin American in origin. Some divide along racial lines, offering displaced "tribes" a place to find community. Older, white congregations have found new life by hosting services in Spanish, Filipino, and Korean. Others consciously deemphasize race, finding strength in diversity. New Song in Irvine, California, offers second- and third-generation Asians a worship experience beyond race, rooted in the primacy of pop culture. At a progressive gathering in Los Angeles called "Tribe," people of many faith backgrounds gather in a drum circle, employing the finest African polyrhythms. Their worship of Jesus combines the best of the French Taize movement with the fervency of drumming from the two-thirds world and the whirling jams of the Grateful Dead. Such fresh, blended expressions of Christian faith can be found emerging around the globe.

There are now 33,800 Christian denominations, "and the fastest growing are the independents who have no ties whatsoever to historic Christianity."[16] David Barrett, editor of *The World Christian Encyclopedia,* sums up the church shift from north to south: "It starts to look faintly ridiculous, you see when the 'respectable' Christians start talking patronizingly about these new 'strange' Christians appearing everywhere. In a very short time, the people in those movements will be talking the same way about us."[17] In an article titled "The Changing Face of the Church," *Newsweek* noted, "For the first time in history, Christianity has become a religion mainly of the poor, the marginalized, the powerless and—in parts of Asia and the Middle East—the oppressed. . . . Amidst crushing poverty, genocidal wars, and pandemic AIDS, Africans find the church is the one place they can go to for healing, hope, and material assistance from more fortunate Christians in the West."[18] Larry Eskridge of the Institute for the Study of American Evangelicals announces, "Christianity is no longer a white man's religion. It's been claimed by others."[19]

The backs of African buses and trucks announce, "God Is Good," "In His Name," and "Abide with Me." Signs above storefronts range from "Thy Will Be Done Hair Salon" and "The Lord Is My Light Car Wash" to "Trust in God Auto Repair." Rosalind Hackett, an expert in African religious movements, notes, "Many people just aren't aware of how active African Christian missionaries are in North America. The Africans hear about secularization and empty churches and they feel sorry for us. So they come and evangelize."[20] Nigerian Archbishop Idahosa put it simply: "Africa doesn't need God, it needs money. America doesn't need money, it needs God."[21] The globalization of the church appears to be a response to the Americanization of indigenous cultures. When world music leads our worship and third-world theologians such as Kosuke Koyama and Juan Luis Segundo help us reinterpret the faith, then the twenty-first-century church may just be starting to get interesting.

9. Post-rational—Experiential

Traditional truths remain truths only when they are vindicated by personal experience.

Andrei Tarkovsky, *Sculpting in Time*

Extreme sports, raves, tattoos. Each offers an immersive, surrounding, full body experience. Top 10 theologians worship *through their senses*. They want to carry hammers. Build houses. Light candles. Smell the flowers. Trek the Himalayas. Add another piercing. In a world of point and click, many are seeking to hold hands with more than a mouse. After a long day of downloading, we may find ourselves desperate for a taste and touch of something that doesn't emit a green glow. Tom Beaudoin finds that "the recovery of experience is especially important for those whose own personal and religious experience has historically been marginalized, particularly women and ethnic and racial minorities in the United States. [Generation] Xers generally find the religious in personal experience, particularly in an emerging form of sensual spirituality."[22] The strictly theoretical seems inert.

That's why sacramental churches are poised for a comeback. The tangible experiences of "smells and bells," candles, incense, bowing, and eating appeal to the next generation. Twenty-first-century worship needs to incorporate the body, whether in bowing, kneeling, and crossing or in adopting the sweaty, heart-pounding transcendence of a rave. Give teens ways to process their God-given drives. The alternative is to drive them out of church, back to the movie theaters, the clubs, and into pop culture. That's why charismatic Christian churches continue to thrive. They never abandoned the emotion or the body, singing with hands in the air and staying open to the Spirit. A Sunday service with healings, prophecies, and uncontrollable laughter can supply the visceral thrills comparable to the best Hollywood roller-coaster ride. Worship at a Vineyard church, an Assembly of God church, or a Church of God in Christ church involves big highs and deep lows—all in the same service. America's enduring religious impulses are populist, anti-intellectual, and irrational.

Church historian Leonard Sweet surveys today's scene and announces:

> The Charismatics, Pentecostals, and the Eastern Orthodox Church have won. Everybody else should just throw up the white flag. None of them do worship services—they do worship experiences. To these believers, worship is not an activity—it's an epic-tivity. It's both timely and timeless. They're experiential, participatory, image-based and connective—everybody else is rational, passive, word-based, and highly individual.[23]

The next generation longs to recover the immersive, unifying, communitarian aspect of the body of Christ.

Yet this is not a question only of style but of content. According to Neal Gabler, American religion was always rooted in entertainment. "Evangelicals preferred emotion to theology. They believed in experiential religion, one in which . . . the sinner had to feel in his very bones the smoldering of guilt, abasement, hope and assurance. . . . The depth of the feeling a testament to the depths of one's faith, the degree of irrationality a testament to the degree to which one had abandoned himself to God."[24] Twenty-first-century expressions of faith will likely be even more emotional, more experiential, more entertaining. But our salvation does not lie in more videos and louder music. Postmodernity demands a change of practice *and* thought. Our new worship must be accompanied by a new message. The commitment to a lived faith will endure only alongside a commitment to thinking differently. In fact, the more desperate need in an era of sensation may be more reflection, deeper thinking, a thoughtful faith. Worship as entertainment attracts but does not satisfy.

8. Post-literal—Mythological

> The Bible with its stories of good and evil, its romance, its poetry, its death and destruction, and its science fiction, is not only rife with ideas for screenplays, it needs to be the basis of the moral imagination of our youth.
>
> Tony Jones, *Postmodern Youth Ministry*

> The heart of Christianity is a myth which is also a fact.
>
> C. S. Lewis, *God in the Dark*

Radiohead's "There, There" video takes place in an enchanted forest. *The Lord of the Rings* and *Harry Potter* present complex universes full of epic battles

I am the Lord thy God. ... thou shalt have no gods before me.

Thou shalt keep the Sabath day holy.

Honor thy mother and father.

Thou shalt not covet thy neighbors:
* house
* wife
* manservant
* etc.

Thou shalt not commit adultry (a little obvious this one).

Thou shalt not steal.

Thou shalt not kill.

Thou shalt not use my name in vain.

Thou shalt not bear false witness against thy neighbor.

Thou shalt not bow down to graven images.

A visual key to the ten commandments.

THINGS GOD WOULD FIND WRONG WITH THIS ▓▓▓.
1. MISSPELLINGS/GRAMMAR
2. OUT OF ORDER ▓▓▓▓ -OK
3. ABR.
4. SKIPPING OVER STUFF.
5. IT'S NOT STRAIGHT. (OR FUNNY)

fought by the least likely heroes. *Spider-Man* shows how a normal teen, struggling through puberty, can still become a superhero. *The Matrix* chronicles a post-technological future in which a reluctant savior will bring hope and deliverance to Zion. Mythology has arisen as the crying need of a world in which the facts have lost their power. Smaller truths (facts) have been superceded by the grander Truth of myths. Modern Christianity wedded itself to a scientific era, reducing faith to a logical, airtight, propositional system. When modernism collapsed, in the eyes of a shifting culture, so did much of the faith. Yet while the Christian metanarrative may have been largely abandoned, big shaping stories are growing by leaps and bounds.

Postmodernity doesn't signal the death of the metanarrative but the rise of anthologies. The next generation wants to shop through a variety of stories and truths before constructing its own metanarrative or mythology. Readers used to the hypertext of the Internet can draw conclusions and freely associate with a wide variety of "seemingly" disparate sources. From a much wider canon come disparate but definite truths. J. R. R. Tolkien fused his scholarship in medieval and Norse legends into a distinctly English myth. The Wachowski brothers blended Japanese anime, Asian martial arts, Eastern philosophy, and the residual strains of Christian mythology into *The Matrix. E Pluribus Unum:* "From many, one."

Previous efforts to harmonize the Bible, to present it as a "unity," actually reduced its fantastic and appealing variety of expressions. We must rediscover how to understand the Bible as a story. It has a variety of storytelling styles: histories, prophecies, aphorisms, songs, and poems. Separating and celebrating the various literary styles will broaden the Bible's appeal and make the message more accessible.

One of the more unlikely publishing success stories has been that of the Pocket Canons.[25] Scotland's Canongate Books "shrank" the Bible into individual books, with unlikely celebrities offering pungent introductions. Nick Cave tackled the Gospel of Mark, Will Self addressed the Book of Revelation, and Bono celebrated the Psalms. British readers used to short trips on and off London's Underground have welcomed the thin volumes. Audiences hounded by short attention spans may stand a better chance of understanding and applying Paul's letters. Rather than picking and choosing verses across Old and New Testaments, readers can thumb through one book at a time, becoming natural exegetes. Bible scholars who tried to get people to consider the *sitz im liben,* the distinct situation and background informing each book of the Bible, should be thrilled.

At the conclusion of *Austin Powers: International Man of Mystery,* Mike Myers resolves one apparent contradiction that has dogged our understanding of the Bible. Are we to relish the freedom Paul emphasizes in Galatians or adopt the restraint evident in Corinthians? When chastised by Dr. Evil as a relic of a bygone era, Austin reframes history: "Now is a very groovy time. It's freedom and responsibility, baby, yeaaaaaah." Austin reconciles Paul's message to the Galatians, "It's freedom, baby, yeah!" with his seemingly contradictory words to the Corinthians, "Shape up, knock it off, keep it in your pants." The recurring problem of isogesis, isolating certain passages from their intended audience and purpose, can finally be breached. Each letter can be understood as a specific message for a specific people with a specific problem. Austin Powers, International Theologian.

In *The Four Witnesses,* Robin Griffith-Jones celebrates the strikingly different visions of Jesus presented by Matthew, Mark, Luke, and John.[26] Griffith-Jones resists the modern inclination to reconcile their conflicting biblical accounts.

Instead, the British rector revels in the contradictions, welcoming the unique artistic voices captured in the Gospels. Postmodern readers have already been trained to question "reliable narrators," such as Kevin Spacey's Verbal Kint in *The Usual Suspects* or Nicole Kidman's worried mother in *The Others*. Four distinct accounts of Jesus' life actually make the overall story much more compelling. For the next generation, the more witnesses the better. Different takes on the same material? Great. Postmodern movie watchers dig the multiple layers in movies such as *Pulp Fiction*. *The Sixth Sense* worked because it demanded (and rewarded) repeat viewings. Complex, tangled narratives, whether in the New Testament or in *Memento*, are preferable to an easily digestible linear story. In fact, *Memento* demonstrates how dicey relying on the facts can be. For now, big, hairy, ridiculous myths trump slippery facts—every time.

7. Post-scientific/technological—Mysterious

Science without religion is lame; religion without science is blind.

Albert Einstein[27]

You *figure out* a puzzle, you *solve* a problem, but you *kneel* in a mystery.

Leonard Sweet, quoted in *Postmodern Youth Ministry*

At the dawn of the twentieth century, science looked like the sworn enemy of faith. Darwin's theory of evolution threatened traditional understandings of the Bible. The resulting culture clash forced people to pick sides in a heated either/or debate. But the both/and views of the twenty-first century allow science and religion to complement one another. The pioneering work of John Polkinghorne reconciled science and theology. Pope John Paul II called Darwin's work "more than just a hypothesis."[28] Biologist Francis Collins, director of the National Human Genome Research Institute, says, "I am unaware of any irreconcilable conflict between scientific knowledge about evolution and the idea of a creator God."[29] He adds that "a lot of scientists really don't know what they are missing by not exploring their spiritual feelings."[30] Scientists? Feelings? What kind of strange alternative universe have we entered? Gregg Easterbrook, writing in *Wired* magazine, declared, "The more scientists have learned, the more mysterious the Really Big Questions have become."[31]

In his *Primer on Postmodernism,* Stanley Grenz points out how filmmaking technology paved the way for this shift in thinking. Cinema is an illusion, a false reality, "a technological artifact assembled by a variety of specialists from a range of materials and with a range of techniques that are seldom evident in the film itself."[32] Yet we regularly accept such a lie as the truth.

M. Night Shyamalan's films have made a mint by "lying" or at least manipulating audiences. He always suggests that the "truth" lies beyond what we can taste, touch, and smell. Fooled by his conceit in *The Sixth Sense,* viewers returned to the theater eager to see what clues they missed the first time around. *Unbreakable* offers a logical, human portrait of superheroes struggling with their identities in our world. *Signs* uses an alien invasion to restore an Episcopal priest's lost faith. Shyamalan is the master of the surprise ending, tying up loose ends in unexpected ways. The overriding secret of his success—offering audiences schooled in logic a chance to revel in mystery.

Even the DVDs for the next wave of films offer tricks, clues, puzzles, and misdirection—from the faux infomercial that starts *Requiem for a Dream* to the fake gear offered on *Fight Club.* Filmmakers demand that audiences "look closer" and think deeper. How interesting that a generation raised in a era surrendered to the "truth" of the scientific method makes movies steeped in the spooky, the surreal, and the unquantifiable. Training in empirical methods and the height of technology only lead to an embrace of the unknown.

Santa Cruz pastor Dan Kimball declares:

> Teenagers crave inclusion in something bigger than themselves—something mystical and transcendent. Many of us treat the youth room as a game-show set and the church sanctuary as a movie theater. Some seeker-sensitive churches removed crosses and other symbols of the Christian faith from the altars for fear of looking too "religious." But it turns out what we've been casting off is exactly what young people are looking for—sensory stimuli that provoke a sense of reverence. A body-mind-spirit experience.[33]

Tony Jones finds role models in unlikely places: "When you walk into an Orthodox sanctuary, you walk into another universe—and this makes sense to the postmodern mind: if there is a God, surely he dwells in a different place and space than we do. God's universe must look, smell, sound and feel different from what we are used to on a day-to-day basis."[34] Historian Leonard Sweet notes, "Postmoderns don't approach life as a problem to be solved, but a mystery to be experienced and lived. . . . That's why ministry in the 21st century is very similar to ministry in the first century—there's a profound openness in postmodern culture to the mystery of the Christian faith and the wonder of the everyday."[35] Poets will prevail in an age of information overload. Artists will be vitally important to slowing us down.

In an instantaneous society with endless info a click away, religions will be tempted to respond to complex problems with pat answers. Theologian Alister McGrath suggests that for believers to preserve mystery they must acknowledge and embrace doubt. "We want to be absolutely sure about everything—the Christian faith included. But no one can ever have this kind of certainty about God . . . so doubt is natural. It's understandable that we should wonder if we have got things right. Doubt becomes a problem only if you let it worry you."[36]

To combat the onslaught of technology, we must slow down, look up, embrace doubt, leave room for questions, and make space for God. Sounds almost like a psalm. Or Bono's celebration of the Holy Spirit in U2's song "Mysterious Ways": "If you want to kiss the sky, you gotta learn how to kneel."

6. Post-sexual—Embodied

The Word became flesh and blood and moved into the neighborhood.

John 1:14 THE MESSAGE

And after my skin has been destroyed, yet in my flesh I will see God.

Job 19:26

Modernism and the Enlightenment boiled down to a battle of competing ideologies, or "isms." Who would win? Communism? Fascism? Capitalism? But the postmodern battleground has shifted from the mind to the body. Legislators argue about abortion, homosexuality, and sex education. Questions about the ordination of homosexuals hound denominations despite their best efforts to avoid them. ABC's *Ellen* paved the way for NBC's *Will and Grace*. Homosexual, bisexual, and trans-gendered people will not go away. Kids will keep piercing and tattooing their bodies despite parents' protests. Some "celibate" priests will undermine the majority of faithful fathers by making children the objects of their uncontainable sexual urges. Teens will continue to sign pledges and practice all manner of degradations while remaining "technical virgins" until we finally address and develop an embodied faith.

The Song of Solomon must be read as more than an allegory of Christ's relationship with his bride.[37] The Bible must be rediscovered as an earthy, sweaty, sexy book. In a culture that celebrates sexuality at every turn, the Song of Solomon stands out as a crucial guide to sacred romance. It affirms our sexuality, the joys of the human body celebrated in marriage.

Surgeon General David Satcher's outgoing report called for "a mature . . . dialogue on issues of sexuality, sexual health, and responsible sexual behavior."[38] Most conservative, pro-family organizations rejected his call. But the Rev. Madison Shockley urges, "Churches, especially black churches, must break the silence regarding sexual issues. Preaching is only one part of what we in the faith business must do. We must offer our youth a frank, honest, thorough sex education curriculum, one that is in keeping with the values of each of our faith communities."[39] Chuck Milian, the singles pastor at Crossroads Fellowship in Raleigh, North Carolina, offers a six-hour dating seminar full of frank talk. "I cannot afford to play a game of pretend. These folks are faced with sensuality on a scale unknown to any previous generation. I have to name the elephants in the room, like pornography and living together outside marriage, because these are options that singles are faced with now."[40] Even *Christianity Today* broke the silence, devoting a cover story to pornography and pastors. The stakes are high; the choices are clear. We can promote abstinence all we want, but for individuals facing fifteen to twenty years of puberty before marriage, frank talk rooted in the gray zone of daily temptations must be offered.

We can't assume that more discussion will lead to more irresponsibility. In fact, one sacrament may already be making a comeback. Some signs within pop culture suggest that the next generation will respond to sexual tension by getting married earlier. The teen sex comedy of a few years ago has morphed into *Just Married* and *American Wedding*. Hollywood stars such as Reese Witherspoon and Ryan Phillippe got pregnant, got married, and settled down. Director Kevin Smith went from a single guy *Chasing Amy* to a married man chasing baby. His marital bliss is reflected in *Jersey Girl*. God's people should welcome this shift and embrace this opportunity to help newlyweds forge a family.

Tom Beaudoin points to piercing and tattooing as a sign of spiritual longings, a way of experiencing spirit *through* body. He writes, "Religious institutions today are unable to provide for deep marking, profoundly experiential encounters. We are a generation willing to have experience, to be profoundly marked, even cut. . . . It could even be said that our indulgence in tattoos mocks the hyper-commercial world in which we live; tattooing is the only way we have control over 'branding' ourselves." He considers bare, pierced navels "theological playfulness about the exposure of a person's center." Expanding on the Hebrew notion of the navel as the center of human fecundity, he says that navel piercing "implies finding the spiritual in the sensual."[41] Thankfully, Beaudoin recovers the hidden history of Christian sensuality. Medieval monks such as Bernard of Clairvaux described prayer as an increasingly intimate kissing of Christ. Teresa of Avila referred to those who seek God as his "lovers." Renaissance sculptor Bernini captured St. Teresa in "divine ecstasy," showing an angel delivering an arrow of divine love that creates a positively orgasmic reaction. Pierced by the love of God. How utterly postmodern (or is it medieval)?

5. Post-racial—Colorful

> Now hear this mixture, where hip-hop meets scripture, develop a
> negative into a positive picture.
>
> Lauryn Hill, "Everything Is Everything"

"At the end of 2002, the secretary of state, the president's national security advisor, the CEO of the world's largest media company, the head of the world's biggest financial services firm, the CEO of the world's largest mortgage lender, the leader of American Express, as well as the globe's most recognized athlete . . . all had one thing in common. Every single one is African-American."[42] Or at least half black. Old either/or categories are now blending into both/and. The 2000 U.S. census reported that there are now more Hispanics, or Latinos, than African-Americans. But what does a catchall category like Hispanic mean? Richard Rodriguez, author of *Brown*, chronicled his changing perceptions of his parents' neighborhood in San Francisco. "A few months ago I would have described the neighborhood ethnically or racially, now it seems to me that it's more important to describe it religiously: These Mexican Catholics lived next door to Chinese Confucians, who lived next door to Russian Jews, who lived next door to Iranian Muslims. . . . Never in the history of the world has such a thing been attempted, that we would be neighbors with one another."[43]

Ghettos arise from differences in race, religion, and economics. Tiger Woods invaded one of America's most impenetrable ghettos: golf. He exploded all notions of what's possible with a set of clubs. Fans of all colors follow him around the world, eager to touch the hem of his greatness. Yet he's been criticized for not being more political, for not boycotting the good ol' boys club of Augusta National and the Masters. Why doesn't Tiger get more political? Shouldn't he advocate more causes?

Born in 1975 to a Vietnam vet named Earl and a Thai woman named Kultida, Eldrick "Tiger" Woods grew up in a post-racial world. Trailblazers such as Lee Elder and Lee Trevino had already broken golf's barriers, wandering in a sometimes hostile desert. Tiger does not need to pioneer. He is a king, raised by a father of Native American, African-American, Scotch, Irish, and Chinese blood, to enter and rule the Promised Land.[44] He represents our arduous and painful past but mostly heralds our blended and colorful future. The same goes for Serena and Venus Williams. Their tennis championships follow the path carved by Althea Gibson and Arthur Ashe. Naomi Campbell, Jennifer Lopez, and Taye Diggs have redefined our notions of beauty. The explosive growth of churches in Africa and Asia has altered perceptions of what a Christian looks like. Our iconic notions of beauty, humanity, and God, forged in the white-washed history of Western art, must change. For people of faith, cut off from visual history, this will be a two-step process. The recovery of images must precede a change of color.

The history of Western art reads like a history of religious art. Greek and Roman statuary gradually gave way to biblical narrative. Icon painters depicted sacred space in this life, on this plain. Giotto, Leonardo, Michelangelo, and Raphael merged classical art techniques with their religious era to create a Renaissance, a rebirth of antiquity. At the time, Catholic and Orthodox churches served as the primary patrons and repositories of visual faith. The Protestant Reformation took a different tack, practicing iconoclasm, the smashing of icons. For Protestants, it's been a bleak five hundred years of visual starvation.[45]

Speaking at the Academy of Motion Picture Arts and Sciences (the home of the Oscars), filmmaker Paul Schrader talked about how his Protestant sensibilities differed from those of his collaborator Roman Catholic Martin Scorsese. When visualizing a scene, Schrader said, "My room is four white walls and a cross. When Marty directs the same scene, his room is full of colors, candles, and statues."[46] The way forward for Protestant artists can come only as they reach back to their pre-Reformation roots. Orthodox and Catholic art is a great place to start.

Sister Wendy Beckett serves as an unlikely guide on this journey, through television programs such as *Sister Wendy's Grand Tour* and *Sister Wendy's Story of Painting*. Who could have predicted that a nun with a yen for van Gogh would become a celebrity satirized on *Saturday Night Live*? How did she develop her expertise? "If you're going to enjoy a painting you've got to set aside time. You must not expect that you can take a fleeting glance and reach a conclusion, any more than you can just look at a book's dust cover."[47] Her contemplative and devotional life contributed to her ability to see. In *Image as Insight,* scholar Margaret Miles suggests that "neglect of images is neglect of contemplation," so for "the untrained eye, eyesight is not insight, just as for the unprepared mind, religious concepts make no sense. . . . Training of both eye and mind is fundamental to the quickening of religious sensibility."[48] In other words, learning to see will enhance our worship, our devotional life, and our spirit.

While art historians question her self-taught "expertise," Sister Wendy's enthusiasm wooed viewers skeptical of both art and religion. She says, "I think everybody's born with a love of art. Even little children at school make mud pies. . . . Art is part of being human. For many people somehow that love isn't activated. They never realize they have a capacity and a need to respond to the beautiful."[49] She views art as an entry point to a divine encounter. "I think art brings you to an encounter with truth and beauty—these are names for God. But they're not synonymous with God. . . . But if you haven't got anything else, art will take you towards a God whose name you don't know."[50] Sister Wendy seems to borrow Paul's engagement with the Athenian marketplace in Acts 17. He observed and commented on their art, finding an altar inscribed "To an Unknown God." Paul began his explanation of Jesus' resurrection with Athens's religious art. Sister Wendy triumphed in the marketplace by taking time to train her eye and sharpen her heart with a deep appreciation of images.

In anticipation of the millennium, London's National Gallery staged a retrospective titled "The Image of Christ." BBC2 followed up with a companion television series called *Seeing Salvation.* Both used paintings to introduce European audiences to a foreign country, "Christianity." Paintings created to communicate theological truths to a pre-literate Christian population now serve as powerful tools in communicating theological truths to a post-Christian population. Neil MacGregor, the director of the National Gallery, says, "The very difficulties Christian artists have had to resolve . . . makes it possible for these images to speak now to those who do not hold Christian beliefs. Christian artists . . .

had to make clear when representing an historical event—the life and death of Jesus—they were not just offering a record of the past but a continuing truth; we the spectators have to become eye-witnesses to an event that matters to us now."[51] In *Painting the Word,* John Drury explains the Christian context and imagery that infuse the bulk of the National Gallery's collection. He also attempts to take the paintings off the gallery walls, restoring them to their original purposes inside the church, within worship.[52] How exciting that professing Christians and art-loving skeptics can take this journey together. The person of faith learns how to see. The skeptical art patron learns how to understand religious imagery. Both bring expertise and ignorance, each needing the other to understand the artists' intentions and God's dramatic story.

British theologian Alister McGrath wonders, "If Christianity is so wonderful, how can its thinkers often manage to make it so wearisome and dull?"[53] To combat the problem, McGrath, in his theological reflection on the cross, has replaced "theories of atonement" with "images of salvation." He points readers toward a cross that worked on multiple levels, accomplishing several tasks simultaneously. He laments, "Some people seem to think that one formula, sentence or analogy contains everything that needs to be said, or could ever be said. . . . But there is always more to the cross than we can imagine. It is inexhaustible."[54] For McGrath, the cross evokes images of a battlefield, a courtroom, a rehabilitation clinic, a prison, and a hospital. It breaks the boundaries of space and time like the best science fiction. It reveals everything wrong in the world like a revolutionary rant against global injustice. The death of an innocent man does not sound like a philosophy to be explained. It served as a dramatic trigger event. Jesus' death (and resurrection) transformed lives and changed world history.

McGrath compares Jesus' cross to Isaac Newton's discovery of light. Newton found that a prism split light beams into a rainbow. The discovery allowed Newton to isolate the individual "parts" or "fragments" that together create white light. Did the discovery of colors make light seem simple or more beautiful, even more complex? By examining the cross as individual components, the entire message grows.[55] It is the bloodiest, messiest, most colorful event in human history. It will take multiple viewpoints, from different cultures, across the centuries before we even begin to grasp the brilliance contained in that blinding act. But God will continue to use whatever means are available—words, music, songs, and stories—to communicate that enduring truth.

We must draw from every color in the crayon box to paint a complete picture of God. In the satirical film *Dogma,* Chris Rock complains about the whitewash that fell over the Bible, leaving out Rufus, the thirteenth and only black disciple. The future church has an opportunity to paint a much more colorful, inclusive portrait. Painter John Nava created a tapestry for Los Angeles's new downtown cathedral. He drew from throughout church history to create a vivid tableaux, a procession of saints of every size, shape, and color. The pope even canonized

Mexico's first saint, Juan Diego, the mestizo Indian who discovered the virgin of Guadalupe. The kingdom of God is finally (and officially) becoming more colorful. Perhaps Paul's famous proclamation that "there is neither Jew nor Greek, slave nor free, male nor female, for you are all one in Christ Jesus" (Gal. 3:28) is slowly being realized. Perhaps instead of "neither/nor," Paul's post-racial vision can actually become "both/and": Jew *and* Greek, slave *and* free, male *and* female, black, white, brown, and every other color under the rainbow.

4. Post-human—Real

> Postmodernism at its best gets us: it preaches the doctrine of original sin to arrogant modernism.
>
> N. T. Wright, Bishop of Durham[56]

American ministers have always been remarkably practical, sensitive to marketing and reaching the masses.[57] Yet when churches try to market themselves, they succumb to a distinctly postmodern temptation to project an unsubstantiated image, which could ultimately damage their standing with the image-savvy generation they're trying to reach. Sociologist Peter Berger explains: "The religious tradition, which previously could be authoritatively imposed, now has to be marketed. It must be 'sold' to a clientele that is no longer constrained to 'buy.' The pluralist situation is, above all, a market situation. In it, the religious institutions become marketing agencies and the religious traditions become consumer commodities."[58] Many churches, in an effort to become "contemporary," have abandoned electric guitars and praise choruses in favor of DJs, drama, and poetry. Five-thousand-member Lovers Lane United Methodist Church in Dallas, Texas, offers five huge television screens, three sound systems, and Broadway lights. Lumicon, a Dallas-based production company, offers a dazzling weekly package of computer graphics, videos, music, and film clips to churches.[59]

We applaud such efforts to become relevant. Yet adopting a style without altering its substance will ultimately prove hollow. Why, during a time when people are wondering what's real, would churches hire image consultants? Jesus did not use folk stories and parables because kids were into them. He was a genuine practitioner of the art of storytelling. Amplified music and snappy visuals may attract attention but still leave teenagers desperately searching for authenticity. Rather than a reel religion, the church must embody a real religion promoted by people they can trust.

Tony Jones, in *Postmodern Youth Ministry,* offers an odd formula for attracting teens: "Boomers wanted 'relevance.' Post modern students want real more than relevant. The church needs to be what it is: a sacred community of persons who follow a mysterious and demanding Lord. . . . When we pretend that we're no different than a hundred other social organizations—we're not being the church."[60] What a strange way forward—stop pretending, stop disguising yourself, stop putting a comfortable face on Jesus. The next generation wants Jesus "unplugged," complete with radical claims, unexplainable miracles, and a savage, bloody death. The future is not paved by relevance but contextualization. The problem with relevance is that it can easily lead to relativism. Contextualization doesn't chase trends; it connects the dots between gospel and culture. May we learn to keep it real.

Confronted by a post-human future, the church will undoubtedly argue that humans should not play God. But an even more compelling and much easier way to enter the post-human future is by acknowledging what makes people different from machines: our fallibility. One counterintuitive way to keep it real is by *celebrating* our sinfulness. Failure, mistakes, and misjudgments are essential and endearing aspects of humanity. We're distinguished from machines by our unpredictability, by our freedom of choice, and most of all by our freedom to fail. To those tired of trying to be perfect, this is a welcome relief. We don't have to be perfect. Only Jesus is perfect. Sin can be presented and embraced as new, very good news.

3. Post-traumatic/therapeutic—Bloody

> I can do you blood and love without the rhetoric, and I can do you blood and rhetoric without the love, and I can do you all three concurrent or consecutive, but I can't do you love and rhetoric without the blood. Blood is compulsory—they're all blood you see.
>
> Tom Stoppard, playwright, *The Oxford Dictionary of Quotations*

Top 10 theology is bloody—not in the scripted battles of pro wrestling or the choreographed carnage of a John Woo film but in the bowels of the Russian Gulag. Or in the persecution of innocent victims in the Sudan. Or in the plane crashing into the Pentagon. It is tainted, steeped in sin, not because it wants to be but because it addresses life that is also bloody.

Jesus' crucifixion serves as an appropriately grisly precursor to recent atrocities. The cross reveals human sadism. Ancient crowds flocked to public torturing and crucifixions. Sports fans' lust for blood in boxing matches or professional hockey looks comparatively mild. Jesus' cross is a shocking and offensive symbol rooted in torture and slow death. It also makes a terrible marketing idea. What corporation would choose a hangman's noose, a firing squad, a gas chamber, or an electric chair as its logo? It would be seen as morbid and sick. Perhaps it is for this reason that even Christians have sought to sanitize it. The early persecuted Christians adopted a fish, a subtle acrostic as a secret symbol. Only after the Roman emperor Constantine abolished crucifixion did the cross become a Christian symbol. But the symbol shied away from the reality it sought to remember.

In the sixth century, Christians placed a figure on the cross, a living, breathing, historical Christ. The arrival of the plague in the eleventh century forced the church to portray and adopt a suffering Christ. People in pain needed to know that their God also experienced suffering and death. In *Dogma*, Kevin Smith mocks a Catholic faith that wants to replace the depressing picture of Jesus on the cross with the friendlier, happier Buddy Christ. Catholic priest Jerome Murphy-O'Connor laments, "The unwillingness of believers to confront the horrible reality of the way Christ died ensured that a realistic type of crucifix did not last long. Today's serene crucifixes are what Christians want to see. . . . The temptation to adopt a vision of salvation that will not make us look ridiculous is ever present."[61]

Yet the scandal, the absurdity, the messiness of the cross cannot be avoided. It addresses the legitimate questions raised by theodicies such as Job or the movie *Signs*: How can God be good amid an abundance of evil? Alister McGrath points readers to a bloody crucifix that endures as a "potent symbol of realism. . . . Any outlook on life which cannot cope with the grim realities of suffering and death does not deserve to get a hearing. This symbol of suffering and death affirms that Christianity faces up to the grim, ultimate realities of life. . . . It confronts the worst which the world can offer, and points to—and makes possible—a better way."[62]

The twenty-first-century church must take up the sufferings embodied by its most enduring symbols. A whitewashed cross, jumping ahead to the resurrection, won't do. The art chapter talked about entering through the pain gate. The chapter on movies revealed that today's viewers are willing to embrace two hours of cinematic pain for two minutes of grace. From *Magnolia* to *American Beauty*, the most profound films make audiences endure tremendous suffering before redemption enters in. The music chapter showed how the gothic visions of Nick Cave passed through murder en route to salvation. Christians must not take a shortcut to Easter Sunday. Blood, sweat, and tears line the road to resurrection.

2. Post-ethical/institutional—Humorous

> There are three things that are real to me—God, human folly, and laughter. Since the first two are beyond our comprehension, we must do what we can with the third.
>
> Jerry Lewis

> It is the test of a good religion whether you can joke about it.
>
> G. K. Chesterton

Is a Top 10 theology an effort to reduce theology and pop culture to quantifiable categories? Perish the thought! List making stems from the irony and irreverence of David Letterman and the obsessive fandom of Nick Hornby's *High Fidelity.* Top 10 theology revels in humor, in self-important lists, in poking fun at institutions that foolishly demand respect. It appears instantly disposable, a defense mechanism rooted in repeated attempts to find meaning and answers in an ever shifting landscape. By appearing casual and unimportant, Top 10 theology demands that listeners pay attention. It separates the reflective from the reactionary, the cultural anthropologists from the cultural critics. It suggests with a completely straight face that *The Simpsons* is the most spiritual show on TV. Like Ethel Barrymore, a Top 10 theologian, believes, "You grow up the day you have the first real laugh—at yourself."[63]

The Bible is full of humor. For the New Testament to open with a long list of the dubious role models leading up to Jesus demonstrates that God has either a great sense of humor or a poor sense of promotion. Why start the Gospel of Matthew with a paradox, introducing the sacred birth of Christ by airing all the dirty laundry? Why bother in a patriarchal society to name "suspect" women such as Tamar, Rahab, and Ruth as Jesus' predecessors? Isn't irony the enemy of sincerity, the committed Christian's closest friend? Patrick Henry reconciles these apparent opposites: "An ironic Christian inhabits a world that is more 'as if' than 'just like,' a world fashioned by a God of surprises. The grace of this God is mysterious, sneaky."[64]

Gregory Wolfe, editor of the journal *Image,* defends irony as much more than the opposite of sincerity. "Used responsibly, irony reminds us of how difficult it is to achieve the transparency of true sincerity. Our hubris constantly undermines our quest to discover and communicate truth, which is why irony can put us in our place." For Wolfe, Jesus is "the supreme ironist." "It is impossible to think of his parables . . . without sensing his playful use of indirection, that teasing form of testing those who encounter him, that is the essence of irony." On the road to Emmaus in Luke 24, Jesus' "innocent" question, "What are you discussing?" inspires a series of events in which "the ironies begin to pile up."[65] Author Annie Dillard suggests that when entering church "we should all be wearing crash helmets. Ushers should issue life preservers and signal flares; they should lash us to the pews."[66] The Bible is a subversive document with a wicked sense of humor that spares no one. Unfortunately, many of its pointed words shoot right over our heads and miss the opportunity to liberate our hearts.

Jesus took an ax to the root of the stuffiest defenders of the faith. That ax was often humor. Anyone turning water into wine could never qualify as a killjoy. Jesus employed dramatic overstatement, creating comic pictures of camels passing through needles. He was a fairly savage satirist, painting vivid pictures of his enemies as whitewashed tombs, broods of vipers, snakes. His words can be read as angry, snarling, or satirical. One wouldn't want to engage Jesus in a game of the dozens.[67] Born under "questionable" circumstances, Jesus undoubtedly heard almost every "your mama" joke known to first-century Palestine. He responded to attacks with sharp, focused comebacks. The targets of his barbs certainly demonstrated no sense of humor. But I bet his "popular," irreligious audiences roared at the broad and vivid brush strokes Jesus applied to those who considered themselves the chosen (or is it the frozen) few.

In *The Prostitute in the Family Tree,* Doug Adams points out how dangerous missing the Bible's humor can be. He suggests that most of Jesus' parables should be read as mirrors rather than morality. Adams treats the tired phrase "Render unto Caesar, things that are Caesar's and unto God, things that are God's" as a punch line.[68] A close reading of Matthew 22:15–22 reveals at whom Jesus aimed his joke. Jesus escapes the Pharisees' entrapment by making them reach into their pockets for a coin. The Romans minted nondescript coins so that the most faithful Jews would not be forced to violate their consciences. So Jesus asks the Pharisees to identify the name and title on their coins. When they pulled out a coin bearing the visage "CAESAR, KING AND SON OF GOD," their shifting morality was exposed. They were bowing down to other gods and carrying around idols. By pointing out two commandments that the Pharisees broke, Jesus undercut their air of moral superiority. Adams suggests that Jesus may have pocketed the coin just as he said, "Render unto God what is God's." He revealed their hypocrisy, affirmed his divinity, and pocketed the difference. Not a bad, very practical (and memorable) joke!

Does this reduce Jesus' words to mere entertainment, a sacred stand-up comedy routine? Neal Gabler argues that American religion has always trafficked in entertainment. The most famous preachers always put on the best show. The gap between televangelist Jimmy Swaggart and his cousin, country entertainer Mickey Gilley, has always been slight. From D. L. Moody to Billy Sunday to Billy Graham to T. D. Jakes, Christian celebrities delight, amuse, and entertain while delivering serious messages. Perhaps an admission that God likes to laugh would provide some welcome relief to kids bored to death by our religious observations.

We hope that despite the "light" nature of many of these points, the main idea will still shine through. We have offered patterns of meaning, big picture ideas of what's going on, trusting you to fill in the blanks. It may require more "faith" on our part, but we trust the sophisticated readers of Generations X, Y, and Z to figure it out. Our overall goal remains the recovery of a Jesus who can be Savior and Lord as well as revolutionary, storyteller, role model, wholly accessible, wholly Other, the ultimate artist, the friend of the poor, the disturber of the peace, and the man in the marketplace, who mixes it up with the people, his people, all people—from every tribe, nation, and tongue. We hope to let Jesus, having been hijacked, bound, and gagged by his "defenders," out of the oppressive box of "churchianity" as we rediscover him in the church of pop culture.

1. Post-Christian—Loving

> We have just enough religion to make us hate, but not enough to make us love one another.
>
> Jonathan Swift

> The Bible tells us to love our neighbors, and also to love our enemies; probably because they are generally the same people.
>
> G. K. Chesterton

How do we proceed as followers of Jesus in a post-Christian culture? Richard Rodriguez says, "I think we are at the beginning of a century in which the points of definition and separation between people will be more theological than at any time since the Middle Ages. . . . I tell young people they better read the Bible, they better read the Koran, they better know how the world is inscribed in sacred literature. Because they are entering the twelfth century and they must confront it."[69] We hope some models for confronting the future have emerged from our matrix. Theology has been far too theoretical for far too long. We have advocated a lived theology, a demonstrated faith. But we also hope you have found a passion for theology "proper"—the direct experience rather than the study of God. Through the prism of postmodernity and pop culture, we find a startling image. What is simultaneously diverse, experiential, mythological, mysterious, embodied, colorful, real, bloody, and humorous? The face of God, which emerges in the matrix. If you're still uncertain, consider a vibrant film that embodies an ethos that never goes out of style.

Twenty-first-century film started with an extravagant look back to the turn of the last century, to a revolutionary era. *Moulin Rouge* is a visual feast, an orgy of experiences that nearly blasted viewers out of the cinema. Critic David Ansen said that it "starts at such a frenetic level I thought it was going to self-destruct before it even got started."[70] He calls *Moulin Rouge* a "deliriously energetic, promiscuously post-modern, tragicomical musical."[71] It's a paradoxical pastiche, blending ancient myths, classic opera, and cheesy pop music. Ansen notes the film's seemingly irreconcilable opposites that shouldn't work. But they do. It's a fully immersive experience, engaging all the senses. Audiences either loved or hated it, probably costing Baz Luhrmann an Academy Award nomination as best director and the Oscar he deserved for creating the best picture of 2001.

Amid the flesh flying and dancers writhing, *Moulin Rouge* celebrated the ancient virtues of truth, beauty, freedom, and, above all things, love. The film re-creates the bohemian spirit, with Bono celebrating the "children of the revolution" on the soundtrack. What kind of revolution (revelation?) did Luhrmann have in mind? Beyond all its pyrotechnical pizzaz, *Moulin Rouge* offers a sweet, sincere celebration of the timeless healing power of love. What could be more simple, more naive than a big-budget musical? Luhrmann calls *Moulin Rouge* a confluence of primary myths rooted in Orpheus, *Camille,* and *La Bohème.* Yet critic Douglas Jones points out the film's unacknowledged source, the inspiration for the film *Camille,* Alexandre Dumas's 1848 novel, *La dame aux camelias.* Dumas's story can be read as a meeting of the prodigal son and Mary Magdalene, a country boy lost in the big city encountering a world-weary prostitute. At the end of the novel, Dumas's heroine Margeurite experiences redemption. "She lived a sinner, and she will die a Christian."[72] Luhrmann's homage to love and sacrifice borrowed from far deeper wells than perhaps the audience realized.

After a frenetic opening designed to test viewers' patience, the story settles down in a rendezvous atop an elephant (of course!). Aspiring writer Christian woos dancer-courtesan Satine with lines from the slightest, most laughable pop songs of all time. Famous "philosophers" like Phil Collins, Dolly Parton, and KISS provide platitudes such as "I was made for loving you," "Love will lift us up where we belong," and "I will always love you." Satine dismisses his musings as "silly love songs." When people of faith proclaim, "Jesus loves you," they sound just as silly. In a world that's been burned by truly bad faith, such a bald statement can sound so empty. Yet Christian's love songs in *Moulin Rouge* indicate a remarkable cultural shift. The dreamer, the lover, the "Christian" serves as the hero. Despite the many objections of science and psychology, doubters like Satine are in decline. Succumbing to his love songs, Satine admits that he's going to be "bad for business." Ethical and behavioral changes arise only after a profound encounter with grace and love. Just in case Satine forgets, Christian writes her a secret song as a reminder of his commitment. When Christian promises, "Come what may—I will love you to the end of time," his eternal pledge cuts through Satine's sacrificial death. Their love soars past sex into a spiritual transcendence.

Yet many people despise the film, finding its style overheated and its plot slight. They are stuck in a past that no longer exists, allowing reason to rule their hearts. Instead of spiritual longing, they see a bohemian artist tossing out tired lines in an effort to get into a prostitute's pants. How can we praise a film that celebrates lust? If you look close enough, beyond the surface provocations, you will see that pop culture reflects a longing for authentic truth, beauty, freedom, and love. Can we put our ears to the ground and find the current rhythms with which to reach even the most skeptical viewer?

We must help the Satines "look closer." They may want to sing, to dare to trust vows of eternal love, but their brains (and hearts) remember too many broken promises. We must court the courtesans, wooing them with silly love songs. They may dismiss us at first, but, as with Satine, that eternal love song will ultimately penetrate even the most jaded heart. Children of the revolution, start singing.

notes

Preface

1. Brian Godawa deals with these questions in *Hollywood Worldviews: Watching Films with Wisdom and Discernment* (Downers Grove, Ill.: InterVarsity, 2002). His appendix on sex, profanity, and violence in the Bible offers a thorough and compelling argument for engaging culture. Atlanta's progressive Art Within theater company answers the recurring question, "How could you cuss for Jesus?" at www.artwithin.org.

2. Tupac, "Me against the World," Interscope Records, 1995.

3. We do not really subscribe to generational theory. Life is too complex simply to draw lines around certain groups: Boomers, Gen-X, etc. Generational names tend to be marketing tools, and we find them suspect as a means of engaging contemporary cultural and theological issues.

4. Kudos to Andy Crouch for challenging this blind spot in "Thou Shalt Be Cool," *Christianity Today,* 11 March 2002, 72.

5. Larry Kreitzer's work stands as an insightful role model. His studies of the Old and New Testament in fiction and film reverse the hermeneutical flow.

6. Some may wonder why a history book such as Chronicles was grouped with more wisdom-oriented literature such as Proverbs. William Sanford Lasor's *Old Testament Survey* (Grand Rapids: Eerdmans, 1982), 508, turns to C. H. Gordon's suggestion that Chronicles offered a happy ending as the edict of Cyrus signaled the end of the exile.

7. Ibid.

8. Jack Nachbar and Kevin Lause, eds., *Popular Culture: An Introductory Text* (Bowling Green, Ohio: Bowling Green State University Popular Press, 1992), 7.

9. See Gene Edward Veith and Thomas L. Wilmeth, *Honky-Tonk Gospel: The Story of Sin and Salvation in Country Music* (Grand Rapids: Baker, 2001).

10. Neal Gabler, *Life the Movie: How Entertainment Conquered Reality* (New York: Knopf, 1998).

11. Ibid., 244.

Introduction

1. John Wiley Nelson offered a comprehensive and early contribution to this field in *Your God Is Alive and Well and Living and Appearing in Popular Culture* (Philadelphia: Westminster, 1976). Priest/sociologist Andrew M. Greeley presented a Catholic perspective in *God in Popular Culture* (Chicago: Thomas More Press, 1988). Greeley tackles artists as diverse as Bruce Springsteen, Stephen King, Linda Ronstadt, Louis L'Amour, and the most

319

Catholic of all pop icons, Madonna. We're also indebted to the scholastic work and witness of Kenneth A. Myers, Quentin Schultze, William D. Romanowski, David Dark, and Tom Beaudoin.

2. Greeley, *God in Popular Culture,* 165.

3. Ibid., 163.

4. From Craig's private conversation with a pastor on the staff of Vanguard, January 2002. Vanguard meets in a converted movie theater and hosts regular gatherings of the Colorado Springs Film Society.

5. Russel B. Nye, "Notes on a Rationale for Popular Culture," in *The Popular Culture Reader,* ed. Christopher Geist and Jack Nachbar (Bowling Green, Ohio: Bowling Green State University Popular Press, 1977), 10.

6. Ray B. Browne, "Popular Culture: Notes towards a Definition," in *Popular Culture: An Introductory Text,* ed. Jack Nachbar and Kevin Lause (Bowling Green, Ohio: Bowling Green State University Popular Press, 1992), 1.

7. Simon During, *The Cultural Studies Reader,* 2d ed. (London: Routledge, 1999), 1–4.

8. Quoted in David Colker, "Race Is On to Get Gay Network on the Air in U.S.," *Los Angeles Times,* 3 May 2002, p. C1.

9. David Lamb, "Ex-Klansman Convicted of 1963 Church Bombing," *Los Angeles Times,* 23 May 2002, p. A1.

10. Erika Hayasaki, "Reading, 'Riting, and Rap," *Los Angeles Times,* 14 January 2003, p. A1.

11. Jean-François Lyotard, *The Postmodern Condition: A Report on Knowledge,* trans. Geoff Bennington and Brian Massumi (Minneapolis: University of Minnesota Press, 1984).

12. The evangelical longing for intellectual respect was reported in lively detail by Alan Wolfe in "The Opening of the Evangelical Mind," *Atlantic Monthly* 286, no. 4 (October 2000): 55–76.

13. From a letter to Wilbur M. Smith, quoted in George M. Marsden, *Reforming Fundamentalism: Fuller Seminary and the New Evangelicalism* (Grand Rapids: Eerdmans, 1987), 13.

14. Scientist/theologian John Polkinghorne entered the humongous gap between popular fascination with the end times and credible Christian scholarship in *The God of Hope and the End of the World* (New Haven: Yale University Press, 2002). Polkinghorne won the Templeton Prize for his important previous contributions such as *Belief in God in an Age of Science* (New Haven: Yale

University Press, 1998). He tries to find a Christian eschatology that is intelligible and defensible in the twenty-first century. While we appreciate Polkinghorne's efforts, we acknowledge that his readership and impact will pale in comparison to the broad reach of Left Behind. Scholars' best efforts cannot stem the tide of emotional and artistic responses ruling Western airwaves.

15. We're grateful to rising New Testament scholar Matt Rindge for pointing this out to us.

16. Artists Bob and Roberta Smith refurbished a hotel in central London with such pithy and subversive phrases. For a more complete discussion of the subject, see the art chapter in this book.

17. This last comment may surprise those who tend to view postmoderns as people who aren't searching for cohesion. We believe that they are. They are just searching for a different set of cohesive ideas, and this cohesion is developed in paradoxical ways. Postmoderns accept the "gray" and are willing to live with conflicting ideas that don't flow in linear ways.

18. Lonnie D. Kliever, *The Shattered Spectrum* (Atlanta: John Knox, 1981), 1–5.

19. Ibid., 2.

20. Ibid., 3.

21. Ibid., 1–10.

22. Thomas Friedman, *The Lexus and the Olive Tree* (New York: Farrar, Straus, Giroux, 1999), 54–55.

23. This idea was inspired by a similar comment in Kliever, *Shattered Spectrum,* 30.

24. U2, "Please," from the CD *POP,* Island Records, 1997.

25. Tom Waits, "Georgia Lee," from the CD *Mule Variations,* Epitaph Records, 1999.

Chapter 1

1. Andrew Blake, *The Irresistible Rise of Harry Potter* (London: Verso, 2002), 8.

2. The idea for this approach was influenced by Susanne Katherina Knauth Langer, *Philosophy in a New Key* (Cambridge: Harvard University Press, 1942), which, while not directly applicative to this field of study, helped us develop a methodological approach that aided our reflection.

3. Eternal thanks and gratitude to Rev. Bob Bonnett, senior vice president of programming for the Hallmark Channel, for introducing us to Bernard Lonergan. We noticed Bonnett's posting

the day before we finished writing this book. Lonergan's notion of "a matrix of meanings" was literally the last thing we added to the manuscript. Talk about divine timing!

4. Mark D. Morelli and Elizabeth A. Morelli, eds., *The Lonergan Reader* (Toronto: University of Toronto Press, 1997), 443–44.

5. Lorraine Ali and Devin Gordon, "We Still Want Our MTV," *Newsweek,* 23 July 2001, 51.

6. Thomas Friedman, *The Lexus and the Olive Tree* (New York: Farrar, Straus, Giroux, 1999), 252.

7. *Joel Whitburn's Top Pop Singles, 1955–1990,* Record Research, 1991.

8. *1 Giant Leap,* DVD/CD, Palm Pictures, 2001.

9. Quoted in Toby Lester, "Oh, Gods!" *Atlantic Monthly* 289, no. 2 (February 2002): 39.

10. Ibid.

11. See Ziauddin Sardar and Merryl Wyn Davies, *Why Do People Hate America?* (Cambridge: Icon, 2002).

12. Friedman, *Lexus and the Olive Tree,* 312.

13. Michael Medved, *USA Today,* 15 October 2001.

14. Daniel Boorstin, *The Image: A Guide to Pseudo-Events in America* (New York: Harper & Row, 1961), 241.

15. Herbert Muschamp, "The Miracle in Bilbao," *New York Times Magazine,* 7 September 1997, 54.

16. Ibid., 34.

17. Bob Smithhouser, "I Definitely Want Heads to Turn," *Plugged In* 6, no. 7 (July 2001): 3.

18. Missy Misdemeanor Elliott, *SupaDupaFly,* Elektra Entertainment, 1997.

19. See www.christiansforcannabis.com.

20. Quoted in Marc Peyser, "All Aboard the Crazy Train," *Newsweek,* 11 March 2002, 64.

21. For an enlightening survey of the demythologizing/remythologizing process regarding theology during the past two hundred years, see Gary Dorrien, *The Word as True Myth: Interpreting Modern Theology* (Louisville: Westminster John Knox, 1997).

22. Thank you to Chuck Slocum of the Writer's Guild for organizing a Reel Spirituality luncheon at Fuller Theological Seminary on this topic. The possibilities for a deeper understanding of the Gospel writers' creative process emerged from our discussion with New Testament scholars and leading television docudrama writers.

23. Tim Ruttan, "Digging for the Truth in Colson's Column," *Los Angeles Times,* 29 March 2002, p. E1.

24. Quoted in Dave Tomlinson, *The Post-Evangelical* (London: Triangle, 1995), 80.

25. Ibid.

26. Telford Work, "Synoptic Star Wars: The Fan Club Strikes Back," *Books & Culture* 8, no. 2 (March/April 2002): 6–7.

27. Ibid.

28. Jeremy Rifkin, "Hyper-Active, Online 24/7," *Los Angeles Times,* 28 May 2001, p. B13.

29. Ibid.

30. Ibid.

31. Barbara Kantrowitz and Pat Wingert, "The Parent Trap," *Newsweek,* 29 January 2001, 49.

32. Anne Quindlen, "Doing Nothing Is Something," *Newsweek,* 13 May 2002, 76.

33. Karen Kaplan, "Kids' Camping Essentials: Boots, Pack, Game Boy," *Los Angeles Times,* 4 August 2001, p. A18.

34. Lorraine Ali and Julie Scelfo, "Choosing Virginity," *Newsweek,* 9 December 2002, 61.

35. Kim Painter, "The Sexual Revolution Hits Junior High," *USA Today*, 15–17 March 2002, p. 1A.

36. National Center on Addiction and Substance Abuse at Columbia University, cited in Paula Rinehart, "Losing Our Promiscuity," *Christianity Today,* 10 July 2000, 34.

37. Quoted in Rinehart, "Losing Our Promiscuity," 36.

38. Andres Tapia, "Abstinence: The Radical Choice for Sex Ed," *Christianity Today,* 8 February 1993, 26.

39. Diana Jean Schemo, "Virginity Pledges by Teenagers Can Be Highly Effective, Federal Study Finds," *New York Times,* 4 January 2001, p. A16.

40. Vanessa Grigoriadis, "Like a Virgin," *Spin Magazine* 17, no. 4 (April 2001): 133.

41. Kathleen Kelleher, "More Teens Are Having Sex, but Don't Always Think They Are," *Los Angeles Times,* 22 January 2001, p. E2.

42. Ibid.

43. Ibid.

44. Kathleen Kelleher, "An Encounter of the No-Strings-Attached, 5,000 Volt Kind," *Los Angeles Times,* 6 August 2001, p. E2.

45 . Ibid.

46. Robert S. McElvaine, "'Hooking Up' Makes a Feminized World More Bound Than Ever by Men's Rules," *Los Angeles Times,* 5 August 2001, p. M6.

47. Brian Lowry, "TV Seldom Depicts Sex Risks, Study Says," *Los Angeles Times,* 10 February 1999, p. B8.

48. Quoted in Steven Isaac, "Teen Pop Star Takes a Memorable Walk," *Plugged In* 7, no. 2 (February 2002): 12.

49. Smithhouser, "I Definitely Want Heads to Turn," 3.

50. Robert Christgau, *Grown Up All Wrong: 75 Great Rock and Pop Artists from Vaudeville to Techno* (Cambridge: Harvard University Press, 1998), 467.

51. *American Pie,* Universal Studios, 1999.

52. Steve Lopez, "Patrons at Real-Life Barbershop Have No Problem with Movie," *Los Angeles Times,* 28 September 2002, p. B1.

53. The president of Spelman College, Beverly Daniel Tatum, addresses this issue in *Why Are All the Black Kids Sitting Together in the Cafeteria?* (New York: Basic Books, 1997).

54. Gregory Rodriguez, "The Future Americans," *Los Angeles Times,* 18 March 2001, p. M1.

55. Lauren Sandler, "The Lighter Side of Racism," *Los Angeles Times,* 12 January 2003, p. E3.

56. Todd Boyd, "History, Hip-Hop Part Ways in 'Barbershop,'" *Los Angeles Times,* 30 September 2002, p. B11.

57. Quoted in Patrick Goldstein, "Action Heroes for a Changing America," *Los Angeles Times,* 28 May 2002, p. F1.

58. Ibid.

59. Quoted in Boyd, "History, Hip-Hop," B11.

60. For a much more complete discussion of this phenomenon, see J. Richard Middleton and Brian J. Walsh, "Reality Isn't What It Used to Be," in *Truth Is Stranger Than It Used to Be: Biblical Faith in a Postmodern Age* (Downers Grove, Ill.: InterVarsity, 1995).

61. Gareth Cook, "At MIT, They Can Put Words in Our Mouths," *Boston Globe,* 15 May 2002, online.

62. Quoted in Michael Cromartie, "A Conversation with Francis Fukuyama," *Books & Culture* 8, no. 4 (July/August 2002): 9.

63. Bill McKibben, *Enough: Staying Human in an Engineered Age* (New York: Time Books, 2003).

64. Quoted in Cromartie, "Conversation with Francis Fukuyama," 9.

65. Colin Ryan wrote his manifesto, "The Anti-Drama of Cinerama," after a particularly potent class discussion of George Lucas's *Star Wars'* prequels. After Craig encouraged his students to resist *The Attack of the Clones* at all costs, Colin responded in writing on 14 March 2002.

66. Ibid.

67. Neil Howe and William Strauss trace the history of pop music and movies and how each generation eventually finds its artistic voice in *Millennials Rising: The Next Great Generation* (New York: Vintage Books, 2000), 244.

68. Private conversation.

69. Graduates of Craig's tiny alma mater, take heart. The only institution to send two grads to the entering class of forty students was Davidson College, a small college with big dreams and disproportionate influence—traditionally, everywhere but Hollywood.

70. For a complete history and background of this provocative festival dedicated to classic cinema and classy conversations, see www.cityofangelsfilmfest.org.

71. Wes Craven, quoted in "The Big Question," *Johns Hopkins Magazine,* September 2001, 24.

72. Thomas S. Hibbs, *Shows about Nothing: Nihilism in Popular Culture from the Exorcist to Seinfeld* (Dallas: Spence Publishing, 1999), 99.

73. Mark Peyser, "TV's Stiff Competition," *Newsweek,* 4 March 2002, 57.

74. Mark Peyser, "Six Feet under Our Skin," *Newsweek,* 18 March 2002, 54.

75. Ibid.

76. Quoted in ibid., 54–55.

77. Ibid.

78. Ibid., 58.

79. James Kelly, "The Year of the Whistle-Blowers," *Time* 160, no. 27 (30 December–6 January 2003): 8.

80. Quoted in Elena Roston, "Penn Ultimate," *New Times Los Angeles,* 23–29 May 2002, 21.

81. John Carney, "Chris Harper Interview," *The Door,* September/October 2000, 31.

82. Quoted in Becky Garrison, "Simon Jenkins Interview," *The Door,* September/October 2001, 2–3.

83. Ibid., 3.

84. Ibid.

85. Ibid.

86. Ibid.

87. Tom Beaudoin, *Virtual Faith: The Irreverent Spiritual Quest of Generation X* (San Francisco: Jossey-Bass, 1998), 62.

88. Patrick Henry, *The Ironic Christian's Companion: Finding the Marks of God's Grace in the World* (New York: Riverhead Books, 1999), 7.

89. Special Edition DVD of *Dogma,* Columbia Tri-Star Home Entertainment, 2000.

90. Quoted in William Lobdell, "Teens' Rite of Passage Can Include Their Faith," *Los Angeles Times,* 19 October 2002, p. B20.

91. Lisa Richardson, "Analyzing the Unchurched," *Los Angeles Times,* 18 May 2002, p. B20.

92. Quoted in ibid.

93. The fount of most knowledge for fundamentalist/evangelical short history is George M. Marsden. Start with his *Fundamentalism and American Culture: The Shaping of Twentieth-Century Evangelicalism, 1870–1925* (Oxford: Oxford University Press, 1980).

94. Quoted in "Campus Seeks to Shed Fundamentalist Label," *Los Angeles Times,* 16 March 2002, p. B19.

95. In sharp contrast to the decline of religion in the industrialized world, Asia, Africa, and Latin America are experiencing profound growth and appreciation of faith. A majority of the Christian community now lives in the two-thirds world. For more about the global church, see the conclusion of this book.

96. Conrad Cherry, Betty DeBerg, and Amanda Porterfield, *Religion on Campus* (Chapel Hill: University of North Carolina Press, 2002).

97. Quoted in Cathy Lynn Grossman, "Charting Unchurched America," *USA Today,* 7 March 2002, p. D1–2.

98. See Jacob Needleman, *The New Religions* (New York: Doubleday, 1970); and Robert N. Bellah, "Religious Evolution," in *Reader in Comparative Religion,* ed. William A. Lessa and Evan V. Zogt (New York: Harper & Row, 1965), 73–87. We realize that later works also deal with these issues, but we have found Bellah's work on religious changes particularly helpful.

99. Thomas C. Oden, "The Death of Modernity and Postmodern Evangelical Spirituality," in *The Challenge of Postmodernism,* ed. David S. Dockery (Grand Rapids: BridgePoint Books, 1998), 19.

100. Beaudoin, *Virtual Faith,* 14.

101. See www.creed.com.

102. Quoted in Bob Smithhouser, "Are They or Aren't They," *Plugged In* 7, no. 1 (January 2002): 3.

103. Quoted in Dan Epstein, "The School of Hard Rocks," *Revolver* (March/April 2002): 61.

104. Tomlinson, *Post-Evangelical,* 1.

105. *Q,* November 2002, online.

106. Walter Brueggemann, *Hopeful Imagination: Prophetic Voices in Exile* (Philadelphia: Fortress, 1986), 23.

107. Ibid., 28–29.

Chapter 2

1. *Q,* June 1999, online.

2. Marshall McLuhan, *Understanding Media: The Extensions of Man* (New York: Signet, 1964), 32.

3. Whether advertising can be viewed as art is a hotly contested subject of debate. As with many issues, how one responds largely depends on how one chooses to interpret what art is. I (Barry) choose to argue that advertising is an art form for many reasons, including the fact that it is a visual, graphic, symbolic form of expression employing a number of varied fine art processes and practices. The argument that advertising exists only because of commerce is a rather weak one because most artists would stop producing art were there not some form of economic incentive to produce it.

4. Mark Fenske, *Brand-New* (London: V & A Publications, 2000), 54.

5. James Twitchell, *Lead Us into Temptation: The Triumph of American Materialism* (New York: Columbia University Press, 1999), 6.

6. Quoted in Hermann Vaske, *Standing on the Shoulders of Giants: Hermann Vaske's Conversations with the Masters of Advertising* (Berlin: Die Deutsche Bibliotek, 2001), 342.

7. Ibid., 343.

8. James Twitchell, *Twenty Ads That Shook the World* (New York: Three Rivers Press, 2000), 11–12.

9. Ibid., 205.

10. Tom Beaudoin, *Virtual Faith: The Irreverent Spiritual Quest of Generation X* (San Francisco: Jossey-Bass, 1998), 97.

11. Ibid., 96.

12. Marc Gobé, *Emotional Branding: The New Paradigm for Connecting Brands to People* (New York: Allworth Press, 2001), particularly 71–102.

13. Ibid., 121, emphasis added.

14. Sherry Turkle, quoted in Cristopher Nash, *The Unravelling of the Postmodern Mind* (Edinburgh: Edinburgh University Press, 2001), 4.

15. Twitchell, *Lead Us into Temptation,* 80–81.

16. For a more complete take on "the decentered self," refer to J. Richard Middleton and Brian J. Walsh, *Truth Is Stranger Than It Used to Be: Biblical Faith in a Postmodern Age* (Downers Grove, Ill.: InterVarsity, 1995), 53.

17. Gina Piccalo and Louise Roug, "Baubles, Bangles, and the Awards Circuit," *Los Angeles Times,* 20 March 2002, p. E2.

18. Christopher Lasch, *The Culture of Narcissism: American Life in an Age of Diminishing Expectations* (New York: Warner Books, 1979), 137.

19. Twitchell, *Lead Us into Temptation,* 19–20.

20. Ibid., 121.

21. Ibid., 87.

22. Neal Gabler, *Life the Movie: How Entertainment Conquered Reality* (New York: Knopf, 1998), 8.

23. See www.brandchannel.com/forum.asp?id=8#more_info, 11 September 2001.

24. Larry B. Stammer, "Organized Religion Slips in Survey," *Los Angeles Times,* 11 January 2003, p. B18.

25. Roger Haight, *Jesus, Symbol of God* (Maryknoll, N.Y.: Orbis, 1999), 86.

26. Ibid., 396.

Chapter 3

1. Quoted in Paul Krassner, "Celebrities, Aren't They Something?" *Los Angeles Times Magazine,* 13 June 1999, 30.

2. Ibid.

3. A fictionalized account of these ubiquitous roadside vendors can be found in Miguel Arteta's 1997 debut film, *Star Maps.*

4. For a scholarly study of how Los Angeles came to define youth and celebrity, see Kirse Granat May, *Golden State, Golden Youth: The California Image in Popular Culture, 1955–1966* (Chapel Hill: University of North Carolina Press, 2002).

5. Richard Corliss, *Intimate Strangers: The Culture of Celebrity in America* (Chicago: Ivan R. Dee, 2000), xii.

6. Neal Gabler, *Life the Movie: How Entertainment Conquered Reality* (New York: Knopf, 1998), 174.

7. Quoted in Krassner, "Celebrities, Aren't They Something?" 31.

8. Edith Hamilton, *Mythology* (New York: Mentor Books, 1963), 16.

9. Ibid.

10. Frederick Hartt, *Art: A History of Painting, Sculpture, Architecture* (Englewood Cliffs, N.J.: Prentice-Hall, 1976), 101.

11. Hamilton, *Mythology,* 44.

12. Joseph Campbell, *The Hero with a Thousand Faces* (Princeton, N.J.: Princeton University Press, 1949), 30.

13. Ibid., 388.

14. Lev Grossman, "Feeding on Fantasy," *Time* 160, no. 23 (2 December 2002): 90.

15. Walter Brueggemann, *First and Second Samuel* (Louisville: John Knox, 1990), 68.

16. I am indebted to the scholarship and friendship of Robert K. Johnston, my professor at Fuller Theological Seminary, for first bringing this to my attention.

17. Corliss, *Intimate Strangers,* 24.

18. Chris Rojek, *Celebrity* (London: Reaktion Books, 2001), 30–31.

19. Quoted in David Colman, "Star-Crazy Magazine Charms London," *New York Times,* 17 March 2002, sec. 9, p. 1.

20. David Shaw, "Personalities Non Grata?" *Los Angeles Times,* 25 September 2001, p. E4.

21. Daniel Boorstin, *The Image: A Guide to Pseudo-Events in America* (New York: Harper & Row, 1961), 198.

22. Ibid.

23. Ibid., 61.

24. Irving J. Rein, Philip Kotler, and Martin R. Stoller, *High Visibility* (New York: Dodd, Mead & Company, 1987), 6–8.

25. Rojek, *Celebrity,* 78.

26. Corliss, *Intimate Strangers,* 32.

27. George M. Marsden, *Reforming Fundamentalism: Fuller Seminary and the New Evangelicalism* (Grand Rapids: Eerdmans, 1987), 91–93.

28. The most entertaining, informative, and essential history of American popular religion remains George M. Marsden, *Fundamentalism and*

American Culture: The Shaping of Twentieth-Century Evangelicalism, 1870–1925 (Oxford: Oxford University Press, 1980). He outlines the beginnings of the tiresome culture wars that have dogged America for the past quarter century.

29. Quoted in Gabler, Life the Movie, 25.

30. Rein et al., High Visibility, 338.

31. Malcolm Muggeridge, Christ and the Media (London: Hodder & Stoughton, 1979), 41.

32. Corliss, Intimate Strangers, 35.

33. Ibid.

34. Boorstin, Image, 155.

35. Corliss, Intimate Strangers, 37.

36. Richard Corliss, quoted in Rein et al., High Visibility, 27.

37. Corliss, Intimate Strangers, 47.

38. Rein et al., High Visibility, 15.

39. Of course, the phenomena crossed over to other fields, as Robert Zimmerman became Bob Dylan, Josif Dzhugashvili chose Joseph Stalin, and Henri Donat Mathieu transformed himself into Yves St. Laurent (Rein et al., High Visibility, 216–17). Rap music continues the trend with James Smith turning "Ladies Love Cool James" into L L Cool J, Marshall Mathers morphing into Eminem, and Alecia Moore rechristening herself Pink.

40. Quoted in David Shaw, "Personalities Non Grata?" Los Angeles Times, 25 September 2001, p. E4.

41. Gabler, Life the Movie, 7.

42. This could explain an odd connection to 9/11—did they attack our freedom or our exports? When we propose "shopping" as the patriotic response to war, then maybe the Twin Towers were a particularly apt choice—a symbol of capitalism par excellence. But then why would Osama bin Laden, a millionaire himself, dare to call capitalism evil? Isn't that the ultimate hypocrisy—one millionaire calling a nation of millionaires greedy? At least we don't masquerade our greed. We celebrate it.

43. Shaw, "Personalities Non Grata?" E4.

44. Rein et al., High Visibility, 155–93.

45. Boorstin, Image, 63.

46. Dave Karger and Mark Harris, "Golden Opportunities," Entertainment Weekly, 18 January 2002, 23–25.

47. Gina Piccalo and Louise Roug, "City of Angles," Los Angeles Times, 13 February 2002, p. E2.

48. Larry Tye, The Father of Spin (New York: Crown Publishers, 1998), 24–25.

49. Ibid., 25.

50. Ibid., 28–29.

51. Gabler, Life the Movie, 96.

52. Ibid.

53. Ibid., 97.

54. Rein et al., High Visibility, 278.

55. Charles Fleming, "The Journalism of Adoration," Los Angeles Times, 20 May 2001, p. M1.

56. Greg Braxton, "'American Idol' Is Fox's Summer Salvation," Los Angeles Times, 3 September 2002, p. F9.

57. Greg Braxton, "From Waitress to an 'American Idol,'" Los Angeles Times, 5 September 2002, p. A15.

58. Christopher Lasch, The Culture of Narcissism: American Life in an Age of Diminishing Expectations (New York: Warner Books, 1979).

59. Boorstin, Image, 232.

60. Quoted in Colman, "Star-Crazy Magazine Charms London," 1.

61. Ibid., 6.

62. Corliss, Intimate Strangers, 274.

63. Ibid., 275.

64. Gabler, Life the Movie, 7.

65. Ibid., 154.

66. Quoted in ibid., 87.

67. Boorstin, Image, 75.

68. Corliss, Intimate Strangers, 51.

69. Quoted in Krassner, "Celebrities, Aren't They Something?" 31.

70. Ron Austin, "Saint Charlot: The Comedy of Charlie Chaplin," Image: A Journal of the Arts and Religion 15 (fall 1996): 112.

71. Corliss, Intimate Strangers, 39.

72. Bill Carter, "Fox TV Finds Another Way to Sink to Top of the Charts," New York Times, 15 March 2002, p. C1.

73. Quoted in "Plenty of Punch Lines for Boxing Has-Beens," Los Angeles Times, 18 March 2002, p. D2.

74. Carter, "Fox TV Finds Another Way," C1.

75. Ibid. Of course, the success of Celebrity Boxing guaranteed a sequel. But John Wayne Bobbitt was arrested for spousal abuse before he entered the ring with Joey Buttafucco. Fox wrangled Chyna, a female wrestler from the WWF, into the ring as a sub.

76. Quoted in Hilary E. MacGregor, "Common Denominators," *Los Angeles Times,* 15 March 2002, p. E1–4.

77. "Plenty of Punch Lines," D2.

78. Nathan Ihara, "Obey? In Step with Shepard Fairey, the Emperor of Ubiquity," *Los Angeles Weekly,* 15–21 February 2002, 33–35. You can view Fairey's evolving series of Andre the Giant at www.obeygiant.com.

79. Rojek, *Celebrity,* 60–61.

80. John Drane devotes an entire chapter to "The Death of Diana, Princess of Wales: Missiological Lessons for the Churches," in *Cultural Change and Biblical Faith* (Carlisle, Cumbria, U.K.: Paternoster, 2000).

81. For more on the Andy Warhol Museum, see www.warhol.org. Great fan sites covering Warhol's life and work include www.warhol.dk and www.warholstars.org.

82. Corliss, *Intimate Strangers,* 233.

83. Check out the fan site www.warhol stars.org.

84. The editors of Time-Life Books, *Turbulent Years: The 60s,* Our American Century (Alexandria, Va.: Time-Life Books, 1998), 42.

85. Ibid.

86. Gabler, *Life the Movie,* 135.

87. Corliss, *Intimate Strangers,* 236.

88. Quoted in Jane Daggett Dillenberger, *The Religious Art of Andy Warhol* (New York: Continuum, 1998), 16.

89. Becky Garrison, "Jane Daggett Dillinberger Interview," *The Door,* March/April 1999, 6.

90. Phyllis McGinley, *Saint-Watching* (New York: Crossroad, 1988), 16.

91. Rojek, *Celebrity,* 97.

92. To his considerable credit, Philip Yancey tries to correct the Protestant suspicion of sainthood in his tribute to the people who helped him endure considerable spiritual dissonance: *Soul Survivor: How My Faith Survived the Church* (New York: Doubleday, 2001). His saints range from writers such as Fyodor Dostoyevsky, Frederick Buechner, Annie Dillard, and Shusaku Endo to divergent statesmen from Martin Luther King Jr. and Mahatma Gandhi to C. Everett Koop.

93. Quoted in Martin Miller, "Lives, Camera, Action!" *Los Angeles Times,* 16 December 1998, p. E3.

94. Dick Pountain and David Robins, *Cool Rules: Anatomy of an Attitude* (London: Reaktion Books, 2000), 19.

95. Ibid., 38.

96. Ibid., 19.

97. Ibid., 165.

98. Quoted in Katherine Turman, "Crucifix-ated," *New Times Los Angeles,* 30 November–6 December 2000, 68.

99. Harold Fickett, "Stories That Will Get You Killed," *Image: A Journal of the Arts and Religion* 15 (fall 1996): 95.

100. Krassner, "Celebrities, Aren't They Something?" 32.

101. Quoted in LaTonya Taylor, "The Church of O," *Christianity Today,* 1 April 2002, 40.

102. Ibid.

103. Ibid.

104. Lynette Clemetson, "Oprah on Oprah," *Newsweek,* 8 January 2001, 40–44.

105. Quoted in Marcia Z. Nelson, "Oprah on a Mission," *The Christian Century,* 25 September–8 October 2002, 20.

106. Quoted in Josh Tyrangiel, "Bono's Mission," *Time* 159, no. 9 (4 March 2002): 66.

107. Ibid., 64.

108. For a much more complete take on Bono and U2's wrestling with faith and fame, see Steve Stockman, *Walk On: The Spiritual Journey of U2* (Lake Mary, Fla.: Relevant Books, 2001).

109. Andy Crouch, "The End of Relevance," *re: generation quarterly* 7, no. 3 (fall 2001): 14.

110. Pountain and Robins, *Cool Rules,* 166.

111. Bono, "God Is on His Knees," *Bread: The Bread for the World Newsletter,* December 2002, 2.

Chapter 4

1. Stuart Maconie, "Ray of Light," *Q,* online archive.

2. Simon Frith, *Sound Effects: Youth, Leisure, and the Politics of Rock 'n' Roll* (New York: Knopf, 1981), introduction.

3. Robert Palmer, *Rock and Roll: An Unruly History* (New York: Harmony Books, 1995), 46.

4. Quoted in Simon Reynolds, *Blissed Out: The Raptures of Rock* (London: Serpent's Tail, 1990), 26.

5. Theodor Adorno, "On Popular Music," in *Cultural Theory and Popular Culture,* ed. John

Storey (Athens, Ga.: University of Georgia Press, 1994), 197–212.

6. Ibid., 202–3.

7. Ibid., 206.

8. Ibid.

9. Ibid., 211.

10. Ibid., 211–12.

11. Frith, *Sound Effects,* 147.

12. Ibid., 281.

13. Tom Beaudoin, *Virtual Faith: The Irreverent Spiritual Quest of Generation X* (San Francisco: Jossey-Bass, 1998).

14. Recently, she has attempted to undermine the significance of statements such as these, which she made earlier in her career, perhaps because her own personal situation has changed or her views have altered somewhat.

15. Susan Black, *In His Own Words: Bono* (London: Omnibus Press, 1997), 30.

16. Ibid., 31.

17. Quoted in Kurt Loder, "Madonna," *Rolling Stone Magazine,* 21 January 1999, 43.

18. Tyler Thoreson, "Marketing God in the New Millennium," *Gadfly* (April 2000): 28.

19. The Pocket Canons (Edinburgh: Canongate Press, 1998).

20. Nick Cave, *King Ink II* (London: Black Spring Press, 1997), 42.

21. Walter Brueggemann, *Texts under Negotiation: The Bible and Postmodern Imagination* (Minneapolis: Fortress, 1993), vii.

22. Cave, *King Ink II,* 139.

23. Ibid., 138.

24. Ian Johnston, *Bad Seed: The Biography of Nick Cave* (Toronto: Little Brown, 1995), 108.

25. Cave, *King Ink II,* 90.

26. Ibid., 138.

27. Nick Cave, *King Ink* (London: Black Spring Press, 1993), 84.

28. Cave, *King Ink II,* 90.

29. Ibid., 90.

30. See Johnston's *Bad Seed* for an in-depth perspective on just how far Cave's selfishness and careless attitude damaged his relationships, both platonic and amorous, as well as how his own lack of self-care led to incredible problems with substance abuse.

31. *The Gospel according to Mark* (Edinburgh: Canongate Press, 1998), vii.

32. Ibid.

33. Ibid., xi.

34. Ibid.

35. Charles H. Kraft, *Communication Theory for Christian Witness* (Maryknoll, N.Y.: Orbis, 1996), 67.

36. Nick Cave, *The Flesh Made Word,* BBC Radio, 3 July 1996, transcript.

37. Ibid.

38. *The Gospel according to Mark,* xi.

39. Ibid.

40. Ibid., xii.

41. Brian Eno, *A Year with Swollen Appendices: Brian Eno's Diary* (London: Faber & Faber, 1996), 293–97.

42. Ibid., 293.

43. Gustav Mahler, Symphony no. 5, performed by the Cleveland Orchestra, conducted by Christoph Von Dohnanyi, Decca Records, U.K., 1989.

44. For an in-depth study of this, see Mark Prendergast, *The Ambient Century* (New York: Bloomsbury, 2000).

45. In a collaboration with Brian Eno, the Irish rock band U2 released an album entitled *Passengers,* comprised of "music for imaginary films."

46. Björk, *Vespertine,* Elecktra Records, 2001.

47. Sigur Rós, *Agaetis Byrjun,* Fatcat Records, U.K., 2001.

48. Quoted in Mac Randall, *Exit Music: The Radiohead Story* (New York: Delta Trade Paperbacks, 2000), 268.

49. Ibid.

50. Joe Brooker, "I Can't Help Quoting You," in *The Message: Crossing the Tracks between Poetry and Pop,* ed. Roddy Lumsden (New York: The Poetry Society, 1999), 15.

51. Randall, *Exit Music,* 269.

52. I am grateful to U.K. theologian Pete Ward at Kings College, London, for the term "liquid church," a theory he is developing as an approach to ecclesiology.

53. Gerald Marzorati, "All by Himself," *New York Times Magazine,* 12 March 2002, 32.

54. Ibid., 35.

55. Ibid., 70.

56. Friedrich Kittler, *DJ Culture* (London: Quartet Books, 1998), 309.

57. Ira Matathia and Marian Salzman, *Next: Trends for the Near Future* (New York: Overlook Press, 2000), 254.

58. For a more in-depth view of this, see Ulf Porschardt, *DJ Culture* (London: Quartet Books, 1995), 373ff.

59. This point would seem to have some important things to say to the contemporary Christian worship scene, perhaps not in this book, but it is definitely thought for reflection.

60. Angela McRobbie, "Thinking with Music," in *Stars Don't Stand Still in the Sky: Music and Myth,* ed. Karen Kelly and Evelyn McDowell (London: Routledge, 1999), 38.

61. Marzorati, "All by Himself," 35.

62. Quoted in Palmer, *Rock and Roll,* 237.

63. Tricia Rose, *Black Noise* (London: Wesleyan University Press, 1994), 2–3.

64. Ibid.

65. Will Straw, quoted in Andy Bennett, *Cultures of Popular Music* (Philadelphia: Open University Press, 2001), 44.

66. Johnny Hallyday is the French Elvis Presley, a huge star in his native France who sells millions of albums and fills soccer stadiums with fans. Yet he is virtually unheard of outside France and a couple other French-speaking countries such as Belgium and Switzerland.

67. Tom Schnabel, *Rhythm Planet* (New York: Universe Publishing, 1998), 10.

68. Matathia and Salzman, *Next,* 255–56.

69. *New York Times Magazine,* 17 March 2002, 8.

70. Timothy D. Taylor, *Global Pop* (New York: Routledge, 1997), 197.

71. Ibid.

72. Ibid.

73. I would recommend the section on the global postmodern in chapter 8 of ibid.

74. This view is very much a product of the idea that a single narrative exists in a particular field that has fueled the modern world, an idea that no longer has currency in our new globalized world.

75. Leonard Sweet, *Quantum Spirituality* (Dayton: Whaleprint Press, 1991), 21.

76. Simon Reynolds, *Generation Ecstasy* (London: Little, Brown & Co., 1998), 9.

77. *The Gospel according to Mark,* xii.

78. There is a lot of work already being done in this area, and I do not need to amplify here.

79. Walter Brueggemann, *Finally Comes the Poet* (Minneapolis: Fortress, 1989), 4.

80. Ibid.

81. Beaudoin, *Virtual Faith,* 155–57.

82. *The Gospel according to Mark,* ix.

83. Ibid.

84. Beaudoin, *Virtual Faith,* 72ff.

Chapter 5

1. Pauline Kael was the dean of American film criticism, the first and last word in what mattered on-screen. Among her devoted disciples was writer-director Paul Schrader, who wrote a moving tribute to her on the sad occasion of her death in 2001.

2. Hollywood pioneer Cecil B. DeMille, the son of an Episcopalian lay preacher, made millions selling sex and salvation simultaneously. DeMille's biblical epics included *The Ten Commandments* (twice), *The King of Kings, The Sign of the Cross,* and *The Crusades.* To his credit, he understood that a proper presentation of the Bible must include plenty of sin. Whether he did it for artistic, theological, or financial reasons remains debatable.

3. Geoffrey D. Black, *Hollywood Censored* (Cambridge: Cambridge University Press, 1994); and idem, *The Catholic Crusade against the Movies, 1940–1975* (Cambridge: Cambridge University Press, 1998) both stand out. Also recommended is Frank Walsh, *Sin and Censorship: The Catholic Church and the Motion Picture Industry* (New Haven: Yale University Press, 1996).

4. Herbert A. Jump, "The Religious Possibilities of the Motion Picture," quoted in Terry Lindvall, *The Silents of God: Selected Issues and Documents in Silent American Film and Religion, 1908–1925* (London: Scarecrow Press, 2001), 71.

5. Ibid.

6. K. S. Hover, "Motography as an Arm of the Church," in *Silents of God,* 48.

7. C. H. Jack Linn, "The Movies—The Devil's Incubator," in *Silents of God,* 273.

8. Richard Blake, *Afterimage: The Indelible Catholic Imagination of Six American Filmmakers* (Chicago: Loyola Press, 2000). See also Andrew Greeley, *The Catholic Imagination* (Berkeley: University of California Press, 2000).

9. For a detailed, biblical argument on behalf of R-rated films, read the appendix "Sex, Violence, and Profanity in the Bible" in Brian Godawa, *Hollywood Worldviews: Watching Films with Wisdom and Discernment* (Downers Grove, Ill.: InterVarsity, 2002).

10. Paul Schrader, "Transcendental Style in Film" (master's thesis, University of California, 1972).

11. Ibid., 10.

12. Ibid., 154–55.

13. Ibid., 164.

14. Robert Bresson, *Notes on the Cinematographer,* trans. Jonathan Griffin (New York: Quartet Books, 1986), quoted in program notes, Los Angeles County Museum of Art, "Retrospective on the Films of Robert Bresson."

15. Anthony Lane, *Nobody's Perfect* (New York: Knopf, 2002), 621.

16. "Retrospective on the Films of Robert Bresson."

17. F. X. Feeney, "Revival Pick," *Los Angeles Weekly,* 28 May–3 June 1999, 98.

18. Quoted in ibid., 98.

19. Roy Anker, "Deliver Us from Evil," *Books & Culture* 5, no. 4 (July/August 1999): 21.

20. Ibid., 20.

21. Quoted in Richard Natale, "A Preference for the Outside," *Los Angeles Times,* 2 December 1998, p. F7.

22. Ibid.

23. Martin Scorsese quoted Schrader on *Roger Ebert and the Movies,* Buena Vista Television, December 1999.

24. Quoted in Natale, "Preference for the Outside," F7.

25. F. X. Feeney, "In Vinterberg Veritas," *Los Angeles Weekly,* 23–29 October 1998, 51.

26. Shari Roman, *Digital Babylon: Hollywood, Indiewood, and Dogme 95* (Hollywood: IFilm Publishing, 2001), 90–91.

27. Quoted in Richard Combs and Raymond Durgnat, "Rules of the Game," *Film Comment* 36, no. 5 (September/October 2000): 28.

28. Quoted in Richard Kelly, *The Name of This Book Is Dogme 95* (London: Faber & Faber, 2000), 5–6.

29. Lars von Trier and Thomas Vinterberg, "The Vow of Chastity," *Los Angeles Weekly,* 23–29 October 1998, 51.

30. October Films, *The Celebration* online, www.octoberfilms.com/thecelebration/dogme.html.

31. Quoted in Stig Bjorkman, "Interview about 'Breaking the Waves,'" www.geocities.com/lars_von_trier2000.

32. Greeley, *Catholic Imagination,* 166.

33. Roman, *Digital Babylon,* 97–99.

34. Howard Hampton started his eulogy for Pauline Kael with this quotation in "Such Sweet Thunder," *Film Comment* 37, no. 6 (November/December 2001): 45.

35. William Goldman, *Adventures in the Screen Trade* (New York: Warner Books, 1983), 49–52.

36. Quoted in Richard Corliss, "Blair Witch Craft," *Time* 154, no. 7 (16 August 1999): 64.

37. Quoted in Patrick Goldstein, "The New New Wave," *Los Angeles Times Calendar,* 12 December 1999, 102.

38. Russian director Andrei Tarkovsky may be the most spiritual filmmaker of all time. His "Reflections on the Cinema," in *Sculpting in Time,* trans. Kitty Hunter-Blair (Austin: University of Texas Press, 1986) can be approached as almost devotional reading.

39. Jeff Gordiner, "1999: The Year That Changed Movies," *Entertainment Weekly,* 26 November 1999, cover.

40. Quoted in Goldstein, "The New New Wave," 102.

41. Gordiner, "1999," 39.

42. David Green, "The 'Fight Club' Debate: Just What Is the Message Here?" *Los Angeles Times,* 1 November 1999, p. F3.

43. For a broad introduction to the voluminous world of anime, chop-socky, and Asian cinema, see Jeff Yang, Dina Gan, Terry Hong, and the staff of *A. Magazine, Eastern Standard Time: A Guide to Asian Influence on American Culture from Astro Boy to Zen Buddhism* (Boston: Houghton Mifflin, 1997).

44. Lori L. Tharps, "Matrix Mania," *Entertainment Weekly,* May 1999, 41.

45. For a much more detailed examination of *The Matrix,* see Chris Seay and Greg Garrett, *The Gospel Reloaded: Exploring Spirituality and Faith in The Matrix* (Colorado Springs: Nav Press, 2003).

46. "Matrix Virtual Theatre: Wachowski Brothers Transcript," Warner Home Video, Canned Interactive, 6 November 1999, www.dvdwb.com/matrixevents/wachowski.html.

47. Quoted in Peter N. Chumo II, "American Beauty: An Interview with Alan Ball," *Creative Screenwriting* 7, no. 1 (January 2000): 33.

48. Ibid., 27.

49. Ibid., 35.

50. Quoted in Gavin Smith, "Inside Out—One-on-One with David Fincher," *Film Comment* 35, no. 5 (September/October 1999): 67.

51. Ibid., 58.

52. *Fight Club,* DVD, Twentieth Century Fox Home Entertainment, 1999.

53. Ibid.

54. Ibid.

55. Ibid.

56. Ibid.

57. Quoted in Neil Jurgensen, "The 'Fight Club' Debate: Just What Is the Message Here?" *Los Angeles Times,* 1 November 1999, p. F3.

58. Green, "'Fight Club' Debate," F3.

59. Tom Beaudoin, *Virtual Faith: The Irreverent Spiritual Quest of Generation X* (San Francisco: Jossey-Bass, 1998).

60. *Fight Club,* DVD.

61. Kent Jones, "White Noise II," *Film Comment* 36, no. 1 (January/February 2000): 38.

62. Mark Caro, "Abundance of Symbols in 'Magnolia' Has Filmgoers Looking for Clues," *Chicago Tribune,* 23 January 2000, sec. 7, p. 7.

63. Quoted in David Konow, "An Interview with Paul Thomas Anderson," *Creative Screenwriting* 7, no. 1 (January 2000): 48.

64. Quoted in Chuck Stephens, "Interview with Paul Thomas Anderson," in *Magnolia: The Shooting Script* (New York: Newmarket Press, 2000), 207.

65. Scott Timberg, "Catholic Block," *New Times Los Angeles,* 4 November 1999, 21.

66. Kevin Smith, "The Marvin Borowsky Lecture on Screenwriting" (lecture given to the Academy of Motion Picture Arts and Sciences, Beverly Hills, Calif., 7 December 2000).

67. Ibid.

68. Quoted in Timberg, "Catholic Block," 23.

69. ABC's Channel 7 *Eyewitness News,* Los Angeles, 9 November 1999.

70. Quoted in Kenneth Turan, "Having Faith in 'Dogma,'" *Los Angeles Times,* 22 May 1999, p. F1.

71. Smith, "Marvin Borowsky Lecture."

72. Quoted in John Brodie, "Mr. Smith Goes to Hell?" *GQ,* November 1999, 206.

73. Quoted in Teresa Watanabe, "Chasing Catholicism," *Los Angeles Times,* 10 November 1999, p. F1.

74. Quoted in Jeff Jensen, "Saving Grace," *Entertainment Weekly,* November 1999, 37.

75. Smith, "Marvin Borowsky Lecture."

76. John Anderson, "New Language of Film: Quick and Fast," *Los Angeles Times,* 30 June 1999, p. F8.

77. Ibid.

78. From Harry Knowles's liner notes to the DVD for *Requiem for a Dream,* Artisan Entertainment, 2000.

79. Gordiner, "1999," 40.

80. Quoted in ibid.

81. Combs and Durgnat, "Rules of the Game," 30.

82. Quoted in Goldstein, "New New Wave," 9.

Chapter 6

1. Quoted in Thomas Friedman, *The Lexus and the Olive Tree* (New York: Farrar, Straus, Giroux, 1999), 45.

2. Mitchell Stephens, *The Rise of the Image, the Fall of the Word* (New York: Oxford University Press, 1998).

3. Two books that detail Philo T. Farnsworth's brilliant discovery and the twisted battle over his technology are Daniel Stashower, *The Boy Genius and the Mogul* (New York: Broadway Books, 2002); and Evan I. Schwartz, *The Last Lone Inventor* (New York: HarperCollins, 2002).

4. Michael Winship, *Television* (New York: Random House, 1988), 6.

5. Cecilia Rasmussen, "'Father of Television' Suffered Travails Worthy of a Soap Opera," *Los Angeles Times,* 13 January 2002, p. B6.

6. Winship, *Television,* 8.

7. Rasmussen, "Father of Television," B6.

8. William D. Romanowski, *Pop Culture Wars: Religion and the Role of Entertainment in American Life* (Downers Grove, Ill.: InterVarsity, 1996), 188.

9. An oft-forgotten fourth competitor, the Du Mont Television Network, stopped broadcasting in 1955 (Winship, *Television,* 19).

10. Friedman, *Lexus and the Olive Tree,* 56.

11. Dominic Strinati, *An Introduction to Studying Popular Culture* (London: Routledge, 2000), 210.

12. James Roman, *Love, Light, and a Dream: Television's Past, Present, and Future* (Westport, Conn.: Praeger, 1996), 149–51.

13. Sallie Hofmeister, "Series Gold," *Los Angeles Times,* 16 January 1998, p. D1.

14. Walter Scott, "Personality Parade," *Parade Magazine,* 22 July 2001, 2.

15. Corie Brown, "TV Chiefs Yell 'Cut' on Costs," *Los Angeles Times,* 18 December 2001, p. A1.

16. Quoted in Anna Quindlen, "Watching the World Go By," *Newsweek,* 26 February 2001, 74.

17. Brian Lowry, "'Entertainment Tonight' and the Cult of Celebrity," *Los Angeles Times,* 7 March 2001, p. F1.

18. Roman, *Love, Light, and a Dream,* 230–31.

19. Stephens, *Rise of the Image,* 26.

20. Ibid., 203.

21. James Twitchell, *Lead Us into Temptation: The Triumph of American Materialism* (New York: Columbia University Press, 1999), 41–42.

22. Paddy Chayefsky wrote the screenplay. Peter Finch played Howard Beale. The quotation can be found in Walter T. Davis Jr., *Watching What We Watch* (Louisville: Geneva Press, 2001), xi.

23. Quoted in Marshall McLuhan, *Understanding Media: The Extensions of Man* (New York: McGraw-Hill, 1964), 269.

24. Steven D. Stark, *Glued to the Set: The Sixty Television Shows and Events That Made Us Who We Are Today* (New York: Free Press, 1997), 3.

25. Quoted in Winship, *Television,* 56.

26. Twitchell, *Lead Us into Temptation,* 102.

27. Ibid.

28. Ibid.

29. Quoted in Stark, *Glued to the Set,* 41.

30. "Copycat Tragedy," *Los Angeles Times,* 30 January 2001, p. F2.

31. "Murder Defendant, 13, Claims He Was Imitating Pro Wrestlers on TV," *Los Angeles Times,* 14 January 2001, p. A24.

32. Stark, *Glued to the Set,* 14.

33. Dorothy McFadden, "Television Comes to Our Children," *Parents Magazine,* January 1949.

34. Magazines such as *Better Homes and Gardens, House Beautiful, Saturday Review,* and *Ladies Home Journal* questioned *Howdy Doody.* Stark, *Glued to the Set,* 18.

35. Marie Winn, *The Plug-In Drug* (New York: Viking Press, 1977), 65.

36. Ibid.

37. Michael Craig Miller, "Does Violence in the Media Cause Violent Behavior?" *The Harvard Mental Health Letter* 18, no. 3 (September 2001): 6.

38. Both quoted in S. Robert Lichter, Linda S. Lichter, and Stanley Rothman, *Watching America* (New York: Prentice-Hall, 1991), 183.

39. One of the most helpful resources that illustrates the contradictory nature of the TV values debate is in the Opposing Viewpoints series. Byron L. Stay compiled a list of conflicting articles in *Mass Media: Opposing Viewpoints* (San Diego: Greenhaven Press, 1999). Stay places articles such as "Television Causes Societal Violence" right beside "Television Does Not Cause Societal Violence."

40. Quoted in Michael Schneider, "Viewers Shrug at TV Code," *Variety,* 26 December 2001.

41. Ibid.

42. Ibid.

43. *Parents Magazine's* scoring code rated the answers: "A) Liar, B) Big fat liar, and C) You may not be perfect but at least you're honest." Found in Daniel McGinn, "Guilt Free TV," *Newsweek,* 11 November 2002, 59.

44. Quoted in Twitchell, *Lead Us into Temptation,* 117.

45. Kevin Maynard, "They Pitch, and We Catch," *Los Angeles Times,* 17 November 2002, p. E29.

46. Christopher Stern, "B'Casters: We're Kidding," *Daily Variety,* 30 July 1996, 24.

47. Sallie Hofmeister, "Fox Eyes Saturday Morning Windfall," *Los Angeles Times,* 14 January 2002, p. C1.

48. Twitchell, *Lead Us into Temptation,* 11.

49. Jack Gould, "What Is Television Doing to Us?" *New York Times,* 12 June 1949.

50. Brian Lowry, "Changing Forces Are at Play in Land of New Behemoths," *Los Angeles Times,* 7 February 2001, p. F1.

51. Ken Auletta, *Three Blind Mice: How the TV Networks Lost Their Way* (New York: Random House, 1991).

52. Rob Owen, *Gen X TV* (New York: Syracuse University Press, 1997), 89.

53. Ibid., 90.

54. David Wild, *The Showrunners* (New York: HarperCollins, 1999), 262.

55. Robert D. Putnam, *Bowling Alone: The Collapse and Revival of American Community* (New York: Simon & Schuster, 2000), 223.

56. Ibid., 224.

57. Steve Mikulan, "Tinseltown Rebellion," *Los Angeles Weekly,* 27 April–3 May 2001, 29.

58. Jube Shiver Jr., "FCC Lifts Ban on Big TV Network Ownership of Smaller Rival," *Los Angeles Times,* 20 April 2001, p. C3.

59. Johnnie L. Roberts, "Cradle to Grave TV," *Newsweek,* 19 March 2001, 40–41.

60. Brian Lowry, "The New Instant Replay," *Los Angeles Times,* 24 April 2002, p. F1.

61. Ibid., F10.

62. McGinn, "Guilt Free TV," 58.

63. Ed Shane, *Disconnected America: The Consequences of Mass Media in a Narcissistic World* (Armonk, N.Y.: M. E. Sharpe, 2001), 163.

64. Quoted in Stark, *Glued to the Set,* 235.

65. Neal Gabler, *Life the Movie: How Entertainment Conquered Reality* (New York: Knopf, 1998), 101.

66. Stephens, *Rise of the Image,* 143.

67. Quoted in Steve Johnson, "Rather Defends Remark after Stem Cell Segment," *Los Angeles Times,* 14 August 2001, p. F7.

68. Gabler, *Life the Movie,* 88.

69. Elizabeth Jensen, "News Still Counts at CNN; So Do Stars," *Los Angeles Times Calendar,* 3 February 2002, 3.

70. Stark, *Glued to the Set,* 232.

71. Ann Woolner, "Big Man Out," *Brill's Content* 3, no. 9 (November 2000): 125.

72. Quoted in Stark, *Glued to the Set,* 250.

73. Quoted in David Bauder, "Face It: Sex Sells TV News Too," *Los Angeles Times,* 11 February 2002, p. F11.

74. Putnam, *Bowling Alone,* 221.

75. Quoted in Diane Werts, "The Small Screen Gets Busy," *Los Angeles Times,* 27 August 2001, p. F10.

76. Ibid.

77. Putnam, *Bowling Alone,* 240.

78. Ibid., 240–41.

79. Ibid., 224.

80. Ibid., 222.

81. Laurence J. Peter, *Peter's Quotations: Ideas for Our Time* (New York: Bantam Books, 1977), 329.

82. Putnam, *Bowling Alone,* 226.

83. Quoted in Stark, *Glued to the Set,* 41.

84. Quoted in Quentin J. Schulze, *Redeeming Television* (Downers Grove, Ill.: InterVarsity, 1992), 154.

85. Stark, *Glued to the Set,* 259.

86. Mark Lasswell and Ed Weiner, "Getting Religion," *TV Guide,* 29 March 1997, 32.

87. Ibid.

88. Greg Braxton, "Closing the Files," *Los Angeles Times,* 17 May 2002, p. F1.

89. Examples range from James Van Hise's *Lost in Space: 25th Anniversary Tribute Book* (Las Vegas: Pioneer Books, 1990), which chronicles all eighty-three episodes of the series in grievous detail, to Robert Weisbrot's *Xena, Warrior Princess: The Official Guide to the Xenaverse* (New York: Doubleday, 1998).

90. Stark, *Glued to the Set,* 41.

91. Jack Miles, "Prime Time's Search for God," *TV Guide,* 29 March 1997, 25.

92. Quoted in Lasswell and Weiner, "Getting Religion," 30.

93. Quoted in ibid., 32.

94. Charles B. Slocum, "The Gospel according to Primetime," *Writer's Guild of America West—Written By* (December 2001/January 2002): 26–30.

95. For a highly detailed analysis, see Chris Seay, *The Gospel according to Tony Soprano* (Lake Mary, Fla.: Relevant Books, 2002).

96. Slocum, "Gospel according to Primetime," 30.

97. Quoted in Lasswell and Weiner, "Getting Religion," 30.

98. Mark Pinsky, *The Gospel according to the Simpsons: The Spiritual Life of the World's Most Animated Family* (Louisville: Westminster John Knox, 2001), 42.

99. Ibid., 8.

100. Quoted in Rick Sherwood, "Q & A with Martha Williamson," *Hollywood Reporter,* 13 November 1998, p. S9.

101. Ibid.

102. Quoted in Rick Sherwood, "Winging It," *Hollywood Reporter,* 13 November 1998, p. S1.

103. Sherwood, "Q & A," 59.

104. Bill McKibben, *The Age of Missing Information* (New York: Random House, 1992).

105. Shane, *Disconnected America,* 146–47.

106. Quoted in Wild, *The Showrunners,* 55.

107. Quoted in Winship, *Television,* 62.

108. Quoted in Wild, *Showrunners,* 124.

109. Ibid., 119.

110. Ibid., 5.

111. Quoted in Lynne Tuohy, "Justice for All, Especially Ages 25–54," *Los Angeles Times,* 3 August 2001, p. F27.

112. Ibid.

113. Ibid.

114. Quoted in Marc Peyser, "'Real World' After All," *Newsweek,* 2 July 2001, 54.

115. Brian Lowry, "Watching the Cash Flow," *Los Angeles Times Calendar,* 22 November 1998, 9.

116. Quoted in Lynn Hirschberg, "The Stunt Man," *New York Times Magazine,* 16 September 2001, 46.

117. Norah Vincent, "'Kidnapped' by Drivel, We Invite World Hatred," *Los Angeles Times,* 7 February 2002, p. B17.

118. Quoted in Jamie Malanowski, "Forget Voting Them Off the Island. They're Just Shot," *New York Times,* 25 February 2001, p. AR38.

119. Charlene C. Giannetti and Margaret Sagarese, "Why You Shouldn't Let Your Children Watch 'Survivor,'" *Los Angeles Times,* 12 February 2001, p. F3.

120. Paul Brownfield, "You Might've Heard of Them," *Los Angeles Times,* 5 January 2003, p. E36.

121. Ibid.

122. Quoted in Peyser, "Real World," 54.

123. Quindlen, "Watching the World Go By," 74.

124. Marcia Z. Nelson, "Oprah on a Mission," *The Christian Century,* 25 September–8 October 2002, 21.

125. Mimi Avins, "Charmed Silly," *Los Angeles Times,* 27 April 2002, p. F1.

126. Louise Roug and Brian Lowry, "Dating Fame Games," *Los Angeles Times*, 18 August 2002, calendar 10.

127. McLuhan, *Understanding Media,* 24.

128. Ibid., 272.

129. Neil Postman, *Amusing Ourselves to Death: Public Discourse in the Age of Show Business* (New York: Penguin Books, 1985), 27.

130. Stephens, *Rise of the Image,* 64.

131. Ibid., 224.

Chapter 7

1. Rebecca Arnold, *Fashion, Desire, and Anxiety* (London: I. B. Tauris Publishers, 2001), 125.

2. Tom Beaudoin, *Virtual Faith: The Irreverent Spiritual Quest of Generation X* (San Francisco: Jossey-Bass, 1998), 43.

3. Ibid.

4. Designers are increasingly aware of the tendency of the buying public to purchase fashion items and create their own "look." One of the trends among designers, therefore, is to offer separate pieces with any number of permutations rather than an item that can be worn only a certain way with certain other items.

5. Dominique Paulve and Marie Boye, *In Fashion* (London: Cassell & Co., 2001), 1–25.

6. Ibid.

7. Ibid., 4–5.

8. Richard Stivers, *The Culture of Cynicism: American Morality in Decline* (Oxford: Blackwell, 1994), x.

9. James Twitchell, *Living It Up: Our Love Affair with Luxury* (New York: Columbia University Press, 2002), 1.

10. Ibid., 6.

11. "Two's Company: The John Walsh Interview," *Independent Newspaper Review,* London edition, 3 June 2002, 4–5. Some might argue that this kind of retreat from mainstream culture is the optimum way to deal with the current times. Our missional task, however, is to be in the world, attempting to engage it in a dialogue about its values, ethics, and choices in light of the gospel.

12. Twitchell, *Living It Up,* 9.

13. Ibid., xv.

14. Arnold, *Fashion, Desire, and Anxiety,* 1.

15. Mica Nava, *Changing Cultures: Feminism, Youth, and Consumerism* (London: Sage Publishing, 1992), 167.

16. Arnold, *Fashion, Desire, and Anxiety,* 13.

17. Beaudoin, *Virtual Faith,* 102–3.

18. Ibid., 102.

19. Greil Marcus, *Lipstick Traces: A Secret History of the Twentieth Century* (Cambridge: Harvard University Press, 1989), 175–76, 383–84.

20. Ibid., 50.

21. Beaudoin, *Virtual Faith,* 103–4.

22. Elizabeth Kaye, "Note Culture," *Los Angeles Magazine,* April 2002, 42.

23. Jean-François Lyotard, *The Postmodern Condition: A Report on Knowledge,* trans. Geoff Bennington and Brian Massumi (Minneapolis: University of Minnesota Press, 1984).

24. Josh Sims, "Memory," *I-D Magazine, U.K.,* the Memory Issue 2000, 110–12.

25. Another issue, related more to the fashion industry itself, is also presented in this "retro-fascination." Angela McRobbie writes in *In the Culture Society: Art, Fashion, and Popular Music* (London: Routledge, 1999), 13–14, that fashion has a dislocated nature at present. While other areas of the arts are seeing walls of division between high and low culture torn down, fashion still functions

very much with a high-culture sense of itself. It is, according to McRobbie, continually seeking to effect a "reconsolidation of the boundaries between high and low with fashion recognized in its rightful place in the cultural hierarchy" (13). With the retirement of Yves St. Laurent, we now see a unique moment for fashion as its connection to those old categories of self-understanding and definition are cut. Retro and its influence on the new generation of fashion designers, such as Alexander McQueen, John Galliano, Tom Ford, and others, offer fashion its moment to tear down the remaining elements of the walls of division between high and low within its genre.

26. Beaudoin, *Virtual Faith,* 100–102.

27. Sims, "Memory," 112.

28. Beaudoin, *Virtual Faith,* 77.

29. Monah Li, "The Making of a Designer," *Los Angeles Weekly,* 4–10 April 2003, 40.

30. *FHM Magazine* (autumn/winter 2001): 164.

31. Cobbett Steinberg, *Reel Facts: The Movie Book of Records* (London: Penguin, 1981), 550.

32. *Room at the Top,* Rank Films, U.K., 1958.

33. McRobbie, *Culture Society,* 50.

34. Ibid., 51.

35. See ibid. for some thoughtful and provocative thoughts in this regard.

36. Christine Gudorf, *Body, Sex, and Pleasure* (Cleveland: Pilgrim Press, 1994), 2.

37. *New York Times Magazine,* 6 December 2000.

38. Lynne Luciano, *Looking Good: Male Body Image in America* (New York: Hill & Wang, 2001), 4.

39. Ibid.

40. Rowan Pelling, "This the Life," *The Independent,* 28 December 2001, p. 4.

41. Elaine Showalter, "Sexual Anarchy, Gender, and Culture in the Fin de Siècle of 1992," quoted in Arnold, *Fashion, Desire, and Anxiety,* 99.

42. Arnold, *Fashion, Desire, and Anxiety,* 122.

43. Beaudoin, *Virtual Faith,* 139.

44. Quoted in Arnold, *Fashion, Desire, and Anxiety,* 122.

45. Beaudoin, *Virtual Faith,* 139.

46. Elizabeth Kaye, "California Zen," *Los Angeles Magazine,* April 2002.

47. Quite a few interior design books focus on interior design and spirituality. For instance, Laura Cerwinske, *Spiritual Style: The Home as Sanctuary* (New York: Thames & Hudson, 1988).

48. *Marie Claire Maison* (February–March 2002): 50.

49. Kelly Klein, *Cross* (New York: Callaway, 2000), i.

50. Quoted in Susan Sherwood, "Because Celebrity," *Harpers & Queens,* April 2002, 152.

51. Ibid.

52. Quoted in Ruth La Ferla, "Religious, Rebellious, or Chic, Crosses Are Forever," *New York Times Magazine,* 20 August 2001, cover story.

53. Sherwood, "Because Celebrity," 51.

54. Clare Coulson, "Holy Muses," *Harpers & Queens,* April 2002, 51ff.

55. Ibid.

56. Ibid.

57. Ibid.

58. Elvis Costello, "All This Useless Beauty," Sideways Songs, U.K., 1992.

59. On a more troubling note, Italian jewelry designer Carlos de Souza designed a collection of jewelry inspired by the cross of Charlemagne (famous as the crusading Holy Roman Emperor). Displaying an element of insensitivity toward those who would view themselves as victims of previous religious wars, he describes the crosses as "good luck tokens for crusaders of the twenty-first century in our daily battles" (Coulson, "Holy Muses," 52). While I echo his sentiment that twenty-first-century life often feels like a daily battle, his choice of words could not be more insensitive in these delicate times.

60. Beaudoin, *Virtual Faith,* 101.

Chapter 8

1. Robert E. Webber has done a fabulous job of outlining the changes in worship initiated by *The Younger Evangelicals* (Grand Rapids: Baker, 2002).

2. From Charles S. Prebish, "Heavenly Father, Divine Goalie: Sport and Religion," in *Sport and Religion,* ed. Shirl J. Hoffman (Champaign, Ill.: Human Kinetics Books, 1992), 47. Hoffman's book serves as an excellent overview of the tension between sports and religion, using primary sources from prior debates about sport as religion, sport as religious experience, religion's influence on sports, and the ethical dilemmas encountered by athletes.

3. *Bull Durham* was written and directed by Ron Shelton, a former minor league baseball player who graduated from Westmont College, a private Christian college in Santa Barbara, California.

4. Harry Edwards, *Sociology of Sport* (Homewood, Ill.: Dorsey Press, 1973), 261–62.

5. James A. Mathisen, "From Civil Religion to Folk Religion: The Case of American Sport," in *Sport and Religion*, 17–33.

6. Some of the most memorable sports moments are collected in book and CD form in Joe Garner, *And the Fans Roared* (Naperville, Ill.: Sourcebooks, 2000).

7. Barbara Ehrenreich, "Where the Wild Things Are," *Civilization* (June/July 2000): 84–86.

8. Brian D. Ellison, "This Is My Bratwurst, Broken for Thee," *re:generation quarterly* 7, no. 3 (fall 2001): 18.

9. Michael Novak, "The Natural Religion," in *Sport and Religion*, 36.

10. Quoted in Mike Penner, "Test of Time," *Los Angeles Times*, 29 May 2002, p. S1–8.

11. Ellison, "This Is My Bratwurst," 19.

12. The most thorough survey of the connection between conservative Christianity and American sports is Tony Ladd and James A. Mathiesen, *Muscular Christianity* (Grand Rapids: Baker, 1999).

13. Randall Balmer, "Is God a Rams Fan?" *Sojourners* (January/February 2001): 21.

14. Quoted in Larry Steward, "The Hot Corner," *Los Angeles Times*, 4 January 2001, p. D2.

15. In 2001, the Dallas Cowboys were named the top sports franchise "brand," worth $274.3 million. The Washington Redskins, New York Yankees, and New York Knicks trailed. Interestingly, three of the top ten teams were European soccer teams—the Manchester United, Real Madrid, and Bayern Munich ("Cream of the Crop," *Los Angeles Times*, 8 February 2001, p. D5).

16. James Roman points out that in 1994, when ABC and ESPN broadcast the first World Cup held on American soil, they superimposed sponsors' logos on a clock occupying the upper left-hand corner of the screen (*Love, Light, and a Dream: Television's Past, Present, and Future* [Westport, Conn.: Praeger, 1996], 132).

17. Larry Stewart, "PGA Agrees to $850-Million Television Deal," *Los Angeles Times*, 17 July 2001, p. D3.

18. Steve Rushin, "Downhill from Here," *Sports Illustrated*, 26 February 2001, 19.

19. Quoted in David Wharton, "Common Touch," *Los Angeles Times*, 6 May 2002, p. D1.

20. Novak, "Natural Religion," 38.

21. Ibid., 37.

22. Rick Reilly, "Corpo-Name Disease: Stop the Plague!" *Sports Illustrated*, 15 January 2001, 80.

23. Ralph Frammolino, "The Heisman Trophy Adds a New Name: Suzuki," *Los Angeles Times*, 14 September 2002, p. C1.

24. Quoted in Houston Mitchell, "Morning Briefing," *Los Angeles Times*, 6 December 2001, p. D2.

25. Steve Henson, "Labor Daze," *Los Angeles Times*, 12 July 2001, p. D1.

26. Mike Dodd, "Selig, Owners behind Eight Ball," *USA Today*, 23 November 2001, p. 3C.

27. Quoted in Ross Newhan, "Selig Says Fail-Safe Point Approaching," *Los Angeles Times*, 17 May 2002, p. D1.

28. "Devil Rays: Best Team That Money Can't Buy," *Los Angeles Times*, 10 April 2003, p. D2.

29. "Million Dollar Madness," *Los Angeles Times*, 17 December 2000, p. D1.

30. Paul Lukas, "Cut the Corporate Clutter," *Civilization* (June/July 2000): 83.

31. Mike Hiserman, "Baseball Sees a World of Possibilities," *Los Angeles Times*, 23 October 2002, p. C1.

32. *Los Angeles Times*, 27 August 2001, p. D7.

33. Jerry Hirsch, "Easton Bats Are Big Hits," *Los Angeles Times*, 27 May 2002, p. C6.

34. These classic quotations were cited in opposition by Mike Boehm, "Adults and Little League: Fodder for a Playwright," *Los Angeles Times*, 4 January 2003, p. E1.

35. David Wharton, "Turbulence in the Air," *Los Angeles Times*, 5 May 2002, p. D1.

36. Mark Starr, "Should Football Drop-Kick Parity?" *Newsweek*, 10 September 2001, 56.

37. Leigh Steinberg, "Seven Ways to Save Sports," *Civilization* (June/July 2000): 77.

38. Diane Seo, "Advertisers Wary of Pricey TV Deals for 'ER,' NFL," *Los Angeles Times*, 16 January 1998, p. D1.

39. "Primetime's Most Lucrative," *Hollywood Reporter*, May 1999.

40. Brian Lowry, "The Big Coin Toss," *Los Angeles Times*, 30 January 2002, p. F1.

41. "Incentive," *Los Angeles Times,* 3 August 2001, p. D2.

42. Quoted in Mike Penner, "Week 12 Breakdown," *Los Angeles Times,* 2 December 2001, p. D13.

43. Larry Stewart, "No Super TV Ratings," *Los Angeles Times,* 5 February 2002, p. D6.

44. Quoted in Ralph Wiley, "Saviors," in *The Gospel according to ESPN,* ed. Jay Lovinger (New York: Hyperion, 2002), 187.

45. Thomas Friedman, *The Lexus and the Olive Tree* (New York: Farrar, Straus, Giroux, 1999), 252.

46. Ibid., 248.

47. Ibid., 253.

48. Kristen Walbolt, "Around the Globe in the NBA," *Los Angeles Times,* 17 November 2002, p. D13.

49. Quoted in "Quotebook," *Los Angeles Times,* 15 February 2001, p. D2.

50. A strange by-product of NBA star status is the requisite rap album. Shaquille O'Neal was the first to make the connection. His manager, Leonard Goldberg, deserves profound credit for crafting an acting career from a 7-foot, 300-pound center. Shaq also added clothing entrepreneur and record label to his coffers. But Shaq Diesel opened floodgates for rappers and dribblers such as Kobe Bryant and Allen Iverson. While none of the NBA superstars has proven a threat to Snoop Dogg or the Notorious B.I.G., the connections between music sales and NBA attendance cannot be underestimated.

51. "Jordan Leaves 'Em Laughing in Toronto," *Los Angeles Times,* 31 October 2002, p. D8.

52. "Injury Sidelines Jordan," *Los Angeles Times,* 4 December 2001, p. D7.

53. Quoted in Mark Heister, "Who's Next?" *Los Angeles Times,* 2 March 2003, p. D12.

54. *Sports Illustrated,* 12 March 2001.

55. David Wharton, "A New Ice Age?" *Los Angeles Times,* 7 March 2001, p. D1.

56. Quoted in Helene Elliott, "Q & A with Gary Bettman," *Los Angeles Times,* 1 February 2002, p. D10.

57. J. Michael Kennedy, "Row, Row, Row—and That's Just the Start," *Los Angeles Times,* 27 November 2000, p. E1.

58. Robert D. Putnam, *Bowling Alone: The Collapse and Revival of American Community* (New York: Simon & Schuster, 2000).

59. Steve Lopez, "Too Many Kids Are Pigging, Pooping Out," *Los Angeles Times,* 2 December 2001, p. B1.

60. Statistic attributed to Anne Flannery, executive director of P.E.4Life, in "To Fight Kids' Obesity Texas Returns to Gym," *Los Angeles Times,* 23 March 2002, p. A17.

61. "31% of U.S. Adults and 15% of Youth Are Obese, Survey Finds," *Los Angeles Times,* 9 October 2002, p. A24.

62. Putnam, *Bowling Alone,* 115.

63. Christopher Lasch, *The Culture of Narcissism: American Life in an Age of Diminishing Expectations* (New York: Warner Books, 1979), 185.

64. Robert K. Johnston, *The Christian at Play* (Grand Rapids: Eerdmans, 1983).

65. Ibid., 111.

66. Ehrenreich, "Where the Wild Things Are," 84–86.

67. Olga Connolly, "Kids' Bodies, Talents Wither on the Vine," *Los Angeles Times,* 10 July 2001, p. B11.

68. Flannery, "To Fight Kids' Obesity," A17.

69. Kevin Sack, "Cash Crunch Imperils High School Football," *New York Times,* 27 February 2001, p. A10.

70. Susannah Meadows, "Meet the Gamma Girls," *Newsweek,* 3 June 2002, 47.

71. Quoted in Joe Donnelly, "Father of the Now," *New Times Los Angeles* 7, no. 37 (12–18 September 2002): 16.

72. Alan Abrahamson, "A New Set of Ground Rules," *Los Angeles Times,* 19 November 2002, p. D5.

73. Quoted in David Wharton, "Generation Gap," *Los Angeles Times,* 7 May 2002, p. D1.

74. Ibid.

75. Michael Brooke, *The Concrete Wave: The History of Skateboarding* (Toronto: Warwick Publishing, 1999), 46–47.

76. Dan Koeppel, *Extreme Sports Almanac* (Los Angeles: Lowell House, 1998), 8–9.

77. Shav Glick, "Crossover Appeal," *Los Angeles Times,* 1 February 2002, p. D5.

78. Quoted in Brooke, *The Concrete Wave,* 106.

79. Kennedy, "Row, Row, Row," E4.

80. Ibid.

81. Greg Johnson, "IMG's Going to Extremes for New-Wave Sports Fans," *Los Angeles Times,* 1 August 2001, p. C1.

82. Martin Miller, "Buzzword X-Plosion," *Los Angeles Times,* 2 July 2001, p. E1.

83. Quoted in Johnson, "IMG's Going to Extremes," C1.

84. Rachel Newsome, "Why Class Is Now Defined by 'Cool,'" *Times of London,* 28 October 2002, p. 12.

85. Ibid.

86. Quoted in Albert Kim and Mark Mravic, "Spotcheck: The IOC's 'Celebrate Humanity' Campaign," *Sports Illustrated,* 30 July 2001, 28.

87. Greg Johnson, "Olympics Scrambles to Bridge Generation Gap," *Los Angeles Times,* 27 January 2002, p. A1.

88. Devin Gordon and T. Trent Gegax, "Dudes and Dinner Rolls," *Newsweek,* 25 February 2002, 48–49.

89. Abrahamson, "New Set of Ground Rules," D1.

90. Quoted in Miller, "Buzzword X-Plosion," E8.

91. Ibid.

92. Ibid.

93. Ibid., E1.

94. Ibid., E8.

95. Ibid.

96. Johan Huizinga argued in *Homo Ludens: A Study of the Play Element in Culture* (Boston: Beacon Hill, 1955) that throughout history "play" has been eradicated from work, law, and religion. Eliminating play's accompanying elements of risk, daring, and uncertainty not only robs citizens of joy but also saps society of innovation and creativity. Let the kids kiss concrete for the sake of their souls—and our future.

97. Ladd and Mathiesen, *Muscular Christianity,* 71.

98. Curtis Krueger, "Radical Move Man," *St. Petersburg Times,* 12 January 2003, online.

99. Ibid.

Chapter 9

1. A major Warhol retrospective drew record crowds in 2002 both at the Tate Modern in London and the Museum of Contemporary Art in L.A., a testament to his enduring drawing power and legacy. In 2002, Picasso had yet another retrospective, this time in conjunction with Henri Matisse, again on display to huge crowds in London.

2. The U.K. art and culture writer Matthew Collings also cites these three artists as a triumvirate of influence in twentieth-century art in *Art Crazy Nation* (Cambridge, U.K.: 21 Publishing, 2001). His reasons are slightly different and much more objective than mine. My inclusion of Pollock came about only after viewing the film *Pollock,* in which actor Ed Harris highlighted, at least for me, the very "Americanness" of Pollock in both the way he presented Pollock on screen as well as in the attitudes portrayed by Harris as he developed the artist's character. Warhol and Picasso were no-brainers. I was tempted to include Julian Schnabel and Jean-Michel Basquiat, but I realized it was because I like them and perhaps give too much influence to their work based on my own preferences and taste.

3. Pollock may be less well known to most but nevertheless is on the public's horizon, particularly since Marcia Gay Harden received an Oscar for her portrayal of Jackson Pollock's wife in the film *Pollock,* released in 2000. He was also featured in a series of Gap khaki ads of great Americans who made khaki pants a fashion must-have in the mid-twentieth century.

4. I use the term *rejected* rather loosely. Picasso's finished products appeared to be a rejection of traditional approaches when in fact they may be seen as a "building upon." He was known for making many copies of his works in more familiar fine art forms and structures, playing with the boundaries until he broke through to something new and different. Perhaps we should say that he, like many others, stood on the shoulders of the giants who went before. Kenneth Clarke the art historian noted that one of the criteria for naming a particular work of art a masterpiece was that it was "many persons thick," meaning that the particular artist had communed with, combined, and mined the talents of his elders and peers. While an artist's work may appear to be unique and highly personal, the unique style is born from an embrace of the artistic community.

5. This is a rather harsh thing to say, and in reality, I find great beauty in much of Picasso's work. My point is that he twisted and manipulated existing ideas, shapes, and forms to fashion a new beauty, a beauty that to some is rather unsightly and troubling to view.

6. Jane Daggett Dillenberger, *The Religious Art of Andy Warhol* (New York: Continuum, 1998) is a great look at this much missed aspect of his life.

7. A good read in this area is a book of interviews conducted with Damien Hirst over the last few years and compiled in *Off to Work* (London: St. Martin's Press, 2001).

8. Quoted in Matthew Collings, *This Is Modern Art* (New York: Watson-Guptill Publications, 2000), 84.

9. The movie was directed by the painter Julian Schnabel, a friend of Basquiat.

10. Taka Kawachi, ed., *King for a Decade: Jean-Michel Basquiat* (Tokyo: Korinsha Press, 1997), 14.

11. Jean-Michel Basquiat, *Basquiat* (Milan: Edizioni Charta, 1999), 126.

12. Not in the classic meaning of that invisible yet intricate part of our beings but as in soul music—that which appeals to the emotions, the very belly of who we are as human beings.

13. Quoted in Kawachi, *King for a Decade*, 111.

14. Basquiat's heroin addiction, however, may ultimately point to some deeper levels of pain at work.

15. Quoted in James Elkins, *Pictures and Tears* (London: Routledge, 2002), 54.

16. David Hockney, *Secret Knowledge* (London: Thames & Hudson, 2001).

17. Julia Blackburn, *Old Man Goya* (New York: Pantheon Books, 2002), a biography of the artist, is enlightening in this area.

18. Quoted in Amy Scholer, ed., *In the Shadow of the American Dream: The Diaries of David Wojnarowicz* (New York: Grove Press, 1999), 235.

19. Tom Beaudoin, *Virtual Faith: The Irreverent Spiritual Quest of Generation X* (San Francisco: Jossey-Bass, 1998), 96–97.

20. Ibid.

21. Paul Cobley and Litza Jansz, *Introducing Semiotics* (New York: Totem Books, 1998), 3–6.

22. Ferdinand de Saussure, *Course in General Linguistics,* trans. R. Harris (London: Duckworth Press, 1983).

23. Will Self, *Face,* online.

24. Collings, *This Is Modern Art,* 219–20.

25. Waldemar Januszczak, "Guess Who's Coming to Dinner?" *Sunday Times Culture Magazine,* 20 April 2003, 4.

26. Howard Finster, *Howard Finster: Stranger from Another World* (New York: Abbeville Press, 1989), 123.

27. Takashi Murakami, *Superflat* (Tokyo: Madra Publishing, 2001).

28. Beaudoin, *Virtual Faith,* 4.

29. John Drane, *The McDonaldization of the Church* (London: Darton, Longman, & Todd, 2000), 155.

30. Walter Brueggemann, *Finally Comes the Poet* (Minneapolis: Fortress, 1989).

Conclusion

1. We can already hear the cries of protest! We acknowledge that this is a huge generalization and that great efforts have been made to reclaim the arts since the Reformation. But we still insist that Reformed theology is intrinsically ill-equipped to confront a largely visual culture, drawn to symbolism and imagery and not as rationally focused as the modern age.

2. The outline of these ideas comes from frequent and ongoing discussions with many involved in rethinking theology and missiology. We're indebted to John Drane and John Smith, who, while operating from very different paradigms, have modeled ways of engaging both culture and theology. We resist using the term *postmodern* theology, because the current social climate has moved beyond the implications of a word like *postmodern*. We direct readers' attention to Frederic W. Baue, *The Spiritual Society: What Lurks beyond Postmodernism?* (Wheaton: Crossway Books, 2002).

3. Carla Freccero, *Popular Culture: An Introduction* (New York: New York University Press, 1999), 13.

4. Ibid., 14.

5. John Fiske, "Cultural Studies and the Culture of Everyday Life," in *Cultural Studies,* ed. Lawrence Grossberg, Cary Nelson, and Paula Treichler (London: Routledge, 1992), 154ff.

6. Michel de Certeau, Luce Giard, and Pierre Mayol, *The Practice of Everyday Life,* trans. Timothy J. Tomasik (Minneapolis: University of Minneapolis Press, 1998), 3.

7. George Ritzer, *The McDonaldization of Society* (Thousand Oaks, Calif.: Pine Forge Press, 1996).

8. Kenneth Clark, *What Is a Masterpiece?* (London: Thames & Hudson, 1979), 9.

9. Rebecca S. Chopp, quoted in Diarmuid O'Murchu, *Quantum Theology* (New York: Crossroads, 1999), 7.

10. Found in Leonard Sweet, *Quantum Spirituality* (Dayton: Whaleprint Press, 1991), 21.

11. Andrew M. Greeley, *God in Popular Culture* (Chicago: Thomas More Press, 1988), 15.

12. Ibid., 17.

13. Tom Beaudoin, *Virtual Faith: The Irreverent Spiritual Quest of Generation X* (San Francisco: Jossey-Bass, 1998), 34.

14. Ibid., 32.

15. Richard Mouw, *Consulting the Faithful: What Christian Intellectuals Can Learn from Popular Religion* (Grand Rapids: Eerdmans, 1994), 28.

16. Kenneth L. Woodward, "The Changing Face of the Church," *Newsweek,* 16 April 2001, 49.

17. Quoted in Toby Lester, "Oh, Gods!" *Atlantic Monthly* 289, no. 2 (February 2002): 44.

18. Woodward, "Changing Face of the Church," 49.

19. Quoted in ibid.

20. Quoted in Lester, "Oh, Gods!" 45.

21. Quoted in ibid.

22. Beaudoin, *Virtual Faith,* 74.

23. Quoted in Tony Jones, *Postmodern Youth Ministry* (Grand Rapids: Zondervan, 2001), 91.

24. Neal Gabler, *Life the Movie: How Entertainment Conquered Reality* (New York: Knopf, 1998), 24.

25. The Pocket Canons (Edinburgh: Canongate Press, 1998).

26. Robin Griffith-Jones, *The Four Witnesses: The Rebel, the Rabbi, the Chronicler, and the Mystic* (San Francisco: HarperCollins, 2000).

27. Quoted in Gregg Easterbrook, "The New Convergence," *Wired,* December 2002, 163.

28. Quoted in ibid., 169.

29. Ibid.

30. Ibid.

31. Ibid.

32. Stanley J. Grenz, *A Primer on Postmodernism* (Grand Rapids: Eerdmans, 1996), 31.

33. Dan Kimball, quoted in Jones, *Postmodern Youth Ministry,* 92.

34. Jones, *Postmodern Youth Ministry,* 97.

35. Quoted in Jones, *Postmodern Youth Ministry,* 203.

36. Alister McGrath, *What Was God Doing on the Cross?* (Eugene, Ore.: Wipf & Stock, 1999), 92.

37. Father Andrew Greeley offers a particularly passionate argument for reclaiming the Songs in "Sacred Desire," in *The Catholic Imagination* (Berkeley: University of California Press, 2000).

38. Quoted in Madison Shockley, "Seeing Sex Education as a Sacred Duty," *Los Angeles Times,* 6 July 2001, p. B15.

39. Ibid.

40. Quoted in Paula Rinehart, "Losing Our Promiscuity," *Christianity Today,* 10 July 2000, 38.

41. Beaudoin, *Virtual Faith,* 78–79.

42. Tim Rutten, "African Americans at the Top: Where Is Coverage and Context?" *Los Angeles Times,* 4 January 2003, p. E4.

43. Quoted in "Where the 21st Century Meets the Middle Ages," *Los Angeles Times,* 6 April 2003, p. E3.

44. Ralph Wiley, "Saviors," in *The Gospel according to ESPN,* ed. Jay Lovinger (New York: Hyperion Books, 2002), 201.

45. For a much broader survey of the tension between art and the church, refer to an earlier volume in the Engaging Culture series: William A. Dyrness, *Visual Faith* (Grand Rapids: Baker, 2001).

46. Paul Schrader, "The Marvin Borowsky Lecture on Screenwriting" (lecture given to the Academy of Motion Picture Arts and Sciences, Beverly Hills, Calif., 29 November 2001).

47. Quoted in Hilary Brand, "A Conversation with Sister Wendy Beckett," *Image: A Journal of the Arts and Religion* 27 (summer 2000): 48.

48. Margaret Miles, *Image as Insight* (Boston: Beacon Press, 1985), 150.

49. Brand, "Conversation with Sister Wendy Beckett," 47.

50. Ibid., 52.

51. Neil MacGregor, *The Image of Christ* (London: National Gallery, 2000), 7.

52. John Drury, *Painting the Word: Christian Pictures and Their Meanings* (New Haven: Yale University Press, 1999).

53. McGrath, *What Was God Doing on the Cross?* 44.

54. Ibid., 48.

55. Ibid., 107.

56. Quoted in "Resurrection Faith: An Interview with N. T. Wright," *The Christian Century,* 18–31 December 2002, 31.

57. For a more complete historical picture, see R. Laurence Moore, *Selling God: American Religion*

in the Marketplace of Culture (New York: Oxford University Press, 1994).

58. J. Richard Middleton and Brian J. Walsh, *Truth Is Stranger Than It Used to Be: Biblical Faith in a Postmodern Age* (Downers Grove, Ill.: InterVarsity, 1995), 43.

59. Sara Solovitch, "Lights, Camera, Religion," *Wired* 10, no. 5 (May 2002): 46.

60. Jones, *Postmodern Youth Ministry,* 90.

61. Jerome Murphy-O'Connor, *Scripture from Scratch*, quoted in a church bulletin, St. Monica's Catholic Church, Easter 2002.

62. McGrath, *What Was God Doing on the Cross?* 117.

63. Laurence J. Peter, *Peter's Quotations: Ideas for Our Time* (New York: Bantam Books, 1977), 439.

64. Patrick Henry, *The Ironic Christian's Companion* (New York: Riverhead, 1999), 1–2.

65. Gregory Wolfe, "Editorial Statement: In Defense of Irony," *Image: A Journal of the Arts and Religion* 25 (winter 1999–2000): 3–4.

66. Quoted in Henry, *Ironic Christian's Companion,* 10.

67. A game of dozens is a cut down contest rooted in the black community—basically "your mama" jokes. This is the source of the rap battles central to the Eminem movie *8 Mile.*

68. For a more complete exegesis of the passage, see Douglas Adams, *The Prostitute in the Family Tree: Discovering Irony and Humor in the Bible* (Louisville: Westminster John Knox, 1997), 7–10.

69. Quoted in "Where the 21st Century Meets the Middle Ages," E3.

70. David Ansen, "Yes, 'Rouge' Can, Can, Can," *Newsweek,* 28 May 2001, 61.

71. Ibid.

72. Douglas Jones, "Seducing the Underworld," *Books & Culture* 8, no. 2 (March/April 2002): 15.

bibliography

Arnold, Rebecca. *Fashion, Desire, and Anxiety.* London: I. B. Tauris Publishers, 2001.

Beaudoin, Tom. *Virtual Faith: The Irreverent Spiritual Quest of Generation X.* San Francisco: Jossey-Bass, 1998.

Blake, Richard. *Afterimage: The Indelible Catholic Imagination of Six American Filmmakers.* Chicago: Loyola Press, 2000.

Boorstin, Daniel. *The Image: A Guide to Pseudo-Events in America.* New York: Harper & Row, 1961.

Corliss, Richard. *Intimate Strangers: The Culture of Celebrity in America.* Chicago, Ivan R. Dee, 2000.

Dark, David. *Everyday Apocalypse: The Sacred Revealed in Radiohead, the Simpsons, and Other Pop Cultural Icons.* Grand Rapids: Brazos, 2002

Davis, Walter T., Jr. *Watching What We Watch.* Louisville: Geneva Press, 2001.

Dillenberger, Jane Daggett. *The Religious Art of Andy Warhol.* New York: Continuum, 1998.

Docker, John. *Postmodernism and Popular Culture: A Cultural History.* Cambridge: Cambridge University Press, 1994.

Drane, John. *Cultural Change and Biblical Faith.* Carlisle, Cumbria, U.K.: Paternoster, 2000.

During, Simon. *The Cultural Studies Reader.* 2d ed. London: Routledge, 1999.

Friedman, Thomas. *The Lexus and the Olive Tree.* New York: Farrar, Straus, Giroux, 1999.

Frith, Simon. *Sound Effects: Youth, Leisure, and the Politics of Rock 'n' Roll.* New York: Pantheon, 1981.

Gabler, Neal. *Life the Movie: How Entertainment Conquered Reality.* New York: Knopf, 1998.

Gobé, Marc. *Emotional Branding: The New Paradigm for Connecting Brands to People.* New York: Allworth Press, 2001.

Greeley, Andrew M. *God in Popular Culture.* Chicago: Thomas More Press, 1988.

Hesmondhalgh, David, and Keith Negus, eds. *Popular Music Studies.* New York: Oxford University Press, 2002.

Hoffman, Shirl J., ed. *Sport and Religion.* Champaign, Ill.: Human Kinetics Books, 1992.

Johnston, Robert K. *Reel Spirituality: Theology and Film in Dialogue.* Grand Rapids: Baker, 2000.

Kellner, Douglas. *Media Culture: Cultural Studies, Identity, and Politics between the Modern and the Postmodern.* London: Routledge, 1995.

Marcus, Greil. *Lipstick Traces: A Secret History of the Twentieth Century.* Cambridge: Harvard University Press, 1989.

McLuhan, Marshall. *Understanding Media: The Extensions of Man.* New York: McGraw-Hill, 1964.

Nachbar, Jack, and Kevin Lause, eds. *Popular Culture: An Introductory Text.* Bowling Green, Ohio: Bowling Green State University Popular Press, 1992.

Niebuhr, H. Richard. *Christ and Culture.* New York: Harper & Row, 1951.

Palmer, Robert. *Rock and Roll: An Unruly History.* New York: Harmony Books, 1995.

Pinsky, Mark. *The Gospel according to the Simpsons: The Spiritual Life of the World's Most Animated Family.* Louisville: Westminster John Knox, 2001.

Pountain, Dick, and David Robins. *Cool Rules: Anatomy of an Attitude.* London: Reaktion Books, 2000.

Romanowski, William D. *Pop Culture Wars: Religion and the Role of Entertainment in American Life.* Downers Grove, Ill.: InterVarsity, 1996.

Schrader, Paul. "Transcendental Style in Film." Master's thesis, University of California, 1972.

Stark, Steven D. *Glued to the Set: The Sixty Television Shows and Events That Made Us Who We Are Today.* New York: Free Press, 1997.

Stephens, Mitchell. *The Rise of the Image, the Fall of the Word.* New York: Oxford University Press, 1998.

Storey, John, ed. *Cultural Theory and Popular Culture.* Athens, Ga.: University of Georgia Press, 1998.

Sweet, Leonard. *Quantum Spirituality.* Dayton, Ohio: Whaleprint Press, 1991.

Twitchell, James. *Lead Us into Temptation: The Triumph of American Materialism.* New York: Columbia University Press, 1999.

index

• ERRORS

There are no ERRORS
that I am personally
aware of in this
~~book~~ except those in
the area of taste.

(These are general
in nature and
cannot be attribu-
ted to anything
in particular)

SERIOUSLY,

THE AUTHOR